YOURS, MINE, and OURS

YOURS, MINE, and OURS

How Families Change When Remarried Parents Have a Child Together

Anne C. Bernstein, Ph.D.

W. W. NORTON & COMPANY
New York • London

Library of Congress Cataloging-in-Publication Data
Bernstein, Anne C., 1944–
    Yours, mine, and ours: how families change when remarried parents
have a child together/Anne C. Bernstein.
        p.   cm.
Bibliography: p.
Includes index.
    1. Stepfamilies—United States.   2. Stepchildren—United States—
Family relationships.   3. Remarried people—United States—Family
relationships.   4. Brothers and sisters—United States.
5. Stepparents—United States—Family relationships.   6. Children of
divorced parents—United States—Family relationships.   I. Title.
HQ759.92.B48   1989
306.8'7—dc19   88-26538   CIP

ISBN 0-393-30668-2

W. W. Norton & Company, Inc.
500 Fifth Avenue, New York, N.Y. 10110
W. W. Norton & Company Ltd.
37 Great Russell Street, London WC1B 3NU

Printed in the United States of America
1   2   3   4   5   6   7   8   9   0

FOR MY FAMILY—
Ringo, Sean, Antonio, Brian, and David

Contents

Acknowledgments

I would like to thank all the people who made this book possible.

I am most indebted to the men, women, and children who will find themselves on these pages: for the time taken from busy schedules and for the courage to take a closer look at themselves and their families. I have tried to be a faithful custodian of their personal stories, the triumphs and the trials, the sorrows and the joys. For many, reading about themselves as "halves" and "steps" will sound odd, technically accurate but emotionally foreign. Like them I use these labels for the sake of clarity, not to attenuate their relatedness. Although they cannot be listed by name, my deepest gratitude goes to them for all they have taught me about stepfamily life. Our time together has given me both information and inspiration. For the laughter and the tears, and the fine, clear thinking, thank you.

Diane Ehrensaft, Jamie Kelem Keshet, and Mary Whiteside have given generously of their time and expertise, reading earlier drafts of this manuscript. My special thanks for their acumen and analyses: their suggestions have made this a better book.

Other contributions become harder to specify. Along the way I have received encouragement, emotional sustenance, help in navigating the sometimes stormy seas of stepfamily life, and advice—literary, demographic, and practical—from many people. I would like to thank Hani Ahmad, Ronald Lee, Barbara Lena, Harry Levine, Laurie Phillips, Lillian Rubin, Barbara Safran, Carlos Sluzki, Jean Sternberg, Emily and John Visher, and Erika Waechter.

So, too, I am grateful to the staffs of the Rainbow and Berkwood-Hedge Schools for taking such good care of my son and making it possible for me to devote the time necessary to both research and write this book.

I owe special thanks to my agents for all their work on my behalf. Marion Young's early enthusiasm for the project, and her continued interest, encouragement, and friendship made this book possible. And Judith Weber, inheriting a book in progress, has been the very model of a *good* stepmother: concerned, available, and a real advocate. All stepchildren should have it so good.

Susanne Kirk has been a gem of an editor. Clear and approachable, she has been a delight to work with. From the early days when her excitement and encouragement about the project renewed my own enthusiasm to the final stages when her keen judgment about organization (and which 150 pages to cut) gave shape to the final manuscript, her contributions have been invaluable. Susan Barrows' support for the proposal for this book gave me invaluable encouragement in the very earliest stages of the work. I am very grateful to her for making this edition possible, and I am delighted for the chance to work with her after years of respecting her editorial talent.

Without my family, however, this book would never have happened. Their contributions, singly and together, go beyond those I can mention here. Had I not become a stepmother and then a mother, it would never have occurred to me to write this book. I thank you all for the inspiration, and for abiding with the reduced standard of living that was the principal support for this research. I am grateful to my stepsons, Antonio, Brian, and Sean for teaching me that the struggle is worth it, that commitment and caring bring rewards that are sometimes obscured by the heat of the fray. And I am grateful to my son, David, for sharing his Mommy with her MacIntosh. All the children have taught me so much about being a parent and a stepparent, a child and a stepchild, a family.

I am most indebted to my husband, Ringo Hallinan, without whose love both book and family would not be. I am thankful to him for so much: for supporting this endeavor by reading and rereading drafts of the manuscript and offering keen editorial suggestions, for covering the home front during intense periods of authorial effort, for all his support during and after the more difficult times in becoming a stepfamily, and, most of all for agreeing to have "one that's ours."

YOURS, MINE, and OURS

Introduction

In a cabin in the Santa Cruz mountains, my stepson, Antonio, then ten, was talking to nine-month-old David: "We all have the same Daddy. His name is Conn. First he married Eda, and they had Sean, and then they got divorced. Then Daddy married Judyann, that's Brian's and my mommy, and then they got divorced. Then Daddy married Anne, and they had you, and they're going to be together a long, long time and live happily ever after."

This baroque family genealogy clearly sailed over David's young head. Part of a deluge of information that he would absorb before he could understand, it underlined the complexity of the family chrysalis that shelters him as he forms his wings. What he heard was a beloved big brother paying him tender attention. He did not yet understand how much more there was in Antonio's statement: that families are fragile and changeable, that Daddy is someone they share and Mommy someone who is uniquely his, and the hint of brotherly envy that David alone would benefit from a fairy tale ending.

The traditional coda to these time-worn legends, marrying and living "happily ever after," is, of course, easier said than done. Even the child whose parents' marriage endures has a complex legacy when he is born into a family that includes children born of previous unions. Their history is part of his inheritance, and his existence changes their lives. Called variously the mutual child, the child in common, and the "ours" child, the baby born into a stepfamily is related to everyone, whether or not they feel related to one another. The promise of having "one that is ours" is that he will tie together fragments of two families and make them one, symbolizing by his very existence their hopes for unity and renewal. Part of his job description, from birth, is to make for "one big, happy family," and like most occupations, this one colors who he will become.

As an infant, the mutual child enters a family ecology that is a variation on the more usual arrangement. Instead of being born to two adults fumbling to become parents together, the child born in remarriage may have one parent who is a greenhorn and another who is an oldtimer at the business of parenthood. Instead of having to learn to share parental love and attention with others who have equal claim to both stars in the family galaxy, the children with whom she shares a home or a parent have staked out orbits that are closer to one parent and more distant from the other than her own path is wont to be, altering the gravitational field that shapes her course.

Like all other living creatures in dynamic interaction with their environments, as she is shaped by, so, too, does she alter the ecology she inhabits. By entering the stepfamily equation, she adds her weight to each of its terms. Because she has been born, her parents will change as partners and as parents together, and her half siblings will feel closer to or more distant from each other, their parents, and their stepparents.

Children born into stepfamilies have a unique endowment. At least one parent and the children from an earlier marriage have endured loss and suffered the grief of losing a loved one to death or a nuclear family to divorce. While marrying again may feel like a new beginning, imbued with hope for a future that will not repeat the disappointments of the past, there is no starting over. The journey resumes, despite interruptions: along the way there are stations marking the first marriage, one or more parents caring for their children separately, and then remarriage. It's all part of the same trip, and the baggage acquired along the way, with souvenirs from every whistle stop, gets heavier as time goes on.

In *Love and Power in the Stepfamily,* Jamie Keshet likens the family formed by a first marriage to a one-room cabin, to which additions are built one room at a time. In an evocative metaphor, the stepfamily is counterposed as a three-family dwelling, in which parents and their children from previous marriages start off in separate units, gradually taking down walls, installing an intercom, substituting one mailbox for three, and increasing communal space as they come to accept, respect, and care for one another.[1]

Stepfamilies have been with us from the beginning of time, although the occasions that create them have changed from the lower life expectancy that widowed young parents over the millennia to the currently more frequent situation of remarriage following divorce. More than a million stepfamilies are formed every year, and current projections are that one child in four will have a stepparent in the home during part of the child's growing-up years. Still more will acquire a stepparent whose home they only visit, however frequently. Yet despite the increasing numbers of stepfamilies and their historical longevity, it is only in the last twenty-five years that studies of stepfamilies have become more common. Jessie Bernard's 1956 work on remarriage, *Remarried: A Study of Marriage,* stood out as a singular contribution to a field that attracted few researchers until more than another decade had passed, and social scientists scrambled to catch up with the demographic groundswell.[2] It was not until the 1970s, when professionals and stepfamily veterans, notably Emily and John Visher, began to write about how remarriage creates families that are different in structure and "feel" from first-marriage families, that romantic dreams that the new families could replace the families that preceded them came to be seen as unrealistic, hindering remarrying parents and their children from becoming "relatives" rather than helping them to do so.

The Vishers point out the inherent problems of stepfamilies: the child must reconcile having a mother and a stepmother, a father and a stepfather, while all the adults involved must deal with one another in the child's best interests, since children can maintain membership in two households. There are "extra" grandparents, aunts, uncles, and cousins. Role definitions are fuzzy, and financial arrangements can be difficult, complex, and a continued cause of stress and resentment.[3] Members of a stepfamily household may not even agree about whom they consider part of the family. In one study, 15 percent of the stepparents did not include a stepchild as "part of your family," even when the child lived with them. Stepchildren were even more exclusive about bestowing family membership, with 31 percent excluding a live-in stepparent from their list of who was in the family.[4]

Any marriage can be seen as a cross-cultural marriage, with the adults coming to the partnership as ambassadors of the families in which they have been raised. Whatever their skills in diplomacy, or lack thereof, they must negotiate how the ways of life to which each is accustomed will be sifted and selected, gleaning from each what will become the "how we do things here" of the new family they create. When that marriage is a first marriage for both, they come to the bargaining table more or less as equals, with ideas and preferences about how to spend vacations, decorate an apartment, prepare meals, or raise children. But the personal preferences of an individual, however ingrained, do not have the weight of established practices that are part of a history shared by two or more people. Remarrying parents bring with them a more pervasive cultural legacy, including not only the family culture in which they were raised, but the culture they created with a previous spouse, a culture that is seen by their children as "just the way things are." Differences may be perceived as a revolutionary threat, challenging the family's very foundation. A single person coming to the bargaining table confronts a team, most of whom see no need to negotiate in the first place. When there are teams on both sides, as when each parent brings children to a remarriage, the competition heats up, with each side lobbying for the adoption of its own constitution.

Stepfamilies are different from the very beginning. When a couple have their first child together, they are a twosome before they become a threesome. In a stepfamily, parent and child may be the original twosome, with the stepparent the newcomer trying to find a place for himself without feeling that "three's a crowd," the stepchild reluctant to let the stepparent in lest he himself then be excluded, and the remarrying parent feeling like the rope in a tug-of-war between them. Stepparent and stepchild have to figure out who they are to each other, especially when, as is frequently the case, the child has a biological parent in another household. Stepparents often feel as if they've been put to work without a job description. And stepchildren, whose pain in losing a parent or fantasy of parental reunion may be drowned out by the joyful peal of wedding bells, may not want to be part of a new family. Torn by their loyalty to their other parent, living or dead, and the family that gave them birth, they are loath to legitimate the claim of this supernumerary, not knowing what to do with yet another "parent," chafing at having to come to terms with a situation not of their own choosing. Sociologist Andrew Cherlin has talked about stepfamilies as "incompletely institutionalized," meaning that roles and norms are poorly defined and unclear, leaving stepfamily members to negoti-ate for themselves how they will behave with one another.[5]

How different to be born into this teeming complexity, peopled by explorers charting unknown territory, than to be born to a "tea for two" couple, a far cry away in the proverbial cozy cottage with its white picket fence. It is these differences that I set out to chart as I began this book, to study how stepfamilies change when they have "one that is ours" and how occupying this unique family role shapes the develop-ment of the children born into stepfamilies.

A psychologist and family therapist long before I was a stepmother and mother, I thought I knew what to anticipate in marrying a man with three children and having a child together. The books I read and my clinical experience in working with other families did teach me a lot, but they did not prepare me for how stepfamily life would feel from the inside. Too often I felt like a terminal case of "do what I say, not what I do," when the passions of the moment triumphed over my intellectual knowledge of family dynamics. Only my husband's support, his insistence that I was a good stepmother, despite my suspicions to the contrary, and his humility in acknowledging that he did not know that he could do as well were he the stepparent kept me from giving in to recurrent feelings of failure.

Becoming a mother changed me as a stepmother. It changed how my husband and I shared parental responsibilities for my stepsons. At seven, ten, and seventeen, the needs and particular niche in the family of each of the older boys differed. So, too, did each have a distinctive relationship with their father and me, and they greeted David each in his own way, accordingly.

And I am a different mother to my son than I would have been had I not been a stepmother first. Like so many people who have not yet had children, I had many ideas about child rearing that have fallen by the wayside. Stepmotherhood reconciled me to not being able to totally patrol our gates, so that the heartless world of toy guns and Saturday morning cartoons has penetrated the haven I would have wanted to create had I more control.

But the story of what it is like to have children from two or more marriages cannot be adequately told based on the experience of one household. As a mother and stepmother I knew how helpful it would be for me to learn more about what worked and what didn't work for families like ours. As a family therapist and a teacher of family process,

I saw the need for more knowledge about this little-charted area of stepfamily life, so that clinicians could help families to anticipate the changes set in motion by having a child in remarriage, enabling therapists to help their clients navigate yet another transition in the stepfamily journey.

In trying to get a fuller picture, I began a study of stepfamilies with children of both past and present unions. I wanted to know how having a child together changed remarrying parents as partners and as parents. How do couples decide whether and when to have a mutual child, and what goes into their decision? What are the stresses and the benefits of having one adult a veteran parent and the other a neophyte? What difference does it make if both of the mutual child's parents have already had other children? And what is it like to start over, when a parent who thought she was done with diapers and the park bench has yet another infant?

And the children. What is it like for children whose parent has another child with a new partner? Does it make a difference if it's Mommy or Daddy who has another baby? How does where they live affect what it is like for them to have a half sibling, since some share the same household, while others commute between households or are occasional visitors to the stepfamily home? How is the impact of a child born in remarriage different if both of its parents, rather than only one, have already had children? Does the new addition bring about any changes in custody arrangements for the older children? And how does the stepchild's birth order in his original family and the age interval between the older children and the mutual child affect how they will get along, both initially and over the long haul?

All families develop patterns in how they relate to one another, creating and maintaining "rules defining who participates and how," the boundaries that give rise to what noted family therapist Salvador Minuchin calls "the family dance."[6] This sequence of shifting alliances and coalitions makes the difference between families that work well, moving with ease and fluidity from one developmental stage to another, and those that get stuck in a frustrating and defeating two-step, locked in a narrow pattern that precludes change.

How then does having a child in remarriage change the choreography of the stepfamily dance: who promenades with whom, and how easily stepfamily members shift to address their partners, address their corners, and change partners to sashay for a turn? How does the quality of the remarriage affect the welcome of its children? Do feelings of allegiance parents have to their children who are already born temper the welcome they accord a newcomer, or do they shift allegiance, depriving the older children of their dedicated concern? Do stepparents become closer to or more distant from their stepchildren when they have their own children? And how does getting along well or poorly with their stepparents change the relationship stepchildren have with their half siblings or, for that matter, with their parents?

Nor does change stop at the door of the home into which the child is born. Stepfamilies necessarily have larger gaps in the fence that surrounds them than do families from an initial union. People who are emotionally central to the children's lives live elsewhere, creating what Constance Ahrons has called "the binuclear family."[7] The children's other parent, another stepfamily, other half siblings, and caretaking grandparents all influence and are influenced by any additions to the stepfamily household. How then does the mutual child play a part in this larger drama?

And what about the child whose birth sets in motion so much change? I wanted to explore what effect this particular position in the stepfamily has on those children who occupy it: how their relationships with each of their parents and siblings are affected by the politics of living in a stepfamily; how their developing sense of self and their ability to form relationships are informed by being a child in such a family; and how they understand and make sense to themselves of the complex families in which they live, where siblings come and go and may have "two mommies or daddies," and parents are differently tied to each of the children.

Who Are We?

Ten years after the Vishers called stepfamilies an "invisible population," we are not so invisible after all. A careful reading of the daily newspaper tells us that families like ours are everywhere. Ronald Reagan has two children from his first marriage and two more in remarriage to Nancy. Michael Dukakis was a stepfather before having children with his remarried wife, and former First Daughter Susan Ford Vance is a stepmother to two children and mother of two more. Popular novelist Danielle Steele has added four mutual children to her teeming stepfamily, which includes two children from both her and her husband's former marriages, while singer-actor Kris Kristofferson has six children from three marriages, in addition to adopting three more on his own. Jane Fonda was the first mutual child of her remarrying mother, only to acquire another half sibling when father Henry adopted a daughter with a subsequent wife. Other mutual children include such luminaries as Franklin Delano Roosevelt, Sigmund Freud, choreographer Paul Taylor, and comedian Robin Williams.

Despite the predictions that soon there will be more binuclear families than nuclear families in the United States, we cannot fully describe the demographics of this growing segment of our population. Demographer Paul Glick estimates that by 1990 approximately one-third of all children will encounter a divorce before reaching eighteen years of age, and one child in four will spend some of the growing-up years living with a stepparent.[8] Trying to tease out from the available statistics just how many of these stepfamilies will have children in remarriage is a difficult task, which is examined in more detail in the Appendix, but very conservative estimates point to at least 1.5 million households with children from both past and present unions.

In seeking to better understand what life is like for stepfamilies like ours, I interviewed whole families, talking with all available family members over the age of three. In most instances, I set the condition that the child of the remarriage be at least three years old, so as to be interviewable, but a few stepfamilies with a still younger mutual child were included, as were adults who, thirty to sixty years earlier, had been the children or stepchildren of their own parent's remarriage.

Without the opportunity to speak with all the members of so many of the stepfamilies, this would have been a very different study. Seeing the same events through different eyes uncovers disparate realities. Throughout this book, the reader will note that parents' and stepparents' accounts of family history do not always jibe with their children's accounts. Stepmothers, for example, are nearly unanimous in thinking that their relationships with stepchildren improved markedly when having a child of their own led them to "lighten up" on the older children. Several of the stepchildren, however, see things differently, missing the attention, however ill-received, shown them earlier and feeling somewhat abandoned by the redirection of stepmotherly overinvolvement. Similarly, both parents and stepparents overestimate the amount of conflict between half siblings, according to the children themselves. And children sometimes see a baby as a terrible burden to a mother who describes herself as delighted by having another child. Taken individually, the pictures of stepfamily life are one-dimensional. Together they create a living diorama, with a depth and richness that a single point of view does not reveal.

I found families to interview in a variety of ways. I began with a modified version of what has been called the "snowball" method of sampling: starting with a small core, like a snowball rolling down a hill, getting bigger and broader as it goes along. I began with a few families with whom I was already acquainted, asking them for the names of other families, and then interviewed those stepfamilies that were most different from those already available. In addition, I advertised for families to interview, both in stepfamily publications and in more general publications of wider circulation. Although the San Francisco Bay Area is remarkably diverse, spreading over nine counties that demonstrate marked differences in socioeconomic conditions, cultural values, religious orientation, and even weather, I included several families from other regions of the country, so as to be sure that my pool of informants was not too geographically limited. In all, I interviewed 150 people, representing 55 remarried households. A fuller description of the population sample whose stories contributed to this book can be found in the Appendix.

The stepfamilies interviewed for this book are a very diverse group of people. While most of the families interviewed were Caucasian and native born, they include blacks, Chicanos, and Asian-Americans as well as some born overseas. A few live in houses that could easily be featured on the pages of *Metropolitan Home* or *Better Homes and Gardens,* with housekeepers or au pairs to help working parents come home to "quality time" with the children. Others are scraping to get by, crowding three full-time residents and visiting children into two small rooms, scrimping for necessities. Most fall somewhere in between, with economic pressure a daily fact of life, but with some choices about how to allot their resources. There are mothers who work full-time outside the home, mothers who work at part-time jobs, and mothers who are committed to being at home while their children are young. There are also a couple of fathers whose income-producing work is secondary to their role as nurturers of their children.

Although professionals are overrepresented in the sample, the work roles of the parents and adult children interviewed are many and various: there are white-, blue-, and pink-collar workers; those employed by labor unions and by large corporations, by municipalities and by the federal government; artists and craftspeople; health care and social service workers, and teachers at all levels, from preschool to university.

Almost all of the stepfamily parents are among the "successes" of remarriage, having passed the four-year mark, by which time two-fifths of all remarried couples have redivorced.[9] The largest group among the families was formed by first-time brides and their recycled grooms, followed by stepfamilies created by a remarrying mother and a single man, with the smallest number of families including parents who each brought children from a previous marriage. The Appendix includes a discussion of how representative these families are of stepfamilies in general.

While there were many anguished tales of difficult divorces marked by prolonged hostility between ex-spouses, and even reports of the child's other parent absconding with the children, all of the families were flexible enough to risk taking a closer look at how they were getting along as a stepfamily. Several of the families had sought help through psychotherapy in navigating difficult periods in the past, but only one of the families was currently consulting a therapist.

In any study that depends on volunteers, there is a self-selection against participants with active problems. A number of families declined to be interviewed on the grounds that talking about how they felt about each other would stir up more than they were prepared to handle. In addition, a few parents and stepparents were willing to participate themselves but refused to allow the children of an earlier marriage to be interviewed for fear of upsetting the children and their other parent.

"Our feelings change according to what just happened," said one stepmother, who, with her husband, decided against his older children participating in this study. "What just happened between them and their mom will really make a difference in how they deal with us. What just happens with us will change the way they are with their mom. At the moment my stepdaughter and I are getting along real fine, but she's good at turning hot and cold. If you hit it at the wrong time, it could get amplified."

So, too, do the results of all the interviews depict a reality that represents a particular slice of time. Using Salvador Minuchin's metaphor of the family kaleidoscope,[10] the shards of stone shift, and the pattern reflected by the array of mirrors changes from a skeletal snow-flake to a richly textured mandala. "I thought about what I said," one woman called me back to report some weeks later, "and I think we should meet again. What I told you doesn't feel true anymore." Yet when I attempted to schedule another interview, she declined. "It was true then," she said, "and is no more or less true than what I might have to say now."

We all have our ups and our downs. During some of the rockier periods at our house, I would return from an interview to lament to my husband, "Everybody's doing better than we are." "You don't know that," he countered. And sure enough, we would pass another mile-stone, the scenery would brighten, and the road ahead would appear less fraught with pitfalls. As it is always easier to see in what ways another's course is ill-advised, so, too, does it sometimes seem that no one else could have it so rough. Like many of the people I interviewed, I have had good intentions go awry and made my share of mistakes. Like them, too, I have found that change travels in time's wake, presenting opportunities for healing and repair, delivering more than it promised, surprising with its gifts.

Interviewing and being interviewed for this book was a powerful emotional experience for many of us. After I had interviewed their children, Ben and Julia told me that their sons had asked them many questions about who in their family was related to whom. Her son from an earlier marriage voiced his concern that the younger boys' needs were put above his own. Although I made myself available to discuss this with them further, they declined, saying that it was a welcome opportunity to discuss among themselves how things were going for them as a family.

When I returned to Ben's office to resume an interview we hadn't had time to finish a few weeks earlier, he told me: "I can see why the kids were all stirred up. The questions are real evocative. For me, it's been a reliving. There are a lot of good things, but an awful lot of pain. I don't spend much time thinking about how I felt in splitting up my first marriage. I have a lot of sense of loss around Josh, not having done it right. Lots of regrets. Day to day I don't let them dominate my life. Yet when I recall them, the feelings are right there. It's not as if I've resolved them and can say, in fact, I did good enough and everything's worked out fine. I think today I'm a little more prepared. The first time I was agitated for the rest of the day. It stirred up an awful lot of feeling, especially around Josh, and my sense of loss, and my sense of having failed him. The feelings were strong feelings, but they're part of me. A part of me that I like to push aside, but they're important. I didn't expect that. It's powerful. It's your life."

"God," exclaimed a thirty-year-old woman, at the conclusion of the interview about the stepfamily in which she had grown up, "you could do this as family therapy. I've definitely constructed letters to each member of the family as I'm talking." I knew that the interviews, like any close examination of important relationships, would sometimes evoke powerful feelings, and tried to leave adequate time to deal with whatever came up, offering to meet further with those who wanted to talk at greater length. While therapy was never part of the design, I hope that the interviews were, when appropriate, therapeutic in the broadest sense of serving to heal.

At the conclusion of our interview, one stepmother remarked, "It's interesting, because I guess I haven't talked to anybody so fully about all these things. It gave me some new things to think about. I guess I'm feeling sorry about the relationship with my stepson," she continued, tears filling her eyes, "and I don't know what to do about it. I guess it's good to at least talk and think about."

I ventured a suggestion. I had not yet met her stepson and could not know what was and what was not possible, but I couldn't imagine it would hurt to tell him that, in the course of the interview, she had felt strongly that she would like their relationship to be better. She sat silently, considering, then spoke: "It's interesting. It could be that this interview could sort of spark something. Maybe we can use it as an opening."

I hope so. I know that I have learned so much from all who so generously shared of their experience that I would like to think that I have given them something in return. For many, knowing that their pain and their joy, their mistakes and their discoveries, their struggles and their successes may be of use to others navigating the same seas made taking a closer look worth the risk. I have tried to minimize that risk, while keeping open the opportunities for welcome change.

All names and identifying information have, of course, been changed to protect the confidentiality of those interviewed, except for specific references to my own family. To minimize the unavoidable confusion of keeping track of complex relationship chains, I have adopted the convention of choosing names that begin with consonants for biological parents and the children of their first marriage. Pseudonyms of stepparents and the children of remarriage all begin with vowels. Because of the small number of vowels available, *Y* is taken exclusively to be a vowel.

Pieced like a quilt from the stories of women, men, and children, the pages that follow trace the design of stepfamily life when a child is born into remarriage. They tell their own stories, while I discover and put into relief the patterns of their experience, the shifting sequence of steps in the family dance.

1

Will We? Won't We?

Deciding Whether and When to Have a Mutual Child

"Brian is five now, and I can see the light at the end of the tunnel," says the man who will become my husband the next year. We are driving down the Pacific Coast Highway to the Point Lobos Nature Reserve, where wildflowers bedeck dramatic cliffs and sea otters clown in the sea below. It is one of those rare times when it is just the two of us, a weekend without his children. I know the "light at the end of the tunnel" is a beacon that signals the end of many years of intensive parental labor. And I am trying very hard not to cry.

Over the past few months of our spending most of our nonworking hours together, there have been other such moments. I've heard the "light at the end of the tunnel" line before. There is also: "When I'm fifty, all of my kids will have left home." A perfectly understandable feeling for a man who has been a parent for fourteen years now, ever since he was twenty-three years old.

I am following my mother's advice for a change. "You don't have to announce to a man on the first date," she told me with some disgust at my lack of guile, "that you're eager to have a baby." So for three months, at each of Ringo's joyous anticipations of a child-free future, I have bitten my tongue. But today, the second such foray elicits a rejoinder. "Well, your last kid may have left home by the time you're fifty," I tell him, "but my last kid won't have." After a long silence, we agree to put the topic on hold.

So opened the series of conversations, private considerations, and mutual deliberation that led to our deciding to marry and to have a child. For me, it was clear that these decisions were inseparable. But the conclusion was far from forgone.

Like many remarrying couples, we were at different developmental stages in our adult lives. I was thirty-six and never married. Although only a year my senior, he was twice divorced and the father of three boys. At the top of my agenda was to have a family, which to me meant at least one child that I gave birth to. What he longed for was time to himself, to pursue the interests that early fatherhood and some years of being a single parent had preempted.

Every remarrying couple not prevented by age or infirmity faces the question of whether to reproduce. Even sterilization, although a stumbling block, can sometimes be surgically reversed. If both partners have already had children, and especially if each has had more than one child and the children are nearly grown, they may quickly agree to forswear a return to the days of diapers and dinosaurs. But when one partner is childless, the matter can be more delicate. Because most remarrying men choose women who are younger than they by more years than their first wives, it is more often she who has not yet had children. She may be taking for granted that, like the childhood jump rope rhyme, "first comes love, then comes marriage, then comes Sally with a baby carriage." He, on the other hand, may associate the failed former marriage with its parental responsibilities and wish for a romantic adult intimacy this go-around. Despite the greater propensity of women to equate childbearing with fulfillment, this decision can be an overriding concern for both sexes. Nor is reluctance to start over exclusively a male preserve. Mothers who have put in their time on the park bench and, after years of deferring personal ambition, just gotten started in work or studies may fear that agreeing to another child will entail an unacceptable postponement of personal goals.

In choosing to love again, perchance to marry, another child may be the farthest thing from the mind of a single parent. Yet the very presence of children throughout the courtship makes the issue a hard one to ignore. As two people become more intimate, and their lives become more and more entwined, the relationship between one's children and one's partner becomes an important criterion in deciding whether to commit oneself to the new relationship. For the childless partner, even one without a pronounced case of baby hunger, continued proximity to the children and responsibility for their care gives rise to nagging questions of what it would be like to be a "real" parent.

It can be uncomplicated. When both partners agree on whether to have more children, the going can be smooth. There are many reasons why a remarriage can be happily childless. Perhaps both people have had their children, who are now half grown or almost adults. They are eager to move on to a new life stage that does not include the care of young children. Or a single parent may reconnect with a person who is childless and pleased to remain so. Infertility is another rising tide that diminishes the numbers of children of remarriage. Current estimates are that one-fifth of American couples are involuntarily childless, and because infertility rises with maternal age, it is more likely to be an obstacle for remarrying couples.[1] With this group, however, the option of adoption keeps the question of whether to have a child that is "ours" an open one.

The Dream that Didn't Die

Many remarrying parents enter the new union with a wish to expand the families truncated by the failure of a past marriage. Parents, especially those with only one child, have often seen their families dissolve before they were complete.

For the single parent whose dream of having more children didn't die, as for their childless counterparts, a partner's desire to be a parent can be an important part of the attraction. Maggie, then a single parent, describes the mutuality with which she and Eliot, not yet a father, approached the question: "I think that part of the reason I was so attracted to him was the way he related to my son, the way he talked about wanting to have children, because I *always* wanted to have more children. It came up very early on that if I were ever in a very stable relationship I would love to have more. And he was certainly clear that he wanted some. There wasn't ever a lot of question about more kids. Never."

"What a Wonderful Way to Show How Much You Love Me"

Like Maggie, many parents of single children always assumed that they would have more children, and a courtship that is going well rekindles their desire to finish the family building they had started in an earlier union. Even for those who thought their childbearing years were over, falling in love again can give rise to a romantic vision of having a child as an important expression of their love and commitment. While the desire for creative collaboration can find other outlets, fantasies of a "love child" may begin to dance in the heads of all but the most confirmed "never again" parents. Even those who eventually decide not to have a baby may find themselves musing about what a child who was the product of their union would be like.

Even disparate agendas do not necessarily lead to conflict or even difficult negotiations. Even a parent who has no special desire for more children may quickly agree to oblige a beloved new spouse. A grateful widower who felt that the three kids he had were plenty was willing to do anything his new wife wanted, despite a surfeit of diapers in his life to date. "Naturally it wasn't as important to me as it was to her," explained a divorced father of two, "because I already had kids. But it was something I could deal with, in that she wanted it. It was something I could handle."

For these couples, there is that moment of reckoning when cards are put on the table and the partners look to see if they've got a match. It becomes part of the marriage negotiations, whether prompted by one partner's craving to be a natural parent or prospective grandparents' concern that marrying a much older man may deprive their daughter of a chance for a family. While childless men were more confident that the single mothers they were wooing would be romantic enough to be persuaded to have another child, many women have vivid memories of the time, place, and manner in which they told their suitors that a baby was an important part of their plans for the future.

Arlene laughed as she remembered how taken aback Sol was to hear that she wanted to have a child: "It had never entered his head that this was going to be part of his new life. He wasn't opposed to it, he had just not considered it. And I told him that it was just out of the question for me not to have a child. I don't think we ever again had a serious talk. I think he just accepted it."

Sol, in his forties at the time, had thought his family was done. "I was initially surprised," he told me, "but I understood it. Arlene was in her thirties. She'd always wanted to have children, and she made it clear that if we were going beyond just cohabiting, a child or children was in her immediate future because her clock was ticking." The father of a fourteen-year-old at the time, he was nonplussed by the prospect. "It wasn't difficult. I loved children. And I wanted to give her anything she wanted. A second family, if that's what she wanted, was okay with me. If she wanted the moon, and I could have gotten it for her, I would have done that too."

While being persuaded to shift gears and travel the common road may be easier for some than for others, those who can do so are not necessarily more in love than their counterparts who require more time and negotiations to work through ambivalence about having more children. Most of the parents in this category were men who saw their children from a previous marriage regularly but did not live with them. Having yet another child, one whom they envisioned raising to maturity, was sometimes also seen as an opportunity to carry through in a way that they had not been able to when the end of the earlier marriage led to their losing the job of parent in residence. The one woman who had thought her family complete but was easily persuaded to enlarge it was, as her partner predicted, "romantic enough" to enlist in his dream of having a child together.

The Second-Chance Child

Because their first ventures into parenthood did not go as planned, parents may approach the prospect of another child as an opportunity to avoid the blunders and burdens of trying to be a good parent while navigating the stormy seas of marital conflict, separation, divorce, or bereavement. It is not their children they are dissatisfied with, it is themselves as parents. For them, a loving remarriage is an opportunity to "do it right," and to have children who will be lucky enough to live with both their parents.

When times have been hard, as they often are for single parents struggling to make a living and meet most of their children's needs by themselves, often in the face of conflict with an ex-spouse, the child of remarriage may seem like a chance at a "dreamchild." Laura, whose relationship with her son, Nathaniel, has long been volatile, described her attraction to Andrew: "My sense of him as coming from this really healthy family really made me want to have a child with him. I wanted to do it right. And having a child with Andrew has been idyllic. He's a wonderful father. He's there 100 percent of the time."

As for many parents who have suffered the insults to self-esteem that can be part of divorce and its aftermath, the chance to have another child gave Laura an opportunity to repair her sense of herself as a "good enough" mother. The reparative motif surfaces in her account of how different she is—more patient, less guilty and ambivalent—with her daughters than she had been with her son: "When I lose my temper at Elena, I don't feel horrible about it. I don't feel like I am being this shrewish mother, who's out of control and always bitching at her kids. I feel that they have a really good life. With Nathaniel, I felt guilt that he only had one parent. I always felt he was deprived."

As with the Chinese character for "crisis" that contains the symbols for both "opportunity" and "danger," so, too, does the prospect of another child signal "opportunity" and "danger" to the parent who feels like a failure. For Ben, who lives with a sense of loss and failure about his oldest son, whom he rarely sees, the idea of another child was fraught with worry: "It scared me because I felt I hadn't done a good job with Josh. I had let the kid be a casualty of my wife's craziness and my obsessive preoccupation with myself. I let him down, so what kind of a father was I?" He had to be convinced to start again, but once he was convinced, the resolve to be a different kind of father emerged: "I felt that Julia was a much better mother than Gail had been. And I was in a better place, too, but it was scary. When Ira was born I had a real clear sense that I'm going to be involved with this kid from the word 'go.' I'm not going to be an absentee father."

Eight years and two children later, he has developed a faith in his own capability as a father. Had he known then what he knows now, he says, "I would have fought harder for Josh. I would have tried to get custody." While the pain in his voice makes the insecurity he describes believable, watching him with his children belies its content.

But What About the Kids I Already Have?

Completing the family building interrupted by divorce or death, wanting to express the love of a new partner through the creation of a child, and seizing the opportunity to rehabilitate one's sense of oneself as a parent all press the remarrying parent toward agreeing to or even lobbying for a child of the new marriage. But regardless of their eagerness to pursue fresh reproductive plans, all see a yellow light of caution: "How will it affect the children we already have?" A parent's vital concern with the well-being of existing children must be balanced with his or his mate's desire for potential children. They ask themselves 'Can we stretch our financial and emotional resources any further?' While all consider how having another child will affect existing children, responses to this yellow light vary. Some stop as the light turns yellow, some merely slow down, and some speed through the intersection before the light can turn red.

The parent, especially of a single child, may worry that having another child is disloyal. When a parent and child have been a tight twosome for several years, entertaining thoughts of having another child may feel like infidelity. The parent may wonder if she can love another child as much and feel guilty about having suddenly to give attention to the baby. This allegiance to progeny, a reluctance to expose them to yet further stresses following the disruptions of divorce or death and remarriage, leads to hesitation on the baby question.

The natural parent worries that a new family will take precedence: to create one would be disloyal to her children, who have already suffered family disruption. "I remember that my wife was real worried," said Arthur, "that I would care more about our daughter than I would about hers, and that Jessica was going to take second place once Annie was born." The weight of this factor is not lost on childless stepparents, who may see their stepchildren as obstacles to their having a much-desired child of their own. Not wanting to create two classes of children in the same family is, however, more often grounds for vigilance than for abstinence.

The interests of the existing children are not always seen as an obstacle to having more. Instead, parents concerned about the deficits of being an only child put having another child in the credits column when calculating the interests of an older child.

While parents and stepparents do worry about how older children will take the birth of a child of the remarriage, and many postpone plans for this reason, few permanently shelve the question for reasons of the children's welfare. For one thing, failure to have a second or later child for fear of sibling rivalry would, taken to its logical conclusion, make for the universality of one-child families. For another, parents find a way to believe that what is best for them is also best for their children. They may decide that their children are too old to be jealous of a baby, only to find out later that even a generation of age difference may not be enough to eliminate envy. They may decide that the impact will be positive, based on "a feeling as a parent that a child would like anything I would like, which is not very realistic." Although few are so candid, one father tells that while his children were considered in the decision, they were not and could not be the determining factor: "We were wondering if they'd like it, although ultimately it didn't make any difference if they liked it or disliked it."

Will This Marriage Last?

Perhaps the most telling question for the parent considering having a child with a new partner is whether that partnership will last. The pain of separation when there are children is surpassed only by the pain of a parent's death, and when conflict remains active between ex-spouses, worrying the wound, even time is prevented from taking its palliative course. For many single parents, the difficult question is not "Do I want another child?" it's "Is this the person I want to be with long enough to raise a child to maturity this time?"

"My ambivalence was about the relationship," explains Richard, describing the process by which his youngest son was born. "I love kids, and I didn't have any questions about my fealty, my willingness to hang in there." The experience of having a child can destabilize any marriage, and many who have experienced marital failure date the beginning of the end to the changes in the relationship set in motion by the birth of a child.

The greatest nightmare for the remarrying parent is that history will repeat itself, leaving him juggling visitation with two sets of children, leaving her to raise two sets of children alone. And it is this nightmare that puts on the brakes for many, delaying a commitment to have another child until the new relationship seems to be on solid ground, prolonging negotiations when there are divergent agendas.

Before examining how parents and stepparents resolve disagreements about whether to have children, let us first look at the stepparent's point of view.

"I'd Always Wanted Children"

In dreaming about their adult lives, children picture themselves as parents, telling themselves what they'll be like as mothers and fathers, even as they bristle at what theirs are like with them. While not all children grow up to be parents, nor do all want to, almost all have rehearsed this identity during some part of their growing-up years. What they don't count on is becoming stepparents before first becoming parents.

In his romantic pursuits, the man whose life plan includes fatherhood is also looking for a mother for the children he hopes to have. The woman who has always planned on having children measures prospective partners against her image of a good father. For either, getting close to a single parent who is loving, dependable, and nurturing to his children can be an important part of the attraction. In courting a single parent, aspiring parents do not have to wonder or worry what kind of parent he or she is hooking up with. They know. She has seen him minister to a sick child or make up nonsense rhymes to entertain an impatient one on a long drive. He has been there while she tells her son how to manage a playground bully or helps her daughter deal with the vagaries of preteen friendships.

Seeing Simon as a good father, taking responsibility for the children whose custody he shared, was a big attraction for Elizabeth. She had never known her own father, and Simon's continued involvement with his children convinced her that "here's a man who, even if it didn't work out between me and him, he would still know his children." Even without the added poignancy of Elizabeth's family history, seeing a parent be a good parent can be an important part of his appeal to a prospective mate who wants children.

A Clear Job Title

Not all stepparents have "always wanted children." Indeed, some never do. But for many being a stepparent itself gives rise to the wish for children of their own. The ambiguity of the stepparent role, feeling an outsider to the elemental power of the parent-child connection, can push the stepparent to resolve the ambiguity by acquiring a more clearcut job title: Mother or Father. Irma describes how she became more and more interested in having a child with Mike: "It wasn't conscious, but I think maybe there was some jealousy in terms of Mike's relationship with Jason, and me feeling on the outside of that and really wanting to fully be a parent to someone."

Stepparents learn from sometimes bitter experience that a stepparent is not a parent. In taking care of their stepchildren, they may make parental moves, and yet the dance may not work the way they hoped it would. The child's steps may not be in sync, or the other parent may come to sashay the child around the floor. One common response is to accept the limits of being a stepparent, and rechannel the urge to parent into a mutual child.

Many of the stepparents I spoke with, especially stepmothers, were so fervently committed to being parents that they would not have married their spouses if the commitment to have another child had not been there. All remarriages that include children are a package deal. Marrying a parent means taking on responsibility for the children of a prior union: accepting their existence and making room for them in the new family. Before taking on the job of stepparent, many not-yet-parents make their acceptance conditional on the opportunity to have a biological child as well.

"Two on Her Side, and Two on Mine"

Jessie Bernard tells us that the remarried have the habit of dividing the marriages of a lifetime into major and minor. For some, the major marriage is not necessarily the happiest, but the one that has produced the most children.[2] While having a child is by no means an unequivocal message about the state of the marriage, a couple may be happier than in their first marriages and want to express their love through a child. Like commingling property or sharing incomes, having a child is a cultural act of joining, a statement of commitment to the union, a demonstration of family solidarity. But motivation is rarely unalloyed. Having a child can also be a rote satisfaction of cultural programming, or even more problematic, an attempt to cement a foundering relationship or a competitive move to produce a family that will outdo the family of a spouse's former marriage: "I wanted to balance the numbers, two on her side, two on mine."

Although competitiveness sounds like a nasty contaminant in a list of reasons to have a child, its presence is not evidence of spoilage. People in remarried families know from experience that marriages come and go but having a child together is forever. Having a beloved partner hesitate or, worse still, refuse to have a child with you when he has done so with someone he says he liked less is hard to accept, especially if that frustrates your own desire for children. One stepmother describes the "really big issue" that her husband's refusal to have children raised for her: "Here for seven years I'm with this man who won't have a baby with me, and yet he's had a baby with somebody else. In the back of my mind, I'm saying 'Why did he have a baby with her, but he won't have a baby with me?' He'd give me all sorts of reasons: he was young, he didn't know what he was doing, this and that reason. It still always made me feel that there was something secondary about our relationship. Even though we both felt that not only was it as good as anything they had, it's much better."

Although tempted to see their stepchildren as impediments to their having a child of their own, especially if partners are reluctant, stepparents can be vitally concerned with the children's well-being and worry that in having a baby they are causing harm to the older children. Feeling responsible for a change in the family not wholly to the children's liking, they may struggle with feelings of guilt about a pregnancy and anxiety about its outcome. One stepmother described a "very nervous first pregnancy," during which she became terribly depressed, panicked, and went to see a psychiatrist for the only time in her life. "I was really worried," she remembered, "about how everybody was going to come together. And I was worried that I had done something irreversible, something very hard on my husband's original children. The girls were teenagers. They hadn't lived with their father for years, and they like their father a lot. He's a very nice father. He's always very reliable to them, very responsible, very attached. And this was the kid that was going to get to live with Daddy. I thought that was going to create rivalry."

Having a child may feel like a ticket of entry for the stepparent who feels like an outsider to the biological parent-child minifamily. In seeing the mutual child as an object of envy by the stepchildren, the stepparent is anticipating the other side: that her ticket of entry will be experienced as a deportation order by the older children. This idea that both stepparent and stepchild cannot feel "inside" at the same time is based on a scarcity model of emotional resources and represents an early stage in stepfamily formation where family membership is not yet taken for granted by all.

The Bargaining Table

For every would-be parent confident that his new partner is romantic enough to have a baby with him, there are more who anticipate a rocky road to agreement. Nor is such confidence always well founded. Ambiguity before marriage can lead to irreconcilable differences after, where partners go their separate ways despite a relatively happy marriage. I did not systematically interview remarried couples who chose not to have more children. Some who make that decision are delighted with their choice, seeing their family arrangements as "the best of both worlds"—part-time parenting without full responsibility. Others are dissatisfied, nursing deep regrets that they honored a partner's feelings, "giving up the chance to have a child that would be ours," like one "second" wife who dreams of herself standing alone at her husband's gravesite, as his children are comforted by their mother.[3]

Yesterday's clarity can yield to today's indecision, and vice versa. And ambivalence can ebb and flow in both partners. For the younger woman marrying a man who has had his family, children may not seem an important consideration at twenty-two; at thirty-five, when her peers have become mothers and her own biological clock is ticking, she may reconsider, only to find that her husband considers this a breach of contract. Again, it is women who want to be mothers as well as stepmothers and the fathers they marry who most frequently see themselves as at cross-purposes in this regard: would-be fathers are more confident that their dreams will prevail, perhaps because remarried mothers are more frequently eager to continue having children, with less need to be persuaded.

When the decision is put on a back burner, each believes the other will come around to his or her way of thinking in the end. Since relationships are always in motion, minds and hearts can be changed, and mutually agreeable solutions can be found, albeit not inevitably. Later problems can be prevented, however, when this negotiation takes place before the commitment to marry. For many the decision to have a child is simultaneous with the decision to be together over the long term. Sometimes reluctance to agree to having a child together reflects, as partners sometimes suspect, ambivalence about being a couple, so that resolution depends on the desirability of remarriage. When feelings about having a child together differ, the party who places the survival of the couple above the outcome of the decision about a mutual child finds a way to make peace with a partner's greater need.

Alice and John provide an example of a remarried couple for whom the decision to have a mutual child was a difficult one. Like many who find themselves with competing priorities, he already had two children and she was childless when they began to see each other. Each knew the other's position early on. It probably came up, recalls John, when "I made one of my hard and fast statements that I wasn't going to have any more children, that I already had my two children, and that was enough for population control." Alice remembers that they put the issue on the shelf until they realized that their relationship was serious. Hopeful that she could persuade him, she was far from certain of the outcome, yet both knew that a negative decision would lead her to seek another partner with whom she could have a child. After two or three years, the question had become a critical one that had to be resolved for the relationship to continue. After seeking therapy, which included the homework assignment of writing out the pros and cons of having another child, John realized it was "inevitable." Devoted to their seven-year-old, he has made peace with his concession: "I've since found out that one is not done with parenting when a child leaves the house anyway. And I can justify the population control as: if you have one child for each parent, then if you have a third child with a second parent who has none, it's zero population growth."

Sometimes it takes a separation to convince a reluctant parent to pick up the gauntlet for another round. At twenty-seven, Adrienne was thrown into a quandary about whether to have a child when her best friend adopted one. For Marv, twenty years her senior and the father of three, another baby was "out of the question." They broke up and she moved out. After six months of soul searching, he asked her to come back, telling her that he was willing to have two children if she wanted to, despite the need to surgically reverse a vasectomy.

Without the prospect of losing Adrienne, Marv would never have imagined having a fourth and fifth child. But it was not just that she insisted. Partings of the way occasioned by divergent reproductive agendas do not often end in happy reunion. Forced to weigh the rewards of the future he imagined for himself against the burdens and benefits of having more children, he discovered his own satisfaction was more congruent with Adrienne's than he had thought. In reflecting on what he had most enjoyed in life, he realized that raising his children was clearly among life's greatest pleasures.

Up to now we have described the more frequent instance of polarized ambivalence, where one member of a couple, usually the remarried parent, is hesitant to have another child, while the other, more often the stepparent, is the one who wants to create a child together. Another dance is, however, possible, when both members of the couple, alternately or together, feel that having another child is something that might be right, but then again, might not.

Edward and Susan were just such a couple. Together for eight years before their son was born, they were both very satisfied with their life with Carl, Susan's son, whom Edward had known from infancy and lived with from the time Carl was three. Susan describes how it took them four years to decide whether to have a child: "We were both very ambivalent. Edward felt that he had been able to be a nurturer because of his relationship with Carl. He felt he was a parent. He didn't have any great need to have a biological offspring. He was also feeling that it was nice that Carl was getting older, and we had more independence. And we realized that with a second child, we wouldn't be able to send him to his daddy in the summer."

If anything, it was Susan who, despite having done it before, was leaning toward having another. "I did have a sadness when I thought about not having another child," she recalls. "It just felt that I wasn't quite finished with that early parenting business." And Edward, whose relationship with his stepson was one of the most wholeheartedly open and mutually loving I witnessed, "never had any great desire to have children." Susan, lobbying in her more positive moments, had told him: " 'You've been a very good parent, but there's this really miraculous period of time that you haven't experienced, and it would be nice for you to watch a newborn become a kid.' Because they're really pretty well cooked by three."

How was the decision ultimately made? For one thing, they decided that, in Edward's words, "It was the more selfish things we might have wanted to hold on to that might have led us to not have a child . . . just the kind of yuppie stuff, I guess," and that not to have a child would deprive Carl of a sibling. But it was outside help that decided the issue, this time from a friend who told them: " 'You guys are trying to make this a rational decision, and it's not a rational decision.' So we decided that we probably would regret it if we didn't have a child, and we probably would not regret it if we did."

Not on the Calendar

While Edward and Susan may feel that they backed into the decision to have Eric, they spent years of rehearsing alternative scenarios and weighing one consideration against another. Accidental pregnancy, on the other hand, may be more accurately seen as backing into having a child, as the child precedes the decision. Current folklore would have it that "accidents" happen only to teenagers, the impoverished, or the uneducated. Middle-class stepfamilies are assumed by many clinicians to think longer and harder about whether to have additional children, to test the marital waters and accustom the children to future family transitions, before having an "ours" baby. I was surprised by how many of these families, older and more educated than most, had to resolve lingering conflict and ambivalence during the pregnancy itself.

While most of the couples in this study who had unexpected pregnancies were divided about whether to have a child together, surprise conceptions also happen to couples in which neither party intends to have more children. Some such pregnancies are terminated, but others continue because of religious conviction or because they occurred when abortion was not legally available. Still others may surprise resolute "no more children" couples into unexpected delight and anticipation.

When both man and woman are open to being parents together, a pregnancy can provide the impetus to overcome fears of commitment to another relationship. Tim and Isabel both welcomed a surprise pregnancy that came soon after their friendship took a romantic turn, at a time that was otherwise probably not propitious to make a long-term commitment. Tim had just emerged from a long period that he describes as "celibate and in my shell" after the breakup of his marriage: "I'd gone through sort of a despairing period about ever having another relationship, and to me it was just fantastic. I really felt this was brilliant. I was prepared to put as much as I could into it. And it was great."

Isabel, although divorced and in her thirties, had not yet had children. "The older I got, the more I thought that I would like to have a child," she explained. "That was part of the reason that I agreed to take the chance of forming a permanent relationship with Tim. I really had to struggle with the decision, because I was adamantly opposed to voluntary single parenthood, and, on the other hand, I knew that entering a new relationship with a child on the way was not a good idea, a dangerous proposition, a real stress. But I did it nonetheless, and it seems to have worked out." Tim is convinced that his record as an attentive parent to his four-year-old daughter was an important consideration for Isabel "when she thought about us spending the rest of our lives together."

For some, moral conviction rules out abortion as a response to an unexpected pregnancy. For those whose ethical beliefs include the right to make a choice about such matters, the dilemma posed by premature pregnancy can be a thornier one, especially if the couple come to the question with different reproductive desires.

Reeling from a difficult divorce after thirteen years of marriage, and feeling pressure by existing responsibilities, including his two sons, who were getting to an age where he felt they needed more of his attention, Jim described himself as "overwhelmed by the rapid change." He hadn't had the breathing room, the time for personal exploration that had been part of the motivation for the divorce. Clearly he was not ready to have another child, and his first response to Inez' pregnancy was to push for an abortion. But to do so would put the relationship at risk in a way he was unwilling to accept: "I didn't think I could handle it, but I certainly couldn't have her do something she didn't want. That would have been a terrible thing for us, and she never would have forgotten it. So the right thing was done."

While Jim was protective enough of the relationship with Inez not to force the issue, others were so convinced that having a child before the marriage was on a firm footing would be disastrous that they applied considerable pressure on partners reluctant to abort. For a few of the families, the subject of another child first came up when an unexpected pregnancy ended in abortion. Typically, at that time, an agreement is made that a second pregnancy, should it occur, would be allowed to go to term.

When Eileen became pregnant the first time, Rick reports, both really struggled over the question of whether to abort. "It felt like the connection was very solid and strong, but it felt too soon to put that task in front of it. But the contract that was really made at that point was that if another pregnancy occurred, she'd have a child."

The second pregnancy, while no more opportune than the first, led to the birth of Eddie, Rick's third child and Eileen's first: "It wasn't an optimum time. Given that he's such a sweetie pie, I'm glad he's here and I have no regrets about it. I honestly don't, even though it's been hell. But the timing was not perfect. Eileen and I were just beginning to become aware of some things that we really needed to work on and see whether we could fix before we invited somebody else to dinner. On the other hand, I didn't feel like it was my right to ask her to choose between no baby ever and no baby now. So I didn't, and I'm glad. I now think it was a good thing that Eddie was born, and there may never have been a right time between us." The issues that had begun to surface when Eileen became pregnant with Eddie continued to erupt painfully, and she and Rick separated when their son was four.

The struggle over whether to have a mutual child can be long, difficult to resolve, and fraught with the threat of separation. One particularly protracted struggle involved yearly pregnancies, both before and after the marriage of Peter and Ellen.

At their wedding, Peter foresaw that the issue of whether to have a child together might dissolve their marriage. "Two things were very, very clear in my mind," he insisted. "One is that I didn't want a baby, and that, second, if the baby is there, I'm going to respond to the baby as I responded to my son Michael, which is the closest I can ever feel. I felt I couldn't cope with another baby. I was not as young as I used to be. By the time the baby is twenty, I'm going to be an old man." Perhaps even more important than his reluctance to have another baby was his feeling of being manipulated by Ellen's repeated pregnancies. "My position about the whole thing is that there is no reason in the 1980s for anybody to get pregnant if they don't want to get pregnant, and I resented that. So it was a question about the relationship rather than about the child."

Ellen's relationship with Michael is one of the warmest, most parental relationships between stepmother and stepson that I observed, yet as the years went on, her drive to have a baby became more pronounced. In agreeing to abortions, she retreated from insisting that she prevail over Peter's objections, sometimes acceding to arguments of timing: they were being evicted, he was out of work. What really made her decide, she reports, was the experience of friends who were also stepmothers. One friend who had been a stepmother to two children for seven years was prevented from even seeing the children when her marriage to their father ended. Another friend, this one in her sixties, had a very good relationship with her stepson, but when her husband died, the son vanished from her life. "I asked her why," Ellen told me, "and she said, 'Because he has a mother.'

"That really made my mind up for me," Ellen continued. "It wasn't a question of me trying to persuade him to do this and getting a 'yes' or 'no.' So I put the relationship on the line, with the hope that it was going to be okay. I decided that I was going to get pregnant and go for it. I kept telling him, and I was taking my temperature. We had a major struggle about that, but I never saw him running to get a vasectomy. He didn't stop. He didn't go to the drugstore. He had some control over it, though he'd still probably maintain it was all me. I said, 'I'm fully prepared to leave. You don't want the baby? Cool. I do.' When I told him I was pregnant, he said 'Congratulations,' as if it were happening to someone else. Then, after he came around, somewhere mid-pregnancy, that was it. You'd think that he'd wanted it from day one and had begged me to get pregnant."

Peter's reluctance to have a second child was serious and built on a variety of concerns. Devoted to his son, Michael, he refused to consider doing anything that might make Michael feel pushed out of a cherished place in his father's life. Peter was also worried that having a baby would lead Ellen to withdraw the affection she lavished on Michael. Perhaps more telling, he feared that history would repeat itself. His earlier marriage had gone sour after childbirth, and Peter worried that he would be left to provide most of the emotional care for his second child as for his first. On the basis of his experience with his first wife, Peter had created a cultural stereotype of American women as insufficiently nurturing and very different from the women of his own European heritage. There were also important financial and career deterrents to enlarging the family. How had he come around? He reports that once the decision was made he slowly came to terms with it. "I'd experienced having a baby and Ellen never had. And it's important that she does. My sister, too, was on her side. She said, 'Who are you to say that she shouldn't have a baby?' "

To see him with their daughter, it is hard to imagine he fought so long and so hard to avoid having her. As he had known all along that he would be, he is as devoted to her as to his son. While his stormy refusals were hardly a vain show, they were only part of the picture. To continue to make love to a woman who repeatedly gets pregnant, who announces her intentions to conceive, and who openly keeps a temperature chart, suggests a certain measure of denial for a man who protests his antipathy to having a child. What we see at work here is the polarization of ambivalence: while she was full-speed-ahead, storming the ramparts of hesitation, any admission of interest on his part would have led to a too rapid resolution. Instead, his interest in having another child was expressed only covertly, in his omission to take responsibility for birth control when it was clear that Ellen could not be trusted to do so.

It would be foolish to assume that all such dilemmas are resolved as happily. While there were several families in which childless women put the relationship on the line, making their continued membership in the couple contingent on an agreement to have a baby, such leverage requires as a fulcrum a relationship that is loving and a man who has some ambivalence about becoming a father again. One can argue that, strictly speaking, unilateral decisions to become pregnant must involve duplicity and deception. Short of artificial insemination, it still takes two to conceive a child. But going ahead with plans to conceive a child with a reluctant partner is a little like buying a used car without checking out the engine. It may work just fine, but you can anticipate a lot of problems down the road. Some gamblers win, more don't. Because I talked only with people who had a child of remarriage and, with few exceptions, only those couples that were still together, the voices of those who decided to forgo that experience, whether happily or unhappily, are absent here.

The Importance of Timing

Regardless of why parents have a child when they do, how soon after the remarriage the mutual child arrives will have a profound effect on how stepfamily members, children and parents alike, ride with the changes that any shift in family membership entails. Patricia Papernow has described stages by which a group formed by remarriage begins to feel like family, establishing its own culture, different enough from what went before that the stepparent feels at home, but not so different that each biological unit feels cut off from its own history.[4] In the

"Early Stages" of stepfamily life, parents and stepparents try to enact the myth of an instant family, making whole what had been broken, healing with their love the wounds of loss, rescuing children who can be seen as traumatized, neglected, or abused. Children, however, hang on to their fantasies that their own two parents will somehow get back together again, aborting the stepfamily.

Later, as reality sets in, stepparents become aware that they are still outsiders, separated from parent and children by the history of life in a family they were not part of, the years of experience they have not shared. Alternating between frustrating attempts to join the family and exhausted retreat, stepparents blame themselves for the failure of the center to hold. Parents face a different dilemma. As the "pivotal insider" to whom everyone turns, they feel that the success or failure of the remarriage rests on their shoulders alone, as stepparents and stepchildren make their unhappiness evident. With "awareness," stepfamily members begin to see that the problems they have in feeling like a family are built into the situation and are not a reflection of personal failure.

The "Middle Stages" of remarriage, when the stepparent mobilizes to bring about changes that lead to his inclusion and the recognition of his authority as an adult family member, can be a pretty tumultuous time, as the stepfamily struggles to forge a culture that is shared by all members, excluding none. When negotiated successfully, this mobilization to action produces a couple that works as a partnership of equal insiders, and each adult can be with each child without one or the other of them calling in a third as an ally. Papernow estimates that it takes five to seven years—and courage, understanding, and lots of support—for stepfamilies to reach "Established Remarriage," when intimacy and authenticity in stepfamily relationships have been achieved, both stepparent and stepchild can feel like insiders, and the primacy and solidity of the couple provide a strong center to the stepfamily.

A Timetable for Arrivals

While accidental pregnancy preempts the question of when in a remarriage to have another child, many couples give a great deal of thought to the timing of their mutual child so as to minimize the shock of transitions for the older children and maximize confidence that the new union will endure. Although the question of how the timing of the birth of a child will affect the marriage and the children already on the scene is important, the answers they arrive at vary enormously.

Putting on the Brakes

Having been through the wrenching business of ending a marriage that has produced children, remarrying parents usually are in no hurry to risk a recurrence of this emotional wringer for either themselves or their children. They prefer to wait until the remarriage feels solid and enduring before taking the gamble of having another child.

Although fewer than half of the families I talked with spent even two years under one roof before their first mutual child was born, of those that did, many cited as a reason to wait the need to get to know each other as marital partners without the demands of an infant. Stepfamily consolidation, allowing the stepparent-stepchild relationship to develop without the complication of introducing a child who would be differently related to the adults, was another reason for delay.

While many families mentioned a desire to have at least one year without an additional child, for some a recognition of unfinished stepfamily business made for more lengthy postponements. It was hard for Alexis to see herself as a mother when being a stepmother had been so difficult for her: "I think I delayed because I was so disturbed by my role as a stepparent. I didn't think I was very good at it, and it made me think I wasn't going to be a very good mother. No one was saying to me 'it's different when it's your own.' " Alexis and Bill were married six years before having a child, both because Alexis needed to bolster her confidence in her ability to be a parent and because she wanted to work through the rough spots in her relationship with her stepdaughters first. "I didn't want to introduce anything that would make it worse for them," she remembers, "and actually, it's the best thing we ever did, because having the additional child made us a family in a way we had never been before." While she feels that her relationship with the older girls improved after her daughter's birth, rather than before as she had hoped, doubtless much had been worked out between her and the girls over the years. In addition, waiting until her stepdaughters were into their teens before having a baby also smoothed the transition for them.

Another reason to postpone beginning a "second" family is to acknowledge the reality that the first marriage may not have ended emotionally, despite a divorce and remarriage. When conflict between ex-spouses runs high and battles rage over the children, one or the other partner may insist that having another child should wait. For Abby and Gabriel, the question had always been when, not whether, to have more children. His had been a particularly acrimonious divorce, during and after which his ex-wife ran off with the children. For long periods he was ignorant of their whereabouts, then each parent alternately "snatched" the children, until he withdrew in pain and concern for his sons' well-being. But the tumult of being denied access to his children made it difficult to move on. In a reversal of the more usual pattern, Gabriel was eager to have babies right away, while Abby insisted that he first resolve the struggle over her stepsons.

"I felt so deprived of being able to raise my own children," remembers Gabriel. "I didn't want to substitute these for the others. I knew I still had to fight for them." But the idea that one set of kids could be a substitute for another was itself an obstacle to having children in his remarriage. Remarried to a man who could not have children, Gabriel's ex-wife would periodically tell him and Abby to have their own children "and leave us alone." Put that way, as a directive from her, it became an impossibility.

For her part, Abby describes how for years "the contention over the children was just the major feature of our lives." Echoes of her own childhood, during which she felt abandoned literally by her mother and psychologically by her father, made her angry at Gabriel for not being more assertive of his right to see his children and be a father to them.

Although frightened by Gabriel's passion about having children, and confused by the repetition of themes from her family of origin, Abby later seemed to regret waiting nine years before having their first child: "I'd have kids earlier. But maybe I'm getting to be a fatalist. Maybe it worked out for the best. Objectively, there's no jealousy and there might have been if I'd had children earlier, but it would have made us a family earlier, so that our own needs and desires would have determined our lives, and not just be reacting to the needs of another family."

There is something to be said for this point of view. Increasing the areas of life over which they felt in control would have made for greater satisfaction over the years. Yet, in the intervening time, Gabriel had slowly and painstakingly rebuilt a relationship with his sons, as both he and their mother had begun a series of mutual concessions that led to a grudging truce. When Abby and Gabriel finally did have their own children, they were in no way a substitute for his sons.

Stepping on the Gas

Even more second marriages than first marriages end in divorce. Recent estimates have it that 55 percent of remarriages end in divorce, compared with 50 percent of first marriages, with 40 percent of divorces occurring within four years of the wedding.[5] Because I selected families who had a mutual child who was at least three years old, all had passed this four-year statistical benchmark, although fewer than half had either lived together or been married more than two years when their first mutual child was born. In this, they represent the larger population of stepfamilies.[6] Despite a recognition that, everything else being equal, it is better to wait until the remarriage looks as if it will last before having another child, most of the families went ahead and had a baby, believing that this time would be different.

For everything else is seldom equal. One important consideration that leads people to hurry their childbearing is their preferences about the age gap between existing children and their prospective half siblings. "I didn't want an enormous gap," explained the mother of a son who would be nine and eleven years older than the daughters of her second marriage. While large age differences are a defining feature of most remarried families with children from both marriages, parents try to minimize the gap, both for the children's sake, so they will "feel like sisters and brothers," and so that their own child-rearing days do not seem to stretch into infinity. In thinking about the children's needs, however, their being closer in age should be weighed against giving the older children time to accommodate to a series of transitions that are made more difficult when they follow in rapid succession.

Even more of a constraint than the children's ages is how old parents are when contemplating a new child. The ticking of the biological clock has become the background music for the social lives of many women in their thirties, who orchestrate their social decisions to its beat. As a family therapist and psychologist studying stepfamilies, I knew that, like broken bones, recombined families take time to knit, and that minimizing change meant minimizing stress for all of us. As a woman of thirty-seven, I didn't feel that I could afford to take that time.

Even remarried mothers, contemplating a second or later child, feel the pressure to reproduce while it is still possible. "I was thirty-eight already," Susan told me, laughing, "and I didn't want to have a child when I was ninety, right?" Although Susan and Edward had been together for more than six years when their son was born, her age added urgency to their protracted consideration of how to resolve the question of whether to have a child. "It was time to make a decision."

While the prospective father's age is clearly less critical than that of the mother-to-be, men, too, feel the need to get on with their procreative plans as they feel the years crowd in. In two of the families in which there was a twenty-year gap between partners, it was the men who insisted that whatever babies they would have be born soon. Citing "the difference in our ages," one father was eager to begin having children well before his new wife was. She elaborated: "I felt I was too young, but he was forty-four at the time, and he wanted children before he was too old."

For stepparents, unaccustomed to the added demands of dealing with infants, the presence of children in the marriage from its beginning seems like a reason to get on with having their own. One stepmother explains: "There was always the responsibility of children, ever since we were together. Which is probably why I wanted mine so quickly. If I'm going to have the responsibility, I might as well have my own, too."

The remarried parent, who remembers the increased freedom that comes with a child's greater autonomy, is more inclined to differentiate between the demands of being a parent to an infant and those of being responsible for an older child, while for the stepparent, being the "real" parent for a change offsets the added rigor of infant care. Amelia describes the difference of opinion between her and Joe about the timing of their son's birth: "His biggest complaint is that we never had any time together, just the two of us. Now he blames that on me getting pregnant, and on having Owen." She laughed. "I blame it on his having two kids before. To me, what's the difference, we never had that initial period of no children. But he said a baby is different than Larry and Kevin were, and that we only had them half time. So his argument was that he would have wanted to have waited longer."

As in any family, the decision when to have a child is subject, too, to pressures from outside the remarried family. An aging parent's illness, and the desire for grandchild and grandparent to know one another, is another frequent incentive to accelerate childbearing plans. What happens in the other nucleus of the "binuclear family," or divorced households linked by having children in common, will be taken up in depth in a later chapter. But competition between ex-spouses can give an extra little nudge to the remarried parent whose ex has gone on to have another child with a new partner. One step-mother could not believe that it was coincidental that her stepson's mother became pregnant just two months after she did; while the timing was close, she had had an earlier, recent miscarriage, news of which had been relayed to his mother by the boy. And Eleanor was explicit about how her plans to defer having a child until her profes-sional training was completed were changed when her stepdaughter's mother and stepfather had a child: "Rick had always been clear that he wanted another child, and he started to want to do it right away. Pamela was already seven, and if we waited until I was done with whatever I had to do, she'd be ten or twelve. And I think Rick felt a little nervous that her mother's household was more exciting for Pamela. Somehow their having another kid solidified them as a family. It's hard not to feel competitive and worry."

It is easy to assess competitive feelings as ill-advised and harmful, but I tend to credit Eleanor with being more honest than most. While clearly it should not be a strong motivating factor in deciding to have a child, making one's own home feel attractive and emotionally com-pelling to the child who must come and go from it is an element for all of the stepfamilies I have met, both personally and professionally. Recognition of this competitive element can temper its abuse; knowing it is there, parents and stepparents can look more closely at what they do, using the child's ultimate best interest as a check to acting out old rivalries.

Deciding Whether to Have a Child Together

All of the parents and stepparents interviewed for this book chose to have a child in remarriage. The choice was not always easy, nor was it always well considered in advance. Those who made a similar choice only to regret it have not made their way into these pages: Many of their marriages have ended and they are unlikely volunteers for such a study. As a result, the voices heard here join in a chorus of satisfaction with having added a mutual child to their stepfamily. Their choices may or may not work for everyone.

When a couple is divided about whether to have a child in remarriage, it helps for each person to explore both negative and positive feelings and fantasies about the prospect. In talking with a partner, each one should assume that both are at least a little ambivalent about having a mutual child and talk about both yearnings and doubts, so that one is not always arguing for and the other taking the case against adding a family member. It is common to assume that telling a reluctant partner about your own hesitations will only add fuel to the fires of opposition. On the contrary, admitting to unsureness of your own can allow the partner who is less interested in having another child to explore any inclination to make a positive decision without fear of boarding a train with no scheduled stops.

The interests of children already born can play an important part in deciding when to have a mutual child and how to make sure that the older children are included in family life. Whenever possible, this means waiting until steprelationships rest on a firm foundation before undertaking to change the structure of the family by introducing a new category of member, allowing previous changes to become well established before creating still another transition. It does not mean permanently shelving a shared interest in having a child together.

Time to Become a Family

The families interviewed for this book confirm that there are some tumultuous times on the way to becoming a successful stepfamily. Clearly it is better to wait until the stepfamily has ripened before having a mutual child. A rapid succession of changes is stressful for everyone. But not all stepfamilies feel it is possible to wait the five or so years it takes before relationships have settled into an easy intimacy. Sometimes a pregnancy occasions the remarriage, sometimes the woman's age presents the risk that putting off attempts to conceive may frustrate the eventual goal of a child together, and sometimes wanting to narrow the gap between children, whether to enable them to be playmates or to shorten the span of years when children will be in the home, makes remarried couples willing to shoulder the added emotional work that having a mutual child earlier on entails.

And work it is. It takes determined effort not to retreat from the often difficult task of clearing a path toward mutual understanding and trust through the thicket of mutual ambivalence between stepparent and stepchild. An infant, with whom acceptance, authority, and affection are not at issue, can be both a distraction and a refuge from unfinished business in stepfamily formation. To give in to the temptation to transfer all effort and engagement in the direction of the mutual child is, however, to set the stage for later strife: splits between parent and stepparent, exacerbated rivalry between half siblings, and an inauspicious emotional climate for the development of mutual child and stepchildren alike.

2

Tipping the Parental Balance

Having a baby ushers in big changes for any couple, upsetting the status quo ante. When a first child is born, the shift is from a one-generation to a two-generation family, with husband and wife learning to be mother and father for the first time, and having to reorganize their marriage to include a child in their intimacy. With a later-born child, the family must make room for the child in their affection and on their agenda, redistributing the attention and care available, making for greater closeness or distance between other family members.

As stepfamilies know from firsthand experience with remarriage, changes can be stressful, even if they are anticipated, desired, and highly valued. Research shows that the transition to parenthood is stressful for almost all couples. In a 1957 study, E. E. LeMasters found that 83 percent of the couples who had recently become parents reported moderate or extreme crises in the first year of parenthood.[1] Subsequent research has shown that both parents undergo profound shifts in their sense of themselves, their role arrangements, and their communication as partners, as well as in their relationships with the families from which they have come and with their friends and colleagues.[2] Marital satisfaction typically declines, as does communication between husband and wife, and for women, so do self-esteem and feelings of happiness and adequacy. Perhaps as a result, the time gap between having a baby and deciding to divorce appears to be narrowing. A 1979 study revealed that 15 percent of all parents were separated or divorced by the time the first child was three years old, a percentage that appeared to be on the increase.[3]

Unlike a man and a woman both having their first baby, stepfamilies, by definition, already have children. Some have courted while taking care of babies. But whether they have children in primary residence or for more limited periods, the remarried couple doesn't bring a new baby into a childless home. As a result, the newborn may not require the tremendous leap childless people must make when they have a first baby. Child-centered routines of regular meals and staying home in the evening may be established, and both adults may be used to having children around and considering the children's needs in making plans.

It would be a mistake, however, to minimize the changes set in motion by the birth of the mutual child just because at least one member of the couple has "been there before" and the other has had a period of serving as a parent surrogate. Even if the children of the first marriage live with you, the needs and demands of a ten-year-old, or even a five-year-old, are qualitatively and quantitatively different from those of an infant. And a full-time child can be a novelty for those who haven't lived with their children for many years. Even parents with joint custody must get used to sacrificing their "off duty" time. With a mutual child, the weeks or weekends of adults-only time when the older children are away with their other parent become a thing of the past.

When a couple has a child in a first marriage, both adults experience a simultaneous change in the roles they occupy, adding "parent," whether mother or father, to their repertoire of relationships and responsibilities: husband or wife, son or daughter, brother or sister, friend, worker and coworker. For stepfamilies in which both partners bring children from a previous union, this symmetry is preserved, for both have been both parent and stepparent before the birth of their child together. In the more frequent case in which only one partner has had a child before, the asymmetry is modified but it persists. One becomes a parent for the first time, but continues to be a stepparent, too. The veteran parent of the pair, however, remains a parent only, perhaps a parent in residence as opposed to a parent who is visited by his children.

Having a child who is both of theirs shifts the balance in the couple as a parenting team, changing who does what for whom and how they see themselves and the other as parents. It forces parent and stepparent to confront their own differences as they become for the first time a team with equal claim to and equal authority over the same child. Being parents together creates patterns of decision making and authority that carry over to the care of all the children. Finally, having a child in remarriage changes the life of the couple as marital partners as well as parents, reorganizing how they spend their time together and increasing the likelihood that the stepfamily will endure.

Unlike the social science laboratory, real life has a habit of confounding the effects of any given change by heaping one on top of another. For several of the families I studied, sorting out the impact of having a child in a remarriage was almost impossible because so many things were changing at the same time. Many were in new living arrangements. As noted earlier, nearly half the couples had a child within two years of living under the same roof. Others made significant changes in their work lives at about the same time their child was born, going back to school or taking on a demanding job that made them less available to all the children. As one stepmother put it, referring to a rating of life changes that predispose to illness, "We picked the top ten things on the stress scale and did them all; it was pretty tense." The year of their son's birth included divorce, marriage, pregnancy, remodeling a house, and the older children's starting a new school. Custody changes, the death of aging parents, dramatic job shifts, and the adolescence of older children can also complicate the assessment of how having a child together changes life for a couple in a stepfamily.

Whatever else is going on, however, the baby's arrival gets most of the credit for desired changes and most of the blame for changes that are disliked. Especially for stepfamilies that have not had time to consolidate before the birth of a mutual child, the child feels like a ticket of entry into the family for the parent whose previous role was exclusively stepparent.

It is this feeling that legitimacy or normalcy will be achieved by having a child together that unleashes tense anticipation of what it will be like to have a family in which the adults are *differently attached* to the children for whose care they are responsible, giving rise to fears that these different kinds of attachments among family members will compromise the care of some of the children. After all, a common idiom used to describe being deprived or maltreated is being treated "like a stepchild."

Varying Attachment

To begin with, we must remember that it is not "love and love alike" in any family. While parents may be meticulously even-handed, they cannot help but respond differently to different children. One child may remind them of a beloved grandparent, another of a ne'er-do-well uncle. Some children may remind parents of themselves as children, while others may be temperamentally different enough to seem like an ambassador from another planet. Temperamental match between parent and child, family circumstances at the time of the birth, physical and personality resemblance, and the parent's hopes and dreams for the baby all shape the evolving relationship between each parent and each of the children. In families that stay together from the conception of their children till death do them part it is not unusual to have one daughter who identifies more strongly with her mother, while another is "Daddy's little girl." Varying attachments are a fact of life in all families.

What is different about stepfamilies is how explicit the differences are and how disproportionate they can be. Even when stepparents have been involved with the child since infancy and the child "likes" the stepparent better than a parent, the child will feel more emotional resonance with natural parents than with stepparents. The difference in attachment will persist, despite attempts to deny it. It is not necessary for steprelatives to withhold care to preserve the "specialness" of the biological tie. The challenge for stepparents and stepchildren alike is to get beyond the loyalty games that equate loving a stepparent with betraying the same-sex parent, or getting close to a stepson with abandoning the son a father may see more infrequently.

Comparing attachments in stepfamilies often feels like a "damned if you do, damned if you don't" bind. If bonds to parent and stepparent are too even-handed, the child feels she has betrayed her natural parent; if the care and attention bestowed on child and stepchild are equal, the parent feels he has abandoned his own child. On the other hand, discrepancies in attachment that feel too great compromise the self-esteem of the parent as nurturer, especially for stepmothers, who are apt to chide themselves as guilty failures for favoring their own.

Few meet the rigorous standards of equality posed by one mother/stepmother: "I used to play a game with myself, and I never lost," says Marilyn, describing how she tested her allegiance to her stepdaughters by comparing it to her attachment to her sons. "When I would check in with myself about how I feel about these kids, I used to fantasize that they all needed rescuing and they were calling to me. I wouldn't know whom to rescue before the other."

Couples who have both brought children to the remarriage have had to struggle with the issue of allegiance and attachment from the time the stepfamily begins. For those families in which only one parent has previously had children, the prospect of a child together introduces a new wrinkle. Before the mutual child arrives, all children have had the same form of relationship with their parent, and all the children have had the same form of relationship with their stepparent. Now, for the first time, there will be a child whose parent is another child's stepparent, and the differences that prospect evokes can be a source of concern for both parent and stepparent.

What Are the Differences?

For a stepparent, the answer to the question "Will I feel different about my own child?" is almost invariably "yes," but the differences range from almost negligible to profound. The more integrated the stepfamily at the time of the birth, the less dramatic the discrepancy in attachment.

After six years of taking care of Leo, Elaine felt their relationship was better than those of most stepmothers and stepsons, because they had worked so hard at it. Elaine loves Leo, she has a good time with him, and yet when she does not feel exactly as she thinks she would feel if he were her baby, she feels guilty, as if there were "something lacking in me." Curious to learn what the differences she couldn't wish away would be like, she sought help in the experience of others. At the supermarket checkout, she compared notes with the man in line ahead of her, himself the stepfather of two children and the father of a two-year-old. "Well, for me," he told her, "I would kill for any of my kids, but I would do it for this one with more passion." "At the time I thought, 'What a weird statement.' And then I thought that was what I felt too. It didn't have anything to do with love, or the degree of love. It's something really more animal."

Before having a child of his own, the stepparent may idealize his relationship with his stepchild, like Andrew, who told of his "ideal vision that there was not any reason why Nathaniel couldn't be as much a son of mine as a natural child. And just having a kid made it clear how different it was. I saw that as something that I didn't really have control over. It's just a fact." It was, however, a fact he felt guilty about, regretting that he was not as committed as a parent, vigilant lest he appear to be favoring one over the over, despite a prejudice he experienced as unavoidable.

The difference is that the mutual child feels more "a part of me" to the first-time parent than does the stepchild, whose early years occurred in the stepparent's absence. For some, the difference is seen as biologically based, with the mutual child as a mirror of the self and a link in a genetic chain to past generations, while the stepchildren are experienced ahistorically and as "not self." Irene explains: "I didn't look at the older children differently, but I did realize that genes make a difference, in that your children are a lot of the grandparents. When Emily acted a certain way, I saw my mother, I saw my father. When Amy would misbehave, I could understand it, because I remember getting in shouting matches with my own mother. I could see that the older kids were like their father in many respects, but they were also like other relatives. When they would misbehave, I couldn't say 'that's like somebody in my family or myself' and accept it as easily. I'm proud of all my kids, but when it's your natural child, there's a little more of you in that person. It's like 'I've done this, it's part of *me.*' " Elaine, like Irene, goes on to qualify the weight given to genetics in explaining differences: "Or maybe it's because you have the kid from infancy. You've been there the whole time. I'm sure people who adopt may have the same thing."

She is right. Being there the whole time, or from early on, is an important part of the difference. The younger the child when a stepparent enters the picture, the closer the attachment will be. The very needfulness of the infant, its dependence on care for its very survival, most effectively elicits attachment in caregivers. Feeding and bathing, drying tears and playing games, the everyday labor-intensive care demanded by very young children is tremendously engaging; it is the stuff of which love and connectedness are made, as the farmer loves the soil he tills, and the Little Prince his flower.

For their part, the younger the children, the more openly they can embrace a new stepparent. In an earlier study on children's ideas about sex and birth, I learned that for preschoolers all women are Mommies and all men Daddies.[4] To get to be a parent, you have merely to eat your vegetables, brush your teeth, and follow the imperatives of childhood until you are grown up. Unless loyalty conflicts are invoked by difficulties between the parents, the bonds between preschool child and stepparent can approximate the parental bond. And it is in these families that the difference in attachment to stepchildren and mutual children is minimal.

Edward is a stepfather who differentiates minimally between his son and his stepson. Many factors go into the lack of difference: He has known Carl since this stepson was a toddler, and he has been a member of the household since Carl was three. He and Susan were ambivalent about having another child, taking many years to come to an affirmative decision, so that by the time their son, Eric, was born, their stepfamily had been in existence for almost seven years and was well consolidated. Also significant, Edward had no burning need to have a biological child. Carl had satisfied a great amount of his parenting urge: "a chance to teach somebody some things and love somebody and reach out and pick this kid up and comfort him and stuff like that."

For Edward, the distinctions are there, but they are not a significant force in family politics. When Eric was born, he discovered the mysterious "something about blood . . . when this little guy came squeaking out of the womb and hit my hand, there was a lot of electricity in that." But the years have given a naturalness to Edward's relationship with Carl. Because Edward feels that Carl accepts and respects him, the "electricity" doesn't have much charge: "Once I get past that, there aren't a lot of implications for making distinctions between the boys, in terms of what my responsibilities are, or whether I love this person and am going to do right by him, take care of him and meet his needs. Those are givens that don't have anything to do with the blood relationship.

"I don't want to exaggerate the blood thing," Edward continues. "I didn't sit there with Eric in my arms and say 'This one's mine.' It's hard to define. I look at Eric and I can see myself in him. In his eyes, I see my mother's eyes. He's got my chin. He's got Susan's feet and my hands. Physically, I can look at him and see the fact that here are two pools of genes that got together, had intercourse, and created a combination of themselves.

"I feel a kinship with Carl, which is all of those elements," he elaborated, "absent the blood. One way to say it is when this child comes out of the womb and it's your child, there's a whole host of obligations and responsibilities that are right there and indisputable. With Carl, they were acquired. I may feel no different about Eric when he's sixteen than I feel about Carl at sixteen: how I relate to him, what I want him to be, what kind of limits, expressions and the rest of it. But for Carl it was an accumulative process, both of us coming to understand that we could invest that kind of blind faith in each other that is a given when the baby is yours. I guess that's what the difference between blood and not blood is. And a lot of people, probably, with their stepchildren, don't ever get to that level of acceptance."

When, as is more usual, the birth of a child to the remarriage leads to a discovery of more difference than one wishes existed, the loss of an ideal vision of the family creates conflict for many stepparents, whether they strive to avoid all appearances of favoritism or indulge the passion of their special tie to their own child. For many stepparents, especially those in the early phases of stepfamily formation, the birth of the mutual child signals the first time that feeling accepted as a parent is not an issue. "The feelings I have toward my kids are really new to me," explained a stepmother who had just told me about the tentativeness in her relationship with her stepsons, even after a decade of intermittent contact. "For the first time I feel really comfortable and accepted. With the boys, I want some show of affection, and it requires some maturity on my part to look at the situation and know that they do care for me on one level. I kind of talk myself through it."

Stepmothers, especially, trace the distance they feel from their stepchildren to the triangle between child, mother, and stepmother. Perhaps because the remarriage rate of divorced women trails that of their ex-husbands, perhaps because of the far more dramatic decrease in their standard of living following divorce, and certainly because women invest more of their sense of themselves in their parental role and responsibilities, mothers continue to be more of a presence in the homes of their remarried ex-spouses than are divorced fathers. "The ex-wife is never ex," complained one stepmother. "She's in your life forever if you have shared custody." Every stepparent must come to terms with the fact that no matter how "terrible" a parent the child's other parent is, the child will have "a certain attachment to her that he will never have to me."

Having a child who has only two parents can be a tremendous relief for couples who have had to negotiate provisions for child rearing among three or more adults. Many stepparents attribute their greater closeness to their own children to the absence of the tension with a same-sex parent. "I don't have the history of having battled around her," said a stepmother, explaining why her daughter is an easier person for her to be close to than her stepdaughters. "I've had her since the Day One. There's not been somebody hanging over my shoulder criticizing me the whole time, which I've had with the girls. Their mother has been constantly criticizing."

One way for a stepparent to cope with his counterpart's being there in spirit whenever the child is in the house is by withdrawing from the child. To the extent that this represents a reconciliation with the limits of being a stepparent, it can be a reasonable adaptation; to the extent that it goes beyond that to give up on the relationship, it can prejudice the development of all concerned. Distressed to discover a preference for their own child, stepparents often struggle with guilt as they strive to reconcile conflicting emotions, perhaps withdrawing from the older children, perhaps papering over emotional gaps with a rigid and inappropriate sameness. It's a balancing act: attempting to neither deny the very real distinction nor express it in ways that are confounding and destructive.

Stepmother's Child, Stepfather's Child

Stepmothers tend to feel more of a difference in attachment to their children as compared to their stepchildren than do stepfathers. Especially vulnerable in this regard are stepmothers who have had no earlier children of their own, who researchers agree seem to have a harder time in stepfamilies than do mothers, stepmothers with previous children, fathers, or stepfathers.[5] Although this may be due to inexperience with children, more telling, perhaps, is the greater confusion about expectations for stepmothers. When, as is usually the case, the mother is the primary parent, children may feel more confused about what to expect from a stepmother than from a stepfather.

Stepfathers are more like fathers than stepmothers are like mothers because their job descriptions are essentially similar: "Wanted: Male parent. Must bring home the bacon, dandle baby on knee, play games with older children, occasionally lay down the law, and dispense hugs and kisses at day's end."

Despite the very real changes in women's and men's traditional parental roles, the trend toward shared parenting is still a minority phenomenon. Women remain primarily responsible for the care of children. The very word *mother* conjures up images of the earth, a source of emotional bounty, nurturance, and life itself. She is the bosom on which to find comfort, the skirt to cling to, the safe haven in which to seek shelter and replenishment. Her primacy and centrality present a dilemma: By definition, there can be only one center. The expression "a face only a mother could love" tells it all. Stepmothers do not offer that level of acceptance, nor, we must remember, do all mothers. But for the child who wants a stepmother to "do everything I want my mother to do and nothing I don't like my mother to do," less than unconditional love is felt as more of a deficit from a stepmother than from a stepfather. "Mothering" means more contact between stepparent and stepchild, and more contact, especially when it entails the traditional tasks of socialization, makes for more opportunities for conflict.

Even in families in which both parents have had children before remarriage, stepmothers seem to differentiate more between their stepchildren and those born to them. Grown children of the remarriage recall how, as young children, they didn't know that not all the children in the family were their father's natural kids, while it was obvious who was and who wasn't their mother's child. Disposed to credit both parents with benevolent intentions, children may see mom as treating their half siblings differently "subconsciously," "not on purpose," or because the older children made it hard for her to treat them equally, even scapegoating her for other problems. Dad, on the other hand, has never given the impression of loving one child more than another.

Because the role of stepmother has many pitfalls, women typically feel that they fall short of their desired job performance. Perhaps this is why stepmothers having a first baby differ from other first mothers in not suffering a decline in self-esteem in becoming a parent.[6] Without exception, all of the stepparents interviewed expressed relief and delight in the comfort of attaching to their firstborn. Most of the stepmothers I spoke with talked about the joy of feeling like a good enough mother at last. Perhaps for stepmothers having a baby, confidence in themselves as parents has nowhere to go but up.

The First Child

There is something about first children that makes for a particularly intense parent-child bond. While this is true in all families, it may be more true in stepfamilies in which the stepparent's firstborn also confers legitimacy as a parent. "Now you're a *real* mother, too," one of my stepsons said to me when my son was born. Greater attachment to a firstborn child does not necessarily mean that child is the most loved, rather that she is the child with whom a parent may feel most connected, most empathic; the one with whom the boundaries may be fuzziest, the one who can push all the buttons.

Mike describes how Ethan, his second son and his wife's firstborn, gets "this adoring love from his mother, it's totally passionate," as contrasted with a "pretty consistent, but I would say more busy and less devoted to him father."

Mike has learned from experience to cool the passion of his attachment to Jason, his own firstborn, and he sees the parallels in Irma's connection to Ethan: "Ethan likes to push her buttons, and her buttons get pushed by him. It's like my relationship to Jason when he was young. Very deep and very passionate, intimate. I have a much more detached relationship with Ethan. When he gets upset, he won't vamp on me; he'll go and vamp on her. That's the negative part. She doesn't know yet how to detach herself enough from her boy." But Irma, too, is more detached with *her* second son. "She knows how to step back with Ezra," Mike continues. "I think it's pretty classical. You go through one kid and with the second kid you know more about how to handle certain emotions. It's the same with me in learning from Jason to Ethan."

All but one of the stepmothers and most of the stepfathers I spoke to identified their firstborn as the child they were closest to, and for more than half of them, this connection felt stronger than the bond with their partners. A difficult choice, this ranking was often reached by contrasting the greater sharing with the spouse to the feeling that the child was the one to whom one's very survival was held hostage; the loss of a partner would be painful but recovery was foreseeable, the loss of a child would be unendurable. "She's very much a part of myself, the one who could hurt me most," said one mother, attesting to the strength of identification with her first child.

When the passion of this connection overwhelms all other family ties, however, the mutual child gets to be looked on as not mutual at all, but rather the "property" of the stepparent, a construction of reality that has dysfunctional consequences for the family as a whole and the child himself.

All My Children

Several of the parents were surprised at how attached they were to the child of their remarriage, especially if the baby was principally the stepparent's idea. Both mothers and fathers fail to anticipate that they will fall so in love with the new child. A mother may be astonished to find she misses their mornings together when her second son goes off to school. A father may expect to be more detached from his second child, thinking that he had stepped back a little from active parenting. Instead, he finds himself fonder of the daughter he had considered a concession to her mother than he'd thought he'd be.

Part of the attractiveness of the parent to his family-oriented partner is his love for his children, which for many single parents has been a lifebuoy in the stormy seas of marital transition. Both parent and stepparent may worry in anticipation about whether "he was going to love our kid as much as he loved his kid." Putting aside the question of "as much as" for the moment, all have been pleasantly surprised. "I didn't really think it was going to happen," admitted Mike, "but I did fall in love with the second child. I was surprised to feel this tremendously deep commitment to Ethan as well as to Jason."

Tom tells how a veteran of divorce can expect to keep his distance from another child, especially when the motivation to have a baby is mostly a partner's: "I thought before I had Emma that I had stepped back a little somehow. I felt that I would be more detached than I was with George." Questioned further, he reveals what may be behind this anticipated detachment: "When Maggie and I split up . . . obviously you get attached to a kid, and that puts you in a very vulnerable position with a woman. And that was not something I wanted to set myself up for again. But then if I'd thought about it, I would have realized that there was no way of getting around it." Even those who have been through it before, even those who don't want to open themselves up to the pain of potential loss, forget how effective infants can be in eliciting attachment in their caretakers.

Whether their love for their "second set" of children is anticipated or a surprise, remarried parents retain a particularly intense attachment to the children who have lived with them during the days of single parenthood. The special feeling of connection to the child who first makes you a parent has been mentioned above in discussing the power of the bond between parent and firstborn child. But the longevity of the connection, the time in the parent's own adult development, and the child as solace in a time of trouble, following divorce or bereavement, all give the relationship between parent and older child an unrivaled intensity. For single parents of an only child, the time between marriages can be very much a case of "you and me against the world," giving that relationship greater importance, even survival value.

While stepmothers are more apt to differentiate between their stepchildren and natural children than are stepfathers, the reverse is true for natural parents. Mothers were less likely to make distinctions among the children when they had cared for all since birth. The sole exceptions were one mother who had been single with her daughter, intensifying their connection, before marrying her son's father, and two mothers each with an older son with whom conflict had been longstanding. Fathers, however, tended to savor the connection to their older children; while they loved the children of their remarriage and did not actively discriminate among their children, a history of being a single parent, feeling alone, guilty, or vulnerable, enhanced the emotional charge of their attachment to the older kids.

For men, the duration of the connection, coupled with a child's being older, a teenager or adult with whom he can talk more than with a youngster, tend to make the child of an earlier marriage the one he names as closest to him. Work patterns, too, enter into this. When a child comes at a time of intense career development, or financial stress and overtime, a child may get less time with a parent who had more to give either earlier or later.

Rick talks of his "special relationship" with Pamela, his oldest daughter and the only child of his first marriage, although he is now the father of four. "It's a little different than my relationship with my other kids. I'm not sure I would characterize it as closer or that having my other kids made my relationship to Pamela closer. Although over the years, it's true, having had the other children makes me appreciate that there is something unique about my relationship with Pamela, because I was so focused on her. And when she was at my house, I had more responsibility for her than anybody else. A lot of it goes back to who I was when I had Pamela, and the amount of my identity wrapped up in her. My marriage breaking up was hard for me. I was really adrift in my life, and I focused a tremendous amount of energy on her. I can remember feeling, sometimes when she was under two, I had the feeling wash over me that being the father of this child was just the most wonderful thing that could ever happen to me. It was a visceral, physical feeling, and I think that had to do with my own vulnerability."

Other fathers, too, describe being more adrift in their lives when their first children were born, so that "he was what I did on the weekends," pitching the ball around, riding bikes, and doing the kind of things that a more established work life and more than one child leave dramatically less time for. Important, too, is the intensity of bonding between a parent and the child who has been a companion through the frequently traumatic times of family disruption. Guilt at causing pain to the child and solace in the child's very existence go a long way toward making that child "the apple of my eye," the "bones of my body."

Having more than one child in the original family does not necessarily dilute the emotional pull between father and children. A father may sometimes feel closest to the younger of two. Perhaps he tries to overcompensate for the fact that the younger child had less time with him. Conversely, he may feel a special bond to the older, as a firstborn, the one he had the longest time with, if divorce marked the end of sharing a household. When bereavement precedes remarriage, the original family may have more emotional pull, as its children now have only one natural parent, while the children born since have another parent who is coequal. Irene tells how her husband, Gene, still identified Daryl, the youngest of her three stepchildren, as "the baby," even after the second of their two daughters was born: "One day somebody says to Gene, 'How's your youngest doing?' And he says, 'Oh, Daryl's fine.' Here we have Emily and Amy, and he's not thinking of her as his youngest. Daryl is still his baby. I thought that was significant. He's had Daryl longer, and he really had a lot to do with Daryl's care, because the mother was sick. He probably had more to do with caring for him than he had with Amy, 'cause I was right here on the scene. Although they played games together, and she helped her daddy in the yard."

In short, older children, despite some of the apprehension to be discussed later, do not seem to lose a parent's love when that parent has more children with a new spouse. If anything, especially with fathers who remain an active part of the older child's life, it is the new child who must win a place for himself.

The Division of Labor

Earlier we saw how the very labor devoted to tending to a child's needs helps develop the bonds of attachment between child and caregiver, be it parent or stepparent. How the work of caring for children is divided between parent and stepparent varies enormously among families: Social class, community mores, custodial arrangements, whether the other natural parent is still living, sex-role expectations, and personal predilections all enter into how much responsibility stepparents take for their stepchildren and how much is left to the partner who is the children's natural parent. Whatever the preexisting division of labor, the rocking of the mutual child's cradle can also rock the boat.

Stepmother families and stepfather families tend to differ markedly on this dimension. While there are significant social trends toward increasing commitment by fathers to the nitty-gritty of children's care, mothers still, by and large, take primary responsibility for meeting the needs of children in families. Psychologist Diane Ehrensaft found that even in the minority of families in which both parents contract to be egalitarian partners as parents, electing to "share mothering," in her terms, women tend to keep the agendas and make sure that everything that needs to get done does get done. As Ehrensaft puts it, "Men *do* mothering, women *are* mothers."[7]

Stepfamilies in which the mother is the natural parent of all the children tend toward an exaggerated version of the stereotypical role division. Because the children are hers more than they are their stepfather's, she is doubly primary. More even than in families with two biological parents, the custodial mother is the emotional hub, the source of nurturance and support, the one in whose hands final responsibility rests.

Stepmother families, however, whether the stepmother brings her own children to the new marriage or not, are tugged in two directions. The stronger ties between parent and child pull the father into a more active role than he might ordinarily play, and frequently a more active role than he did play with his children before the end of his former marriage. But counterposed to the biological pull toward greater paternal involvement is the sociological pull toward female responsibility for children. Sociologist Nancy Chodorow has demonstrated that little girls, mothered by women in a culture that defines child care as women's work, develop a capacity for nurturance and a stake in mothering that far exceeds their brothers' interest and cultivated ability in this area.[8] While few if any little girls go to bed at night and dream about the day when they will be stepmothers, there is something about being the female adult in a family that includes children that pulls for the exercise of the templates for mothering formed in childhood.

And fathers, being grown-up boys who were also mothered by women, are far more ready than mothers to step back and allow a stepparent in. Frequently, they not only allow stepmothers to share responsibility for their children, they expect that a new wife, as a woman, will take on tasks that they had not considered rightfully theirs in the first place. Even when a man is a committed egalitarian as a single or joint-custodial parent, he may discover that his new wife comes up with parental responsibilities that he had not yet considered.[9]

Dotting the "I's" and Crossing the "T's"

Having a mutual child necessarily makes changes in how a parent and stepparent function as a team of caregivers. The addition of a new member always requires shifts in the organization of a family, and the demands of infant care can strain prior arrangements about who does what and when. As we saw earlier, negotiations about having and caring for a child together can be lengthy and laborious.

When a parent had thought he was "finished" with having children, a stepparent commonly contracts to do most of the work. Seldom are the negotiations as explicit as the contract one father, a union man, made with his wife to split responsibilities on a sixty-forty basis: "My philosophy was that if I could convince Irma to pick up most of the shitwork, and I could sit around the house and bounce him on my knee, I was going to do it. It was up to her to figure out what she wasn't going to do and convince me. It was up to her to come back with a counterproposal that made sense in terms of our lives."

More frequently the contract is implied. Perhaps typical for stepmother families is the story of Alice and John, the father of two daughters. Alice was very mindful that in having their daughter, John was making a concession. She describes her strategy: "I said, 'Look, I'm willing to do more of the work, because I'm the one who's pushing this, and you've already done it.' The general theory was that I'd take on more of the logistics, the day-to-day hassle. We would share responsibility, but if there was some spillover, it was going to be my job." Behind her willingness to take on more of the responsibility, competing with her desire to be a mother to a child, was her fear that John would feel imposed upon: "I have always been very concerned that he will resent her, the little one, because it was my idea to have her."

If Alice is typical of most stepmothers and an occasional stepfather in promising to do "more than her share," John is typical of most of their partners in knowing, from the vantage point of experience, that such plans are abstractions, and that real children and their real needs cannot be so neatly divided. "There were announced plans," he told me, "and there were unannounced plans. The announced plans were Alice saying 'This is my child. I sort of forced this on you, and I will take the major parenting role.' The unannounced plans were my saying 'I can't simply have a child and ignore it and put all the work off on the other person.' Alice's plans, as announced, were made because she was afraid I would resent the child terribly. Versus my knowledge that it was going to be my child, whether I wanted originally to have one or not. That was not going to be a lot different, once the child was there."

In earlier times, and in social classes or communities that value shared parenting less, it was and is more common for stepmothers to carry through on their intent to take on the major responsibility for a child they see as existing primarily at their urging. Speaking of twenty years past, Gene describes how Irene didn't "allow," but then changes it to "ask" him to share the chores of child care. "When the girls were coming along, I remember Irene telling me, 'Don't worry, I know you've gone through this. You don't have to worry about changing any diapers,' something like that. So, I kind of enjoyed sitting back. Although I'm not . . . I changed diapers for these kids, too. When you need to help out, you help out. Especially an old salt like me." Years later, he regrets that "I'm not as close to the girls, like I'd like to be. That's because Irene has taken over."

Approaching a Middle Ground

Couples approached sharing child care from two directions, and their paths seemed to cross somewhere in the middle. Committed egalitarians whose first children had been born in the late sixties or early seventies set a more traditional course with their second set of offspring, whereas mothers who had shouldered most of the work and fathers who had missed out on too much of their older children's early lives moved in the direction of more equity.

Maggie, whose husband Eliot just assumed she would take more responsibility for their children, didn't really think about how it would work day in and day out. Having shared the care of her older son with his father on a more rigorously egalitarian basis, she attributes the change in her current arrangements to the changing times with their attendant peer pressures: "There were a lot of pressures in the early seventies to coparent. This is hard to say, did you hear me hesitate? I think the main difference is me. In the early seventies, when George was little, I really and truly wanted to share parenting. I thought it was absolutely the most important thing in terms of changing sex roles. I don't think I was fanatical, but I really believed that, and I don't think I believe that in the same ways now. I'm willing now to take most of the responsibility in child rearing and trust that who Eliot is as a loving, nonsexist person will come through. He doesn't have to take care of our children half of the time in order for them to learn that."

It is not just the tempering of ideology with time, as any banner must be tailored when experience informs belief, nor does the difference lie wholly in how the eighties are unlike the seventies. Having children in her thirties, as opposed to having them in her twenties, also entered into Maggie's greater willingness to assume major responsibility for child care, selecting a flexible job in order to take her baby with her to work: "I loved that and wouldn't have wanted to give that up. I wouldn't have wanted to give them to Eliot. They felt so precious to me. I guess that's age. George felt extremely precious, but at that point I had the whole rest of my life and I might have had four or five more children. By the time Aileen came along it was quite a bit later. I wanted to spend as much time with her as I could."

Fathers who had been equally sharing parents the first time around had, by and large, had enough. More involved in their work lives than

earlier, partly because of the greater financial pressure of supporting
more children, often in two homes, they were less willing to do it again.
As Mike put it, "It was not going to be fifty-fifty. I was not interested
in fifty-fifty anymore. I'd seen that movie." Not a complete renegade,
he estimated that the current balance of labor for his and Irma's first
son was sixty-forty and for their second sixty-five–thirty-five. And, he
reasoned, since he still had more responsibility for his oldest son, who
is with them half of the time, it balanced out. "Was it really so rigid
as all that," I asked, "with a 40 percent time commitment for one of
their children and 35 percent on the other?" "No," he admitted, "it's
just when I don't feel like doing something, I say 'I've already done my
35 percent this week.' "

  While stepmothers tend to lean over backward, committing
themselves to do most of the work because they fear their husbands'
resentment about being reluctant repeat fathers, a father's initial interest in having more children is not the most significant factor in
determining how much responsibility he will take for the everyday
care of the children. Social class, financial stress, work pressures, and
perhaps most important, a desire not to repeat an unhappy earlier
experience are all more influential. A father who felt his first wife
was somewhat neglectful may find a second wife who nurtures their
child to be "beyond my wildest dreams," not requiring him to fill
the breach while encouraging his partnership. A man who felt that
the coparental arrangement with his older child's mother was competitive and alienating may be willing to "do a lot more work around
the house than your average father," but not take on again "the
overriding responsibility" for a child.

  While several of the stepmothers who volunteered to do most of
the work find that the balance is not as skewed as anticipated, other
stepmothers who have seen their husbands as active, engaged parents
of older children are disappointed by a man's refusal to be as "hands
on" with the children they share. Resentment can set in even if things
work out to be pretty consistent with plans.

  Seeing a man as a very involved and doting parent to his children
during courtship creates expectations in his second wife that can lead
to later disappointments. A stepmother describes her surprise at finding
that so much of the infant care for their colicky first son fell on her:
"I'd always seen Simon spend equal time with the kids, but they were
older when I saw them. With an infant, Simon definitely sees the

mother as primary. I'm not saying he leaves it all up to the mother to do, but he definitely takes a back seat."

With men who have never taken an active role in child rearing, the balance can be more skewed and the disappointment more intense. Traditional sex role expectations, more exaggerated in working-class families, seem to change more slowly for men than for women. A stepmother, now a part-time retail clerk over the initial objections of her husband, a bus driver, describes how her expectations, minimal as they are, were not met: "It sure wasn't anything like what I pictured. I guess when we would talk maybe it would be mostly me talking and saying 'Jeez, I hope you do this, and I hope you do that.' I thought my husband would help a whole lot more than he is. I thought that he'd help me with the baby, changing diapers, getting a bottle or two. Just giving me a rest sometimes, and it didn't happen. I don't think he understood why I was the way I was, being so angry and tight. My husband is strictly going to work and coming home. I was the wife who was to stay home and watch the kids."

Perhaps the fathers most committed to spending more of their time with their second set of children were those who felt they had lost something the first go-around by having just such traditional expectations. One father who took on a more active day-to-day parenting role with the child of his second marriage than he did with his older children included the dissolution of his first marriage in the disadvantages wrought by the earlier division of labor. John told me: "At age twenty I was more involved with what roles the father plays and the mother plays. We had somewhat advanced ideas for the time of how fathers should be more interactive with the children, partly because I wanted to have a better relationship with my kids than I had with my father. But I still held a lot of traditional ideas: I would work, I would expect meals to be ready for me when I got home . . . leading not insignificantly to separation and divorce. By the time Angela came along, my thinking on what I should do, if not what I wanted to do, was quite different." Despite his initial reluctance to have another child, he is an active parent, perhaps to avoid the marital tension that imbalance had created in his first marriage.

Even more common among older fathers is the desire not to miss out on the intimacy that more direct involvement with children creates. Ingrid describes her husband Jack as being of the opinion that young fathers are "lousy" compared to older men. "Young men are so self-absorbed, and so concerned about their career, and making it, that they don't always appreciate the valuable moments with their children. He didn't want that to slip by with these kids, so he was a real participant."

Jack himself is "continually impressed that I was a much better father to the younger kids than I was to the older: more tolerant, more loving, and I gave them much more time. Which I view primarily as a function of my age." Despite his decreased tolerance for noise, and "the randomness, the disruptiveness of kids," in his late forties and fifties, he prefers to spend time with his family more than he did in his thirties, when the older children were small. "My second set of kids were tougher on me," he told me, "but I was a better father to them."

Unlike the men described earlier who had shared parenting equally with their first set of children, putting their work lives in a holding pattern, this group was somewhat older, reaching maturity in the fifties and devoting their energies when young to building a career. Given the chance to be a father to a young child again, aware of how quickly the years go by, they elect to be more of a participant in the care of the children of remarriage, enjoying it more because they are more involved. Despite their greater participation in child care, this group of fathers does not sign up for the fifty-fifty contract that some of their younger counterparts had undertaken years ago and not renewed. Traditional gender roles had been stretched but not redefined.

When a stepmother who wants a child convinces her husband to have another by promising to do most or all of the work of child care, she is reinforcing the traditional division of labor. Stepfathers in the same position, making the same offer, are more likely to propose a fair division of labor, as sex role expectations and the desire for an additional child become countervailing forces, moving the man toward more involvement.

For one such couple, the original plan was that Eli would raise their baby, a prepregnancy fantasy that fit in fine with Nancy's plans: "I'd raised these two kids. I'd had all these years of single parenthood. I was ready to be out in the world. And Eli had traveled around, had no connections for all those years. He was ready for home, the apple tree, and the baby. Now where," she laughingly concluded, "did that go wrong?"

She answered her own question: "Here I was pregnant. My energy was down. I gave up the idea of taking the bar exam for another year.

How were we going to live? Someone had to work to support the baby. I was not of a mind to establish a career at that point, I was growing a baby. So Eli began getting very worried about this, and working hard and making connections and getting a job."

Despite the failure of the original plan for a role reversal in child care, by the time their daughter was two years old, they both described the arrangement as "equal when both are home." "More and more it's gone back to the original fantasy," Eli told me. "I am more of a primary caretaker, because I'm more attached to Ilona. And she needs less overall, so what she needs, I can support." Two years later, when their daughter was four, they separated. Their joint custody arrangement includes more time with Daddy.

The need to make a living is a given in family life, and how a couple divides child care responsibilities depends on how their work lives are structured. For Eli and Nancy, his greater ability to earn a living precluded his being their daughter's primary caretaker in her first years. For another couple, a more unusual pattern prevailed: She was the one with the steady income and a career that she had worked for all her life, so he "looked forward gratefully to the opportunity" to be his son's primary caretaker as he had been his daughter's. Work also becomes a factor in changing patterns of child care over time, most frequently as men who have devoted more time to their children in the early years pull back when they feel that they are "losing it professionally."

Perhaps the most prepared to share the hands-on care of their mutual child are those couples who have been together years before his birth and shared the care of the children one or both brought to the marriage. "We'd already had a child and we had shared a lot," Susan said, describing Edward's involvement with his stepson for more than six years. "When we talked about having a child, I said 'I'm not into this for my own thing. I've never been a full-time parent by myself, and I'm not into that now.' It was almost offensive to him, because we had never done anything in the house that way." "We committed ourselves," Edward told me, "to the notion that this was a shared job. It wasn't 'If we have this child, you're the mother and it's a mother's job to raise children.' I don't believe that."

Yet even for a couple like Susan and Edward, a commitment to shared parenting is limited by the pull of traditional role definitions, a force like gravity that shapes their decisions and their actions in ways that are not always taken into account. Susan, not unhappily, describes some of the limits of the equality: "It was always understood that he would be as involved as he could under the assumption that I would be nursing. I planned to take off a bunch of time, because I wanted to and he thought it was a good idea too. He was supportive of it, financially." Edward added, "Within the framework of the fact that I work five days and she works three, the notion of shared responsibility of parenting has been pretty much borne out." So, too, does the reciprocal influence of work and family get played out in every family; and in most it is the woman who tailors her work schedule to fit her family responsibilities, while her husband's choices are made to fulfill a primary commitment to creating a sound financial foundation and fostering a work-based identity.

Ready for an Encore?

However a couple elects, or is constrained by circumstance, to divide responsibility for caring for children and stepchildren, becoming parents of a mutual child demands a series of adjustments. Having made those adjustments, are remarried couples sufficiently satisfied to have yet another child?

Whether because a first-time parent wants more than a single child or because both parents' images of the ideal family requires that a sibling be close in age to the new child, the question of when to stop making babies is an issue for many. In thinking it through, parents weigh their own needs, their work and family obligations, and the needs of their children: the older children who have already had to adapt to a half sibling and the mutual child whose enshrinement in the family pantheon may make the entrance of a possible contender unthinkable.

As in families whose children share two parents, stepfamilies are influenced in deciding how many children to have by the experience of their childhood. Somehow each parent's ideas about the "right" number of children to have frequently corresponds to the number of children in their "families of origin." Eliot and Maggie, for instance, both come from families of three children. With two children with Eliot and a son from a former marriage, Maggie finds herself more ready to stop baby making than Eliot, who still feels one child short in his life plan.

Where each parent was in the lineup of siblings also enters into the reckoning, as they strive to reproduce what they liked about their own childhood and to avoid what they had loathed. For example, the youngest in a family of very much older children may be clear that she does not want her son, whose half siblings ranged from thirteen to seventeen when he was born, "to be put in that position." When a parent has suffered the death of a sibling in childhood, the need to have more than one child takes on an even greater and dreadful urgency. "My father openly told me that if he didn't have other children he would have killed himself when my brother died," explained Ellie, "and I couldn't help but think 'What if something happened to Erica?' Now for Bob it would be devastating, but he would have Polly and Nila, and I wouldn't have anybody."

The desired ultimate size of the family, more than anything else, was the ruling factor for those who planned the number of children in their remarried families. One mother is typical of those who stopped at one mutual child. "My attitude is: The fewer children you have, the more attention you can give them. You never have enough time to do all the things you want to. As far as I'm concerned, with a larger family you have to spread it even more, and I see my kids as needing a lot of attention."

While being part of a stepfamily influences remarried parents in deciding how many children to have, the results of that decision are not always predictable. It is the meaning attached to the various relationships, rather than the fact of stepfamily status, that tips the balance. Sometimes the mutual child is the result of a compromise between a remarried parent and his previously childless partner: although presumably "finished" with childbearing or child rearing, he consents to "just one" more to assuage the baby hunger of his new wife. Additional children may have been ruled out by prenuptial agreement.

Those parents who had full-time custody of their older child are more likely to see themselves as completing their family with only one child in remarriage. In contrast, families in which the stepchildren are with them only every other weekend or less are more reluctant to stop at one. For them, the single mutual child seems to be virtually an "only" child. While natural parents are more likely to "count" all the children in figuring whether they have satisfied their desire for progeny, stepparents with longstanding, affectionate relationships with their stepchildren also see less need to continue having children, if their "ideal" family consists of the conventional two children.

Even when parents feel that a mutual child needs siblings, finances may prohibit another baby. Stepfamilies, many of which are already burdened by supporting children in two households, often decide they can't afford a second or third mutual child. While families differ enormously in what they feel they can and cannot afford, and in what standard of living they regard as acceptable or necessary, each assesses what another baby would cost, and if the price is too high, forgoes the opportunity.

In addition to their number and the financial obligations they entail, stepchildren can serve to limit the size of the remarried family by reminding adults that children need care beyond the most tender years. Having three or four children at two-year intervals, a first-married couple can harbor the illusion that when they are all in school the parents will enjoy clear sailing. Because they are often so much older than their half siblings, stepchildren are a dramatic illustration to their elders that children require work well into their teens and beyond. "You look at it and say," said one stepfather, "hey, these kids are not just work now, they're going to be work down the road." Even those who would love to have another *baby* decide that they do not really want yet another *child*.

Having children from previous partnerships is not always an obstacle to having two or more children in remarriage. For example, a mother with one child from a first marriage and two children from her second may refuse to consider herself as having reached her ultimate goal of three children because "I don't have three in one family," despite the fact that all three live with her. "In some ways," said another mother, "there are only two children in this family, because the first two are ten years apart." Deciding that it "would be really nice" for her daughter to have a sibling that she's close to, she and her husband went on to have another child. She recognizes that it has taken away from her son, now fifteen: "It's taken up so much of my time that I don't give him the time he needs. In some ways I think it's unfair to him that I had these children, and that was one of the arguments against having a second baby, but ultimately we felt it shouldn't be because of him that we didn't have a third child."

Both parents and stepparents are inclined to reason that if they have one child together, they should have two. Even parents who are reluctant to have any children may agree to two in a "package deal," either to avoid having an only child for those who disliked being one or to give to the child of their remarriage what they themselves valued highly in childhood: the experience of growing up with another child.

Stepparents who have not yet had a second child can be even more insistent that their first requires a full sibling. While the mutual parent may be more inclined toward a second to reduce the prima donna tendencies of the first, the first-time parent thinks ahead to the time that the stepchildren will be grown and the mutual child will be an only child, for a longer interval than is usually the case in families in which all children have the same parents. "In a few short years," said one stepmother, "my son is going to end up as an only child. By the time he's seven, it's going to be just him. Not when he's an adult, but now."

Having a second child together can also be seen as a means to correct the overinvolvement of a mutual child and the parent whose first child he is. For one family it was a cancer scare, precipitated when they discovered a lump on the neck of their three-year-old, that accelerated the momentum toward having another baby. "It just freaked me out so much," recalled his mother, "that I decided that we needed to have another kid, that I had too much invested in this child. Even though I knew rationally that this new kid was never going to replace Alan if something happened to him, I felt that there were too many eggs in that particular basket." She is not alone. A stepparent's recognition of the intensity of his involvement with his only biological child stirs in many the desire to temper that intensity by having another.

Because remarriages often involve partners more distant in age than first-married couples, the discrepancy in their ages also enters into the decision of how many children to have and when. When the age gap widens, an awareness of the older partner's reduced life expectancy enters into the calculations. Twenty-one years separate Jack and Ingrid. As Jack tells it, "Ingrid wanted a second child very badly. She's always worried, as have I, that I will die many years earlier than she. She wants family to be with her." Because older men also tend to have older children, a stepmother's desire for another child may be fueled by a refusal to be upstaged in the reproductive arena by adult stepchildren. "There was a drive for a second child," Alexis told me, "that I was unwilling to abandon. Bill was perfectly happy with one, and very concerned about his age. I foresaw his desire for any other babies being satisfied in grandchildren. I didn't wish to have my stepchildren's children be the surrogate for what ought to have been my other child. So part of that was that it was my turn first."

To hear many of the couples interviewed talk about factors to weigh, negotiations, and compromise, it might seem that each child always represents a deliberate decision, carefully made. However, second or later children, like their older brothers and sisters, often "just growed." For some families with unexpected pregnancies, a second mutual child was not only not planned but went counter to an original plan for just one child together.

Just as babies frequently arrive without being planned, so too do planned babies fail to materialize, raising the question of whether to adopt. Stepfamilies that plan a second, or for that matter a first, mutual child may give up after years of trying, as the older children become ever farther in age from their would-be siblings or half siblings, and the parents begin to feel older and less energetic.

Menopause is one way to settle the question, unplanned pregnancy is another, and separation is a third. Remarried couples, like couples in first marriages, sometimes find that their desires about whether to have a baby, or another baby, are irreconcilable, and like all irreconcilable differences this one can end in concession, giving up, or deciding to pursue the agenda with someone else, whether the prospective partner is waiting in the wings or is yet to be recruited.

Coming to Terms with Differences

For all parents and for all children, there is at least some small difference in the quality of attachment between a relationship that starts in infancy and one that begins between an adult and a child who has been on this earth for some time when first they meet. Accepting that difference is an essential part of coming to terms with the reality of being in a stepfamily. Just as stepchildren can envy the special love they see their stepparents bestow on their own children, so, too, do stepparents often wish to be as important to their stepchildren as are the children's own parents. As the years go by, and stepfamilies develop an integrity of their own, stepparent-stepchild relationships come to have a sense of durability; each is secure that theirs is a lifetime connection. Yet, it is also a time of grieving, for even as their contact and affection makes "holding on" possible, they must also "let go" of wanting the other to be as much theirs as a "more biologically entitled" parent or child.[10]

Though some difference in attachment is inevitable, there can be small differences, as in the stepfamily that is well established by the time the mutual child is born, or enormous differences, as in the story "Cinderella," the quintessential caricature of a stepfamily. While we know that the birth of a mutual child occasions fewer changes in families in which both partners are experienced parents, most stepfamilies that go on to have a child in remarriage consist of one parent who is a veteran and another whose mutual child is a first child. A previously childless stepparent's urgency to have a child can, unfortunately, intensify difference and requires a redoubled effort to strive for fairness without denying distinctions. Research on sibling relationships shows that rivalry and hostility between children is greater when there is clear parental favoritism.[11] The greater the passion with which a stepparent strives for natural parenthood, the more fertile is the ground for dramatically different treatment. With effort and awareness, however, this ground, however arable, need not be cultivated.

What this means in practice is that the stronger the imperative to have "one that's ours," the more time and attention must be devoted to enriching "unnatural" pairings. It is tempting for stepfamily members to gravitate toward constellations that feel familiar and comfortable: for stepchildren to turn to their parent, and stepparent to devote himself to the mutual child. Especially in stepmother families, where biology and tradition conspire to wrap mother and child in a cocoon of rapture, sustained effort is necessary to maintain the tender connections between stepparent and stepchild and to establish the newborn as a truly *mutual* child, so that the repeat parent does not become a minority shareholder in what must be a joint enterprise.

Part of what makes any partnership work is a clear contract about who will do what. While zealous negotiators bargaining for an agreement to have a child may promise to do all the work, there is no way to share a household and relinquish all parental responsibility. In planning how to divide child-care responsibilities, couples in stepfamilies have much to count in the reckoning: work commitments, unequal motivation to have a mutual child, the wish to do things differently than in a prior marriage, and responsibilities for the older children.

How happy parents will be with the division of labor will depend primarily on what each expected would happen when they decided to have a child together. If things turn out as anticipated, everyone is pleased. If expectations are unmet, frustration and anger can fester. A forthright and far-reaching discussion of who will do what, when, and for whom allows each parent to bargain for a mutually acceptable roster of responsibilities, minimizing the inevitable surprises that occur when plans are put into practice.

3

Parents Together

Becoming a Team

When a couple have a baby in a first marriage, both become parents for the first time. The "job skills" they bring to the task of caring for their child may vary: One or both may have grown up with much younger siblings or one, more often a woman, by virtue of having grown up female, will have thought more about herself as a prospective parent and how she wants to raise her children. Nonetheless, they embark together on an adventure that neither has experienced before.

For couples who are both parents already, the child of remarriage may feel like "starting over" with "a first child for us." While they may feel like new parents because parenting together is new, both "know more what to do." Having a child with a different spouse may feel fresh and exciting, yet there is a symmetry to the samenesses and differences each parent experiences. The novelty lies in creating a different kind of partnership.

Veterans and Novices

In a remarriage in which one partner has had children before and the other has not, having a child involves an asymmetry that is central to how the couple makes the transition to being parents of a mutual child: One is becoming a parent, as opposed to a stepparent, for the first time, while the other is repeating an experience that is in many ways familiar.

Established remarriages in which a stepparent has been an active participant in the care of children mitigate this asymmetry. Eleanor, a stepmother who had lived with her stepdaughter half-time for seven years before her daughter was born, felt as much a veteran parent as her husband. "I think we had less anticipation, maybe a little less fear, maybe a little less excitement, than our friends who were having their first child. Even though it was our first child together, it wasn't the first child we had raised. We were more relaxed and ready for it."

When stepfamilies have not had time to consolidate before the birth of the mutual child, asymmetries can be more dramatic, especially if being a parent has not always been part of the stepparent's life plan. This is the stuff of which comedies are made, as witness Isabel and Tim's early days with their son, Ivan.

Isabel remembers: "It was a riot. Tim said, 'You don't have to take any of those classes, I've done it all before.' Then Ivan was born and Tim was quarantined for a week with strep throat. Here I am with a baby, and no idea what you do with a baby. I'm in the kitchen sterilizing bottles. Luckily, when you buy a paper diaper, you can only put it on frontward or backward, and no matter which direction you put it on, it works. You could have written a Woody Allen or Lucille Ball comedy. I did a lot of silly things. I wasn't a particularly protective mother, it just never occurred to me that I could just leave him in his crib occasionally. I thought you had to watch a baby all the time. One day Tim comes in and there I am soaking in the tub, and there's Ivan, in his little Moses basket, and Tim just burst out laughing."

Like Isabel, many stepparents who have infants for the first time appreciate having a veteran parent on hand. If novices appreciate the unflappability of veterans, their greater equanimity in the face of the myriad crises in a child's early life, veterans, for their part, enjoy the sense of wonder the novice brings to the experience of having a child. Eliot's wife, Maggie, describes how he "walked around with that aura of miracle, which I didn't have so much the second time. It's an incredible experience that can never be repeated." Veteran parents may also appreciate the benefits to the child of having a first-time parent with a tremendous amount of energy to put into the child.

But the asymmetry between experience and enthusiasm is not without its drawbacks. The very same parent who appreciates his partner's vigor, relieving him of the labor-intensive aspects of being a parent, may be concerned about the blurring of boundaries between first-time parent and child. The tendency of the stepparent to become enmeshed with his own child is exacerbated when the mutual child is the only child of the remarriage, so that it is a matter of one person having an only child and the other multiple children.

In such families, the veteran parent may find the responses of the novice "neurotic," with a hesitancy to discipline the child adequately out of fear of alienating the child or inflicting psychological damage. "On the negative side," Barry said, describing a closeness between his wife and their daughter of which he is critical, "there is more of a clinging relationship between the two of them. In some ways it's a love-hate relationship, where they get so close to each other that they're in each other's hair. Then they scream and yell at each other. Many times it's much easier for someone who does not feel as close to April to work with her and get rational responses from her. For example, I'm out for the evening, leaving Emma to take care of April, April will be asking Emma to do this for her, 'read to me,' do this or that. With me, April's reaction is more, 'I better find something to do, because my papa's probably going to watch a football game on TV or do something else.' "

Veterans also get impatient with what they see as novices' excessive anxiety. One father, whose wife's first daughter was his third, complained: "You have to be reassuring them that because the kid is coughing a little, it doesn't mean the kid is going to choke to death." He, too, describes how the difference in emotional intensity devoted to a first child can be a source of tension in a couple: "With a second or third child, you know that unless you have extraordinary bad luck, they're going to develop fine. When you have a first, every little thing there is to worry about, you worry. So the parent who worries less tends to feel that the parent who's worrying too much is being neurotic about it, even though the experienced parent was probably just as 'neurotic' when he or she was dealing with a first. So, there's a strain there, no question about it."

Another strain born of the gap between repeat parent and first-timer comes when the novice continually defers to the veteran on questions about the children, a pattern that I found only among stepfathers and their partners. This becomes an irritant to mothers who are already feeling burdened by their responsibilities as the only natural parent of an older child or children and by the greater duties they almost always assume for the care of the baby. While a stepfather who's been around children for a while is not likely to feel the complete novice, he considers himself inexperienced with children who are younger than his youngest stepchild was at the time of their becoming a family. Most first-time fathers see their wives as more expert in baby care than they themselves are, simply by virtue of their being female. This difficulty is compounded for stepfathers, who know their child's mother has already mothered children. Fielding a lot of questions, such as "What about a bottle?" "Do you think he needs changing?" can become an additional burden, creating more work for a mother who had hoped her husband would be more of a partner when they had a child together.

Becoming a Parental Team

When two people are parents together, they form a team. Like other groups of people embarking on a new venture, parents need practice before they can feel that they are pulling together instead of moving at cross-purposes. In the course of making decisions, both anticipated and unforeseen, they discover unexpected areas of disagreement, and even when ideas are in harmony, implementation can be an issue.

Remarried couples have already teamed up to care for the children of earlier unions, but having a child together changes the way the team works. A baseball team is not suddenly called upon to play football, but a shortstop may have to play second base, or a right fielder can be called upon to fill in in center field. The changes go in two directions, both toward more unity and cohesion as a parental unit within the family and toward new recognition of differences, as the stepparent, feeling newly entitled and newly passionate about decisions, discovers that tensions around child care were not all the fault of some scapegoated outsider.

If it has not happened before, as stepfamily members accommodated to one another over time, the birth of the mutual child can lessen a parent's defensiveness of his own authority, allowing the stepparent a greater role with all the children. Leslie had always been clear with Everett that her daughter, Denise, came first. Having their son, Oliver, changed her defensiveness in the face of his disciplining Denise. It also led to her acceptance of Everett as a parent to both children. "I always thought," she told me, "if anything happens to me, I want them to go to my mum, both of them. But now it's different. Even Denise, I don't know if I'd want her to go home. Up until a year and a half ago, I would have thought, because Everett's young, I wouldn't want to burden him with them. But now it's a different thing. He's just their dad. So, it would be like taking his arms off or something."

More of a surprise, for many couples, are the differences that emerge now that they have a child who is equally both of theirs. In dealing with children who have a parent living elsewhere, the remarried couple can exaggerate their likemindedness, seeing dissension as originating outside their gates, in a combative, critical, or irresponsible other parent. In having a child together, they look forward to finally being able to make decisions about how to raise a child without having a third party involved. Power plays between members of the couple now occur in a different arena, as perceptions of who is loose and who is strict, who is indulgent and who withholding, begin to nudge out money, job decisions, vacation plans, and household cleanliness as areas of contention. "The other things we disagree about," one stepmother said, referring to her husband, "occasionally politics, the setting of the thermostat, which one of us is more extravagant, are minor compared to the intensity of the issues about the children." Stepparents who despair of passing on their values to their stepchildren, acknowledging that the children "come from another family" and are "not my blood," must finally come to terms with how their values differ from those of their new partner. Especially when being a stepparent or noncustodial parent has intensified the desire finally to "do it my way," finding that negotiation is still necessary can pop many a balloon of wishful expectation about the child with only two parents.

Another difficulty in forging the kind of parental team that fits with prenatal fantasies of doing it differently and doing it "right" is the evocative pull of the familiar, eliciting the repetition of patterns from former marriages. Eleanor describes how her husband, Rick, falls into deferring to her about decisions concerning the children, as he had to his former wife, and then resents it when his withdrawal leads to her taking over: "There's more room for him to make decisions, mutually with me, around our kids, but part of his pattern with Judy was to let her make decisions, because it was easier than fighting. Then, when he lapses into that pattern with me, he gets resentful. Sometimes I think we have conflict, not because it's really there or necessary, but because he hasn't been assertive."

When each parent asserts his position, and differences are addressed, resolution is possible, and team formation occurs. One detour around differences, regardless of which children they pertain to, is to divide up parental responsibility into "his" and "hers" children. While parents are not equally attached to each child, even in nuclear families, stepfamily bonds can be more skewed. As discussed earlier, a parent may feel closer to an older child, while the first mutual child is most tightly connected to a previously childless stepparent. If the mutual parent is the father, a normally occurring pattern in any family, whereby Dad devotes more time and energy to older children while Mom takes care of the baby, is further accentuated by stepfamily patterns in attachment. One father describes how, seeing his wife become more and more involved with the baby, he spent more time with the older children, so that they would not feel neglected. As an interim arrangement, this can work out quite well, but if, years later, one adult is consistently doing 90 percent of the care of one child, while the ratio of involvement between the other adult and child is skewed in the opposite direction, rigid alliances are created that can bring trouble. Not only is each child then deprived of the resources of the other adult, but parents can find themselves at odds, each championing a child, as unresolved conflicts between the adults are detoured into sibling struggle.

This does not mean that differences cannot or should not exist. In most instances, a stepparent feels more entitled to set policy for his own child, whereas his authority with his stepchild is derived from his partner. Arthur describes how, despite a very real closeness to his stepdaughter, who is remote from her natural father, he feels there are limits to his authority with her: "It was always clear that Marie was in charge of Jessica. I would never, and still would never, tell her to clean her room or, except in Marie's absence, make rules. She certainly listens to me now, but I was very much an accessory parent, however much she accepted me, and however much I liked doing it. I was perfectly competent to take care of Jessica, but it was always filling in, and that's not true for the others." He has never liked the way his wife loses her temper with his stepdaughter, with storm clouds of tension building up to a thunderous mutual hysteria, but when it happens with his daughter, he is moved to intervene. "I don't have the feeling that Marie has special rights to Annie, but I do feel that she has rights to Jessica that I don't have, and that she can do with her more what she wants." One grown stepchild noted the pattern, typical of most of the families, that his stepmother "had a lot of feelings about what to do with us, but my dad would take more initiative on what to do with the older than with the younger kids. It wasn't an equal balance of their judgment on how to handle us."

Patterns of responsibility developed before the birth of the mutual child will linger. Especially when custody is shared, a former wife can insist that father, not stepmother, be responsible for their child's needs. He will continue to be the one to call the school guidance counselor to get his daughter into a class, to arrange her violin lessons, or to do other of the myriad tasks that he tends to slough off on his wife when it comes to the care of their younger children. Stepparents, for their part, now find that they have responsibilities for their own children that are obligatory, whereas previous care of their stepchildren, no matter how extensive, may have seemed optional. In setting priorities in the face of competing demands, it is too easy for the press of obligations to leave less and less room for what seems optional. Especially in stepmother families, where gender role and biological primacy are at odds, making the father the primary parent of the older children, parents can drift into a division of parental labor by child.

In families in which both parents have had children before remarriage, having a child together is not as dramatic a change as when one partner was previously childless. Both adults are already parents, both are already stepparents, so no new roles are introduced. Yet being parents together, equally of the same child, brings its own accommodations. For couples with joint custody, it may be the first time in years that they have full-time a child with no other parent to provide relief for adult vacations or family emergencies.

For noncustodial fathers, even those living with their stepchildren, having a mutual child is a chance to be "a normal parent" for the first time in a long time. Seeing her husband with their child can reassure a mother-stepmother that he is, after all, a good father. Diane describes how she feels much more positive about Steve as a father since their daughter Angie's birth a year before: "I've gone through periods of being the Mother Hen, protecting her chick and doing all the wrong things. I never saw him in a normal parenting relationship before. His daughter Jenny would come over here, and it would seem like lovey-dovey, and I would resent that. I was feeling 'Ugh, you're yelling at Beverly all week, then Jenny comes over and . . .' He'd just go, 'Well, it's just different.' He really cares about Beverly, but it's not always easy. She gives him a lot of flak. He'd play the role of being real amenable, and then he'd get fed up. Now, we're all doing this together, and it's real nice. I think he's a real good Daddy. He really cares about his kids, and he spends time."

Doing It Differently the Second Time Around

All parents, with the wisdom of hindsight, can see things that they would have done differently in raising their children. Given an opportunity to have another, parents resolve to keep what they liked in their child-rearing repertoire and discard and revise the rest. Whether intentionally or not, they will be different as parents to the children of their remarriage.

There is a sense in which no two children have exactly the same parent. Every second child benefits from her parents' experience with their first. The child of his parents' middle age gets a different set than his sister, born in their youth. Every daughter knows that her parents are different with their son than they are with her. And every stepchild feels that his stepparent is different with her biological children. "You can appear to have the same parent, and yet have a different parent," said one woman, now in her early thirties, referring to her stepbrother's idyllic relationship with her father. "He really had a different father in him than my sisters and I had. Partly because he got him at a different stage in my father's life and went through different experiences with him. Partly it's a different person because it's with a different mate, or in the absence of a mate."

The difference in mate goes a long way in accounting for the differences in how parents are with the children of their first marriage and those of subsequent marriages. A cooperative team operates differently than a competitive one. And each partner evokes certain potentials in the other, creating a new set of conditions. A father, for example, who is relaxed and seems unconcerned when teamed with a highly organized, overinvolved mother may become much more structured when paired with a mother who is more prone to let things go. Any parent has both strengths and weaknesses, areas of special concern and areas of relative lack of interest. Partners can evoke their opposite in the other, or organize a mate to move in their own direction. Jack, for example, attributes how he is different with his second set of children primarily to the differences in his marriages to the children's mothers: "I think it's due to the nature of the parents, the closeness of the parents. Ingrid and I really work at consensus regarding the children. My first wife and I simply accepted the fact that we had different views. Ingrid guides the children more than my former wife did and gets me involved in guidance."

Mothers see themselves as less different with their children born of different marriages, perhaps because, as primary parents, they have more influence on child-care styles and values than do the fathers involved. Older and wiser, they may relax if they were formerly overinvolved and overprotective, or, conversely, they may become more cautious and worry more, taking themselves as parents more seriously in their late thirties than they did in their early twenties. "We saw repercussions that we simply didn't see when the others were in those years, and we found ourselves bothered by things at a much deeper level than we had been earlier," said Marilyn, concluding that "being younger is an easier time to parent than when you're older. You know too much."

With mothers, it is often the child who creates a different mother for herself than her older siblings had. Here again, the idea of complementarity, the evocation of "the other half" of the pattern, describes the evolving mother-child relationship. Melanie tells of how different she was with her second son than she had been with his older half brother: "With Paul I sat and sang to him every morning from five in the morning until eight, eye contact the whole time. But with Yale, I didn't feel like talking to him. I don't know why. I would hold him and feel like I wanted to have this internal communication. I'd say to myself 'Why don't you sing him songs?' I just didn't want to. I wanted to be quiet with him."

Being a single mother has its ups and downs, and learning to share a child with another parent can bring both relief of the burden of shouldering all the responsibility and a sacrifice of the freedom of making decisions by oneself. When a mother has had a hard time feeling in charge, particularly with a son, having a man around to support her in setting limits and an "easy" baby can feel like having "died and gone to heaven." Stepfathers who have been critical of their wives as mothers of an unruly son attribute their wives' difficulties to the stress of being a single parent to a child distressed by the trauma of separation, divorce, or death. Having a mutual child rehabilitates these women as mothers in their husbands' eyes. "She had a difficult time with her first child," Evan said of Melissa, "and what she learned from that made her a better parent with Eric and Eda. That continues up to this day, where Melissa still has all these frustrations and difficulties dealing with Donny, and is very confident and straightforward dealing with Eric and Eda." Andrew, similarly critical of the raging battles between his wife Laura and her son Nathaniel, set in contrast his view of Laura as a mother to their daughters: "With Elena, she was absolutely wonderful. She did and still does put in a lot of time and love and effort. I feel very good about our parenting with the girls, although it's very labor intensive."

Unlike the beleaguered mothers just described, a single mother who has felt successful in raising a child alone may chafe over having to confer about everything with another parent, feeling less clear about what she is doing and less good as a mother to the children she shares with her husband. Partly due to the difficulty in emerging from the tight twosome of single mother and only child, the greater difficulties with later children can also revolve around differences in the gender of the child or its temperament. Arthur describes how Marie has a harder time with their daughters than she does with Jessica, her daughter from an earlier marriage: "Annie is a lot more like me, and she doesn't know what to do with her. In some ways that's fascinated her, but it's also intimidated her."

Fathers, more than mothers, attribute the way they are different with the children of remarriage to differences in their partners. While both mothers and fathers credit greater maturity and the changing times as factors in how they are different as parents with the younger children, fathers also put more emphasis on how the changing role of work in their lives shapes them as parents. As noted in the earlier discussion of the division of labor for child care, the older fathers who were climbing the ladder when their first set of children were young consider themselves much better fathers to their younger children: more tolerant, more actively loving and giving of their time and attention. In contrast, some of the younger fathers who were conscientious about sharing child care fifty-fifty with their first child have now developed lives that are more work-focused and less child-centered. As parents of more than one child and people who have been parents for years and years, their interest and energy for child-centered activity is at a lower ebb for their younger children.

Stepparent's Review: "My Partner as Parent"

Stepmothers, while they give their husbands generally good notices as fathers to their mutual children, also let drop hints of surprise that the overindulgent Daddy of her stepchildren is a reformed character with his younger children, a change that is met with mixed reviews. The picture that emerges for many is that of a father who, in his wife's eyes, is too lenient and more protective of her stepchildren and more strict and less available to the children they share.

The refrain from this stepmothers' chorus is oft-repeated. Able to be more detached from her husband's child-rearing values when they were applied to her stepchildren, she now finds herself more critical of him as a father. Elizabeth, for example, explains: "Before, when it was not my children, I didn't have as much at stake. Now if he uses a judgment that I don't agree with, I'm much more sensitive to it." Like many of the other stepmothers, she sees Simon as much more of a disciplinarian with her sons, harder on them and shorter-tempered than she ever remembers him being with her stepchildren. Surprised with him, she is also surprised with herself, seeing an unanticipated role reversal: "In Simon's old age," she laughed, "I think he's turned the other way. I find myself stepping in and taking the other point of view, which is being the more lax. Whereas before, with his other kids, I'd always seen him being the one that was lax."

Dad's tightening up is not always seen as negative. Instead, a stepmother may think her husband is a better father to their children precisely because he is not overindulgent, "letting his kids walk all over him," a position taken more often by fathers who have visitation but not custody.

Although some fathers do become successively firmer with each child, regardless of whether that child is from a previous marriage or a current one, noncustodial fathers continue to be more protective of the children who have lived through divorce. One father, who was willing to have his four-year-old mutual child interviewed, initially refused to let me interview his older children. His wife complains that he lacks all conviction in disciplining the older children, as opposed to the children they have together, a difference she attributes to his need to compensate for the divorce. For many fathers, this includes an attempt to make up for the hard times that precede divorce, which usually follows upon years of tension and conflict. A father who was not available in the early years of an older child may see "the real difference in what he was able to do for his child and what he does for our children," and that difference may "bother him a lot," complicating his relationship with the older child in the present, interfering with his ability to say no.

A noncustodial father can also be stricter with his mutual children out of a desire finally to have an influence over a child's upbringing in a way not possible with older children. Not being there on a day-to-day basis to pass on his own values, he has frequently had to restrict himself to expressing his standards to the children's mother, who may or may not share them. As a result, the things about the children of his first marriage that bother him are blamed on their not having grown up in his household, and having another child, for whom he is a daily presence, can lead to an intense effort to make his influence felt. Alexis tells how Bill is "more intense than I think necessary: Whereas the older children had a somewhat erratic religious education, these children go to church. Bonnie and Judith had little sports activity, these children are athletic. It's both positive and negative. Being more intense is a negative, but being a more present parent is a positive. He's around more." His determination is not lost on his older children, now adults. Bonnie describes how her father is different with her half siblings: "I think when you have children, there are certain things that you think went wrong with them, so it's like you've got another chance. I don't think he's changed that much, but I see him pushing Enid in ways he never pushed us. In a certain way it's bad for Enid, because she may end up having the least close relationship with him of any of his children."

Some of a stepmother's disappointment in her husband as father to the children they have together may be due to having gotten to know him as a father to his older children, since fathers typically do become more involved with their children after the labor-intensive early years. One stepmother describes having had more respect for her husband as a father before their son was born: "I never knew what kind of thing you have to do when you're a parent." She laughed. "And when I started having to do them for Ira, I realized how little Will did. It made me think that he was a Disneyland type of father. He's great for entertainment, but he's real short on discipline and responsibility and things like making sure their teeth are brushed. And I never noticed that before because I never thought about having to do some of those things."

While it would be a mistake to assume that all or even most stepmothers are critical of their husbands as fathers to the children they have together, those who have seen their husbands as single parents or joint custodians tend to feel that their own children are getting a less involved father than their stepchildren had. For many, this is anticipated as "part of the deal." Disappointment is a question of expectations. Those who are most dissatisfied made assumptions based on seeing their husbands as active fathers to older children, assumptions that were never called into question by deliberate negotiations before having a child together.

Parent's Review: "My Partner as Parent and Stepparent"

Repeat parents, for their part, gave rave reviews to their partners who were first-time parents. Almost without exception, they were enthusiastic about the stepparent's entry into "real" parenthood.

Seeing a partner apply standards consistently, doing unto her own child what she has done unto her stepchildren, can also rehabilitate her in her partner's eyes as a stepparent. Before they had their daughter, John sometimes felt that Alice very much wanted to be with him and that his daughters were some of the baggage. Her insistence that they develop good eating habits, learn table manners and consideration of others had been, in his eyes, an effort to make things as comfortable for herself as possible, given the bargain she had struck. Seeing her apply the same standards to the daughter they share made him revise his assessment of her dealings with the older girls as unlovingly dutiful.

If the mutual parent has a criticism of the stepparent, it is as a stepparent, not as a parent. Seeing her husband head over heels with his baby sometimes makes a mother wish he could be as loving to her children. While mothers tend to chafe more that their husbands do not love their stepchildren as they themselves do, fathers are grateful that someone is willing to come in and pick up the other handle of the rickshaw. While many mothers think very highly of their husbands as stepfathers, fathers are more generous still to their wives as stepmothers, recognizing the greater investment of time and energy typically devoted to the children by a female stepparent. One widowed father of two in no way changed his mind about his wife as a mother when their own two children were born. " 'Cause I liked what she was doing with the older kids. She was capable and insightful. She saw things I didn't. She was certainly concerned about them and took them as her own." Whatever his children's complaints, he didn't think any less of her. "There were times when she was protecting her cubs from the older kids, so to speak, which for the most part was fair. In any case, I would side with her. The older two had no squawk coming. As far as I'm concerned, they had a life with a single parent as one alternative, or one with two parents and with everything running smoothly. And that's what they got, and it's the better of the two choices."

Even the criticism of stepparents as parents to their mutual children is not entirely negative. In a partner's eyes, having their own child can be a sobering dose of reality, dispelling the stepparent's idealism about what he would do when finally imbued with the authority to make child-rearing policy as an equal. In his own as in his partner's eyes, the stepparent gets his comeuppance in having his own child. Amelia describes a family ski trip with another remarried family. Both her husband, Joe, and the mother in the other family agreed: If one of the teenagers left his gloves home, the parents would give him theirs. Amelia and the other woman's husband, a stepfather to her children, took the position: "Let them ski without gloves and they'll learn next time to remember." But when Amelia thinks about her son, Owen, she thinks she'd probably give him hers.

Tempering Justice with Mercy

In disagreements between parents and stepparents over the children, stepparents frequently find themselves the voice of reason, insisting on limits and consistency and consequences, while parents, with their greater emotional resonance with the children, find compelling empathic grounds for making exceptions and stretching the rules.[1] Elaine's experience as a stepmother for eight years before her daughter was born convinced her that her husband, and all her friends, were more tolerant with their children than she could be as an "outsider." Even then she attributed this difference to their knowing the children from infancy, when the babies were so needy and depended for all their needs on their parents, creating an indulgence that outlasted its necessity. The birth of her daughter convinced her of the validity of her observation: "I've discovered these reserves of patience that I never suspected were there and always feared would not be. I'm still very indulgent, and I'm sure I always will be much more indulgent with her than I am with Leo. With Leo, there's always this kind of intellectualization. I say, 'Okay, wait a second, this kid is needy because of this and this, and I'm going to respond this way.' Whereas with her, it's more immediate, more of an emotional response."

The birth of the mutual child gives the stepparent an unanticipated glimpse of how his partner feels about his own children, a response not lost on a spouse who has previously felt misunderstood. Joe describes the change in Amelia's attitudes catalyzed by the birth of their son: "She understood this incredible bond that occurs, and how you can become sort of irrational when it comes to your own kids."

Learning firsthand the nature and power of the attachment between parent and child can dispel, for the first time, the stepparent's feelings of rivalry with the children for the affection of the parent. As for many other stepmothers, especially those who are considerably younger than their partners, the years up until her daughter's birth had been difficult for Alexis, who was sure that her inability to cope as a stepmother would be the undoing of her marriage. "At the most primitive level, they represented my husband's love for another woman, that he'd had another marriage and that he'd loved her enough to have these two children. I wished they never existed, all of them. It was hard emotionally, because I always did feel second to them." Alexis describes the sense of revelation in suddenly understanding "how you love your children, and how it's different from anything else. It made me understand that there was no rivalry. You don't love your spouse as you love your children. And I understood that total lack of objectivity about them. You think they're God's gift, and they are. It made me more open-hearted toward my stepdaughters. And I had an all new understanding of Bill, and all new affection for him, really for putting up with me during the time when I was the bitchy critic about the miserable children who dumped towels on the bathroom floor."

Empathy for a partner as a parent extends beyond understanding the passion of his attachment to diluting criticism of his parenting skills. In becoming a parent herself, the stepparent learns to "criticize no man until you have walked a mile in his shoes." Not being a parent herself, the stepparent typically has "idealistic views" of what she will do when she finally has the authority and control to implement her ideas about child rearing. Grand schemes for after-school crafts activity or regular and extensive outings get balanced against a parent's need to be alone sometimes, as the stepparent discovers that it is harder to implement schemes than it is to hatch them. And it is much easier to spot inconsistency in discipline than it is to practice consistent limit setting with children. Many of the stepparents I spoke with confessed to feeling far more expert on how to raise children before they had their own. "I would tell Mike that you have to be consistent," laughed Irma. "I would say I was rigid, not consistent, with my stepson, Jason. And when I had my own kids, I understood that it's not always possible to raise your kids the way you think you should. And it made me feel more kindly toward Jason, because I used to be so mad at him all the time. Then I could see that my kids were manipulating me in the same kinds of ways." If the proof of the pudding is in the eating, being a parent teaches the palate a new range of tastes.

In addition to increasing compassion and tempering criticism of stepchildren, or using his emotional responsiveness to his own child as a measure of how to respond to his stepchild, parenthood teaches the stepparent how to say yes when he wants to say no. Learning that an adult stepchild will be accompanying them on vacation may not thrill a stepmother, but thinking how she would feel after not seeing one of her own children for a year allows her to empathize with both father and daughter enough to be more relaxed about unexpected intrusions and more tender toward her husband's instinctive permission as opposed to her more removed restraint.

Being with a child from infancy also gives a parent, however untutored, an understanding of child development that meeting that child later on cannot provide. If you have seen a child through the transformations of learning to speak and to move on his own steam, achieving one after another of the skills necessary for self-sufficiency, you have a sense of how far he has traveled and how far he has yet to go. Stepparents, unless they have been there from the beginning, lack that first-hand developmental knowledge. As a result, their expectations of maturity in the children are frequently unrealistic.

Their own children teach stepparents about the inappropriateness of their expectations of their stepchildren at the same ages. Alice remembers with guilt her lack of developmental insight: "When my daughter was five, I was more aware of the limitations of a five-year-old, having watched her get there, than I was when Paula was coming into my life as a five- or six-year-old. My tendency is to have too high expectations for kids, period. I'm more aware of the limitations with my own child, and more aware that I was probably too harsh with the older kids, or too firm, too rigid, whatever, a lot of the time."

Although the vantage point of the stepparent differs from that of a parent, it is not without value. Parents who are also stepparents, and in the best position to compare, find that they are able to think more clearly about their stepchildren. Not so wrapped up emotionally as with their own children, stepparents credit themselves with better judgment and greater clarity, seeing what a parent may refuse to see, acknowledging, for example, the adult sexuality of a grown stepchild when both parents put on blinders.

The greater distance of the stepparent can be an asset to the parent, whose own ambivalence and guilt about causing his children pain can lead to equivocation and a failure to function effectively as a parent. One father remembers how his second wife was put in the "unfair position" of "almost solo parenting the kids. Because I wanted to be their friend. I wanted their support and love. I felt that I had done them dirty. I woke up to this stuff, obviously, but those patterns are pretty insidious." Clearly, the obstacles to a stepparent's acting effectively as a single parent to stepchildren are enormous, and as long as this father did not support his second wife in laying down the law, the need for structure in the family could not be met.

The greater objectivity of the stepparent can only be an asset to the team of parent and stepparent, however, if their positions are not polarized: Parents must temper their empathy with a concern for justice and stepparents must moderate with nurturance their campaign for fairness.

The State of the Union

Having a child together changes a couple as marital partners, not just as parents. Unlike first-marrieds, remarried parents have already had some experience of how having a baby can profoundly alter a marriage. Memories of a first marriage that deteriorated with the arrival of children can lead to dire expectations that must be first overcome before embarking on a second go-around as a parent, fighting against a feeling of déjà vu when inevitable parallels appear. Communicating often and well is the most effective immunization against stress-induced changes in the relationship. The best predictor of the adjustment of both mother and father to birth and parenthood of a child, in remarriage as in any marriage, is the quality of the marriage before the child is born.

Asked how having a child together has affected their marriages, most couples I talked with found it a unifying experience. Parents' having very different careers, for example, can mean that children provide a vital common project that brings a man and woman closer together, but only if they are both active participants in the children's care. "Enhanced, enriched, frantic, busy, exhausted, overextended, the usual phrases," Alexis reeled off, describing how her marriage to Bill had changed with the birth of their daughter. "It's been a lot of fun." The camaraderie of a labor-intensive task, when undertaken in tandem, can bring new levels of closeness. Seeing themselves and each other mirrored in the child they have made together can also serve as a kind of narcissistic glue; in their enjoyment of the child's existence, they find grounds for greater appreciation of each other.

That doesn't mean that the mutual child does not, like any child, put a strain on the marriage of his parents. While most couples felt their relationship had deepened, so too was it more stressful. The typical picture is less money, less time for each other, and less sex. The theme of more pragmatism and less romance echoed through the interviews, as couple after couple talked about how life had become caught up in what one called "the high-function mode" of problem solving and task sharing, who's picking up whom, what, and where. While most are conscious of making an effort to be together and talk about things other than the mechanics of daily life, fun and sensuality, if not a casualty of having children, are relegated to the background. Especially when the older children are not at home all the time, the small ones can seem, as in one father's description, like "great black holes. They absorb a tremendous amount of energy. They throw off a great deal of energy, too, and there are days when we are totally exhausted." While much of this is true for all families having a young child, stepfamilies are frequently accustomed to time for adults to be alone together, or just alone, when older children were with their other parent. Having a full-time child, without even an occasional weekend off, is a major change. "Now the new issues," according to one father, "are how to have a family, how to pursue a career, and how not to have a heart attack by the time you're forty-six. How to be a whole human being and have a hell of a time."

Beyond the exhaustion and the practical problems that are the lot of almost every parent, remarried couples are also prey to the echoes of past marital battles, especially those that hint at a repetition of patterns involving parents and children. Men, especially, seemed to fear that history will repeat itself. The husband whose wife has already left her first husband and taken the children may worry that she will repeat that scenario with him. Happily remarried fathers whose previous wives lost interest in them after their older children were born fight feelings of neglect and rivalry as they watch their new wives fall head over heels with a firstborn. Many of the new mothers among the stepmothers did confess to "overdoing it a little" in their involvement with their babies, shortchanging "couple time," and even "getting a lot of my huggie-cuddles from my little one," leading to greater distance from their husbands.

Women, both mothers and stepmothers, were more distressed by unmet expectations about how their husbands would share responsibility for the children, rather than that the future would echo the past. When a woman is taking primary care of her child while her husband functions principally as a provider, doing occasional backup child care, she will be resentful to the degree that she expected things to be otherwise. One stepmother/mother said, "Our marriage is really different than I thought it was going to be. I think having our son was disillusioning to me. I found that I had married a very traditional kind of male. He's not really macho, but he has this sort of 'this is a woman's job and I shouldn't do it' that really came out around parenting." This division of roles can lead to very separate lives, as another woman describes: "We're off in our own little world and we meet in our world together. But that world together right now is real tired. We don't have a lot to give each other."

Criticisms of each other as parents, of course, contribute to marital tension. Criticisms range from those directed at a father for insufficient involvement with a mutual child and at a mother/stepmother for overinvolvement with the same child, to those leveled at stepparents of either gender for different treatment of their own child, as compared with their stepchildren. The resulting triangles of parent, stepparent, and mutual child and parent, stepparent, and stepchild as a source of marital disharmony will be discussed at greater length later.

But whatever strains and joys having another child brings to a remarriage, there is unanimity on one score: Having experienced the emotional costs of marital disruption firsthand, remarrying parents and their partners are highly sensitized to how hurtful ending a marriage can be to adults and children alike and have become deeply committed to preventing the demise of the current union. Since the divorce rate for second marriages exceeds that for first marriages, the people I talked with threw salt over their shoulders as they talked about how having a child made them feel their marriages were now permanent, prefacing their statements with such disclaimers as "That's a little silly to say in this day and age."

Silly or not, couple after couple talked about the importance of the mutual child in cementing the remarriage, involving them more in each other's heritages, families, and traditions and providing a reason to ride out the rough times. Remarriers are frequently more hesitant even than the never married to make commitments that experience has proven fragile. Irma tells about how gradually she and Mike eased into feeling settled with each other: "For all those beginning years we were sort of doing this dance where we'd move a little closer, and then a little further apart. I remember how when we first started living together, everything was 'This is yours in the property settlement. This is mine.' One day we bought something, I don't remember what, and my stepson was with us, and he said, 'Whose is that in the property settlement?' " She laughed and added, "So we stopped doing that.

"Sometimes I think that having kids," she continued, "means that when you have fights, or when things aren't going right, you don't have that quick response: 'I can leave this any time I want to.' There's much more impetus to work things out. And that's a good thing. I like the feeling of family and commitment to the family. I don't always like all that goes with it, but I'm real glad I have my family."

Couple after couple reiterated this theme: Some felt that their relationship would not have survived if they had not had children, and others simply that the children had served as a brake to any impulse to say "Oh, the hell with it." While demographers sometimes theorize that the higher divorce rate among remarried couples reflects a greater willingness to leave an unsatisfactory marriage, I found a group of born-again monogamists, especially among the divorced parents and their partners, who declared themselves "very conservative," thinking "people should never divorce." "Before the baby was born," Tom told me, "one or the other of us were free to leave, and that's just not the case at this point." Even those who are themselves married for the first time learn from their partners' experience. Tom's wife, Eva, agreed with him about how having a child made their union a permanent one: "Seeing how painful it's been for Tom affected me. I would not want to share our daughter, and I would not want her not to have her dad, so this is just going to have to work out." And both parents and stepparents have witnessed and shared the pain of the older children: "You know better than anyone else how difficult it is to raise a child as a single parent, and you don't want that to happen to your kids." Despite the higher rate of divorce among the remarried, demographers confirm that having a mutual child reduces the probability of divorce, while having stepchildren in the home makes marital dissolution more likely.[2]

With the wisdom of hindsight, a few of the divorced parents think that if they had known then what they know now they might have worked harder to make the first marriage an enduring one. Jerry, a father and stepfather who was one of many to surmise that without their mutual children he and Betsy might not still be together, talked about how the changing times and his own greater maturity gave him a new perspective on the commitment that having children entails. "I think we like each other a lot, but there have been periods when there's been a lot of struggle and the balance was tenuous. That whole business in the sixties, that the worst thing a family can do is stay together for the kids, that's a bunch of bullshit. There are worse things you can do. If it's really horrendously awful, yes. But if there's a basic friendship, so what if it isn't everything you ever wanted it to be. You have a responsibility to the kids. I'm glad we're together for lots of reasons now, but there have been times when one or the other of us could have said, 'The hell with it, I don't need this garbage.' I know it's true for me, and I think it's true for Betsy, that having gone through the divorce the first time, and seeing what it did to the kids, and what it did to me losing access to my kid, it would have to be a pretty awful situation for me to be willing to pay that price again." The theme that emerges is that having a child together, and making the child's interests and each parent's own attachment to the children a priority, allows couples to ride out the bad times that are a feature of most marriages, so that when the tides change, they still have a craft that can ride the waves.

Putting the Couple Front and Center

A loving, enduring marriage gives solidity to the stepfamily, providing security for all the children, who benefit from its stability even when voicing a desire for parental reunification. Couples whose first source of emotional solace and companionship is each other will create a stepfamily that endures. Feeling supported by a partner is the best storehouse of emotional strength for a stepparent who frequently must draw upon unsuspected reserves of generosity. Solidarity on the marital front also gives parents the ability to be loving to their children without holding them too near, meeting their needs for closeness with another adult rather than directing them to a child who can be easily drafted, to his own detriment, into a coalition with one parent. The alternative, when a stepparent turns to the mutual child for warmth and companionship, while across the gymnasium the mutual parent teams up with the child of an earlier union, is a blueprint for trouble. Anger and disappointment are then diverted from marital dissatisfaction to complaints about the children, who hold tenaciously to the "specialness" that keeps them immature or pseudomature and mirror the tensions that remain unresolved between their parents.

Making your partner your principal ally within the family means making sure that marital issues are dealt with head on. But how to parent together must also be placed on the agenda. In having a mutual child, stepfamily couples must confront their own beliefs about how to raise children, unmasking the differences between them that masqueraded as the handiwork of previous partners. When there are only two parents to weigh in the balance, differences in heft become apparent. Despite the greater experience of one parent, when veteran and novice alike share both expertise and enthusiasm, negotiating differences to create unified policy, they become an effective team as parents, finding solace in solidarity and power in partnership.

4

Being a Parent to Children New and Old

In having a child, remarried parents juggle hopes and fears. Hopes for an opportunity to learn from past mistakes and create a happier or more enduring family vie with fears that a new child will add insult to the injury of children hurt by divorce or bereavement. Remarried parents frequently anticipate that the older children will feel envy, jealousy, and resentment about their having "another family." While all of these do occur to some extent in most families, parents who imagine the worst seldom find their fears realized. More often, parents are surprised and delighted that the children, at least at first, are happier, more excited, and more affectionate than expected. But despite the older children's excitement at the birth, and the opportunity to be an adored older brother or sister, the mutual child occupies a position in the evolving family that is unparalleled. He alone is equally the child of both of the adults in the household. Both parent and stepparent are sensitive to the implications this privileged new role may have for the other children.

Especially when children visit or are in joint custody, the arrival of a baby in a household in which they have previously been an only and occasional child makes it "feel more like a whole family" to all. "There wasn't a family over there before," said one fifteen-year-old, referring to the time before her father and stepmother began having children eight years before. Parents whose children visit also feel, now, that they have a "real" family again. Gabriel described how his daughter's birth "minimized the degree to which I could be the uncle that's always having a party" when his sons come to town.

Yet despite parents' best intentions and most fervent efforts, their older children are bound to have mixed feelings about the baby's arrival. Joy in the formation of a newly "real" family mingles with disappointment at having to further let go of any dreams of reuniting the original family, or reawakens feelings of loss in a bereaved child. The appearance of more stability in the household and delight in the mutual child is weighed against the "added wear and tear" of introducing an infant to an already overloaded system. Recognizing the unique relation the younger child has with both of the adults in the household, the older children may fear eviction from the center of parental love and attention.

However the scales are balanced in the stepfamily before his arrival, the birth of the mutual child introduces an unknown into the equation, the impact of which will, first of all, depend on the equation itself. The effect that a new child born of remarriage has on the relationship between parent and child of a previous marriage depends on what was happening between the two before the baby's arrival: How secure the older child was in his parent's affection beforehand and whether there has been time to integrate other changes in the family, so that new members can be added to the stepfamily without consigning the older children to the periphery.

When the children display envy, jealousy, and resentment, which happens with any younger sibling, parents are likely to see an older child's envy as directed, not at the baby, but at the family subgroup created by his birth. Determined to make sure that the older child does not feel left out, they counter the child's own tendency to draw a tight circle around the nuclear threesome. Describing her own sadness at learning, as a child, that the father of her two younger sisters was, in fact, her stepfather, Maggie remembers "from that day forward, I always felt the family was my mom and stepfather and my two sisters, and that I was an outsider." Now the mother of three children, one from her first marriage and two from her second, she is extremely conscious of how George may be feeling in her home. "It's so similar, you know, two of the children being with the mother and father who all match, and then this one kid. So when he says things like 'Aileen is my half sister,' there's a part of my heart that kind of scrunches, 'cause I want him to think of her as his sister." She is aware of bending over backward to indulge George's whims, zealously avoiding his feeling peripheral to the household in which he alone comes and goes.

Conscious of his position, the older child may vie with his stepparent over who can be closer to parent and mutual child, a strategy that only seems worth trying when the children share a mother. It is painful for all concerned when the older child retreats from the nuclear minifamily, but it is most damaging to the child who is allowed to do so. When a twelve-year-old enters the living room and sees his mother and stepfather on the couch with their two children and walks on by, later telling his mother, "You were a unit," he breaks her heart, but it is he who is most isolated by this reading of the family reality.

Mothers are the most sensitive to the possibility that any of their children will feel less a part of the family than the rest. Laura describes her worry that the threesome of her husband and daughter and herself excluded her son, just by existing: "We were all related in this way, and I was related to Nathaniel off to the side. As much as I tried to include him in the family picture, he didn't want to be included. Because he was angry at Andrew and Elena, and angry at me for making the situation, when before it had just been the two of us. I have a really clear image of us, of Andrew and Elena and me, as this circle that Nathaniel was outside of . . . he refused to come in. His solution to that has always been 'I'm going to break up that circle and make it like it used to be.' "

What Stays the Same

Many children and parents report with conviction that their relationships are unchanged by a new baby, while the rest are divided among those who report an improvement, a deterioration, or a mixture of the two. How, in the presence of often sweeping changes precipitated by adding a stepfamily member, can parents and children insist that nothing has changed between them? When children are old enough to be looking outside the family for companionship and entertainment, especially if the baby is born to the household they visit, they may find that consistency and stability follow in the gentle wake of the mutual child's birth. Bonnie and Judith were fourteen and sixteen when their father and stepmother had their first baby. Both girls agreed, as Bonnie put it, "Dad and I have always had our own relationship, and it's always been what it's been. Having Enid affected it hardly at all." When there are ten or more years' difference between the children, too, the older child may be better able to understand that the differences in how the children are treated are related to the difference in their ages.

When all the children share a household, or even when the older children are in joint custody, residing for long periods with each parent, the children can feel that they are "all in one boat," for good and for ill. Even when the new children change the family substantially, an older child can perceive his tie with his parent as substantially the same as his half siblings'.

A firm sense of the parent's love, established over years of care, and a continuing commitment to set aside time together, can give the child enough emotional ballast to not feel blown aside by the addition of a half sibling. One young man who is the mutual child of one marriage and a stepchild to his parents' new mates found no significant differences in how his father was with him and with his sister, eight years older, and how his mother was with him and a younger sister and brother, born when he was twelve and seventeen. Responding to my question as to how his relationship with his mother changed when she had children with his stepfather, he replied: "I don't think it really did change. She had to physically spend more time and energy on them, but she managed to still have plenty of time to help me with my book reports and all that. I'm not quite sure how she did that, but she did. I don't see myself being any different than the younger kids, except that I was more of a single child." About his father, he said, "Again, we're both his children, regardless of who our mothers are. I think we fall into the same category."

Despite a parent's effort to be inclusive, stepchildren in the same family differ in how attached they become to the children of their parent's remarriage. Perhaps the best predictor of which older child will be receptive to the younger child is the pattern of alliances between parents and children in the first family. Even before the original family was broken up by divorce or truncated by death, each parent had a different bond with each child, and each child had different allegiance to each parent. When divorce occurs, differences in attachment can become polarized further, with one child blaming the mother and the other the father for the separation, so that each parent may have camp followers among the children. With remarriage and the birth of a mutual child, the older children may divide along the lines of their initial alliances. The child who is most closely allied with the remarried parent will feel more like a sister or brother to the baby, while the child who is estranged from the mutual parent tends to be alienated from the mutual child as well.

Parents with More to Give

A sense of being "Daddy's favorite" or "Mom's special one" can survive the addition of other children who are obviously less favored. Even for children less assured of their singularity in their parent's affection, the arrival of the child of remarriage can strengthen their own bonds with the parent they have in common. Having a baby can soften parents, rekindling their ability to nurture. Tom recalls how having a daughter with his second wife broke down his "standoffish-ness" with his son, who was eleven at the time: "It put me more in touch with smaller kids. I was very close to George when he was small. I wouldn't say we drifted apart, but your relationship does change when they get older. Somehow being in touch with another small kid opened some doors or something. Otherwise you get to be all business."

Many parents use the occasion of the new child to reminisce together with the older ones about what their lives were like at the same age. This can also be an occasion to talk about some of the difficulties of their early lives in a way that elicits self-acceptance and empathy with their younger selves. Susan, for example, thinks it was important for Carl to see what she was like with his small half brother Eric, ten years younger: "Carl was three when his father and I separated. We talked about how he could imagine what he went through by imagining what it would be like for Eric, who was a vivid reminder of what three-year-olds are like. It kind of allowed us to talk about some things in a different way."

Either because they are happier to have a family that feels "complete" at last, or because the need to take care of a baby leads to a reduced work commitment, mothers especially report that they feel they have more to give an older child after having another. Sometimes it is the remarriage, rather than the mutual child, that lifts a depression and permits the parent to be more loving to all. Fathers, especially, when they have not had much access to their children, find that being a day-to-day parent makes them feel like a "real parent" at last, giving them a new sense of self-confidence that extends to their dealings with all the children.

Parent and child also come closer to each other when both are smitten with the baby. "There's been an emotional closeness in watching them take care of her," said Nancy, describing how affectionate her older children are with the baby, "and seeing how she loved them, that's been quite wonderful." From the child's point of view, sharing child care with a parent can give them "something in common" during years when they might be moving farther apart. For a twelve-year-old girl, taking care of eighteen-month-old Evan was an avenue to more time with her father, who she speculated would otherwise be outside playing with her ten-year-old brother during their weekends together.

Children who visit the remarried household, especially, are impressed with how much more like a family it feels after there is a full-time child around, imparting a sense of stability and security that feels valuable. Now in his early twenties, Dan feels that "one of the main things that I've gotten out of my relationship with my father and stepmother and the children was a need for and respect for a family unit, which I don't think I would have gotten without that."

How much visiting children want to feel a part of the remarried household has everything to do with how they feel about their own parent, primarily, and their stepparent. But both parents and children agree that the mutual child gives the older ones another stake in the family, a stake that is especially powerful for children for whom he is an only sibling. Fathers without custody are cognizant that the strength of their bond with their older child, and even their bargaining power with their former wives, are enhanced when they can provide brothers and sisters to an otherwise only child. Ben confesses to "consciously using that in a manipulative way" to increase his son's visits: "I'll kind of guilt trip his mother and stepfather about getting him out here so he can get to know his brothers. They're the only brothers he's going to have, because his mother's had a hysterectomy. That has a lot of power. I know it means a lot to him, and I like thinking of him with the other kids."

When children change custody, unless child-care demands are oppressive, the presence of younger children in the household can help in integrating them into the new family unit, providing a "family focus" that is less available in adults-only households. Peter was fourteen when he moved in with his father and stepmother, whose daughter was then two. He has "great memories of really being involved with baby-sitting and taking care of her, and doing things with my family that only happen when there's a little kid in the family, like going to Disney World, going to the beach. Whereas if it was just me there, as a fourteen- or fifteen-year-old, they wouldn't have done those things. So I think it contributed to the closeness of the family."

Normalizing the Older Child

Perhaps one of the greatest boons that having another child confers is to rehabilitate the older child as a normal kid in his parent's eyes. Susan illustrates the process of rethinking the developmental history of a first child who experienced an early parental separation, a reevaluation that is set in motion by watching another child develop who has not been exposed to the same family disruption: "What's interesting to me is that a lot of the stages that Carl went through after the separation I always attributed to 'Oh, it's because of the divorce.' When he was real cranky or a pain in the neck or whatever. Now I realize these are just stages kids go through. Eric was just impossible over the holiday, just awful. I realized that if it had been Carl at this age, I would have been going, 'It's the divorce.' I always explained everything by the divorce, when in fact it's just that kids are a pain in the neck sometimes."

This "normalization" of the older child is not limited to the past. In rethinking earlier formulations about a child, the rehabilitation can be extended to the present day. Melanie, for example, by watching five-year-old Yale go through some of the same problems that eleven-year-old Paul did at the same age is newly confident that "they're transitional problems, they're part of growing up through childhood," a position she could never muster when Paul was five. "I can then look at the problems that Paul is dealing with now and say, 'Oh, this must be approaching adolescence, or it must be some cycle, or it'll pass.'" Comparing her two sons, one of whom is being raised with the advantages of a stable two-parent home, and finding similarities, Melanie looks to developmental factors to understand her children's behavior instead of blaming everything on the divorce, blaming herself for being a working mother, or blaming her ex-husband for not caring enough.

If watching a mutual child develop normalizes a parent's perspective on a child who experienced death or divorce in the family, so too does watching a parent with a much younger child give the older a different perspective on that parent as a parent. Seeing a parent make the same mistakes with another child in another marriage, a grown or near-grown child can develop some distance from the struggle, sorting out what she likes in his child rearing and what she would change, given the choice, and not becoming as "mean-spirited" about confronting him. Part of growing up in any case, seeing a parent as just a person, with strengths and faults, capable of pleasing and disappointing, can be accelerated when there is an opportunity to observe how he is with children who are removed in age or residence.

Mixed Blessings

"You don't want the *National Enquirer* headlines? 'Brother Beats Brother and Sister. Brother and Sister Kick Older Brother Out of House.' " Bruce, in his early twenties now, apologizes that he has no such stories about not getting along with the children of his dad's second marriage, parodying what he thinks I have come to hear, as he tells me how attached he is to his eight-year-old half sister in particular. And he is telling the truth, or *a* truth, anyway. Yet in his wisecracking telegraphic version of the structure of the family, he also conveys the ambivalence of many older children who have to share a parent with other children whose second parent is not their own.

For some, being less the object of parental concern is a relief. Parents of an only or youngest child may treat him as younger than he is until he is no longer "the baby of the family," then immediately treat him as older. One father of an eleven-year-old and an infant realized that he had treated his son like a baby until his daughter was born. The period of strain between him and the boy, who was unwilling to confront him directly, eased when he transferred his "infantilizing" concern to a genuine infant.

From the older children's point of view, especially if they are well into their teens when the mutual child is born and have a parent who is intensely concerned with them, sharing that concern can feel like having a burden lifted. A man who labeled his dad "fairly intense and really hardheaded" talked about how nice it was to have somebody to share that intensity with. "If he didn't have my two sisters, he'd be on me all the time," he said.

Noncustodial parents, usually fathers who feel deprived of contact with their growing children, may have a harder time "letting go" when their teenagers want to spend their leisure time with peers. Having younger children at home can give the older ones some breathing space, the latitude to make some choices for themselves. Bonnie, who was sixteen when her half sister was born, is hard pressed to think of any way in which her life was made more difficult by the birth: "I think when you're in high school or college you don't really care about having your parents super-super-super involved in everything you're doing. Having them have another child takes a little bit of attention away from you. If I'd been younger when Enid was born, I probably would have resented her. As it was, there's the sense that if I don't make it home for Thanksgiving this year, well, they have Enid. It's not like they're going to be by themselves on a family holiday, because they've got the little kids. Even now, I'm recently married and I want to be there for the family occasions, but if we can't, they've got their own little sub-family group too. Which is nice for everyone, I think."

Despite the expression of relief by many, the diminution of parental attention can feel like more of a mixed blessing to the older children, especially when they are living in the home or are of an age to be. Teens and preteens may revel in being out from under a watchful parental eye, but too much freedom can feel like neglect. They need to feel that trying their wings is a hard-won achievement, not that they are being bumped out of the nest. In thinking about how their lives might have been different if their parent had not had a child in remarriage, they think, "He would have had more time, but I don't know if I would have used it; I might have been busy with my friends." Seeing a parent nurture a much younger child can have a regressive pull, especially if the older child feels that he has not gotten what he needs from that parent. The older child then vacillates between celebrating his independence and signaling his neediness. The same eighteen-year-old who chafes at being referred to as one of "my three kids" by his father—"I'm one of his offspring but I'm not a kid"—can show disappointment that he is not included in an Easter egg hunt with his three-year-old half sister.

When children are closer in age, approximating the differences between children who share both parents, parents entertain the common set of worries about sibling rivalry, wondering how to reassure the older child that he will not be pushed aside by the younger. But parents of children who are eight or more years apart tend to feel the time has come to dethrone "his majesty the baby." "The realization that they're not the most important thing in somebody's life came at an appropriate time for them," observed Richard, whose older children were ten and twelve when he had a son with his second wife. "They were full-bodied people, they were already on their way to having more of an adult focus." Even when the older child is not entirely convinced that a parent has adequate resources to nurture all, explicitly protesting his parent's love for another child, the parent may think that the second child is an effective antidote to the "King Tut" or "spoiled brat" tendencies of the first. Mike, after detailing the polarization of the family that took place following Ethan's birth, still held that the "positive side" of having this second child "was very important for Jason to get a sense of his relationship to the universe" after being the center of attention in the households of both remarried parents.

While some parents applaud the object lesson in an older child's not being the center of the universe, many feel spread very thin and regret not being able to give more to all. When the mutual child "comes first the way babies do," a mother may find herself too exhausted to take an evening a week with each of her older children, as she had before. Two years later, when the baby is no longer as demanding, she may try to renew her special time with the older kids, only to find that one or more have come to an age where being alone with Mom is not as much fun as being with friends. "Keith stood me up," said Nancy, referring to her efforts to reinstitute weekly dates with her twelve-year-old, "and it was heartbreaking. I was back and where was he?"

"It pulled me in all different directions," John recalled, "because I always wanted to spend somewhat equal or at least quality time with all three children. It is very difficult when you have one that demands so much attention. I remember being somewhat tired and not having the energy that I felt I needed to do an adequate job with the older girls." Like several of the fathers, he was much less confident of his ability to be a parent to teenagers than to younger children. Another father who admits to taking "less interest in their personal lives and what was going inside their brains" attributed this change, not to his having "new kids," but to his older children's becoming teenagers. "I really feel with all my kids that I'm just a totally incompetent parent for teenagers. I fear the teenage years of my kids. I don't understand it. They get picked up by the cops, consider suicide. If they can get through it without these horrible things happening, thank God for small favors."

Despite the ability of teenagers in all kinds of families to make their parents feel incompetent, they still do need parents. Because their needs are less obvious, less compelling, and even repudiated by the teenagers themselves, it is easy to overlook them. They know, however, that they miss having parents available to participate in activities with them and lament that "the kind of things that I'd like to do now, we have to wait until the people who are one year old are up to my age before we do them. And then I won't want to do them." Indeed, they can become bitter about needs, never voiced, not being met, voluntarily choosing not to make demands of parents they see as overburdened even as they hold that exhaustion against them. Or they may scapegoat the children of the remarriage for changes in parental availability that happen to coincide with their arrival, as, for example, when a father triples his work load to pay for his older children's college tuition at the time that his younger children are being born.

Even when parents extend themselves, young people who feel deprived by not having a parent around all the time and envious of their siblings who do may, nonetheless, choose not to visit. Tony, for example, feels "sort of short-changed by not having a father around all the time. But I found that there was no reason to spend any time with anybody but my friends. The only reason I see my mom all the time is that we live with each other. It's sad. I wish I could have a father around so I could see him for five seconds."

These teenagers and adult children feel distanced by their parent having a child with a new partner, while others feel as close as ever, or at least as close as they care to be. What distinguishes the two groups are the strength of the parent-child bond before the mutual child enters the family, how well the child feels his needs have been met along the way to his current station in life, and how the parent manages to balance the emotional budget when accounts payable include children separated by different developmental needs, another parent they do not share, and, perhaps, primary residence.

How Many Children in All

In the emotional economy of the family, how much the mutual child changes what transpires between a parent and his children from a previous marriage hinges on the sheer number of bodies that must be counted in the reckoning of time and attention. When the child of the new marriage means that there are three, four, five, six, or more children in all, the impact differs greatly from when an only child gains a half sibling. For the large family, a new baby may feel like "a drop in the bucket." Nonetheless, when material or emotional resources already feel spread too thin, the baby may be held accountable for the scarcity.

Joining a Crowd

Many children in large families, with the exception of the reigning "baby," tend to downplay the impact of the child of the remarriage. Like Judy, whose mother had five children with her father and four with her stepfather, they tend to judge that overall "there was so much going on in my household that you really didn't get very much sort of individual anything from my mother." Number six differed little from number five.

When it is mother who has the additional child, children are more apt to sympathize with the stress of added responsibility that another child entails. A number of the older children judged that the baby was a plus for everyone in the family except Mom, a judgment the mothers themselves do not share. One man remembers the birth of his second half brother as "a pretty stressful time," because his mother added three stepchildren and a baby to the two children she already had, "a quantum leap" that left her "frazzled." Even when the baby comes to be appreciated as "a wonderful, super person" who gives her parents "tremendous joy," there is no question that adding a baby to a family, especially one dealing with a rapid succession of other changes, adds wear and tear. For an older child "one more person, more sleepless nights, a more crowded, noisy house" can add to the sense that there is not enough attention to go around, especially when the needs of the newborn become a greater point of focus than the progress of the older child.

Parents, for their part, can feel spread pretty thin by trying to meet the needs and demands of a number of children. "Certainly the larger the family got," said Gene, "the less close I was able to be with any one of them. If I had any one of these kids all by himself or herself, I would have devoted all the time to that one kid. It would have been completely different." Instead, having three children before being widowed, remarrying, and going on to have two more, he found that "all of a sudden I'm now playing baby games with them, the same as I did with the older kids, probably at a time when if I didn't have them I'd be playing older games with the older kids. I still had time with the older kids. I'd be playing chess with Daryl at the time I'm playing blocks with the girls. I had to become thinner. I didn't mind doing all of that, but I probably didn't do enough of either one because there were too many demands. But that's the way things were. I'm sure the older kids probably wanted some of my time when I was playing with the younger ones and vice versa."

But it is the older ones, not the younger, who usually feel short-changed. The children already born see themselves as a given, whereas the much younger children, especially if they have a different parent, are considered optional, intruders who must be made room for but who literally take the food off your plate. "For a few years I remember Christmas being real lean," remembers the oldest of six, "and I thought, 'Here the kids are, I don't see Mom and Dad like I used to, we don't have the things here that we used to.'" Comparing her friends' parents' availability to participate in high school activities with how unavailable her own parents were, she blamed it on their having their three mutual children.

It is the youngest of the first group of children (one of whom was described by his older brother as "uprooted from being the youngest, the most spoiled, the one with the most attention, to being socked in the middle"), who is likely to do the most comparing and complaining. "There's no way," a former "baby of the family" said, "that my dad could have as strong and close relationships with the five of us as he could have with the three of us." Even a child who felt that his parents did "a good job of divvying up attention" among six children resolved to do things differently in his own life as an adult. The stepfather of one child, he and his wife devote all their energy to her, rather than try to divide their love and attention between even two.

"You and Me Against the World"

On the other end of the scale from these families with five to nine children are those that add a mutual child to an only child household. When the remarriage is consolidated before the birth, and especially when the single-parent phase of the family life cycle has not been a prolonged one, the transition from one to two children is more like a "first" family than any other configuration and in any other circumstance. Edward, describing how he and Susan approached having a child after seven years together, said: "There was no question that a considerable amount of our attention was going to go to this new baby, and that Carl was not going to have the undivided attention of two people, but there were two people. We felt that whatever needs Carl had we ought to be able to meet them with two adults on the scene. One to take care of the baby, and one to take care of the big guy, if it came to that." What makes the two child–two adult family seem adequate to meet the needs of both children, however, is that in this family stepfather and stepson had developed their relationship to the point that both children were not clamoring for their needs to be met by the same parent.

In contrast, children who have been the only child of a single parent for a long time have a harder time sharing, first with a stepparent and then with another child. Helen Reddy's song, "You and Me Against the World," often sung as a love song, was written about being a single mother; it is a love song to her child. The tightly coiled connectedness of this twosome, sometimes passionate, always intense, makes it difficult to open up to newcomers, as both partners protect their emotional territory in the heart of the other.

Leslie and her daughter, Denise, were such a twosome. Not yet eighteen when Denise was born, Leslie was essentially a single parent until she married Everett when Denise was four. Denise's father, who worked elsewhere, was with them on weekends at first, but by the time she was three they had broken off their relationship, and he had ceased visiting Denise, saying it was too painful to be around Leslie after it was over between them. "We had such a closely tuned relationship," says Leslie, "it was just us, there was nobody else to consider. I'm very much 'only me can tell her anything.' I was like that with her father, I was like that with my mum, and it was very difficult for me to deal with letting go and letting Everett in."

While Leslie concludes that Oliver's birth, when Denise was almost six, was "probably good for her because I was too close to her," she feels guilty for not being as available to her daughter as she was before. "She's the one who gets the short end of the stick," Leslie told me, heaping undeserved criticism on herself. "On the other hand, as I always tell myself, 90 percent of the time she's here, she likes to sit and read. Lots of times when I say 'Shall you and I do something together?' she'll say 'Oh, Mom, I want to go to so-and-so's house.' "

Because they were so close, Leslie thinks they "could tell what each other was thinking, it seemed like, when she was little. I know I do wrongly, I put myself in her position so much, and it ends up she's thinking something completely different. Then I'll be shocked: 'You mean she didn't want to do this?' " Leslie is aware enough to know that the greater distance between them is age appropriate for her daughter, but she persists in feeling guilty about enlarging their family beyond the two of them, favoring her daughter to make up for her not getting what she used to get. "I'll say 'Oh, Denise could get this, Denise could do that.' Thinking of special things to do for Denise. Just because Oliver gets so much of the everyday stuff, time and energy. If we have a plan and she wants to do something else, I'll let her do that. It's crazy. Every time I go to the Emporium, the only thing I buy is for Denise. Just silly things. I'll go and say 'Oh, Denise would like that.' "

This pattern of guiltily indulging an older child occurs for many long-single parents of an only child and continues for many beyond remarriage and additional children. Part of the indulgence is treating the child too much like a peer. Having been, as Mike describes his single years with Jason, "my primary relationship, the most intense relationship I have ever had in many ways," the child is given a great deal of power. Jason, for example, "was very interested in controlling who I went out with," Mike continues. "If he didn't like a person I was going out with, it had a great impact on me. He very much wanted me to be with someone, because that's what I really wanted to do. He wanted to be very supportive of that, but on the other hand, he wasn't sure how much sharing he wanted to do of Papa." Papa's marrying a woman who had been Jason's friend before she'd been Mike's partner was an easier transition for Jason, who continued to be the only child in the lives of the four adults, parents and stepparents. However, Mike described him as "too used to center stage," reporting that Jason "freaked out" with jealousy, at nine, when Mike and Irma's son Ethan was born, despite Jason's having lobbied for a sibling for years.

While many of the only children welcomed a half sibling as the only brother or sister they would ever have, several cling to the memory of the lost romance with Mom or Dad. When the intensity of being alone with a parent has been there for a long time, it is hard for the child to give up. "She agrees with me a lot," said nine-year-old Denise of her mother, Leslie, ruing her lost influence, "but she used to agree with me very much." While it may be in their ultimate best interest to be demoted from premature adulthood when a parent remarries and has another child, forming a group of "the children" into which they are newly thrust, the loss of status can smart.

Mother's Child, Father's Child

> I'd really like my Daddy to have another kid. I want to be a big sister. But I don't want my Mommy to have another baby because it would live with us, and I'd have to share all my toys.
>
> *[Jenny, age seven][1]*

Does it matter if it is mother or father who remarries and has another child with a new partner? Children who have had a half sibling in only one household answer with a resounding "yes." "For me, the family has always been Mom and all her kids," remarked one twenty-year-old, whose mother had two children by her first marriage and a third with her second husband. Like the inner-city kids who told their teacher that their mother's children were their "real" sisters and brothers "because you come out of the same stomach," children who share both a mother and a household feel more connected than those who have intermittent contact based on a visitation schedule with their fathers. The biological connection during pregnancy can be impressive evidence of maternal primacy. Susan, for example, feels that Carl's presence at Eric's birth was more significant than if he had been present at the birth of his dad's child, because "he may have been able to think, this is exactly what I went through, 'cause here's the same woman." And, from the child's point of view, a teenage boy speculates that he would be closer to a child born of his mother: "When I think of Owen, I think I'm his brother, but I think of him as more Amelia's than my dad's. My dad didn't have him inside him for nine months. So I think he'd be more of a brother if my mom had him, not necessarily that I'd like him any more or less."

Children who visit their fathers are unanimous, however, in preferring that it be their father who has more children. A seven-year-old girl is glad that her mother was not the one to give her a half sibling, because "she would be holding it all the time." Another girl, at fourteen, concurs, saying that she "probably wouldn't like it as much, because I'd probably have to be around them all the time, you know, and take care of them when I wanted to go out or something." Looking back at twenty-four, a young woman, also a visitor in her father's remarried household, which now has two more children, thinks of what it would have been like if her mother had had more children, and is adamant: "Oh, my God, that would have been awful. Maybe because we lived there. It's not something I could imagine. Having to share a household would have been a lot harder." Despite thinking they'd feel closer to their mother's child, none of the children whose fathers had had a mutual child expressed any desire for their mothers to follow suit.

These children fervently believe that having a baby takes more away from what a mother has to give an older child than what he would lose from his father. Scott, fifteen, whose mother has a baby girl and whose father has two children with his stepmother, has had it both ways. He explains the difference as resulting from gender roles in child care: "Because usually the mother is the one who takes more care of the baby than the father. So the father is not the actual one that's having it. So it won't be taking as much away from you. I suppose if you have a really good relationship with your stepmother, more than with your father, then it's different. But if who you're wanting attention from is your father, then I'd say it's much better if it's your father's side."

Most of the children in his situation, with both mothers and fathers who have gone on to have more children in remarriage, find that whether the mutual child is Mommy's baby or Daddy's baby makes little difference. What matters to them is the custody arrangement and how they feel about their stepparent. All are agreed that sharing a household makes them feel closer to the new child than intermittent visits. When, however, the older children are in joint custody and have spent substantial periods of time in each home, most take the position, with sixteen-year-old Carl, that "it's the same. They're part of the family. They're happy to see you when you come, and sad when you go. It's pretty easy to get to know them again."

In thinking about the advantages and disadvantages of a mother or a father having more children, how the older children get along with the stepparent who is the mutual child's other parent weighs heavily in the balance. "I think it has everything to do with whether you like who they're remarried to," said Pamela, fifteen. "Because if you don't like the person that your parent is living with, then I think you'll resent your parent. Especially if they have a kid with them. Because then it's like this little kid is tied to you by the person that you don't even like. I think that would really be bad. Other than that, I can't really see any difference, because if you think about it, Eleanor is my second mother and Arthur is my second father. So basically I don't think my dad's kids are less my sisters and brother than my mom's daughter."

Both Carl and Pamela, in this regard, are typical of those who have come to know and trust their stepparents over many years before the baby is born. In remarriages that have children earlier on, there is a trend, most clearly observable when both parents bring children to the stepfamily, for all the children, from all the marriages, to see stepmothers as more likely to play favorites than stepfathers. In preferring that their mothers not become repeat parents, even though they may approve of their fathers' already having done so, children may be generalizing from their experience with their stepmothers, expecting a similar loss in time, energy, and emotional investment from their mothers were they, too, to have more children in a new marriage.

A Different Parent

So far our attention has been on how having a mutual child will affect the relationship between parents and their children from a previous marriage. Looking at the flip side of the coin, how then does having been a parent before change the way parents relate to the second set of children? For some, it is difficult to sort out the effects of being a repeat parent from those of being an older parent. All agree, however, that they are more relaxed with their second set of children. Gene, for example, recalls that his experience with his older three children made the younger two "a piece of cake: It didn't represent so much anxiety to me, since I'd already had three kids through these ages."

In Chapter 2, I discussed how noncustodial fathers find themselves trying to make up for lost time, being the parent to their mutual child that circumstances prevented them from being to their older children. I would be talking with a man about his children and, time and again, he would call the first of his mutual children by the name of his first child. When I brought Ben's attention to this name shuffle, he was struck: "I don't make that slip so much anymore, but I still have to be vigilant about it. So that's the sense of Ira being my second chance."

Seeing the "second" family as a replication of the first one does not occur only with the first child of the remarriage. There are ways that parents behave similarly to the first children of each marriage, and they go on to treat the second child of each union in ways that display striking parallels. Linda, now twenty-one, commented that for her father, "There's a definite parallel between Jane and Amber, and between me and Eve. He says things to them that he doesn't think about first. There's a lot more bickering going on between them. He even always gets me and Eve mixed up on our names, and always Jane and Amber. Never Eve and Amber or Jane and me."

Noncustodial fathers are not the only parents who see having a child in a new marriage as a chance to start over, to remedy the "mistakes" made last time. "She told me she wanted to do it right this time," Greg said, referring to his mother's second son. "She feels very guilty for the way I was raised. Meaning I lived in twenty-six houses before I was ten. We were on welfare for a long time." Critical of his mother for "spoiling" his half brother, he attributes her indulgence of the younger boy's whims to a "zealousness" to compensate for past lapses.

Greg, whose relationship with his mother is a good one, is critical of her for behaving differently with his half brother than she did with him, effectively endorsing the kind of mothering he himself received. Nathaniel, on the other hand, lambasts his mother for the ways in which she is the same with her daughter as she was with him. "You're letting her get away with murder," he tells his mother. "You know that's going to make her into a person who always thinks she can get her way." When Elena was a baby, Nathaniel would scream at his mother when the baby cried, "Nurse her. She's hungry." Or "change her," insisting, from his own sense of deprivation, that his mother do better, even with an envied rival, than she did with him.

It doesn't take being a stepchild to make an older child a vigilant parent-watcher, comparing how a younger child is being raised with his own upbringing. But parents expect to be under greater scrutiny when their children are from different marriages. They anticipate greater resentment from the child, who brings to bear knowledge of another way of doing things gathered when he lived with both parents, and greater criticism from the child's other parent. While the older children are looking hard for differences between themselves and the new crew of children, parents are trying desperately to find similarities, to build the bridges that will enable all of their children to feel that they're in the same family.

What Parents Can Do

For parents who have children with more than one partner, making all the children feel like family to one another takes effort and planning that begins during the pregnancy. Being sure that the right person breaks the news to the older children lays the groundwork for their being able to look forward to having a half sibling. Hearing the news from the mutual parent, who can then assure them that they will lose neither his love nor his availability, rather than from a family member more likely to amplify their fears, goes a long way toward allowing them to comfortably anticipate the birth. Giving them time to explore their own worries and fears without condemnation, asking questions and testing allegiance, sharing fantasies about how life will change for them, are all part of preparing the older children for the arrival of the mutual child.

Whether a parent who is happily remarried and pleased to be adding to the family feels she has more to give to all her children or, despite wanting the baby, she feels like the rope in a tug-of-war of competing demands, each child needs to know that there is some time that is his alone. When demands multiply, it is often difficult to set aside time for all. However modest the minutes or hours allotted may be, the payoff is great, preserving each child's sense that he is important to the parent whom he must share with yet one more person.

Encouraging his child to have a direct relationship with his partner, and his partner to have a personal tie with his child, frees the parent from the thankless position of constantly being called upon to adjudicate conflict. When stepparent-stepchild tensions are not always routed through the parent whose love and allegiance each craves, they must work out who they will be to one another between themselves, creating the family feeling that cannot develop without one-to-one contact.

Parents can do much to create feelings of kinship among their children, even when half siblings are separated by thousands of miles and a generation of years. Pictures, stories, encouragement to think of each other as family, and closeness to the parent they share instilled a feeling of sisterhood between the youngest mutual child of one Iranian-American father and the daughters he had left in the old country, despite their having lived together for a total of six months. Making sure that each child feels well connected to you as a parent enables them to feel connected to each other.

Children who are out of the household most of the time must be allowed time to reconnect with their parent before being expected to divide their attention among other family members, whose allegiance may feel less vital. Handling time together when it is infrequent can be a delicate problem in diplomacy for the parent everyone wants a piece of. From the point of view of the mutual child, the prospect of a visit from a parent's older children is exciting, but also threatening when it conjures up feelings of rivalry for possession of the shared parent. The emotional climate in the household churns as the arrival comes closer. The shared parent is eagerly awaiting a chance to see the children he sees too little and is perhaps distracted from the child whom he sees every day. The parent who is also a stepparent may be anticipating conflict with her stepchildren or abandonment by her husband for the duration of the visit. Both adults are hoping to get the reentry process over with as quickly and as painlessly as possible. And all this excitement has as its center somebody else: somebody bigger, somebody whom the mutual child may adore in a way that often feels unrequited, somebody whose claim to her parent historically precedes her own, and, she fears, somebody who will displace her, however temporarily, as the center of his attention. "No," she may insist, "I don't want to share him with them. I don't want them to come. I want to be with my daddy just alone." She needs to hear that, while it is all right for her to feel that way, her half siblings and her parent get to see each other so seldom that it is hard on all of them. She gets to see the parent all the time and can have special time with him before and after her half siblings visit. With this kind of preparation and reassurance, by the time the older children arrive, the mutual child will be most interested in being with "the big kids."

We have seen that children of a parent's past and present marriages, although rivalrous, also have much to offer one another. When the children fight among themselves, the challenge for the parent is to avoid always blaming the older child for conflicts between children of grossly disparate ages, difficult as that sometimes is. While bigger kids must not be allowed to hurt the little ones, neither are they the villains in the piece. Their lack of a developmental perspective in looking at the behavior of the mutual child is only partly a failure of understanding. More telling is their need for assurance that their parent's expanding his circle of love and care leaves plenty of room for them at its center.

The single most important task for the parent who is having children in remarriage is to instill this assurance in his older children. Feeling displaced in that parent's affection will not only interfere with the older child's acceptance of the new addition, but, as will be more fully developed in the next chapter, will contribute to strife between stepparent and stepchild, detracting from general family satisfaction for all. For children whose primary residence is elsewhere, this means steady, dependable time in the stepfamily household, and for visitors and residents alike, it means creating opportunities for each child to be the center of the parent's attention, at least some of the time.

5

A Basis for Comparison

*Stepparents with Their Children
and Their Stepchildren*

When Brian, the youngest of my three stepsons, was almost nine, and my son David was fifteen months old, Brian caught me by surprise. As he helped with the breakfast dishes, he asked, almost offhandedly: "Would you rather have David for a baby or me for a stepson?" Taken aback, I paused for a moment and said, "I'd rather have David for a baby *and* you for a stepson." But Brian was not to be satisfied with this diplomatic, albeit honest, rejoinder; he insisted I had to choose. "I wouldn't want to choose," I admitted, "but if I had to, I'd have to say 'David as a baby,' because I'd feel really sad to never have a baby. But I'd rather have had you as a baby, too." Brian protested, "No you wouldn't. I took a long time to come out, like thirty-two hours." That wouldn't deter me, I countered, as David had taken even longer, a fact he disputed, only to be sent to his father, whose eyewitness account of both births could be relied on.

The debate on the circumstances of each boy's birth was a diversion from Brian's real concern: Now that I had my own child, how important was he to me? Would his needs have as much priority? How much did I care? Could he trust me with his affection now that he had a rival with a different claim on my heart? Before, I had been a stepmother to all three of the children in the family, now, would my being a "real mother," in their words, change what went on between me and the older boys?

A Ticket of Admission

Stepparents who have previously not felt accepted find a new legitimacy in being related to their stepchildren by way of the mutual child. Steprelationships are given permanence by the addition of a person to whom both "steps" are indissolubly linked. Eliot described how his wife's cancer scare led him to reflect on the impermanence of his tie to his stepson before his daughters were born: "You start worrying, and you start to say, 'What if Maggie was not around?' George would always have a permanent relationship to me, because his sister is my daughter. I remember that very strongly, that sense that 'George is part of my family, even if I'm not related to him by blood.' He will always be part of my life, no matter what else happens. Whereas if it was just us, I might be gone."

Even if stepfamily integration has not progressed very far along its developmental course, there is consensus that the mutual child is, at least initially, a great integrator. When tensions rage between stepparent and stepchildren, the baby forms an unbreakable link that makes one family out of two camps. One embattled mother insists that, despite her wish to protect her children from her husband's displeasure with them, their son has "made us a family of five, instead of a family of three and a family of two: me and my husband, and me and my kids, with me stretching trying to bring them together. The baby's done that. The connections between the older kids and the little one are so strong I can't imagine us separating that way."

Indeed, the baby is the only family member who feels equally "a part of all of us." Her father and mother are brought closer together as, finally, the parents of the same child. And her siblings, in the typically concrete thinking of children, may measure the relative strength of her blood lines, concluding that as the only person to share blood with every person in the family, she belongs to them, too. Here, at last, said one stepmother, was someone that everyone "could love, kind of equally, without any of the hang ups of a "step-relationship."

It is the equality of family members claims to relatedness, not sharing a gene pool, that puts the mutual child in this position. Indeed, adopted mutual children seem to play a similar role in the stepfamilies they join. An eight-year-old was told by his mother that his father's newly adopted baby boy was not 'really related' to him because they have different mothers. Surprised by his stepmother's comment that her new son was no more related to *her* than to the older boy, he abandoned his reserve and embraced the infant as a brother.

Even when both parents have already had children, the stepparent-stepchild relationship shifts to make the stepparent more of a parent. Diane, for example, found that her stepdaughter, Jenny, began to see her differently after baby Angie was born. "I'm more of a mother, not just a mother to Beverly, a person highly competitive with her who's the same age. She could think, 'Dad just got this other family, with a seven-year-old girl to replace me.' With the baby, I think she sees it as more of a whole family, and I'm just the mother of it." Ben, already a parent when he married Julia, echoes this theme that having children together made him "the Dad of the family" in a way he had not been before with his stepson: "I felt that I didn't have rights with Jeremy. Then we had the kids together. Okay, the kids in the house are the kids in the house, that includes Jeremy." And Lowell, from the stepchild end of things, remembered feeling his stepfather was "more of a father figure and less of a stranger" after his mother gave birth to a son.

All family members agree that the mutual child's birth helps to make the stepfamily more of a family. Perhaps to feel more like part of the family, stepchildren at this time occasionally change the way they address their stepparents and frequently change the terms by which they refer to them. Denise, a five-year-old who barely remembered her natural father, began to call her stepfather "Daddy" when her mother was seven months pregnant. "Cause when the baby comes it'll be confused if it hears me calling him 'Everett,' " she told her mother. Especially when the stepchild is outnumbered by the mutual children, she will feel more a part of the group if she refers to her stepparent as "Mom" or "Dad" when talking to the younger children. "When I'm at my mom's house," explained Pamela, "to my sister I'll call my stepfather 'Dad,' like to the kids here I call my stepmother 'Mom.' It makes it easier, and it makes me feel closer to the other kids."

The increased empathy of the stepchild for the stepparent is matched by a surge in the stepparent's empathy for the stepchild. Finally feeling like a permanent member of the family with a legitimate and defined role, the stepparent becomes more relaxed about his place in his stepchildren's affection, accepting the hierarchy of attachment as inevitable. As Elaine explains: "I love the fact that I'm this kid's mom. I came to terms with the fact that I was never going to be Leo's mom. I would be a very significant person in his life and in many ways would reap benefits from the relationship that his own mother wouldn't. And yet I wanted that experience of being the Mom, of being the person who provokes somebody else to cry when you close the door. It feels good to feel really important in that way. I've always known that there was a hierarchy, and that as much as Leo loved me, the hierarchy goes Mom and Dad, and then Stepmom and Stepdad. I think I've accepted it much more graciously, now that I have a baby of my own." Becoming reconciled to this reality eases the way for a more mutually accepting relationship between stepparent and stepchild.

A Window of Vulnerability

While having a mutual child can make a stepparent more understanding, more relaxed, less demanding, and less critical with his stepchild, he does not necessarily become less vulnerable to that child. His self-esteem is often more at risk with his stepchild than with his natural children. Even adults who appear remarkably self-possessed and self-assured can be more easily wounded by the insult of a stepchild than by that of a natural child. Arthur, for example, describes how he gets "paranoid" with his stepdaughter in a way that he never, ever gets with his own kids. "The real wonder of having kids of my own is that I'm never paranoid," he said. "I never wonder if they like me or not. And it's much more likely with Jessica that I will get in a snit because I think she doesn't like me enough, or that she treated me badly. I never think about my kids treating me badly. If they do, I yell at them. But I'm much more vulnerable to Jessica. Over the years, I've been more likely to feel that she was being mean to me in some way." And over the years, he has been able to hear his wife's voice of reason, helping him to untangle himself from what else was going on with Jessica, not overreacting to her slights, real and imagined.

With his own child, a parent can hear the child shout "I hate you" at him and know that it is anger speaking, that there is a firm base of love and attachment that binds them and that will outlast the heat of the moment. With his stepchild, however, the stepparent knows that they are together by accident, as it were, and that the child presumably would like nothing better than the stepparent's disappearance as a welcome precursor to the reunification or resurrection of his original family unit. While stepparents' assumptions about their stepchildren's anger are frequently exaggerated, they are not completely wrong. Unfortunately, a stepparent's vulnerability fuels his stepchild's aggression, which in turn exacerbates the stepparent's aggressive wish that the child disappear; round and round they may go in a cycle of mutual aggression and exclusion, a circle with no identifiable point of origin.

What the stepchild wants more than anything else is for his stepparent not to be so vulnerable to him. He does not want to feel that his anger can hurt an adult; when it does, his own power can frighten him. "She can't deal with what I have to say, and she's never allowed me to say it and feel that I didn't destroy her," one adult stepchild said of his stepmother. Another, also in her mid-twenties, thinks that talking to her stepmother of their difficulties would "scare her to death: This might be just some illusion, but whenever I'm alone in the room with her, I feel that I'm doing something to her, that I have all this power. I just feel that I don't want to have a conversation with her. I don't want to hurt her."

Her younger brother, remembering the early days of their dad's remarriage, opens a window to explaining their stepmother's vulnerability, however exaggerated in his sister's eyes. "Now that I think about it I don't understand why, but I'd let mean things slip out at her. I was kidding around, and she took it badly. She and Dad were really concerned about the first kids liking her." What was behind his needling? He laughed. "I just wanted to let her know I thought about her in some kind of way, that I wasn't totally ignoring her. I'd just call her a sort of insulting name. Maybe subconsciously I was being aggressive, but back then I just thought I was playing around with an older adult, being sort of bitchy and precocious to get a rise out her."

Being a portable free fire zone can make stepparents oversensitive to their stepchildren's onslaughts, both real and imagined. Having their own children can make for a striking contrast in feeling accepted, with the confidence of being loved and needed serving as a shield against stinging criticism and hateful outbursts. This confidence can also make stepparents less apt to "personalize" the behavior of their stepchildren as directed toward them in a negative way.

A Basis for Comparison

For stepparents who are first-time parents, having a child provides a basis of comparison, a way to reassess their relationships with their stepchildren. Aware of how much more attached he is to his own child, he expects that his stepchild experiences this contrast as a loss. Eliot, for example, projects a resentment on George, who was eight when his half sister was born: "He saw me as a stepfather, who was not quite a father but who was involved with him, and there I was holding and loving this little baby, in a way I never had with him."

George, like other children who compete with their stepfathers to complete the circle of mother and baby, vied with the baby's dad over who would hold the baby when. When his remarried father also had another child, George became the "only floater in two stable families," leading his parents and stepparents to worry about his feeling "betwixt and between." If the stepparent finally gains full family membership with the birth of his own child, the danger is that the stepchild will feel excluded by the creation of a nuclear minifamily within the larger stepfamily.

The exclusion of the stepchild is not in anyone's ultimate interest. While the stepparent, especially, may cherish the quiet moments when the couple is alone with its younger child, without, for example, the intrusiveness of a teenager putting in his two cents as to how the family should handle its taxes, he knows from his own experience how awful it feels to be pushed to the periphery of the family. So, too, does he realize that emotional or physical exclusion would harm his partner, the child's parent, their marriage, and his own child, who would learn that children are disposable in this family, as well as the stepchild.

How welcome the children feel depends in part on how their stepparent acts toward them as compared and contrasted with how they see the stepparent behave with his own child. But whether the child stresses the differences or the similarities, and how she feels about whatever differences do occur, will depend both on the prior relationship between stepparent and stepchild and on how the stepparent balances the needs of all the children.

Many children find that there is no essential change in how they and their stepparent get along after the birth of the mutual child. And downturns and upturns in the relationship are not necessarily attributed to the newcomer to the family. While children sometimes scapegoat the mutual child for a parent's reduced availability, which may be due to shifts in his work commitments, adults sometimes misread changes in a child's behavior as due to the baby's birth when developmental factors are more influential. One young woman, fourteen when her father and stepmother had their son, thinks that she got along worse with her stepmother "because I was a teenager and not because of the baby." An independent youngster whose friends left high school before she did, she longed to be on her own and chafed at "living with parents," despite having chosen to live in her father's remarried household.

When the stepfamily is well-established and stepchild and stepparent have comfortably worked out their relationship, the arrival of the mutual child is minimally disruptive of the status quo. Edward's relationship with his stepson Carl became closer, exciting Edward's longing to have been a part of Carl's life before the "scarring" of parental divorce: "It made me wish that I'd known Carl from zero to three. It would have been nice to watch that 'how do my hands work,' and learning how to walk, and what words were. All that stuff that's pretty neat that I didn't have with him."

Pamela, fifteen, also found continuing love and mutual respect in her relationship with both of her stepparents after they had children of their own. Speaking of her stepfather, she said: "I don't think it really changed him either. It's still really a fine line whether he calls me his daughter or not, and he does. I mean he's really sensitive about whether I want him to call me his daughter or not. He didn't get any less interested in me, when he had his own. He does take a certain amount more initiative with Ellie, of what he thinks Ellie should be doing. That's only natural, because he couldn't really do that with me. He can't come into my life and make me his kid without making sure that's what I want." While she recognizes distinctions in his relationship with her, as compared to that with his daughter, the meaning she attributes to those differences is a positive one: He is not favoring his own child, he is respecting her wishes.

In Pamela's view, what matters most for a child whose parent has another child in remarriage is whether she likes her stepparent. In saying it would be "really bad" if a parent were to have another child with someone his older child didn't like, Pamela infers that such a child would resent both his parent for tying him to the disliked stepparent and the new child who embodies that tie. While disliking the baby's parent doesn't doom the relationship between the children, neither does the baby necessarily improve things between stepparent and stepchild. Scott, for example, at fifteen, sees his stepfather as more a burden than an asset to his overworked mother. Critical of the remarriage, he doesn't want the attention of the stepfather he does not respect, and states flatly that "he has no authority over me." Yet he is very fond of the baby of that remarriage, delighting in taking care of her and describing himself as "closer to her than Mom is sometimes."

Shifting Stepparent-Stepchild Relations

Pamela and Scott represent the poles in a continuum of acceptance, authority, and affection between stepparent and stepchild. For most children, who fall somewhere between these extremes, the birth of a mutual child to the stepfamily sets off a series of shifts that change the nature of the relationship between stepparent and stepchild. Some of the changes occasioned by the addition are clearly perceived by all as a plus. The stepparent who becomes a first-time parent frequently is more available for "family time," as opposed to jealously guarding the inviolability of "couple time." For example, Joe observes that his wife Amelia probably takes more responsibility for his two boys than she did before their son was born, but resents it less. She agrees: "I think it oriented me more to family life and being home; because I was home anyway with Owen." Previously resentful that their social life as adults was curtailed by having to stay home with the older boys, she now finds that she can be there for all the children because having Owen created in her "the mother mentality." Several stepmothers who either stop or cut down on work commitments after having a baby report being more available to all the children as the at-home parent. And several families in which the adults used to take at least some vacations without the older children revise that practice when there will be a child with them in any case.

Stepparents who become first-time parents, especially if the mutual child is born to a recent remarriage, are near unanimous in claiming that they "lightened up" on their stepchildren when their own child was born. Among the stepmothers was a sizeable group who were relieved "finally to have children of my own," after years of wanting a child and not knowing whether their partners would eventually agree.

Some recognize in retrospect that their stepchild was a ready target for the frustrations they felt at not having a clear parental role, and in the words of one such stepparent, "a lot of the difficulties I was having with my stepson were really difficulties with my husband. It was just easier to let them out on my stepson."

Both stepmothers and stepfathers describe themselves as less jealous, more empathic, and less critical of their stepchildren when they had a baby. Because their self-esteem is less tied to their effectiveness as a stepparent, they are less focused on finding fault and less emotionally reactive to the older children's misbehavior. "When I had my own child I didn't put so much weight on what the older kids did," Adelle said, reporting how, after her son's birth, she felt closer to the stepdaughter who helped in his care and more distant from her stepson, "but not more negative: By that I mean that it didn't matter to me as much the things that he did in public. Before the things he would do just drove me crazy because I felt that people figured he was my kid, and 'How could you allow him to do those things?' Somehow when I had my own baby, I just assumed that the world knew this one was mine and those weren't. A really irrational kind of thing."

Irrational perhaps to think that the world could distinguish which of the two boys she had given birth to, but for the strong majority of stepparents the opportunity to feel like a "good enough" parent to the mutual child allowed them to be less insistent on remolding their stepchildren in the image of their own particular child-rearing philosophy. They raise their voices in near unanimous chorus that by virtue of their being less solicitous, less zealous perhaps, as stepparents, they have improved the emotional climate markedly. Dismissing their old expectations of being more of a parent to a stepchild as unrealistic, they see disengaging as a step in the right direction.

But developing a more appropriate set of expectations and gaining developmental knowledge, greater empathy, and self-confidence are not the only reasons first-time parents "lighten up" with stepchildren. The more dramatic needs of their own, smaller children are an often welcome distraction from the more fragile and difficult process of getting to first base with the older ones. They put more effort into a baby who is theirs, because these efforts are better rewarded. As Adrienne put it: "I got so much more back from the little guys than from the big kids, and I worked so hard, not to parent the big kids, but to be some sort of adult friend to them. They were teenagers, and I was getting so little back that I backed off. It improved things that I wasn't trying so hard." No longer did she plan elaborate birthday parties and solicitously prepare their favorite meals, or be sure to be there every night and help them with their homework. In other words, she eased up on the campaign to make them like and appreciate her, and like so many overzealous wooers, she found that the objects of her affection moved closer to her when she was no longer chasing them.

Like Adrienne, other stepparents who pull back find that as their efforts diminish, the absence is noted, leading indirectly to an appreciation not elicited by their bounty. Adrienne continues to care as much about the welfare of her stepchildren even as she does less for them. With "less of an edge," a less resentful, happier person, she is more enjoyable to be around, and her slacking off on the campaign to win their hearts eases their feeling of being caught in a loyalty conflict between her and their mother.

Not all stepparents, however, see having a mutual child as improving their relationships with their stepchildren. Stepmothers whose stepchildren visit are less available to be "camp director" when there are full-time children in the home. When the age gap between the children is large, especially when there is more than one of the little ones, family activities may be centered at an age level that makes the older children opt out, cutting down on the opportunities for contact between stepparent and stepchild. An important factor is where the children live most of the time, as "lightening up" seems more likely to improve the relationship between a stepparent and stepchild when they do not live together. Sociologist Anne-Marie Ambert found that stepmothers who have a first child tolerate *visiting* stepchildren better, perhaps because they now feel like part of a parental team with their husbands.[1] The children may appreciate that their stepmothers are no longer trying to compete with their mothers over who is the better parent.

For children who live with their stepparents, especially, the underside of "lightening up" is withdrawal. Ambert reports that the relationship between a stepmother and her full-time stepchildren seems to go downhill when she becomes a new mother, protective of an intimacy with her own child that may make the older children's daily presence feel like an intrusion. For these women, and the occasional man desirous of this intensity with his infant, "lightening up" may mean the relief that accompanies détente rather than a real warming trend in the family's emotional climate. Stepfathers, because they are usually not the ones to provide most of the hands-on care for the children, are less apt to feel this tension, and stepparents, both men and women, whose mutual child is not their first make no mention of becoming less invested in their stepchildren when they have a child in remarriage. According to Ambert, stepmothers who had children from both past and present marriages were among those who felt most attached to their stepchildren, both resident and visitors.

A Child's-Eye View

How do the children themselves feel about the claims of so many stepparents, especially those whose mutual child arrives early in remarriage, that having their own child made things better between themselves and their stepchildren? Some would agree, citing their stepparent's becoming more understanding and less critical. Judith, for example, finds it hard to decide whether the improvement is a result of her stepmother's having a child or of her and her sister's growing up, but credits both: "She says that having her own imperfect children made her understand more of my father's feelings toward us, and she became more accepting of us. Over the years, we're closer. I'm more accepting of her, and she is of us, too."

But while stepparents stress the up side of being less engaged with their stepchildren following the birth of a mutual child, more of the stepchildren emphasize the drawbacks. Stepparents who talk about being happier and therefore pleasanter to be around may not be the same ones whose stepchildren complain they are busier, more pressured and stressed, and therefore a harder person to grow up with, but there is overlap. Children who have felt especially close to their stepparent can feel abandoned when the stepparent transfers his energy and attention to his own child, whether in a wholesale fashion or merely in response to the more compelling needs of an infant. One stepmother, herself a stepchild, recalled how she felt as if she had lost a friend when her stepmother became a mother: "My mother always dressed me in saddle shoes and proper clothes, and my stepmother let me wear patent leather shoes and nice clothes, much more fashionable. So I thought she was *wonderful*. And then she started producing all these *children*. Her back hurt, and she had to stay in bed a lot. The children were crying all the time, and she didn't have any energy for them, so I took care of them." After an initial glorious year of living with her father and stepmother, she found that "the fun was over when she had the kids." For this family, the issue was not favoritism, but rather that having children so depleted this stepmother that she had less to give to everyone, withdrawing from the stepdaughter, who was left to pick up the pieces, returning to her own mother, whose own second batch of children had progressed beyond the more labor-intensive stages of infancy and toddlerhood.

Most stepchildren find that the birth of a mutual child provides an apparent opportunity to research a topic of compelling personal interest: How would my stepparent be different with me if I were his "real" child? Dedicated parent-watchers, they are vigilant to signs of different treatment. When a stepparent passes muster on this most difficult of tests, his stock with the older child soars. Scott, in observing his stepmother as a mother to his ten-years-younger half brother, decided that she was an "equal opportunity" parent, and their respect for each other was firmly established: "She saw that I was responsible, helping with the kids, and that I have some mature qualities about me. And I learned that she was giving them the same kind of attention that she would give us. So it wasn't like she was just doing whatever she would do but not as well as if we were her kids. It was like we were her kids."

Most children, however, find that their emotional seismographs register marked differences in how their stepparents relate to them as compared to the mutual child. In families in which both parents have children from previous marriages, the children of each are accustomed to seeing their stepparent relate to another child in a qualitatively different way than to themselves. Even with the best efforts of all concerned, different levels of attachment are almost universal, the primary exceptions being stepfathers who have been with their stepchildren since very early childhood and had no burning desire to have their own child. Despite seeing these differences as natural and inevitable, and even when essentially satisfied with how they get along with the stepparent, children are disquieted by the differences they observe. Ginger, now eighteen, remembers her stepmother's voluble excitement about the birth of a daughter seven years earlier as "a bit hard: It was obvious that it was exciting because it was hers. I'm sure she made very conscious efforts not to exclude us, but I knew that it was something that was special for her, that this kid meant something else, meant more to her than I did. And not that that necessarily was wrong, because if I had to weigh things out, for some terrible reason, my dad is my father and there is a stronger relationship with my father than there is with Andrea. But still it was difficult."

An unusually astute observer of relationships, Ginger notes the greater emotional ease and expressiveness between mother and daughter. Although registering that she is treated with more respect than seven-year-old Addie, she notes that her stepmother is both more affectionate toward and readier to yell and scream at the younger girl. Not certain how much of the difference to ascribe to the biological relationship and how much to its duration, Ginger recognizes that "when I was Addie's age she'd only known me for two years and didn't care for me and love me the same way yet. At that point neither of us knew that she would be spending the rest of her life with my dad, most likely, and that we would be family, or that we'd ever be as close as we are now." While Ginger thinks Andrea worries more about Addie than she does about her and would be more traumatized by losing the littler girl, "In terms of everyday worries and concerns about how I'm doing in my life and how Addie's doing in her life, I think those are equal."

Ginger has integrated well the differences in attachment, recognizing that they are understandable, reciprocal, and not of great magnitude. But what Ginger had to fall back on, four years of an evolving relationship with the woman who became her stepmother, is not available to all children in her position. When there has been less time for attachment to grow between stepparent and stepchild, the latter may perceive that a mutual child "is more important to her" or is liked or loved more, with the good reason that her stepmother "had no one else to love, no one of her own." The needier the child, as with one bereaved eight-year-old whose father remarried a year after her mother's death and had another child less than a year after that, the more she may have to deny the unequal distribution of emotional resources. As an adult, this woman recalls that "I very much wanted my stepmother's love, and felt I had to earn it in some way that I didn't understand, because I didn't have to earn my mother's love. I didn't allow myself to notice that I was never going to get it, not anything like what she had for those other children." Far from experiencing the younger children as a disadvantage to her, however, she found an emotional refuge in the younger children, mothering them as she wished to be mothered. In retrospect, she wishes only for more time to mourn for her mother, more time to come to terms with her step-mother, and to accommodate to "never getting to be the center of the universe again."

Children whose mothers had died were among those who felt most pushed aside by the birth of a child to a remarried parent. "Their needs came first, to the point where I felt that maybe I was getting salami and they were getting roast beef," recalled one woman, whose father and stepmother had two children when she was a preteen. This meta-phor seems drawn from how she remembers the distribution of food in the family. Special foods were prepared for one of the babies, in response to a food allergy, and the older girl hungered for the specially prepared delicacy that was served only occasionally to the older chil-dren, but yearned in silence. As an adult, she is not certain of the reality of her deprivation, but her emotional memory of not being nourished seems more connected to unresolved grief about losing her mother. A mother herself, she now knows "that you have to take care of a child, but as a child you don't see that. You don't see that all the parent's time has to be devoted to the newborn." But even if she had known then what she knows now about child development, the issue is not, as she acknowledges, the realities of the family economy, but the meanings inferred by each of the participants.

Even within one family, two children will study their stepparent's behavior with a new child and will construct very different pictures of what the differences are and what it all means. In the words of one father, who was startled to learn from his adult child that he had perceived a pattern of discrimination throughout the years, "If you want to look at it through a certain kind of eyes, you can see anything you want; if you want to become jealous you'll find a way." Take, for example, a family with two older children, their father, stepmother, and two children born of the remarriage. The stepmother maintains that "I don't think I treated them any differently. I did not favor my own actual children. I reared them with the same rules, regulations, the same values." Although acknowledging that it was easier to be physi-cally affectionate with a child that was hers from infancy, she hugged them all. Her husband essentially agrees, seeing any distinctions as inconsequential.

The oldest son agrees with his dad. Because he is very appreciative of what his stepmother did for him as a child, he also values the changes that being a mother wrought in her: "I think it calmed her down in that it gave her a broader outlook and more perspective on the rest of us. She continued to take care of us all and raise the younger ones too. When I compare that to just taking care of myself, it's a real hard job." Queried further, he admitted that "there must have been some sort of favoritism with those two, it would have been impossible for her not to do that, try as she might." Was the favoritism evident? "Well, I wasn't looking for it." In contrast, his younger brother, whose relationship with their stepmother had been more conflictual, found glaring evidence of discrimination at every turn: "When I'd see them getting things, even when they were justified," he admits, "I'd think 'Where are those rules now when we have some new players?'"

Critics-in-Residence

Vigilant for signs of discrimination, stepchildren often find much to criticize in their stepparent as a parent. Even when there are not obvious signs of favoritism, the older children's vantage point allows ample opportunity for observing the inconsistencies to which all parents are prone. Teenagers, who are beginning to think about how they themselves will be as parents, are especially willing to engage their parents, and even more so their stepparents, in philosophical debates about the correct line to take with the younger children.

Less cognitively mature and more competitive for nurturance, younger children find fault as a way to deal with their own pain. Liam, for example, was seven when his stepmother gave birth to a baby. Displaced as the youngest of his father's two children, he expressed his distress by criticizing and contradicting almost everything his stepmother, Ina, did or said. When his father or Ina's mother brought her breakfast in bed, just days after the cesarean birth, Liam protested: "Why can't you make your own breakfast? You're not sick, you just had an operation!" Later, if the baby fussed during feeding, Liam would inform her: "He's not hungry." When she dressed his brother, Liam told her, "He's too hot," when she put him down after a feeding, "He's still hungry." Liam's message, "You're an inadequate mother," masqueraded as a statement about her mothering of the baby when it was he himself who felt inadequately mothered by the stepmother whom he saw as a competitor for his father's affection. Returning from his mother's house, in his weekly joint custody rotation, he complained to his dad that he and his sister had decided that Ina "gets her way all the time." If she asked her husband to get her some more soup as she ate dinner while nursing the baby, Liam tried to counter the pattern he saw as indulging Ina, protesting "You shouldn't make him get it for you, it hurts his back." Although Ina knew that Liam's complaints came from his own neediness, the constant onslaughts at a time of mutual vulnerability created distance between stepmother and stepson. For her part, she felt deprived of the opportunity to enjoy her first child unmolested by criticism. For Liam, his whole world felt turned on its head, as he had to renegotiate his position in the family. "Baby, baby, baby," he complained, "we can't do anything we used to do because of the baby."

The older child's career change to critic-in-residence is most severe when the mutual child interrupts the early phases of stepfamily development, prematurely distracting stepparent and stepchild from establishing an independent relationship. Nine when Ethan was born, Jason was a vociferous critic of his stepmother's and father's child-rearing practices, which became yet another arena in spiraling family confrontations. His stepmother remembers Jason as a twelve-year-old doing "a whole lot of psychologizing about what we've done wrong in raising Ethan: We've made him spoiled. He was always giving us his pet theories about how you raise children and what he's going to do when he's a parent." Three years later, Jason is not only older, his families have reorganized so that each new couple presides over its own household. Jason can no longer divide his father from his stepmother, his mother from his stepfather, bringing together his parents as the primary adult grouping. As a result, he has also backed off from trying to be a third parent to Ethan. "He's really relaxed a lot," Irma chronicles the change: "We went out to dinner the other night, and Ethan was being just awful. Jason used to not be able to handle that. He called last night, and said 'How's Ethan doing?' And I said, 'Well, he's not as bad all the time as he was last night.' He said, 'Well, I was wondering, but I've learned to ignore it and let you handle it.'"

When the parent-stepchild relationship has had time to mature, the child is more relaxed in searching for signs of discrimination, but he never completely lets down his vigilance. That stepchildren whose relationships with their stepparents are loving and mutually respectful are not immune from this awareness of discrepancies is a testimony to the universality of older children thinking that younger ones are overindulged, a tendency found in families with no "steps" at all.

But the less children feel that their own needs for nurturance and belonging are attended to by their stepparent, the more they search for the tangible evidence of a pattern of discrimination. Because, in addition to having a parent in common, half siblings each have a parent they do not share, differences in child-rearing practices are usually ascribed to the "other" parent. By criticizing the upbringing of the younger child, the older is demonstrating his loyalty to his own, unshared parent; he is saying "What you are doing with my little sister is not as good as what my father and mother did with me." When one young man criticizes the way his father and stepmother are bringing up their daughter, his father hears the results of his son's being raised primarily by his ex-wife. "He did not have as structured an environment as a child, which has a great deal to do with the philosophy or even the temperament of the different mothers. As a result, he may have differences of opinion about certain freedoms, or the lack of certain freedoms given to our daughter."

While stepchildren's criticisms of their stepparents as parents are often exaggerated by hypervigilant and legalistic criteria, they are far from groundless. In a generational split, stepparents whose children are now all adults attest to an evenhandedness less frequently claimed by those whose children and stepchildren are currently still in the home. This reflects a growing understanding of stepfamily issues in the last decade and an abandonment of the mythology that stepfamilies can be just like the idealized nuclear family, with everybody loving everybody, immediately and equally, unwilling to acknowledge distinctions in an "as-if" playing out of unfelt expectations.

"It made me less available to them," said Ellie, "I just couldn't do it all." Like several of the stepparents, she set clear limits with her stepchildren following the birth of her children. "Erica was my number-one concern. That's what it was, and that's what it was going to be, and to expect anything else would be to set yourself up for something that would never happen." No longer would she cover for the older girls' mother, who had been used to leaving them with Ellie when she had a problem at work. No longer would she put herself out to attend distant dance recitals. Her stepdaughters have noticed her reduced availability. They'd like more time with her, but say nothing.

For many of the older children, the "lightening up" of the stepparent is a bust, not a boon. They feel noticeably demoted, deprived, and jealous of the time and affection lavished on the baby. Seeing a stepparent lavish affection on his own child is particularly poignant for those older children who temporarily found in their stepparent a surrogate source of love and care denied to them by a parent who is far away, deceased, or emotionally ill-equipped to nurture. These stepchildren recall what they used to get and feel that the baby has "split up the family" even as it joined it in perpetuity. Jealous of the attention devoted to the baby, they compare not only what is comparable but what is incommensurate, feeling slighted when the same standards of justice are not applied equally to a one-year-old and a ten-year-old, a three-year-old and a nine-year-old.

Even when the older children do not see their stepparent as actively discriminating, the mutual child can symbolize a parent's defection to a new family, mobilizing the older children to reclaim their parent by redefining family divisions. Jim, in his last years of high school at the time his father began having more children, began actively to challenge his stepmother's authority, after being the one of Adrienne's three stepchildren who was closest to her. "It came out two years ago," Adrienne recounts, "that in his mind the family was divided between Dad and the big kids and me and the little kids. All three of them felt that this was something their dad had done for me, and that the little kids were primarily my children. And my husband said, 'No, that's not true. They're as much mine as they are Adrienne's, as much mine as you three are.' And the older kids were shocked by that." To make their dad every bit as much their father as he had been before, they divided the family in two, with each group of children belonging to one parent only, creating more distance between themselves and their stepmother.

Bridges or Barriers

While either stepparent or stepchild can create distance following the birth of a mutual child, the baby can also be a bridge, bringing them together, as the adult appreciates the big brother or sister in the child. For some children, helping with child care is a deliberate strategy employed to stay close to both parent and stepparent. Michelle, at eleven, knew that when her father and stepmother had a child there would be changes, changes she was not sure she would like. "I thought that Adelle would have to spend a lot more time with Evan, and that my father would not be able to see me as much anymore. I was looking forward to changing his diapers or something so I could be with them, because I was afraid that I wouldn't be as close to them anymore. Now that I look back, I don't think that would have happened anyway, even if I hadn't been that aggressive." Now, when her stepmother spends time with Evan, Michelle is with her, "and we usually talk or whatever." The explicitness of the strategy, which she judges a success, comes out in her advice to other children who might be undergoing similar changes in their families: "I would tell them 'You better start spending time with the kid. If you end up spending time with him, then the parents are left out, so they have to spend time with you.' "

Whether or not the decision to be an active caretaker of the mutual child is a deliberate strategy on the part of the stepchild, sharing in the care of a younger child can be a bonding force between stepparent and stepchild, increasing both mutual empathy and respect. Kathy was twelve when her father and stepmother had their child. The youngest of her sisters and stepbrothers, she was also the child who was most engaged with the infant. "With Marilyn," she later said, speaking of her stepmother, "there was an element of that woman-to-woman thing, because she could rely on me to help with Anita. I was kind of attuned to Anita. If we were sitting around as a family, I would always hear her first if she cried. So I would imagine that, between Marilyn and me, there was something that just has to do with our both listening for the same cry."

If how the older children are with the baby can endear them to their stepparent, so, too, can their hostility or subversion further alienate the adult. When the older children hurt the little ones, their stepparents wish they weren't around. Displays of displeasure at the mutual child's existence, egging one of the little ones to exclude the other, or encouraging them to keep secrets from their parents also breed resentment in stepparents. Some begin to question the wisdom of a marriage that involves stepchildren, as did Alissa, whose stepdaughter's initial boycott of the family and "big stink" over the baby's name made her "so mad about it I thought that, despite the new baby, if they could annoy me so much and make me so mad at the circumstances that I had put myself in, I might still get a divorce."

While stepparents can be put off by how their stepchildren are with their little ones, they are also very vulnerable to criticism from the children. Alice, for example, is deeply concerned that her stepdaughters have a good opinion of her daughter, which in turn depends on their thinking well of her as a parent. "I need their approval. Having yelled at them for years, I need for them to feel like I'm doing a good job with their sister. I want them to like her, for her to be the kind of person they enjoy being with, and not feeling that she's just a useless crock, any more than the average seven-year-old."

Different as a Parent

How are stepparents different as parents to their own children because they have been stepparents first? Perhaps the concern of many stepparents about how they will be addressed by their own child symbolizes their worry that the stepfamily pattern will take over, depriving them of the chance to be a "real parent" after all. Alexis, for example, "thought things like 'My kid will call me Lexie, because all anybody ever calls me is Lexie.' " In the scheme of things, of course, such titles pale into insignificance, but they can still pack an emotional wallop. My son, who at two and a half to three used to amuse himself in his car seat by reciting litanies, knew that the following could always be depended on to engage my attention: "You're Sean's stepmother, you're Tonio's stepmother, you're Brian's stepmother, you're my stepmother." And I wondered, how much would his wanting to be just like his brothers estrange him from me?

Depending on the age of the stepchild when the stepparent joins the family and the amount of time the child spends in the remarried household, the longtime stepparent can feel like a veteran, even with a first child. As the years and months have gone by, they may realize, like one woman, that the stepchild was probably "the guinea pig." As a first child herself, she dismisses this as inevitable: "Your first probably gets the worst of it."

Real-life experience with a child forces the stepparent to clarify his values about how to raise children, not from his armchair but from the front lines. This reevaluation of beliefs is not so much philosophical as reactive: what behaviors do I like, what do I dislike, what could be improved, and what can't I stand? The opportunity to shape the development of his stepchildren, while very important, is limited by his being the one cook too many, perhaps, or by his arriving late in the child's life. The mutual child, in contrast, can appear to be a tabula rasa, a chance to put into practice dearly felt convictions. With no competing household, the stepparent knows he will have more influence on his own child, but may underestimate the role of his spouse in creating the behavior he objects to in his stepchild, choosing to blame instead the parent who is his predecessor rather than his partner.

Understanding the development of their new child from his experience with "the guinea pig," especially when he is basically pleased with the way the older child has turned out, a stepparent is less alarmed by and less condemnatory of behaviors in her own child that she has seen before. For Elizabeth, having her own boys has tempered her judgment of her sixteen-year-old stepson: "When Ted was six, eight, ten, I remember seeing what I now term as 'typical destructive boy behavior,' and at the time thinking 'How abnormal! Why does a boy have to break something?' Well, now I have two boys, and the little one will take anything apart that can come apart. I see it as creative. . . . Now that it's my child, of course, I'm not as judgmental, because I can remember Ted doing it, and he's turned out as a delightful, normal human being."

On the one hand, the stepparent is more zealous, intent on shaping behavior in his own child that he feels powerless to elicit in his stepchild, eager to impress an agenda upon his child more energetically than he—lacking a certain legitimacy—could justify imposing on his stepchild. On the other, he is more relaxed about the long-term consequences of behavior that used to ring his alarm bells, viewing what he once saw as offenses as normal and ephemeral. He therefore feels both more permission to set standards and less need to intervene restrictively.

How then does his experience as a stepparent affect his ability to set limits with his own child?

As a stepparent, he derives his legitimacy as a shaper of family policy from his partnership with his stepchild's parent. While a single parent may be eager for help in taking care of the children, he frequently is not entirely willing to share responsibility for making and enforcing decisions. If the mutual child arrives before the authority of the stepparent is established, his being "second in command" becomes part of the new family structure. Certainly the stepparent, looking forward to full parental legitimacy with his own child, frequently fears that his child will learn defiance from his stepchild. More often he neglects to examine how the frustrations of feeling ineffective with his stepchild translate into a style of exercising authority that communicates, if subtly, that he doesn't fully expect to be met with compliance. The twin dangers of learning parental authority from experience with a stepchild are that the stepparent may veer too far toward overcontrol, determined to brook no resistance now that there is finally a child who can be raised from day one, and that he may veer too far toward undercontrol, feeling powerless and giving way to undesirable household norms.

Another liability of having a mutual child before stepfamily relationships have had time to develop into truly personal connections is that the *sturm und drang* of the early stages of stepfamily life can create an emotional force field that sets tempers on a hair trigger, intensifying the affective climate in which the baby spends his earliest years.[2] "The frustration of hitting my head against the wall," said Ina, "contributed to giving Alex a much angrier mother than he would have had under other circumstances. I was madly in love with him, of course, but there were times, especially when the older kids were getting into one kind of trouble and then another, when I felt like I was living in a pressure cooker. And I let off steam with him, overreacting to typical two-year-old behavior, for example, or letting him see me explode at the older kids. I wanted his start in life to happen under calmer circumstances, but I couldn't keep my cool when so much anger was coming at me. I'd like to think that if I hadn't been a stepmother, or if the bigger kids were not more than ordinarily angry and out of control, that I could have been more even-tempered with Alex."

Interrupting Vicious Cycles

As in any triangle, the emotional distance between half siblings is a function of the distance between stepparent and stepchild. Perhaps because the triangle of stepparent, stepchild, and mutual child is the most delicate balance of all stepfamily triangles, vigilance is necessary to avoid the vicious cycles that can spiral out of control if not interrupted early.

Researchers who study siblings have found that the children's behavior with one another depends on the mother's treatment of each.[3] If she favors one, all are unhelpful and unsupportive of one another. Poor relations among half siblings also stem from preferential treat-

ment. Seeing his stepparent favor his own child, the stepchild takes out
his anger on his half sibling, attacking him as "a spoiled brat" and even
enlisting him more openly in guerilla warfare against his own parent,
as when Liam told Alex to "say 'fuck you' to Mommy." Alex, even at
four, knew "I can't do that," yet he was not above flaunting his priority
with his mother to further enrage the older boy.

As the boys fought, Ina found herself less and less sympathetic to
Liam. Originally empathic with his feelings of displacement when, at
seven, he ceased being Daddy's baby, she found that his constant
criticism of her as a new mother, begrudging her any assistance in
recuperation, created a distance between them that was exacerbated by
his openly wishing her son were dead. When Alex, whose response to
being the target of so much anger was to provoke more of the same,
started up with Liam, Ina felt she had to stop Liam from hurting Alex
before dealing with her son's initial misbehavior. Liam, convinced
there was no justice for him where Ina was concerned, continued raging
at Alex, telling him he wished he could kill him, which further mobil-
ized Ina to protect her son from her stepson. Alex, frightened, hurt,
and determined not to be the victim, became expert at pushing Liam's
buttons, and the cycle continued.

There are, however, many opportunities to interrupt the cycle,
setting these relationships on a more favorable course. Ina could spend
time alone with Liam, giving them more opportunity to share good
times, without the divisiveness of Alex's presence, which offers her an
easier avenue to affection and appreciation and convinces Liam that he
matters less. While intervening in the boys' fights, she could be firmer
with Alex, persuading Liam that he stands a chance of a fair hearing
and reducing his anger. Although it is sometimes hard for parents to
accept, even children who battle often do better together when the
adults are not around. Maximizing opportunities for the boys to have
good times together decreases Alex's anxiety in Liam's presence, dimin-
ishing his provocations, and increases Ina's affection for Liam, as her
image of him as the victimizer of her baby recedes, leaving in its wake
a more realistic portrait of a child who is feeling deprived.

Stepparents, especially stepmothers, who are uneasy with the older
children magnify the threat their stepchildren pose to their own little
ones. Images of the older children hurting the baby are common,
perhaps in reaction to the stepparent's own occasional wish that the
family had started as the traditional "first comes love, then comes

marriage, then comes Alice with a baby carriage" variety. While step-children do, at times, act out their resentments by becoming physically aggressive with the children of a parent's remarriage, the stepparent's protectiveness tends to increase rather than decrease the older child's resentment and, consequently, his aggression.

The more intent he is on creating an ideal environment for bringing up his own child, the more resentful the stepparent will be of the disruptions visited upon his household by stepchildren who, because of turbulence in their family history and particular developmental storms, bring intensity and conflict into the family home. Yet the paradox is that the more controlling he tries to be, the more he orders people around, the more turbulence and conflict he will create, troubling the waters he'd hoped to still. A more adaptive solution is to separate the essential from the nonessential.

But where is the line and how does one find it? Sometimes the conflict is not between stepparent and child, but between stepparent and parent, now both parents of their mutual child. The undesirable habits that the stepparent finds so offensive in the older child may be "just the way kids are" to the parent who's been with him since birth. Nor is there unanimity about how children should be, what they should do or not do. A stepparent's irritation with his stepchild can mask real differences he has with his partner, as conflict with the child feels less dangerous than opening the issue of divisions between the parents themselves.

Even when a stepparent and stepchild are close, adding the mutual child as the third point of a triangle can create its own strains, as the stepchild feels pushed away from his stepparent, and the mutual child clamors for exclusivity with the parent he can claim as his alone. In his study of stepsiblings, William Beer has noted that parental evenhand-edness toward children and stepchildren is itself unfair, as the children have unequal entitlements.[4] Dad's children may protest his stepchildren calling him "Dad," for example, as an infringement on their presumptive rights to priority with their father. Mutual children can also be protective of their entitlement: "My sister may have two dads, but at least I come first with the one I do have."

For Ethan, as a five-year-old boy, Oedipal issues give a developmental boost to his attachment to his mother, Irma, that is already intensified in most stepfamilies in which the stepparent has not had children from a prior marriage. When his half brother Jason is around, Irma can't give as much attention to Ethan, and Ethan is fiercely possessive of her. Mike, the boys' father, reflects that Ethan's claim on his mother is amplified because "Jason isn't nice to him all the time," making Ethan more reluctant still to share his mother with the aggressor.

The flip side of Ethan's possessiveness is Jason's sense of loss. Now fifteen, and almost ten years older than Ethan, he remembers that he and Irma were "very, very close before Ethan was born. She didn't have to give her love to another child, and she would do things with me more. I began to be mad at Ethan for taking that time away from Irma, and therefore she and I would fight." Or he and Ethan would fight first, and Irma would break in to rescue Ethan. The cycle continued, as Ethan would then withdraw from Jason and make stronger claims for Irma's attention. Both these moves further estranged Jason, fueling his resentment and motivating further aggressive forays toward Ethan.

From the vantage point of having yet another half brother, and nearly half a dozen years since he was an only child, Jason tries to be philosophical: "I try to accept that she is the mother of these two young kids, and I have to learn to have a relationship with her on our own terms and . . . one I can have. It's hard, because she definitely needs to be their mother. And she's not *my* mother. She says that she has three boys, and that's basically true. As I get older, I don't need as much attention. I'd rather be off alone with myself or with my friends. But there are times when I can see that if the kids weren't there, she'd be able to do certain things with me that she can't. It's not her fault. She has a right to have her kids, and I have a right to try and learn on my own to understand that and have a relationship with her."

Picking on Ethan to protest feeling abandoned by Irma was Jason's "subconscious," as he would put it, strategy to feel connected to the family, albeit in conflict rather than harmony. Whether the older child approaches the younger as a rival who must be squashed or a source of love and connectedness in his own right, the aim of the stepchild is to avoid his own exclusion by preventing the mutual child from becoming the center of a new nuclear family. The more the parent and stepparent prevent the older child from feeling pushed out, the more harmonious will be the relationship between the half siblings.

The triangle of stepparent, stepchild, and mutual child is pivotal in the family nexus. The stepchild's relationship with his stepparent spills over into the sibling bond, for both good and ill. While the stepparent, anticipating resentment, may try to regulate the contact between the two sets of children, the key to ensuring a good sibling relationship is to work through the strains between stepparent and stepchild.

For stepparents, this means tuning an ear to hear beyond the surface criticism of the stepchild to the hurt child within, not overreacting to the aggression that cloaks the stepchild's fear of exclusion. It also means not withdrawing from the sometimes frustrating job of being a stepparent. It is not easy to strike a workable balance between caring concern, on the one hand, and overinvolvement, on the other, but it is well worth the effort.

While acknowledging that they are more deeply attached to their natural parents than to their stepparents, many stepchildren long to be loved and cherished by their stepparents as their natural children are. Stepparents, especially stepmothers, report that their relationships with their stepchildren improved as they stopped trying too hard to be a parent, a change that many date to having their own child in remarriage. They say things like, "I realized I was never going to be his mother," or "She had a mother and didn't need another one," but all rate their pulling back as a positive change in how things went with their stepchildren. The children, however, disagree. Instead, they see themselves as having lost something with the diminution of interest and attention, even when the stepparent thought the attention was unwelcome.

Encouraging one-to-one relationships between all family members is the best protection against the destructive patterns described here. While stepparents may find it tempting to have the children's parent deal with their stepchildren, stepparents who relate to their stepchildren only through an intermediary never develop the authority or the intimacy with the youngsters that make a house a home. Stepparents who encourage a direct relationship between stepchild and mutual child, minimizing their own attempts to regulate contact between the children, also permit them to feel like brother and sister, rather than adversaries in a struggle for limited parental love.

Although pivotal, the triangle of stepparent, stepchild, and mutual child does not operate independently. A stepparent can also be seen as a member of a triangle including parent and mutual child, and another in which he is linked with parent and stepchild. The quality of the relationship between any two people in any family is intimately connected to how each relates to all other family members. A mother's relationship with the child of her remarriage will have a lot to do with how she sees her husband relate to his stepchildren, and in a similar vein, the quality of their marriage depends on the ability of the couple to work as a team, with stepchildren and mutual children alike. And this chain of relationships that depend on other relationships continues across the threshold of the remarried household, as people who reside outside the family home can weigh heavily in the stepfamily equation.

6

The Hole in the Stepfamily Fence

"Who did the invitations for our Labor Day Picnic," asked twelve-year-old Chris, as his family shared a meal at the home of friends. Puzzled by the vehemence of his question, his father, Patrick, and stepmother, Emma, wondered what the matter was. "Whoever did them really messed up," Chris continued. "You forgot to invite my mother." "We didn't forget," they explained, "we generally don't invite her to our parties." "Well, I asked her to come," said Chris, just before running out the door to collapse in tears. When Patrick left to comfort him, he learned that the day before his ex-wife had talked with Chris about how nice the picnic would be and how disappointed she was not to be able to attend. Furious at the boy's mother for putting Chris in this position, he assured his son that he had done the right thing under the circumstances. Later, he called his ex-wife to let her know of Chris's distress and his own anger, and asked her not to attend.

The next day, the morning of the picnic, Chris and his older brother Terry were watching cartoons with Evan, Patrick's and Emma's four-year-old. The horseplay reached the point where Evan asked to be released from Terry's grip. "You're hurting me," screeched Evan. "I am not," defended Terry, not loosening his hold. Emma, responding to her son's screams, entered the room and asked Terry to let Evan go. "I'm not hurting him." Terry held his ground. Emma tried to explain that it was important for Evan to feel in charge of his own body, and that he not be touched when he didn't want to be, pain or no, but Terry kept talking over her. Not looking at her, he refused to acknowledge her, "I'm not listening. I don't have to talk with you if I don't want to." The morning ended with everyone screaming at one another, and Patrick reflecting, sadly, "I think we're getting the fallout from yesterday." Their experience shows how a mutual child, along with his parents and half siblings, can be swept along in the chain of events linking stepfamily members with influential members of their larger network.

When family therapists talk about the couple as "architects" or "executives" of the family, they refer to the power, influence, and authority of the two adults who start a family to set policy, shaping the structure of the family they produce. As "architects," the remarried couple cannot start from scratch; theirs is a job of remodeling, making alterations and additions to the existing structure without forcing the current occupants to vacate the premises during construction. As "executives," they do not preside over a start-up venture; rather, their opportunity and their challenge is to officiate over the stressful transitions of merger, which is frequently seen by at least some employees as a takeover.

As the relationships between the children of an earlier marriage and a current marriage are so dependent on how each relates to both members of the stepfamily couple, so too are all of these vulnerable to pressures from outside the stepfamily household. Ex-spouses, grandparents, and other kin make alliances and enter coalitions that shift the nature and quality of stepfamily pairings, affecting how stepchildren come to terms with their stepparent and helping to determine their response to new children in the remarriage.

Even when a previous partner has died, his memory and the family from which he came remain a palpable presence in the stepfamily. Unresolved mourning can delay or disrupt stepfamily integration, as the child who has not mourned the loss of his parent is not free to form new attachments. In the far more frequent cases in which stepfamily formation follows divorce, the ex-spouse is a living, breathing, opinion-producing member of the "new extended family" created by remarriage. The ramifications of his actions and reactions, how he feels about his own life and the stepfamily of his former partner, are powerful and far-reaching, both for good and for ill.

"If I had a relationship with a past boyfriend," says one stepmother, describing the permanence of the relationship between ex-spouses who have had a child, "what he brings into it is, maybe, the planter that his previous girlfriend made, or a quilt that I can easily stick in a closet. You can't do that with a kid. A kid is there, and not only is he there, but then this other person is there, who under any other circumstances you probably wouldn't have anything to do with. Suddenly, at these significant occasions, birthdays, or your wedding, or your having a baby, all of these things become something to involve this other person."

Most parents and stepparents fail to anticipate the extent and durability of the influence of an ex-spouse on the stepfamily household. Whether intrusions are blatant, as in the two families in which ex-wives walked into their former husband's new homes, giving a tour of the premises to visiting grandparents without so much as a "by your leave," or are confined to the emotional baggage that the child carries from house to house, the child's other parent has a powerful effect on what happens between the four walls of the stepfamily home. Clinical practice has taught me that sons are fine deputies in continuing their father's side of the struggle with their single mothers, and research shows that divorces that end marriages without ending conflict between the partners can continue to have a detrimental effect on children.[1]

Even in the most amicable divorces, there is an inherent competition between two women who are mother and stepmother to the same children, between two men who are father and stepfather. Even without animosity, a mother's attempts to remain responsible to her children when they are not in her home can be experienced as patronizing by both the children's father and their stepmother. From the mother's point of view, the children are always her children, and when they have a problem, it is hard to be uninvolved. But to the stepmother, and even the father, the mother's instructions on child care convey a message: "You are not competent to take care of business." Fathers are less likely to feel the need to stay in charge of their children when they are with their mothers. The way that stepfamilies experience the child's other parent as a problem seems to split along gender lines, with complaints about mothers as intrusive, committing "sins of commission," while father's "sins" are those of omission: neglect, abandonment, inconsistency, and lack of support.

Competition between households in divorced families can take many forms. Parents may compete over who is the better parent, who the children love most or want to be with the most. Families may compete over who can provide a more "normal" home for the child, as part of the struggle for the children's love and loyalty, as well as with a view toward the child's best interests. Jessie Bernard has commented that when the marriages of a lifetime are evaluated, what counts most in the balance is not who was most beloved, but which marriage has had the most offspring.[2] And second wives, more than their male counterparts, have felt their need for a mutual child magnified by the desire to match or outdo the reproductive capacity of a predecessor. "When I think about it, I get a sick feeling," one woman told me, "but when I found out I was having a third child, inside I said 'Ha, ha, I have more children than she did.' The rational me knows I'm not being punished for something like that, but I irrationally think that that's one of the reasons I miscarried, so there's something bound up in that."

When divorces get dirty, children are painfully torn between their parents, both of whose love and acceptance they dearly need. Sometimes families are split, as when one child accepts a stepmother in order to stay close to her father, while another keeps a wide berth while siding with his mother as a damsel in distress. Coalitions can follow old, predivorce family patterns, as in one family in which one child is hostile to his stepmother, whom he sees as having caused his mother much grief, while his sister, who was always closer to their father, has become a good friend to his new wife. Not surprisingly, the older child has a negligible amount of contact with his half sisters by his father's current marriage, feeling no more attached to them than to, say, a cousin's children, while the second is a more integral part of her father's remarried family.

In studying divorced families, Constance Ahrons observes that the relationship between ex-spouses deteriorates with remarriage, especially if it is the husband only who remarries, making it more difficult for the children to accommodate a stepparent and any children born of the remarriage.[3] On the other hand, children are happier and more comfortable in the stepfamily if they know that their other parent is content with the postdivorce life he has made for himself. At seven, for example, Jenny became a lot more responsive to her father's stepfamily once her mother remarried. Before then, her stepmother remembers, she "detached herself a little more from this, as a survival mechanism" to allow her to come and go from the household in which her stepsister and their half sister were full-time residents. "It used to be that on Sunday night she couldn't wait to go home: 'Let's go, Dad, let's go.'

Now it's 'Can't I stay longer?' I can't get her out of the car anymore. Those last minutes to leave are the hardest. She's become more attached here."

Even when competition is neither overt nor pronounced, children struggle with feeling disloyal to their parent when they open up to a stepparent. P. Lutz, in a study of teenagers in stepfamilies, found that 55 percent liked their stepparents better than their other parent, and 40 percent of the youngsters experienced this preference as stressful.[4] Clifford Sager, psychiatrist and coauthor of *Treating the Remarried Family*, tells stepparents feeling besieged by a stepchild to first suspect that the child is demonstrating his allegiance to his other parent.[5]

As an older child, a fifteen-year-old boy is better able to reflect on the process of becoming closer to his stepmother as he became less protectively concerned for his mother. "We didn't have a very good relationship with her, but now she's just like a second mother to us," he told me. What changed? "I guess it was more just getting used to it, and learning more about her. And my mom started feeling really happy. In the beginning it was real hard for her, she was always by herself. But then after she started having boyfriends and got married, it became a lot easier to accept it."

A parent who is content enough, strong enough, or generous enough to give permission for a child to accept a stepparent creates a more navigable path for all concerned. Looking back, Judith describes how her mother made it possible for her to adjust to the changes in her father's remarried family: "I was very upset when I learned about my father's remarriage. But my mother always did anything she could to encourage us to have positive feelings toward Alexis. And she also had a big impact on how both of us accepted their kids."

Rocking the Cradle Rocks the Boat

Pregnancy, like remarriage, sends tremors throughout the binuclear family, creating shifts in how members of each household relate to one another, as well as unsettling the household that expects the addition. Ex-spouses who have managed to remain the primary unit within the stepfamily kinship network are finally challenged when a remarried couple themselves become parents together. Mike tells how, before having children with Irma set in motion a chain of events that led to reorganizing the family, there was a way in which joint custody made his ex-wife, Brenda, his first mate, figuratively as well as literally: "I think I resolved to continue to have my relationship with Brenda through raising Jason. When we went our separate ways as lovers, we were totally fused, on a daily basis, dealing with Jason. We really did a lot of great parenting together, synchronized, coordinated policies. So, even though she'd gotten married, and I'd begun living with Irma, the primary unit was Brenda and myself. For years we'd discuss things before we would inform Irma on my side and John on hers. Irma got more and more uptight about it. Later on, that arrangement blew up in my face." Having children together made it obvious that Mike and Irma had to rely primarily on each other in making decisions for their own home, creating more separation between households.

The presence of a mutual child in one household, when the older children move back and forth between households, increases the disparity between the children's two homes, especially when one parent is remarried and the other single. Ken and Ronny are brothers, sixteen and thirteen. Both find striking contrasts between their two homes, one of which includes a single mother, while the other houses their remarried father, stepmother, and three-year-old half brother. Both boys find that the more populous their dad's household becomes, the more they gravitate toward their mom. Ken, the older, is drawn to his mother out of solicitude, because she is more alone. Ronny, on the other hand, finds that his mother is more available to him than anyone in his dad's household: "My mom's unmarried and doesn't have a lot of kids, so her life is more centered on us. Here, it's more like you have to do more things on your own. At my mom's house, she does a lot of things and helps you."

When both partners in a remarriage have children, the population density can vary still more between households, with a child being an only child with one parent and "one of a mob" for the other. The attraction of peers and playmates, on the one hand, vies with parental access, the opportunity to be the "center of the universe," on the other. When children go back and forth, they may get the benefits of both. Yet being the only child in joint custody when both remarried parents have had more children can entail its own difficulties, as each transition focuses attention on who is a part, and how much a part, of each family. Both of George's parents, who have shared his care since their divorce ten years earlier when he was three, are concerned about how his occupying this singular position may be hurtful to him. His mother says that while George seemed to be pleased at the recent birth of his father's daughter, she has her doubts. His father echoes this concern: "Basically he ended up being between two families and not really fully a part of either. His mother had this family that basically had small kids, and I had basically this small kid, and he was this kind of odd apple."

For the ex-spouse who is not reconciled to the separation and divorce, news that the stepfamily is expecting a baby can be "the nail in the coffin" of any dreams for reunification. For a few of these families, the time of announcing that a baby was on the way was among the worst in the history of their divorce, provoking nasty brawls. One couple both remember that their son's impending birth was difficult for his ex-wife, but their accounts of how she received the news contradict each other. "I think her response was very cool," remembers the husband, "but I could just sense the realization that this was the end of whatever dream she had of getting back together, because I think she held on to those for a long time. She didn't show too much, probably something to the effect of 'I hope you two will be very happy.' "

Compare this with his current wife's memory of the same event: "He told her on the phone. She went completely wild. She was screaming and crying and carrying on. She was really thrilled that I didn't have a girl. She was really threatened, she said to him that I was going to have the girl that she had always wanted to have. But she acted very differently afterward. She stopped trying to get him back. She went into this deep depression, that it was definitely over, and gave up the assaults on him."

Even long-divorced couples who harbor lingering resentments may find that for one of them to have another child brings a change in the emotional climate, altering relationships between ex-spouses and between the parent and stepparent of the same sex. For the ex-spouse, the baby legitimates the remarriage, making the new partner a peer in a way that was not necessarily recognized when the remarriage was without issue. Stepparents may find that their partner's former spouse acknowledges them for the first time, speaking to them on the phone, offering congratulations, and even sending gifts. All these responses bespeak a coming to terms with reality, albeit not without ambivalence. One stepmother described how her stepdaughters' mother sent her an elaborately needlepointed album when her daughter was born, followed immediately by a demand for increased child support.

The nature of an ex-spouse's response to a pregnancy and birth in the stepfamily is largely determined by how happy she is in postdivorce life. When the ex-spouse has initiated the dissolution and is happily settled in a new life, she can feel genuinely joyful that her former partner has also found a satisfying union. Mike tells how happy his ex-wife was to hear that he and Irma were having a baby: "She was quietly praying, I think, that this man whom she loved very much should get his act together and his life together, because after we broke up I was really wrecked for years. So she was very supportive of my getting together with Irma, and very happy all along the way."

Not longing for more children permits the ex-spouse to be gracious and inclusive about the mutual child. Bonnie remembers her mother's response to her half sister's birth as "always happy: She was very secure in knowing that the last thing in the world she wanted to do was have more children. I don't think it upset her because she wished she was having another baby of her own, or she was too old, or she was married to someone who didn't want to." And Bonnie's stepmother, Alexis, remembers the girls' mother as "always very wonderful about our children. She sent baby gifts, she sent flowers to the hospital and called me there. I have always found it disconcerting that she is as fond of Enid as she is. She's invited her to her house, without me, to visit her sisters and her own friends. And Enid likes her a lot. There are occasional family photos, at graduations and things, where she is holding whatever baby there is at the time." Because both of the original partners are happily remarried and content with their lives, Enid is included by her half sister's mother as a delightful opportunity to have a friendship with a child who is not her responsibility.

While the remarriage of both parents helps both children and original spouses accommodate to changes in each household, it is not necessary for ex-spouses to have new partners for them to be genuinely welcoming of a new child in their child's stepfamily. One single mother, for example, tells that her daughter's having two half brothers in her father's household has been wonderful for her: "She gets to be a big sister, and they just adore her and look up to her. With me, she gets a lot of attention. It's been just the two of us for many years, and there she gets to be part of a bigger, bustling family. It gives her some relief from how much of a hothouse it can be for her to grow up with just me. We're so close. I always felt sorry for her when she was mad at me and there was no one else to go to." Because she is not looking

to her daughter to fulfill her needs for companionship or prove her
worth as a parent, she can give the girl permission to open her heart
to new members of the family.

In many ways, not all of them overt, children get a message from
their other parent about how they should respond to a mutual child in
their stepfamily household. When five-year-old Patty, who had been
told by her father and stepmother that baby Ivan was her brother, came
back from her mother's house, she reported: "My mother says he's not
my brother, he's my half brother." Although this is technically correct,
the message she received was that she should qualify her attachment
to the infant and hold herself back from feeling a part of her father's
family.

The other parent considers his own children a given, as contrasted
with the mutual child of his ex-spouse's remarriage, who is seen as an
option. Parents' and grandparents' fears that the birth will be disruptive
and distressing to their children, communicated to both the expectant
couple and the children, broadcast a message that the children will lose
something as the family expands. One man's ex-in-laws told him that
they thought it was unwise for him to have another child with his third
wife, because it would be too hard on their grandchildren. He recalled
with them that they had not had the same concern for his little girl
from his first marriage when their daughter was pregnant with her sons.
Similarly, Ellie described how her husband's ex-wife "said something
about Nila not being the baby anymore. I said, 'Well, she's still the
baby when she's at your house. She doesn't live in my house. And the
baby's an actual baby. If she were a third child in another family, it'd
be the same thing.' " But it would not be the same thing, for a third
child in a first family would bear the same relationship to both parents
as the preceding two children. He would not have another parent, who
is no relation to the third child, to let him know she thinks the baby
is depriving him of something.

Even a parent who is "trying to help" can set up negative expectations that reverberate later on. Irma, who has always felt supported by
and friendly to her husband's ex-wife, had her own worries amplified
by how the ex-wife talked to her son about Irma's pregnancy: "I was
concerned that Jason would feel very jealous. I was really concerned
that he would be with us half time and feel left out or bad that this
other child was with his father all the time. His mother, I think in
trying to help, told him that a mother loves her own child more than

she can ever love someone else, and it sort of set it up that Ethan was always going to be more important to me than him. And there were a lot of problems between me and Jason after Ethan's birth."

So many of these anecdotes refer to mothers' responses to their ex-husband's having another child in a new marriage because women are more involved with their ex's remarried families than men are.[6] They appear to be more threatened by a stepmother's pregnancy and show their distress more often than do fathers in a parallel situation. In perhaps the worst example of using the children as pawns in a postmarital battle, one mother responded to her ex-husband's becoming a father again by telling the children "Daddy doesn't love you anymore," when he called to say he couldn't pick them up because he was at the hospital awaiting the birth. Instead, because it was Saturday and "his weekend," she deposited them at his doorstep, knowing that no one was home.

While not typical, such behavior reflects women's heightened vulnerability following divorce. "She was afraid that if I established myself in another family, I would stop paying child support," said one father, referring to his ex-wife. Although her fears were not borne out, her concern is not irrational, given that over half of divorced mothers do not receive regular child support, a figure that increases with time since the divorce.[7] Perhaps out of fear of receiving less child support, several ex-wives took the occasion of the mutual child's birth to request more, reasserting their continued importance in the family and its economy.

Some parents who have been inconsistent or lax in keeping to a visitation schedule shape up after a mutual child is added to their ex-spouse's family, religiously adhering to schedules after years of disappointing children driven to tears by being stood up or waiting long hours for an overdue parent. Or a joint custodial parent who has had less time with the children than was permissible under the terms of the original agreement reverses the pattern, demanding more time lest the children get to feel more firmly based in their stepfamily as it acquires a new, unifying member.

Changes in Custody Arrangements

Any change in the stepfamily network can catalyze still other changes. Shifts in custody accompanied the birth of the mutual child in several of the stepfamilies I interviewed, who joined the ranks of the 10 to 20 percent of all children Marilyn Ihinger-Tallman estimates change residence after the initial postdivorce custody settlement.[8] Although experts who work with difficult divorces report that parents may give up on custody battles that have raged for years when they have a child in a new marriage, parents who have had mutually acceptable, workable custody arrangements sometimes press for full custody when they are expecting another child.[9] While fathers, too, are prone to imagine that it is possible to forget the past, mothers are more frequently in a position, as custodial parents, to pull for having their older children with them more of the time when they are expecting another child.

Melanie, for example, sought to reduce her son Paul's visits with his father in preparation for Yale's birth. "I had a terrible fight with his dad about visitation," she said, based on her desire for Paul to get used to her new husband so that they would have a relationship established before the baby's birth. "I wanted him to remain in this house and become really incorporated with this new family." Years later, in therapy because of the conflict between her husband and son, who had come to live with them full-time, she recognized that part of what made things difficult was her denial that they were a stepfamily: "I thought if we pretended that this was the nuclear family, and that he was a part of it, and pretended that that other out there didn't exist, that it would go away and we'd be fine. We could put up our white picket fence, and it would be . . . fine. But it didn't work out that way. I denied for a long time that we were a stepfamily. It's funny. Even though Paul can be a real pain in the neck to have around, for instance, if we go on a family outing, I'd really push him to come along. I still wanted him there, because it was like my *three* children. This was my family. And if someone came up to me and said, 'Oh, you have two kids,' I'd be quick to correct them. 'No, I have *three* kids.' It was important that all my children be there."

While fathers generally don't have their children with them enough to pretend that all the children have only one home, some with joint custody bargain to have more access when they are expecting a mutual child. Joe, for example, used his financial clout and the superiority of his local school system to induce his ex-wife to move closer to his current home, moving into a more equal share of physical custody of Larry and Kevin when Owen was born.

Still other shifts in custody are modified by consideration for the stepfamily's needs to accommodate to the changes involved in having a new member. In our family, Tonio's and Brian's mother decided during my pregnancy that she wanted them to be with her half-time, alternating every week, after having seen them for years on Wednesday nights and Saturday through Monday. With the help of a family therapist, we negotiated to delay the change until a month after David's birth, so the boys would not be spending more time away from us just as he arrived. We explained to them that the reason for the delay was that we wanted them with us more because their brother was about to be born, with the hope of minimizing any fears they might have that he would be displacing them. Similarly, Susan delayed for a year Carl's departure for his father's home across the country, so that he would be with her when her second son was born, postponing implementation of their agreement that he would spend two years with his dad before returning to her for high school.

While remarried parents welcoming a mutual child press for all their children to be together as much as possible, mothers sometimes get more than they have bargained for and fathers less than they expected. Among the group interviewed, two stepfather families had natural fathers leave the area without the older children and two stepmother families had natural mothers move long distances, taking the children with them. Mothers who left town did so to follow a new husband or to move to their own parent's home. Fathers left to accept an attractive job offer or to explore more promising work prospects. Diane thinks, however, that having another child with her new husband allowed her daughter Beverly's father to feel free to move, as he looked in their direction and saw Beverly set up in a new family.

Not all changes in custody that occur around the time that a mutual child arrives are initiated by the adults. Children themselves may elect to change households as those households are reconfigured. The family-centered atmosphere of the remarried family that includes more children can be very attractive to older children. A teenage girl who had sided with her father in an ugly divorce moved back with her mother after a couple of years in his "bachelor pad," drawn by the warmth of her mother's home, which then included three younger brothers and sisters, her grandmother, stepfather, and, in quick succession, four half siblings. "I started going there after school. I was very close to my grandmother, and all my brothers and sisters were over there. And then my mother started having babies, and I usually liked the babies. So, there was much more of a home life. The kids, my grandmother, food, everything. I finally moved back there."

Home life, however, has its pluses and minuses, and babies can be a drawback as well as an attraction. Janet went from house to house, seeking time to be a child herself and not a substitute caretaker. When her mother's second husband drowned, leaving her a widow with two toddlers, in addition to Janet and her brother, Janet was left to care for the children when her mother went back to school. A year later, her father remarried and she leaped at the chance "to be with Daddy. I liked the attention, also, of not having to compete with these little babies that my mother had just produced. I had one year before he started having babies." Her stepmother, who had been a special friend to her, became an ailing and overwhelmed mother of two, and Janet again was left as chief diaper changer and bottle washer. Two years later, she responded to her mother's invitation to move back in with her.

It is not only onerous child-care responsibilities that drive children to change residence. All the other reasons why children change custody can occur at this time too. Most commonly, adolescent boys, deemed unmanageable by their mothers, are sent off to live with Dad. Or stepparent-stepchild conflicts may escalate, aggravated perhaps by the new triangle with the mutual child, to the point where the child elects to reduce the time he spends in the stepfamily, either moving in full-time with the parent who has no small children or reducing visitation. "Not having me stuffed down her throat ultimately really improved everyone's relationships," said one woman, referring to her stepdaughter, who stopped commuting between households at fourteen, choosing instead to stay with her mother. "But for a time it really wrecked her father. He felt rejected, and it took a long time getting over it. They're closer now, though, without all the frictions and bad scenes."

Relations Between Households

While the mutual child changes the balance between households in the binuclear family, sometimes catalyzing a series of changes in the membership of each, what it all looks like to him will depend on the amount of contact between households and the feelings people in one home have toward the other. How much the children of remarriage have to do with their half sibling's other parent varies enormously from family to family. At one end of the spectrum, Pamela's mother and stepfather are named in her father's and stepmother's will as the guardians of their children. "It's not as if we're that close," said Eleanor, her stepmother, "but how many people can you ask to take your three kids. Few people we know have lives that are flexible enough. And it made Pamela feel very good that her family would stay together as a family."

When the adults remain on good terms, their half siblings' other parent can feel like part of their extended family to the mutual child. Jason, for example, describes his mother's relationship with his father's younger son as an "aunt-nephew" one, "only because my family is very close-knit." His father, Mike, thinks that his ex-wife feels his son Ethan is part of her extended network, and although he doesn't know if Ethan himself would call her part of the family, she "intrudes in his life in a positive way." Yet stepfamily members may differ among themselves in stressing connection or separateness between a mutual child and his half sibling's other parent. Irma, for example, differs from her husband, expressing disappointment in how Jason's mother relates to their mutual children, contrasting this with a family they're close to in which the older children's mother takes the little kids on outings. "Jason is so in love with the baby, Ezra, that she made a point of coming over and seeing him, 'cause her son loved him so much. But she's busy. She went back to school. She's just at such a different point in her life than we are."

Children of remarriage who visit their half sibling's other parent often develop affectionate and independent relationships, which flourish when allowed to occur out of their parents' presence, and whatever lingering tensions and jealousies that entails. One nine-year-old has for years visited her older sisters at their mother's home. She plays with their old dolls, accompanies them to visits with friends of that family, and likes their mother and stepfather a great deal. Everyone in the family thinks that having the opportunity to know one another well is in the best interests of all.

Mothers, more than fathers, are likely to extend themselves to their ex-spouses' mutual children, as they are more likely to remain active in their own children's lives, even without custody. "I hope in a couple of years you'll think of sending the children down here," one mother said to her daughters' stepmother about the latter's small children, "I would really love that, and I know the girls would." But even parents who make an effort to form a relationship with their children's half siblings make distinctions among them when there is more than one. For the most part, they will have more contact and more of a personal relationship with the oldest mutual child, partly because the age gap between their own children and the first half sibling is narrower. Elizabeth compares the relationships between her sixteen-year-old stepson's mother and each of her own two sons, finding a dramatic difference: "Barry's mother sometimes has Eddie, my six-year-old, over to spend the night, and they'll do something the next day. Eddie's just grown up with that, much more than Alan, who's three. She hasn't put out as much energy toward Alan, just because her own life is so demanding."

The children of remarriage, often intensely curious about their older siblings' hidden life in another household, are eager to know more about their siblings' other parent. They ask to be taken in when the older children are being picked up for and dropped off from visits, or during custody rotations, and engage in friendly conversation when given the opportunity. When the older children are proud of the little one, recounting things he's learning and what they've taught him, their other parent will already have a store of anecdotes about their half sibling. Getting to know each other will help both the mutual child and his half siblings' other parent feel more connected to the children who are so important to both.

If the adults are willing to cooperate, the older children generally take the lead in regulating the amount of contact between the mutual child of one parent's remarriage and the parent they do not share. When she was about eight, Patty had invited three-year-old Ivan to her mother's house on several occasions, before deciding that one way to gain advantage in their struggles for territory in their father's house was to restrict his access to her mother's. Although her father and stepmother had put a lock on her door, preventing Ivan's getting into her room to mess up her things, territoriality was a live issue in this family, where the remarried household chafed at her mother's intrusiveness into their home, sensitizing Patty to think in terms of limiting access and building boundaries.

When such issues of boundary keeping and territoriality create tension between households, hospitality may be limited or ill-received. While Ivan's mother sees the relationship between her son and Patty's mother as minimal, but good, this is only because she has been able to conquer her initial reluctance to permit them to have contact. "He went out to dinner with Patty and her mother tonight," she told me. "I always wondered what I was going to do when the occasion arose, because she and I don't get along. I always said, 'I'd never let him go over there.' Then, the first time it came up, I said 'yes.' If I put his interests first it was the only obvious choice, for both Patty and Ivan. She obviously wasn't going to drop him into the middle of the freeway, so it wasn't a question of safety. It would have been childish of me to say 'no.' "

It is not easy to say to a child, or stepchild, "I am sending you to visit your other parent, but I don't trust him or her to take care of my other children." Even when parents do have serious questions of the other adult's abilities as a caretaker, if the age difference between the children is sufficient, they may have enough trust in an older child to feel confident that a younger half sibling will be well taken care of on a visit to the older one's other parent.

That is not to say that all stepfamilies are on sufficiently good terms with the other household to make independent contact between the other adult and the children of remarriage possible. When I asked about the relationship between nine-year-old Edna and her older sister's and brother's mother, their father, Thomas, told me there was none: "Ellen was adamant. She said, 'I don't want her to see Edna.' It was stated expressly. 'She's been a thorn in my side. She can't share at all.' "

Ellen agrees that it has been by design that the two have never met, but she sees it as more a question of protecting her daughter from a noxious influence than of limited generosity. "I don't want her anywhere near her. I don't trust the woman. I've seen what she's done to her own kids, God knows what she'd do to mine." Ellen recognizes, however, that Edna has difficulty in making sense of the tension among the adults.

Edna herself has adopted her mother's line about the older children's mother: "Donna and Jack's mom is always making things really hard for them. They're grown up now, but it used to be that whatever they did made her mad. Now, she just makes it difficult for them to visit. She doesn't come down here, they always have to go up there. So, I don't like their mother." Not only does she join her mother in condemning theirs, she extends this portrait of their mother to the older children, claiming "Donna and Jack like their dad better than their mom." Even if this were true, and Donna and Jack neither confirm nor deny her allegation, this alliance of condemnation within the family they have lived in for years fans any lingering embers in their conflicts over loyalty to their mother, whatever her failings. Difficult as it may be to create, the more benign the picture the mutual child can have of his siblings' other parent, the less the potential for forming coalitions within the family that make the stepchildren's allegiance to their other parent a crowbar that pulls them from its midst. This does not, however, mean creating an unrealistically rosy picture that would be still more confusing.

It is not always the stepparent who is most reluctant to have his child know his partner's former mate. Unresolved angers may keep the mutual parent from wanting any contact between his ex-spouse and his new children, and painful divorces may leave an embittered former partner unwilling to have any contact with the remarried family. Again the children take their lead from the adults, protecting the parent who seems most in need. Dan, for example, has on several occasions tried to avoid having his mother come in contact with his father's children. His mother has been direct about how she wanted him to insulate her from anything to do with his father's life, including the half siblings born when Dan was in his late teens. "When I'd say things at first, she would adamantly say 'I don't want to hear about it.' Now it's just kind of like 'that's nice.' She doesn't create waves about it, she's not thrilled by it."

The silence in his mother's home about his father's family is mirrored in the younger children's lack of curiosity about his mother. Their mother says that four-year-old Oren hasn't really registered that Dan's mother exists, while Esther, at six and a half, includes her in the family history, telling her father that if he marries her, she'll be his third wife, but never asks questions. "He is their brother and they talk about him all the time. They just never seemed curious about where he went or what his family was like." Each side of his family acts almost as if the other half of Dan's life does not exist, leaving him to integrate by himself how each is meaningfully a part of him.

Mutual Children in Both Households

When both of his parents have had children in remarriage, the older child can try to create a bridge between the two children as a way of making his life feel more "of a piece." Leo, who had "always" wanted a brother or sister, got one of each within two months. He enjoys having "somebody to play with." Even while they're infants, he finds it fun taking care of them, and he likes it that they're so close in age: "I wanted it actually that way. I can tell the other parent what's new about each one. Like when Irina first turned over, something like that, I'd tell my mom."

For Leo, comparing and contrasting the accomplishments of his half siblings is a way to bring each household into the other, a unifying thread, weaving a connection between the two halves of his life. For Elaine, his stepmother, the constant comparisons are difficult, even though, as the mother of the older of the two babies, she is at an advantage in what she experiences as a competition. The comparisons that give Leo a sense of connecting the two babies that are so important to him, despite their lack of contact, feel intrusive to Elaine: "I don't really like to hear very much about what's going on. I don't care. It happens especially when he's first come back, because then I get a long report on what his brother's doing. Interestingly, as he was going back to his mother's the other day, he said, 'I can't wait to tell my mother what Irina's doing. It's like when I come over here I like to tell you all the things that Ira's doing.' "

Although parents and stepparents find comparisons invidious, some parents actively encourage friendships between their mutual child and the child of their ex-spouse's remarriage. As a stepchild may want to build a bridge between households by connecting the mutual child of each, their parents may choose to increase their older child's feeling of family connectedness by following the same strategy. After years of trying to promote a friendship between his oldest mutual child, Alissa, and Ellen, his ex-wife's daughter, Rick reports that at seven and eight years of age the girls are inviting each other to slumber parties and playing more than they ever have. "The reason we promoted it was for Pamela," he said, referring to his fifteen-year-old. "I always wanted her to feel that she had an integrated family. We always called Alissa and Ellen 'sister's sisters,' because while they didn't have any real blood relationship, they were both their sister's sister. I want Pamela to have the sense that she didn't have a separate family here and a separate family there, but all of her siblings were somehow of a piece."

Having a personal connection with a half sibling's half sibling can do much to minimize competitiveness between the mutual children as rivals for their big brother's or sister's affection. Building their own friendship can also help each feel more connected to the older half sibling they share. Anita, now eighteen, is the mutual child of the remarriage of a divorced mother and widowed father. Her mother's older sons have another half sister, Ursula, less than a year older than Anita. "They grew up with a real curiosity about each other," reports Peter, the older of the two boys and fifteen years their senior, "having common brothers. Yet they weren't related to each other, and didn't know each other."

"Her parents did not allow us to speak, more or less, when we were young," remembers Anita. "So I was intrigued, because there was this girl who I wasn't allowed to know, just because I was my mother's daughter." The intrigue provoked feelings of rivalry, at least for Anita, who continued: "I remember really trying to impress Peter. I wanted him to think that I was really neat. Because his other sister is the same exact age, there's been a lot of competition between us."

When the girls were about sixteen, they conspired to meet. "We had a blast," Anita said, "but it was really weird. We'd say, 'Well, my brother Ron,' or 'my brother Peter,' and then we'd realize, 'We both have the same brothers.' We barely knew each other. We told people we were sisters, because it took so long for people to understand the relationship, and we had fun doing that. We wrote for a while, and she came here to visit. She'd stay at Peter's house, and I was jealous of that, because they'd do things together that I didn't get to do with him, even though we live in the same town."

Her feeling of connection transcends the contact made during their time together. Anita emphasizes the relationship with Ursula, partly as a way to intensify her connection to her brothers, since both girls feel the older boys were not as available to them as they would have liked, having shared a home for at most three years in early childhood. Yet Anita realizes that she and Ursula, despite telling people they are sisters, "did not feel like sisters. We bought each other friendship rings. They fell apart, which was interesting. But I think it was neat for both of us. There was this person sitting there, who was my brother's sister, but who was not related to me. We're a lot alike. And we both weren't close with our brothers, because when they weren't here they were there, and when they weren't there they were here. So they drifted between, and neither of us got a lot of time with them. But she has memories, much more vivid memories of them. I don't know if that's because she doesn't have any other brothers and sisters, and I do. I don't remember them at all." In reaching out to Ursula, she is attempting to fill in the parts of her brothers' lives that were a mystery to her, striving to strengthen her ties to the elusive boys she has always wanted to know better.

"Building Bridges or Building Walls": Grandparents and Stepgrandparents

Ex-spouses and their new families are not the only relatives who continue to have a profound influence on how relationships within the stepfamily unfold. Grandparents can build bridges or they can build walls, in the words of Emily and John Visher, speaking of the power of the older generation to influence to what extent stepfamilies will be integrated or polarized, inclusive of all or exclusive of some members.[10]

Stepfamilies normally entail a population explosion of relatives. Instead of having two parents, there may be four caretakers for at least some of the children. Instead of four grandparents, there may be six, seven, eight, or more. In what may be a world's record, Pamela reports having thirteen grandparents whom she knows and sees with some regularity: Because both her parents are themselves children of divorce, they bring four parents each, plus a maternal great-grandfather; her stepmother adds two grandparents and a great-grandmother, while her stepfather has only one living parent. All have been a part of Pamela's life.

"Is My Child's Stepchild My Grandchild?"

Stepgrandparents vary enormously in how fully they accept a child's stepchild as a grandchild. In the families I talked with, stepgrandparents were most welcoming and inclusive of the child when they were not yet biological grandparents and there was only one child to take into the family. For several of these families, parents report that their youngster became their in-laws' "first grandchild, period," making no distinctions between this child and the children born to their own son or daughter, to the point of writing him into their will as an equal inheritor with all the other grandchildren. A child may feel closer to stepgrandparents who have opened their hearts and their doors to him than to a parent's parents with whom he has little contact.

The amount of contact between the generations has a lot to do with how grandparental the relationship is between children and their stepparent's parents. When interaction is rare, there is little sense of being a grandparent. This is best illustrated in one stepmother's contrasting her parents' involvement with her stepchildren as opposed to her sister's stepchildren. Because she lives two thousand miles from her parents, they have seldom seen her stepchildren. "They'll ask about them on the phone, know what they're doing, very concerned," she told me. "They have a sense of them being part of my life, but they don't have any personal relationship with them." When her stepchildren were visiting Florida, she asked them to call her folks when they were there. While she was hurt by their failure to do so, she realizes that there really was no relationship between them. In contrast, her parents make no distinctions between her sister's two stepchildren and three children "because they all lived together, and my folks saw them all equally often."

When there is a chance for steprelatives separated by a generation to get to know one another, the arrival of a mutual child raises the issue, if it has not been raised previously by the presence of stepsiblings, of distinctions in the distribution of love, attention, and material goods among the grandchildren. Again the range is enormous. For most of the families, grandparents made an effort to be inclusive but do not claim to be evenhearted, even when they are evenhanded. Nor do stepgrandparents come in perfectly matched sets. One stepchild contrasted her stepmother's mother, who clearly played favorites, with her stepgrandfather, who never did. Despite this, most of the parents and stepparents appreciated their parents' or in-laws' efforts and did not expect a total absence of distinction.

Speaking of his in-laws, Joe said, "Let's put it this way, they treat Larry and Kevin as a normal grandparent would treat their grandchildren, but they treat Owen excessively. So, they overdo with Owen, and they are really good with Larry and Kevin." This picture is not uncommon, especially among those becoming biological grandparents for the first time with the birth of the mutual child. Gene applauds his in-laws' reception of his three children: "Her parents were great. They accepted the older three kids as their grandchildren. They fussed over them and treated them like grandchildren. Of course, when Emily was born, this was what they had waited for all their lives, their own real granddaughter. But it didn't change their treatment of the older three as part of their family. It was really very nice." His wife Irene essentially agrees, recalling that although her parents were good grandparents to Gene's children, when Emily was born, the first child of their then-thirty-seven-year-old daughter, her father said, "Now I can die in peace."

Even the best-disposed stepgrandparents sometimes have to struggle to be fair when they feel more bonded to the grandchildren they have known since birth. Arthur, for example, describes how his mother deals with feeling different about his stepdaughter than she does about his daughters "by fairly frequently talking about how there is no difference." Although he gives her credit for making an effort to minimize differences, they do occur. In divesting herself of her estate, for example, to protect her assets from possible nursing home appropriation, she put her money in trust for the two younger girls, partly because their age meant the funds would be tied up longer. "She's felt terrible about it ever since," Arthur continued, "and keeps talking about how bad she feels and she hopes Jessica doesn't think anything of it. None of the kids knows anything about it, but she worries. And when she was making out her will, she asked us if we wanted Jessica to be treated like the others. We said 'yes,' and she did."

Stepparents are frequently more critical of their own parents for not fully accepting their stepchildren as grandchildren than are the children's parents. Arthur, for example, objected to his mother's making a distinction in her will between Jessica and his daughters by stipulating that her jewelry would go to the younger girls, only to be told by his wife, "Forget it. She's got a right." And it is in the area of legacies that distinctions come most to the fore.

While some stepgrandparents accord full inheritability to a single stepchild, none of those with two or more stepgrandchildren included them as equal inheritors with their natural grandchildren, a decision with which most parents and stepparents had no quarrel. One father, for example, speaking of his in-laws' having left some money to the children of his second marriage, found this single distinction in their treatment of the two groups of children a reasonable one: "They had some money set aside for the boys' education, which was fair. There was no reason why they had to split that up four ways because we had the two older kids." This pragmatism, a concern that when bequests are modest slicing the pie in more pieces leaves less for each, seems to make a difference between including and excluding stepgrandchildren from equity in inheritance. Factoring in one more seems to make less difference than adding a group to the list of beneficiaries, and omitting just one feels more excluding than a reduced commitment to those who will have company in not inheriting.

Sometimes stepgrandparenthood becomes an abstraction, not through neglect, but by direct renunciation of the role. This abdication is often motivated by opposition to their child's marriage, whether because they disapprove of the partner chosen or because they worry lest, in taking on the raising of another's child, their own child will be burdened. In describing how her parents made their different commitments to her child and her stepchild very clear-cut, another stepmother said: "They have a grandchild and their son-in-law has a son. That's it. Very early, when we got married, and it rubbed them the wrong way, they made a statement that they didn't want his child shoved down their throat, he was not their grandchild, and blablablabla. Our attitude about it is that he has grandparents and it's their loss. We've more or less sheltered him from my parents. He understands that I have a strange and a strained relationship with them, so that anything that occurs doesn't provoke much contemplation on his part." In listing his grandparents and how frequently he sees them, her stepson doesn't mention her parents. As he is not their grandchild, so they are not his grandparents.

Grandparents' Loyalty to the Children of the First Marriage

Differences in biological connectedness are not the only grounds on which grandparents make distinctions between the children in stepfamilies. Many a stepgrandparent, for whom the mutual child is "the apple of her eye" as a first grandchild, still differentiates less between the two children than does her counterpart, the natural grandparent of both children. For the majority of the stepfamilies with living grandparents, the parents of the mutual parent were seen to favor the children of his first family over those born to the remarriage. Some of the older children get to be the "apple of their eyes" on the same basis as does the mutual child: by being the firstborn grandchild. When a grandchild has been "the first and only" for a long time, opportunities for intimacy exist that are unrivaled for later arrivals, especially if they arrive en masse.

Frequently, too, grandparents have spent more time with the older children, taking care of them as young children while the middle generation were single parents, either full- or part-time. Melanie, for example, says that her father definitely favors her oldest son: "He was close to him for his first two years. My dad writes to Paul weekly, and he can't even spell the little one's name right." No wonder grandparents feel closer to grandchildren they have helped raise during the years when their child needed their help. In that interregnum, the child may well have been seen as traumatized by parental death or separation, a victim, in his grandparents' eyes, who needed their solicitous care and protection. The children that come later, born of their child's remarriage, with two parents inside a picket fence, are seen as less in need of their attention. In any case, the grandparents are older, less energetic, and have a harder time with the rough and tumble of small children.

As a self-appointed protector of a grandchild against the inferred wickedness of a stepparent, a grandparent can have a tremendous influence on how the child deals with his parent's remarriage and any subsequent children. The grandparent who can welcome his child's new spouse, conveying to his grandchild that the newcomer is a trustworthy person of good will, gives permission to accept the stepparent. Alternatively, the grandparent can enter into a coalition with the child, preventing the formation of a stepparent-stepchild bond and sowing the seeds of suspicion and resentment to accompany the birth of a mutual child.

Daryl, for example, had his grandmother constantly on hand to convince him his stepmother was not looking out for his best interests, pointing out, especially when his younger sisters came along, that she was giving them preferential treatment. His paternal grandmother had cared for Daryl during the year between his mother's death and his father's remarriage. According to Daryl, Grandma "made no bones about" favoring the three children of her son's first marriage: "It's nothing personal against Emily and Amy. She saw that we needed someone on our side, and she was going to be that person, because she felt no one else was going to do it. She'd see them getting things, or time and attention that we didn't get, and that just infuriated her." So outspoken was she about her slant on things that she catalyzed his resentment and helped create for him a picture of the family reality as one of discrimination.

Grandma's distorting lens reflected a picture of deprivation wherever it focused. As a boy, Daryl had loved camp and admits that he probably wouldn't have chosen to forgo his camping experience to accompany his parents and the two younger children on vacation excursions while the three older kids were in camp. He enjoyed the break from family life, and the younger girls, too, went to camp when they were older. Still, he "couldn't help feeling just a little hurt that they would take them off and do things with them that they wouldn't do with us. It was almost like 'We'll get these kids out of the house, and we'll go take our vacation.' It might not be fair to think that, but of course Grandma was always there to point that out."

Now in his mid-twenties, Daryl recognizes that Grandma's suspiciousness and distrust helped keep him at odds with his stepmother and created distance in his relationship with his younger sisters. "It's time to set those things aside," he says, noting that he is now more able to see things from his stepmother's point of view and can talk to her about matters on which he has long kept silent. As a child, however, he had been too dependent on his grandmother to forgo her fierce allegiance, making him what Emily, the family's first mutual child, called "Grandma's little warrior inside the family."

Grandparents and other significant relatives can either facilitate or disrupt the developing integrity of the remarried family. By entering into coalition with one member of the stepfamily, most often one or more of the first batch of children, grandparents prevent the children from developing a workable relationship with a new stepparent and any subsequent children. By enlarging their circle of care and concern to include a child's new spouse, and the children she brings with her in remarriage, they help stepfamily members avoid becoming locked into adversarial positions, where the interests of children of the present marriage are seen as prejudicial to those of the children from prior unions.

Grandparents can and will feel differently about each of their grandchildren and stepgrandchildren, regardless of whether they are full siblings, stepsiblings, or half siblings. They can, however, be prevented from translating differences in attachment into obvious favoritism. Letting grandparents and stepgrandparents know the probable consequences of making distinctions allows parent and stepparent to create a plan that works for their family. For some stepfamilies, this can mean asking grandparents to refrain from a generosity that cannot be evenhanded. For others, in which each child is equally the recipient of grandparental attention, albeit from different grandparents, a more laissez-faire approach can work. When a grandparent enters into a coalition with a grandchild against a stepparent, however, parents must mobilize to interrupt a pattern that creates ripples of estrangement, affecting both their own marriages and their children's relationships as half siblings.

The Blessing Across the Divide

Former spouses have enormous power to bless or to curse the fortunes of the remarried family. For children whose parents have separated, home spans two households, so that a stepfamily is only a part of a larger system of linked families. Feeling at home in both households and at home in an identity that blends their inheritance from both parents is made easier or more difficult for their children by how divorced spouses manage their continuing relationship as parents. When emotional divorce has not accompanied civil divorce, and marital attachment and hostility survive separation and even remarriage, children are caught in the maelstrom and new partnerships are endangered by old entanglements. Unresolved mourning for a decreased partner and parent also impedes new attachments, making caring for a stepparent or welcoming a new baby a symbol of disloyalty to the original family.

Even enduring intimacy, the "Perfect Pals" relationship between ex-spouses described by Constance Ahrons and Roy Rodgers as the most friendly of all divorced family styles, can be a problem to the consolidation of the new stepfamily, which is why a step back to "Cooperative Colleagues" usually attends remarriage.[11] Following family therapy occasioned by battles between his wife and his pubescent son, one forty-year-old remarried father who had continued to make all of the decisions about the boy with his mother, excluding both her new husband and his new wife, came up with this advice to others in his situation: "While you have a commitment to the mother of your child, you're getting married and you have a commitment to your wife that should be primary. You have to be clear about who the players are and where your alliances are." Being more connected as a parent to his ex-wife than to his new partner led to "a terrible mixup."

Children need to feel that "it's okay with Daddy" to accept a stepfather and that "it's okay with Mommy" to embrace as a brother Daddy's new baby. The child who is told by one parent that the other's new child is "not your sister, she's only your half sister" is deflated and put on guard. To then open himself to feeling fraternal to the little girl is to risk betraying a still more vital connection, the primary bond with the parent he fears to displease. With a parent's blessing, attachment and affection between half siblings can thrive; without such approval, ambivalence is heightened and efforts toward closeness alternate with distancing maneuvers.

More than anything else, children are free to relax into the remarried family, maintaining old relationships and accepting the new, when they are confident that their other parent, remarried or not, is happily resettled in his own life. Having one apparently miserable parent enlists children's protectiveness; to then fervently embrace stepfamily life in the other household smacks of disloyalty. Only when they are assured both parents are "taken care of" are children free to enjoy the benefits of both of their homes, taking from each its unique contributions, and giving of themselves unstintingly, confident there is enough caring to go around.

Children whose parents manage to rebuild separate homes, so that each is satisfied in his life apart, have a tremendous advantage. Here, too, gender differences come into play. Children worry more about their mothers than about their fathers, and with good reason. Divorce patterns have produced an underclass of single women and their children, as incomes plummet for women when they are no longer married. In addition, fewer divorced and widowed women than men remarry. Women are more prone to respond to an ex-husband's remarriage as yet another abandonment, a day of mourning for the lost dreams of the first marriage, even if they have been the ones to initiate the breakup. For men, the wedding of an ex-wife may be cause for celebration, releasing them from responsibility, emotional or financial; they may not recognize that remaining angry is also a way of keeping the first marriage going.[12] Similarly, the birth of a baby in an ex-spouse's remarriage seems to be taken harder by women, even when they themselves do not want any more children. Children are exquisitely sensitive to their parents' emotional states, and they pick up on the message that Mommy is hurt when Daddy remarries or when Dad and stepmother have a mutual child. How then to rejoice in what causes distress to so important an other?

Divorced parents who manage to put their hurt and anger behind them, working together to make policy in the best interests of their children, enable each other to build new families. Their children have permission to greet a stepparent as an additional resource, not a replacement parent. They can welcome a mutual child as someone to love who will also love them, not primarily as a competitor for their parent's love.

To give these gifts to their children, divorced parents must learn to communicate clearly and directly, not detouring messages through the children. This can be done even when parents cannot fully put the past to rest, as long as they are both dedicated to shielding their children from the lingering embers of their resentments. Mutual respect, both in how they speak about each other to their children and in how they behave when together in the children's presence, is essential. If they are also mindful of boundaries that require more social distance than they were accustomed to as marital partners, divorced parents can prepare the groundwork on which each can build a successful stepfamily that nourishes their children and subsequent children alike.

7

What's in a Name?

Children's Understanding of Steprelations

At sixteen, Sean appeared in his school play and the family went out for ice cream afterward to celebrate. His mother had flown in from her home five hundred miles away. Because he had recruited Brian, then seven, to play a bit part, *his* mother, too, was present. When Sean's friends asked who everyone was, he told them: his dad and mom, his two half brothers and his first stepmother, and his second stepmother, me, who was then pregnant with his third half brother. "I felt weird," he later told us, even in our much-divorced community.

When David was, in his words, "four and five-sixes," he told me that for his fifth birthday he wanted another mommy: "I want you for a mommy and another mommy, a real mommy and a stepmommy." He was unresponsive to questions about why he wanted another mommy, although he did know that a stepmother would be "either very nice or very mean." All three of his brothers have "another mommy," and he told me, "My first brain tells me I'll have a step-mommy when I get big."

In this chapter, my focus is on how children in the stepfamilies I have studied make sense of the cast of characters in their complex family networks. Judith Wallerstein and Joan Kelly have commented that children in remarried families are faced with an array of relatives that rivals a Russian novel in its complexity, but without the opportunity to refer to a diagram in the frontispiece for assistance in figuring out who's who.[1] Children are not alone in having difficulty unraveling the tangles in the threads of stepfamily relationships. Social worlds exist in large measure insofar as and in the way that we define and make sense of them. People, as physical beings, exist beyond refutation; we are palpably physical creatures. But family is an idea, a social construct that describes a group of people having a defined set of biological and social relationships.

The idea of family and the social definitions of family roles are an essential part of the organization of any culture. Within each culture, consensus exists about kinship terms, the relationships they describe, and the obligations they entail. However, because most people have no workable definitions of what a stepfamily is and how its members might be expected to behave toward one another, stepfamilies are an anomaly in our construction of reality. Persistent attempts to think of the stepfamily as just a little bit different from the "normal" family are always mistaken.

At the same time, both participants in stepfamilies and the people who study them are faced with the urgent task of understanding what is going on. Without a road map, it is difficult to navigate the transitions in stepfamily development and to help individual members mature. Without an adequate social conception of what stepfamilies are, lacking norms or terminology beyond what we are forced to borrow from the kinship relations of nuclear families, workable definitions are just in the formative stage.

Living in a stepfamily forces children to construct the meaning of the family relationships of which they are a part. Children, the most "naive" stepfamily participants, that is, those with the least cultural baggage from the world of nuclear families, are better able than adults to suspend preconceptions, attempting to understand a social situation as it is perceived and experienced. At the same time, the immaturity of their intellectual skills can make the task a challenging one, so that the child's efforts to make sense of her family will change with her developing cognitive abilities. Intellectual development, however, is not the whole story: What the child has been told, how she feels about family members, and how her own family is organized will color her thinking about who they are to her.

Piaget's Model of Children's Thinking

Swiss developmental psychologist Jean Piaget's model of the development of children's thinking helps us to understand the dilemma of the
young child trying to make sense of relationships that entail a level of
abstraction beyond his grasp.[2] Piaget regards each child as a philoso-
pher who works at making the universe intelligible. Children ask themselves and others: What makes it night? What is a dream? What is a
family? A brother? And, if one is part of their own family, a stepfather?

In growing up, children attempt to piece together answers to these
and other questions, to explain to themselves the whats and hows and
whys of the events that surround and involve them. They use all the
resources at their disposal: what they themselves perceive with their
senses, the information given them by others, and their own style of
putting the puzzle together. As children develop, they shape the world
in terms of their own level of understanding and then restructure their
understanding when they take in information that doesn't fit into their
old view of the universe.

A central point of Piaget's model of development is that children
tend to assimilate information to their current level of understanding.
Children take the information provided by experience and direct teaching, process it, and create their own versions of what a family is, who
is in and who is out, and whether it all matters. Each new level involves
inferences of increasing complexity.

Piaget identifies three major stages in cognitive development
beyond infancy: preoperational, concrete operational, and formal operational thought. A preoperational child builds mental maps based on
her own sensorimotor experiences; she solves problems by intuition.
She cannot assign objects to categories. Asked to define an apple, she
is likely to say, "It's to eat," but she cannot group it in a larger system
with other things to eat. As she moves into the next stage, which
generally happens any time between the ages of seven and ten, she
learns to think systematically and generally about concrete objects. Ask
her about an apple now and she will say "It's a fruit."

What the preoperational child knows is not simply a matter of
information and misinformation. It is difficult to believe that children
have somehow been told the answers they give; rather, it appears that
children who wonder about or are asked questions that are beyond their
grasp simply make up answers. Their answers represent assimilations

both from the content of experience and from the structure of thought, as when a three-year-old whose own father is a stepfather offers the following definition: "A stepfather has steps on the toes, but they're like skis."

Fully understanding kinship, even in more traditional families, requires the child to coordinate a series of relationships, since any given person's relationship to the child may depend on his relationship to a third person. For the young child who has not yet grasped the conservation of identity, this is a formidable task. It is not obvious to the preschooler that however much my appearance may have changed as I grew and matured, my identity is constant and my sense of self is continuous. It is only when I recognize that you and I are the same people we have always been that I can sort out the network of relationships of brothers and sisters, much less half siblings, stepsiblings, and stepparents.

Jimmy is three years old. After our interview his mother handed him some of his baby pictures for him to show me. He looked at a picture of himself taken two years earlier and said, "That's Mikey." Mikey, his younger brother, closely resembled the infant in the picture. Anyone might have made the same mistake. His mother corrected him: "I know it looks like Mikey, but that was you when you were a baby." And Jimmy asked, "That was me when I was Mikey?"

For him, appearance is all-important in determining identity. We can imagine that children's thinking goes something like this: If I used to look just like my brother, perhaps I used to be my brother. Not until six or seven do children let go of the belief that magical transformations are possible. In a study by Lawrence Kohlberg, most four-year-olds said that a girl could be a boy if she wanted to, or if she played boys' games, or if she wore a boy's hair style or clothes.[3] They also claimed that a cat could be a dog if it wanted to, or if its whiskers were cut off. By six or seven, most children were insistent that neither cat nor girl could change species or gender regardless of changes in appearance or behavior. They had learned that identity is permanent and cannot be disrupted by apparent transformations.

Experience does not always rectify beliefs. As in play, for young children things can be what they wish them to be. The very young do not know that thoughts are not real events outside their heads. Children's thought is egocentric. Untutored in the art of considering other people's points of view, they cannot imagine any perspective other than their own. Jimmy may insist, for example, that while he has a brother named Michael, Michael has no brothers.

At about seven or eight, children begin to see the forest as well as the trees. They begin to see the other person's point of view, to realize that if I have a sister my sister must also have a sister, and to put things together according to how they relate to the whole in which they partake. They begin to avoid contradicting themselves, wonder how what's necessary differs from what's possible, and recognize that chance plays a role in events.

These changes in thinking do not happen all at once. Precausal explanations do not vanish overnight to be replaced by logical, scientific thought. Instead, children's growing awareness that there are points of view other than their own begins an overhaul of their old ideas, which are lined up, taken apart, examined for coherence and reassembled. The attainment of concrete operations is a time of conceptual house-cleaning, a time of transition during which old thought patterns mingle with the new.

For the child whose thinking is becoming operational, the world is full of laws. Concrete operations require that we stop focusing only on a limited amount of information. Children capable of these mental actions can focus on several aspects of a situation at the same time. They are sensitive to transformations and can mentally reverse a sequence of changes, concluding, for example, that a ball of clay rolled into a snake can be measured against another ball by transforming the snake back into a ball. They can organize objects into classes and understand which classes are included in more general classes. For example, they can now tell you whether there are more roses or more flowers in a bunch of a dozen flowers, eight of them roses. Children's reasoning that is connected with their actual beliefs, grounded in the direct evidence of their sense, will be logical at this level. Comparisons, relations, inclusion, ordering, and measurement of concrete objects are well within their ability. What they cannot yet do is reason logically about ideas or hypothetical statements based on premises that they don't believe.

Not until eleven or twelve or later, and the development of what Piaget calls formal operations, do children become capable of making deductions about abstract concepts and systematizing their own beliefs. Now, for the first time, they can reflect on their own thought. They can develop theories and test them against reality and can think about thinking. Confronted with events and attitudes that are not easily interpreted within their existing ideologies, they see the contradictions as a call to reevaluate both the evidence and their own beliefs. They begin to be concerned that their beliefs be consistent and that their actions match their ideas and values.

No longer is the truth absolute and mechanistic. The context of an event contributes to its meaning. Earlier a lie was always bad; now a lie that saves a life may be seen as virtuous. Before, a child could think that an attack directed at him had to be the direct result of his own immediate action or be a reflection that he is bad or unloved. Now, the motive for the assault can be located in events that occurred in another time and place. The ability to formulate and make deductions from hypotheses that are contrary to fact liberates thinking about relations and classifications from their concrete and intuitive ties. Systematic problem solving becomes possible only when all the possible solutions are considered and tried. Formal operations allow the thinker to combine propositions and isolate factors in order to confirm or disprove a belief.

With Piaget's ideas of how children's thinking develops as a lens, children's ideas about stepfamily relationships become more intelligible to us as adults, as we trace the interplay of experience and imagination in how they construe their complex family networks.

Can I Draw a Stegosaurus Now?

While children vary widely in how curious they are about the kinds of families they live in, parents report that their mutual children become most openly curious at about four or five years of age, trying to sort out who is related to whom and how. It is then that children typically begin counting and sorting family members into children and adult, males and females. With children born into stepfamilies, the added complexity of those present and those absent comes into play, so that a four-year-old may continually refer to the number of family members that are around at the time. "If there are two empty chairs," said Adrienne, describing how her daughter takes account of her half siblings, "she'll say 'If Bev and Judy were here, they could fill them. There'd have to be another chair if David were here.' "

Two children within the same family will differ dramatically in how many questions they ask and at what age they begin to comment on how family members are related. An eleven-year-old, for example, is described by her mother as "accepting the little realities of her social life as a state of nature," while her younger sister is a fountain of questions, asking about her half siblings' mother, "Who is she to me?" and "Why doesn't Daddy live with her anymore?"

A child shown photo albums from early on will come to identify his father's absent son as a brother, even though he has met him only once and their only contact is long-distance phone calls. Any steady state is more easily understood than erratic changes. And the more they know about the older children's whereabouts when they're gone, the less preoccupied they will be with their comings and goings. When a stepchild is back and forth between houses at frequent intervals, the mutual children who have been to the other home are well aware of where he is. Although they may cry when the older children go, there is no mystery when such departures are routine. Unlike adults, who have expectations of family life that include all members' sharing a household full-time, children born into stepfamilies can accept such arrangements as a fact or life.

Typical of preoperational thinkers, many of the younger children I spoke with said they didn't know what a family was, although all could list the members of their own families. Those who would venture a definition said that a family is "people," or "something a lot of people live in, a lot of people." According to one five-year-old it is "people living together," or, as one four-year-old puts it, "You love all together." Residence and caring continue to be the criteria young children employ, moving on to definitions that consist primarily of a list of familial roles with the attainment of concrete operations, such as defining a family as "a husband and a wife, and usually two or three children." As they enter their teens their definitions become more philosophical, engaging issues of meaning and purpose.

Understanding what is meant by "step" relationships involves a similar progression, but it is not universal. In families where the older child's other natural parent is out of the picture, this prefix may play no part in family life, and younger children may learn late, even in adulthood, that both parents did not produce an older sibling. Sometimes parents delay giving their mutual child information about an older child's parentage for fear of giving him a weapon that can be used against that child. Leslie, for example, does not plan to tell Oliver that

Denise had another father "until he's much bigger" than four. "If it comes into conversation, of course, we'll talk about it, but I don't want to make any differences. If it were brought up, then it would be like 'Well, this is my mum and dad.' I would really hate that to come in. It would be like a power thing that would be easy to use." Others delay giving this information because they think the child is too young to understand, leading him to fantasize that their lives run on parallel tracks. In one such family, one mother described her son as echoing her stepdaughter's stories, assuming that all her relatives are also his: "After Barbara finishes her story about 'My grandmother this and my sisters this,' Anthony will say, 'Well, my grandmother this and my sisters and brothers,' making up a story just like hers."

More usually, however, when relationships are explained to them, children use the vocabulary before they can accurately construct its meaning. Steprelationships may be seen as part of everyday family life, as when David, making a Playdō family of worms, identified them as "the mommy, the daddy, the brother, the other brother, and the stepsister," but use of "step" vocabulary does not imply conceptual understanding. At two, my son could verbalize that I am his brothers' stepmother. At three he was still asking if I was also *his* stepmother, and when told I was not, would ask "Who's my stepmother?" Feeling deprived, he would insist he wanted to have one, too, while Brian shook his head incredulously. Not yet four, David still did not grasp what was meant by the terms that had been part of his vocabulary for two years. When I explained to him that Brian was not with us that week because his mommy likes to spend time with him, David responded that Brian had two mommies. I attempted to clarify, saying that Judyann is Brian's mommy and I'm his stepmommy. David seemed surprised, "You mean she's his *real* mommy?" I nodded. "You're *joking.*"

When family members are defined perceptually—for example, a sister is "a girl in your family" or a mother is "somebody who takes care of children"—it is difficult for children to differentiate between mother and stepmother, sister and half sister. For most of the three- to six-year-olds who are mutual children, a stepparent is another parent, for example, Aileen, at four and a half: "I don't know what a stepfather is, but it's another father. And Eva's a stepmother. Another mother." Or Amos, at four and a half: "Jeremy has two dads. One is ours." There is a recognition of a difference, but no articulation of that difference. Owen, at three and a half, said of his brothers, "I don't know why they have their mom." At four and a half, Ethan says a stepmother is "something kind of like a mother," but when asked what the difference is replied, "That's a hardie. Can I draw a stegosaurus now?" Aileen, more venturesome at the same age, suggested that her brother had two houses: "Because fathers can't live together and mothers can't live together. There has to be one mother and one father, so the stepfather and the plain mother live here, and George's stepmother and real father live there." The first attempt at distinction usually involves this use of the word *real* as the antonym to *step*. So that a stepmother becomes "a mother that's not really your mother."

At first glance it may appear that the propensity of the younger children to begin their definitions of stepparents as supernumerary parents is the result of their being mutual children, not stepchildren. Stepchildren are certainly more likely to make distinctions between a parent and a stepparent. Unfortunately, I could make no comparisons between stepchildren and mutual children of the same age. Because families interviewed had to have a mutual child who was at least three years old, and because the transition from divorce or bereavement through single parenthood to remarriage and another child usually takes a number of years, children in this age range are less likely to have both a stepparent and a half sibling. Previous work suggests, however, that even stepchildren may first think of a stepparent as an additional parent. While studying children's ideas about sex and birth, I learned that for preschoolers all women are mommies and all men are daddies. To get to be a parent, you have merely to eat your vegetables, brush your teeth, and follow the other imperatives of childhood until you are grown up and, by definition, become a mommy or daddy.[4] If all adults are parents, a stepparent might then be conceptualized as "a Daddy that's not really yours."

Asked to explain how their parents and siblings got to be members of their family, the smallest children attribute magical powers to wishing and wanting. Children frequently describe their parents as being their parents because "he wanted to be my daddy," which can be extended to explain the relationship with siblings, as when Erica, at four, insists that Nila "just came out born, and she wanted to be my sister, so when she grew up she was my sister." Who came out of whose "tummy" also figures prominently in their explanations of why older children have a different mother, while paternity is harder for them to account for. It is obvious to Erica that her half sisters live elsewhere, and she claims she has never wondered why, "because they didn't come out of my mommy's tummy."

Another characteristic of this egocentric early stage is that the younger children, from the age of three, can tell how each family member is related to them, but often have some difficulty in telling how the others are related to one another. They cannot yet assume the role of the other, to see relationships from another perspective. It is as if *brother, sister, father,* and *mother* are just labels people have. Oren, at four, knows that Dan is his brother, but it is not at all clear what he understands that to mean, since he identifies his dad as Dan's "cousin," denying that he could be Dan's dad too, and says that this adult half brother has a father who lives "in the same house as he is." Erica, at four and a half, identifies her mother as her half sister's "friend," but later says that her sister is her mother's "child," albeit in a different way than she herself is.

Like the young child who can tell if there are more red beads than blue beads, but not if there are more red beads than wooden beads, these youngsters are not yet capable of keeping categories constant and look to nonessential clues of appearance or activity to make distinctions among relations. Often three- to five-year-olds will explain that their full siblings are related to them in a different way than their half siblings because one is bigger than the other. "Ken," says Alana, at four and a half, is "my other brother," who got to be related because "he was born in my family." Asked if he was her brother in the same way or a different way than her younger, full brother, she replied: "Different, because he's bigger than Aaron." I asked if there were there any other differences. "That Ken can do more things than Aaron." I reminded her that she had said Aaron was related because he lived with her and that Ken didn't live with her. "He's still my brother, and he doesn't live with me, because he has a different mom than mine."

Some of the fundamentals of steprelationships can be grasped relatively early. Eve, at six and a half, could explain that her mother is her half brother's stepmother "because they're my dad's children and not my mom's children." And Ina, while unable, at five, to distinguish in any way other than size between her older sister and her teenage half sister, could add another distinction when she was six: "Pam is here half the time and at her Mom's half the time." In these middle years, both stepchildren and mutual children start to explain relationships in terms of history, often beginning with an account of the initial marriage, the offspring it produced, the divorce, and the remarriage and its offspring.

At this level, quantification and measurement of relationship play an important part. Beverly, for example, at seven and a half, describes a stepfather as "part of your family, but it's not your real father. He's *part* of your father and your real father is *all* your father." Blood-relatedness is often depicted quite concretely in terms of sharing blood, flesh, or genes. Thus, a half sibling may be described as "someone who has half your blood and half someone else's blood," or, by a girl of ten, "I just think of her as my sister. I mean flesh and blood, half of her at least." "Step" is also interpreted very concretely as in "a step removed from," so that Angela, at seven and a half, defines a stepmother as "a step away from who is your real mother," and Tamara, at ten, describes her stepfather as "kind of like a step over" from a father. There were no systematic differences between stepchildren and mutual children in how those in this age range defined family relationships.

Preteens and teens begin to give explanations of relationships that are multidimensional and well-reasoned. They can coordinate a network of relationships and take different points of view, so that relationships are seen as reciprocal and contingent on other relationships. They do not need to trace the historical sequence of family events to give a coherent definition of a given relationship. Instead, they can abstract the essentials, integrating the impact of affection and social convention, without getting the various strands tangled. A half sibling is now "someone born through your stepfather and mother or your stepmother and father," according to one twelve-year-old.

Understanding from the Heart

If a glass can be described as either half full or half empty, so can steprelatives be described as more like or more unlike blood relatives, depending on how a child feels about them. So that a seven-year-old may begin a definition of a stepmother with "They're nice to you," while a nine-year-old who omitted her stepmother from the list of those in her family, when asked how they are related, will say, "I'm sort of not," going on to say that a stepmother is "another mother who didn't have you," defining by negation. Those children with basically positive feelings toward their stepparents tend to make distinctions while minimizing difference, like Carl, at sixteen, who says his stepfather is "the same thing [as his mom], at least for me, helps bring me up, helps raise me." In contrast, Bert, also sixteen, says, "I think of her as a stepmom . . . I think that always, no matter how hard you try, unless you don't like your mom, you have some resentment toward a stepmom." Even children in the same family will have strikingly different definitions of a stepparent, based on the differences in their attachment to the parent who remarries, as when one sister defines a stepmother as "a woman who marries your father who is not related to you," while another, speaking of the same woman, calls her "a friend, a really good friend, and the mother of my sisters." And a daughter who remains loyal to the father who left the family may accept her stepmother, extending herself and reaching out to the older woman as a way of staying close to her father, identifying their child as her sister, while her brother, who was their mother's defender in the family drama, may deny any relatedness to either.

Paula, at eighteen, reflects the warmth, achieved over the years, although not without struggle, of her relationship with her stepmother in her definition: "the woman my father met after being separated with my mom and fell in love with. Technically she's my stepmother because they got married, but she's also my step*mother* in the sense that she mothers me." Whereas Brendan, at fifteen, cynically defines a stepfather as "someone that is married to your mother for the second time." He laughed. "Or the third time, I guess, or fourth or fifth."

When a mutual child explains what a stepparent is, she is talking about her own mommy or daddy, and her definitions generally reflect the greater empathy with the role based on their greater closeness. "I was going to say a second mother," explained Anita, at eighteen, "who is not by birth your mother but chooses to mother. She may not choose to, but has married your father, and is therefore stuck with that job."

Definitions of stepparents are especially loaded for stepchildren, because they raise questions of loyalty. The same child may alter how he thinks of his relationship with a stepparent, giving differing accounts to others, even the stepparent himself. One day when Brian was seven, he told me angrily, "You don't have sons, or stepsons, only friends," yet before the month was out he held my hand to his face and called me his "Annie Mommy." Even steprelationships that extend back to the child's infancy must be differentiated from the biological ones the child fears disavowing. Jillian at first defined Irina as "like a second mother," after saying that "she's married to my father, and she's given birth to my two half brothers and half sister, and I've lived with her for thirteen years." She then catches herself: "Even when I say that, I don't really think of her as a mother. I guess I really do, and that's just me using that she's a stepmother against her . . . I've lived with her for a long time. She's just really another mother when I'm here." But then she catches herself again: "She's not really another mother. That's mean to my mother, but she's like a second mother." More than any other family roles, mother and father tend to pull for exclusivity: It's okay to have more than one child, grandparent, aunt, or sister, while to think of more than one person as a mother or father smacks of treason.

If loyalty conflicts can color stepchildren's definitions of stepparent, so too can rivalry serve as an emotional pollutant in their understanding of half sibling relationships. The most problematic half sibling relationship seems to be between the youngest child from the previous marriage and the oldest child from the current one. The youngest stepchild, having difficulty in emotionally coming to grips with the addition of children to the stepfamily, can make bizarre differentiations between the first mutual child, who displaced him as the baby of the family, and subsequent children, whose birth is not experienced as disruptive. Nancy, at nine and a half, clearly distinguished between how related she felt to four-year-old Elaine and seven-month-old Abbot. Elaine is clearly labeled as a half sister, which is defined as a "sister that's not really your sister." Abbot, however, is "my real brother. He's not like my half brother or half sister or something like that." When I asked her what made the relationship different, as she had said that they were both the children of her father and stepmother, she continued: "I guess it's just like the age or something. Because before my dad married her, she didn't have Elaine yet. So I guess when Abbot was born, then he would be my real brother." My questions continued. "I guess what makes Abbot my real brother is they had him after they were married." She then proceeded to tell me that Elaine, too, had been born after the marriage. Yet Abbot, she insisted, was her real brother, in the same way as her older, full sister, Brenda, was her real sister. Elaine, however, whose birth when she was five must have felt like more of a displacement, was in a category all her own: interloping half sister.

Mutual children in stepfamilies also construct relationships differently, denying either difference or similarity, depending on the emotional loading and circumstances. Two extremes are represented by Orianne, the seven-year-old eldest mutual child in a family marked by some tension between her mother and adult half brother, and Alexander, twelve-and-a-half, the only mutual child in a stepfamily to which both his parents brought older children.

Orianne does not spontaneously include her adult half brother in her family, but when asked if anyone else was in her family, quickly adds, "my *big* brother." She not only "is not so sure" her mom and her brother are related, she goes further, denying the natural relationship between her father and his eldest son: "He grew up with the same father, except he was a little different from a real brother, so he has a different mother." Asked how he got to be her brother, she continued: "because his father died, and my father had to marry again. So he married my big brother's mother, and so he became my brother." So that while her father is her brother's father, "First he had a different father, but I don't know *anything* about that."

Alexander, on the other hand, goes to great lengths to minimize distinctions in a family to which both parents brought a child from a previous union. Speaking of his father's relationship to his mother's daughter, he says: "He's really like her whole father, but he's not really her father. I think he's starting to believe that and she's starting to believe that he is, and I can see why. They're so tight and their birthdays are only one day apart, so they can't be that far away from each other. . . . I wouldn't call it a stepfather-stepdaughter relationship, I'd call it a father-daughter relationship." When asked the distinction, he elaborated: "In that kind of relationship, they're not understanding each other, getting into a lot of quarrels, not listening to each other. That would really be considered a family that has some steprelative, who really doesn't know how to take the place of a real father or mother."

In looking at how emotion colors children's thinking about stepfamily roles, we encounter the role of family structure in how children think about family relationships. First, children with both full siblings and half siblings make more distinctions than those with only half siblings. Witness Bruce, at thirteen, who corrected his mother's statement that they had a lot of children by adding, "But they're all steps and halves." Here is his rundown of the family (Figure 1): "Scott is my

brother. Tim and Janet are my stepbrother and sister. Josh is my
stepdad. Carin and Don are my real parents, who are divorced. And
Don married Anna and together they had Ethan and Ellen, my half
sister and brother. And Carin married Josh and had little Alice, my half
sister."

Contrasted with this is the practice of most of the single stepchildren, who refer to their half siblings almost exclusively as "my little
brother" or "my sister," using half only to respond to queries about how
they are related "technically." Pamela, for example, at fifteen, says,
"My sisters and brother who are half sisters and a half brother, but
that's not really how I feel. Because I don't think about them as half
sisters and half brother. That's just to point out that they're not born
by my mother and my father." Jason, also fifteen, illustrates how for
the child whose only siblings are half siblings, the half is played down:
"Ethan is my half brother, which means that through my father he is
blood-related. That makes him half, because Irma and I don't have the
same blood, but loving-wise I would consider him a brother, just like
anybody else. He has my same blood. Although he and I have gone
through rocky stages, both of us love and trust each other very much.
I mean he was my first brother, so that definitely was a big thing for
me. We don't look at him being a half brother, or me being a half
brother as anything different than, say Ethan and Ezra, who are full
brothers."

Mutual children are less likely to make distinctions among their
siblings than are the older children, whose consciousness of being in
a stepfamily is more acute. None of the mutual children that I interviewed spontaneously identified a half sibling as such until queried
further about relationship, whereas several of the stepchildren did so.
The mutual child would often insist, like one eighteen-year-old, "I
never think of them as half anything. It's just technically that's the
relationship." When differentiating degrees of relatedness, the mutual
child is more likely to counterpose "full" to "half" siblings, unlike some
of the children from earlier marriages for whom the distinction is
between "half" and "real." For these older children, a reference to "my
brother" or "my sister" that lacks a name or birth order qualifier, like
"my younger brother," always refers to a full sibling. Sixteen-year-old
Larry, contrasting his thirteen-year-old brother, Kevin, from their
three-year-old half brother, Owen, demonstrates how the children of
both of one's parents are seen as more of a fact of life, whereas the

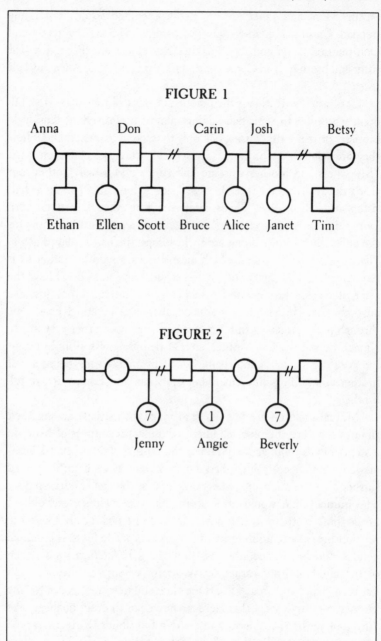

FIGURE 1

Anna   Don   Carin Josh   Betsy

Ethan Ellen Scott Bruce Alice Janet Tim

FIGURE 2

Jenny   Angie   Beverly

mutual child is more of an optional addition to the family: "For me, my brother has always been my brother, so I don't really think about who he is. I just kind of accept him. I never thought about what it would be like without him, because he's always been there."

An example from my own family illustrates how a child feels more related to someone who has been related since birth: When my stepson Brian was seven and I was pregnant, he said that the baby would be his stepbrother. When I explained that my son would be his half brother, just like his then-sixteen-year-old brother by his father's earlier marriage, Brian protested: "Sean's not my half brother. He's been my brother a long time."

Just as siblings that have always been there are experienced as more of a given, and, therefore, more fully related, siblings whom one has known from the time of their birth are experienced as closer than stepsiblings who are encountered as somewhat developed entities. Scott, the sixteen-year-old brother of Bruce, whose family is mapped in Figure 1, describes his feelings: "Halves I feel are much closer than steps. It's by blood with the halves, and also with Ethan and Ellen and Alice, I've been with them since they were babies, and with Tim and Janet it's been kind of coming into conflict. It's been like trying to stick an anvil into wood. It took a while for us to get used to it. We'll never be quite as used to Tim and Janet as we are to Ethan and Ellen and baby Alice. I feel like these are just like brothers and sisters."

How old the child is when his stepsiblings enter his life also influences how related they are likely to feel. Cataloguing his family, Lowell, as an adult, runs down the list: "my three half brothers, my two half sisters, and I have a brother and two sisters that are, I guess, a step-brother and stepsisters." Later questioning revealed that one of the three half brothers was, in fact, another stepbrother, the child of his mother's second husband, who shared a household with him when he was four and the older boy was six. Contrasting this boy to the three children of his second stepfather, who were teenagers at the time of his mother's third marriage, Lowell explained: "He's just my brother, one of my primary siblings."

While the emotional ties to half and stepsiblings are usually clearly differentiated, the language used to describe them remains confusing. Children use *half* and *step* almost interchangeably for quite some time, often continuing into adulthood. The youngest children maintain that there is no difference, and seven- and eight-year-olds say "it's kind of the same thing." In striving for consistency, children may insist that their *step*parent's baby must be their *step*sibling. It takes cognitive maturity as well as emotional reconciliation with family realities to sort out why children born to a stepparent before remarriage are related to them in a different way than those who share a parent with them.

Unfortunately, Cinderella still serves as a reference point by which children gauge relationship. Here is Alissa, at eight, trying to figure out if there is any difference between a half sister and a stepsister: "I'm not sure. Well, if I'm saying this right, from Cinderella: Cinderella's mother came with daughters to be her mother, and those were her stepsisters." Asked if that was the same situation as with her older sister, she replied, "Different. Well, maybe it's not different, because my dad kind of came over, but I think it might be still the same, but Cinderella was already living."

Mom's Child, Dad's Child

Whether the parent they share is a mother or a father is seen as a criterion of the strength of the tie to a half sibling by children who are in primary custody with one parent. Beverly and Jenny, both seven, have a one-year-old half sister, Angie (Figure 2). Beverly lives with her mother and stepfather, who is Jenny's dad. Jenny visits every other weekend. Jenny originally identifies baby Angie as her stepsister, then corrects this to half sister. When asked how Beverly is related to Angie, she says, "I guess it's just her sister." Asked if she thought Beverly was more related to the baby than she herself was, she said, "I guess it's almost the same." Beverly, on the other hand, originally identifies Angie as "my baby sister." In describing how Jenny and Angie are related, she tries to balance the sameness and difference: "That's her stepsister, and it's part of her sister, and it's the same thing. I'm kind of related that way to Angie." This prompts her to correct her initial formulation: "It's Jenny's sister too, it's her real sister, not her stepsister."

One adult stepchild told of learning from her inner-city schoolchildren that a father's children were stepsiblings and a mother's children just plain brothers and sisters, because "you came out of the same stomach." Her own eleven-year-old half sister echoed this approach when she told me, "Well, a stepsister is your father's daughter, and a half sister is your mother's, but it might be vice versa." This reasoning is echoed by Barbara, who contrasted her paternal half brother, with whom she lives full-time following the death of her mother, with the "two sisters and a bigger brother which are my real sisters and brother. Anthony's not actually my real brother, because Edith's my step-mother." What makes the older children "real" is that "they were born to my real mom," although all the children had different dads, making them all half siblings. Asked why having a father in common made a sibling less "real" than having a mother in common, this nine-year-old said, "He was born from somebody else, Dads don't have babies," despite an earlier assertion that "all people have to have dads." Like others her age, Barbara is very concrete in her thinking: Seeing is believing, and paternity is still too abstract a concept to have equal weight with the more observable connection between mother and child.

But the sex of the parent is not the only, or perhaps even the primary, factor in these assertions of "mother right." None of the children in joint custody, including several whose mother and father both had additional children, felt that their closeness to a half sibling depended on whether the relationship was on the maternal or the paternal side. Sharing a household, growing up together, more than anything else, is what makes children feel connected to one another.

The Extended Stepfamily

One morning when we were having breakfast with my husband's brother and his family, Tonio, then thirteen, asked if Natty, Kate, and Morghan were David's "stepcousins." Basing his reasoning on the common confusion of half sibling with stepsibling, he explained: "I thought because he's my stepbrother, he might be their stepcousin." His uncle reminded him that David is his half brother, and I went on to explain the kinship of cousins: "Cousins are only related on one side of the family. Since you're related to these cousins through your dad, not through your mom, and you and David have the same dad, David is related to Natty, Kate, and Morghan exactly as you are." "So would I have stepcousins?" Tonio asked. "My brother's children are your stepcousins." "Oh," Tonio brightened, the light bulb clicking above his head, "Greg and Mark."

When we look beyond parents and stepparents and their children to the larger family network, relationships become still more complex. There never seem to be enough precise terms to describe some kinds of relatedness. Nor is there a social consensus about what constitutes relatedness in stepfamilies. It is no wonder, therefore, that for the child, figuring out whether his mother is related to the stepsister he acquired through his father's remarriage is no simple matter. And in response to questions, children struggle to put the pieces of the puzzle together in a way that feels internally consistent.

Essentially the solution to the question of who is related to whom is arrived at via one of two strategies. The first is to apply the same criteria used by the child to define the family: household membership and propinquity. Children of remarriage using this approach recognize the distance between themselves and their half siblings' relatives. In explaining whether they are related to their half siblings' other parent a three-year-old will say, "No, 'cause she's not in our family," and a four-and-a-half-year-old will elaborate, "No, because she didn't live with me ever." At eight, a girl answered the same question by pointing to behavioral criteria: "I'm not related to Lili because I don't go to her house to spend time like Pamela does." When there is no contact between the mutual child and the extended family of the first marriage, the question is simplified: It is harder to conceive of being related to someone when, according to a seven-year-old, "I never even saw her."

But not all children are as exclusive in their concept of relatedness. Some of the children demonstrate a remarkably expansive definition of family. Greg, for instance, at seventeen, includes his mother's boy-friend's children, whom he has never met, in listing family members. Although he feels estranged from his former stepfather, he includes the older man's mother as "a real grandma, real family." Inclusiveness, as an approach to claims of kinship, stems either from affection or from striving for conceptual consistency.

Frequently, children have a firm conviction that relatedness must be reciprocal: If my mommy is your stepmom, then your mommy must be my stepmom. Even children who see themselves as not related to their half siblings' other parent try to find a way of claiming kinship with the older child's other half siblings. At eight, Alissa knows she is not "really" related to Pamela's half sister from her mother and stepfa-ther's marriage, "But when we were younger, we used to call each other "half half sisters," she told me. Her younger sister, Ida, at five, in trying

to figure out her own relationship to "Pamela's sister," labels her "my
stepsister," even claiming Pamela's mother as her own stepmom.
When I asked her what made her father's ex-wife her stepmom, she
told me, "She didn't have me." I, too, didn't have her, I reminded her;
was I, too, then her stepmom? "No." She laughed. "She didn't have
me, and I *see* her sometimes." No matter how inclusive they are
inclined to be, children have to draw the line somewhere. For example,
Ike, at seven, claimed his mother's first husband as his stepdad, but of
that man's new wife he said, "She's not related at all."
  Children are slow to recognize time's arrow in their understanding
of relatedness. Angela, at seven, reported that "I never met [her older
half sisters' mother], but I think she is sort of like my stepmother. But
she really isn't, because I have a real mother right now. She's sort of
my stepmother." Amber, at eleven, addressing the same issue, says that
they aren't related "anymore." When queried further, she says, "I
guess she never was."
  How and why people are related can be difficult to untangle even
for children at the brink of formal relations. Witness this bright eleven-
year-old, attempting to figure out if Yale, his mother's younger son, is
related to his father's stepson: "Is he? Let's see . . . I'm related to my
dad, but my dad isn't. . . . When you marry, do you become relatives?
I don't know. If now my stepmother is related to my dad, then he
would be related, but if not, then he wouldn't be?" I then asked if his
dad is related to Yale. "He has to be, because he's my brother and this
is my dad. I don't know how it would be. I don't know what it would
be called." The idea here seems to be that two people who are both
his "blood" relatives must be related to each other, but that one of his
relatives by marriage may not be related to another of his "blood
relatives" if he is the only link.
  One solution to the question of who is related to whom, used even
by children who are quite small, is to divide the concept of family into
"our little family" and "our big family," "the four of us" or the "seven
of us," with the latter including half siblings who no longer live at
home. "Our big family" then becomes easily expandable to include the
other parent of the older children, as well as grandparents, cousins, and
other traditional members of extended families.
  When a culture lacks words to describe so many of the relationships
in the extended family of divorce and remarriage, conceptual handles
are unavailable, for adults as well as children. For instance, there is no

name for the relation of the present and former spouses of the same person, no name for the relation between a parent and his children's half siblings, no name for the relation between children who are each the half sibling of the same child.[5] And the vocabulary of kinship we do have is itself inadequate to denote the relationships it does name: For example, the word *stepmother* is used to describe any woman married to one's father, whether she is seen once a year or every day, whether she has principal responsibility for raising a child or is a friendly occasional visitor, and whether the natural mother is in the picture or not.

While part of the difficulty for children in figuring out who is related to whom in stepfamily relationship networks may be due to their slowness in understanding the time factor in this genealogy, it would be a mistake to attribute this, or other holes in their conceptualizing, exclusively to intellectual immaturity. Rather it reflects an arbitrary assumption of our culture that the kin of the current marriage are related to the progeny of the former, while the offspring of the current union bear no relation to the kin of their older half siblings. Children's "mistakes" underline the slowness with which social categories adapt to contemporary trends in American kinship patterns. Those children who insist on a reciprocity of relatedness with the kin of their kin may, like the little boy in "The Emperor's New Clothes," simply be reporting reality as they perceive it: a kinship structure enlarged by divorce and remarriage to create what has been called "the new extended family."

Talking with Children

Knowing that children will not fully understand the complexity of stepfamily relationships is no excuse to avoid talking with them about matters that affect their daily lives. First, answering children's questions honestly and clearly, matching the information given to their ability to comprehend, lays the groundwork for a trusting relationship between parent and child. Knowing that their questions have been responded to honestly helps them to continue to ask questions, trusting parents to help them sort out confusion and dispel worry.

For confusion can lead to worry, as it did for the little boy who thought that he would have to live half the time in another house when he was bigger, like his brother whose joint custody arrangement meant that they shared a home only half the time. Knowing *why* the older boy left, that he had a daddy in another house and they wanted to spend time together, could reassure him that an arbitrary eviction was not on the way for him.

Confusion can arise, too, when children lack the words that enable them to process differences they perceive, as when a young girl senses that her father is different with her than with her sisters. When she is told that he is her stepfather, she has a way of thinking and talking about a host of observations that had theretofore been both unsettling and undefinable. When the discovery that a sibling is a half sibling or a parent is a stepparent is made indirectly or by chance, the secretiveness involved gives rise to feelings that the family status of one or the other family member is somehow shameful.

Frankness about the nature of stepfamily ties allows people to feel good about the relationships they can and do have, whereas secrets imply that "something is the matter." The tools and the opportunity to talk about relationships help dispel disappointments and enlarge possibilities. At a recent dinner at his cousin's house, David surprised me by stating, "I have three half brothers." On the way home, Brian said something about having a "real brother," and David countered with "Brian's not in the 'real family.'" Their dad and I then insisted that both were part of the "real family" and both were "real brothers," but the matter was far from closed.

No sooner had we entered the door than David threw himself on the couch, sobbing inconsolably, "I only have half brothers." Told what David was crying about, Brian went in to say, "I'm your brother, David." When David calmed down, I asked him how he heard about "half brothers," a new word at our house, despite all the talk about my being the older boys' stepmother. His cousin Neil had told him that Billy, his uncle's and aunt's toddler, is Neil's half brother, and that he, David, is a half brother to all of the bigger boys at our house. Did he know what made Brian his half brother? I asked David. "Yes," he replied, accurately, "because he was born from Judyann."

This gave us an opportunity to talk further about what makes two boys brothers. "Sharing the same parent or parents is only one of the things that makes you brothers," I said to David and Brian. "There's also living together, knowing each other from the time David was born, loving each other and fighting with each other, all the things that brothers do, and you can't get much 'realer' than that."

Such discussions will go on over the years, helping each boy sort out how family politics shape their brotherhood. As with anything else that children learn, there will be things that they understand now and complexities they will not be able to grasp until later. Yet to withhold all information until complete comprehension is possible deprives them of the opportunity to make things better between them now.

8

How Old Was I
When You Were Born?

The Impact of the Age Gap
Between Half Siblings

In all families, children worry about losing their special place in the family when a new child is born. In all families, every child's relationship with each parent is different from her brothers' and sisters'. In stepfamilies, however, the baby not only has a unique relationship with his mother and father based on their hopes and expectations and the emotional flavor of their union, but also has a relationship that is *structurally* different. The older child knows that her stepparent is her half sibling's "real" parent. The new child is seen as luckier, surely, in living with both parents, and the suspicion goes, more valuable because he's related directly to both. His birth hammers a final nail into the coffin of the older children's hopes that this new marriage won't last and their own two parents will reunite.

A fourteen-year-old boy typifies the replacement worries that plague older children as they anticipate the birth of a mutual child: "They want to have a baby, and I know that if they do, it will be just like a replacement for me. That's because I only see my dad on weekends, and since he would see the baby more than he would see me, he'd probably grow to like it more than he likes me."[1] In contrast, after the baby is born, most stepchildren discover unanticipated joy in his arrival, however much his existence underlines their own sense of deprivation. "It's especially wonderful now because I have a brand new sister, who's only two weeks old," said Kenny, at twelve, "and I love taking care of her. Of course, I can't help thinking how lucky she is that she's got these two parents who are staying together—parents who hold hands and who'll go to her class plays and go shopping together for her first bike. I'd say she's a bit luckier than I am, with my parents divorced."[2]

The birth of the child of remarriage realigns the relationships among siblings and stepsiblings, and from the child's point of view, with both parent and stepparent. But the displacement the children fear when such a birth is an abstraction is seldom matched by actual events. Parents seldom prove as disloyal as children anticipate, despite the distracting pragmatics of baby care, so that the children's deepest fears are not realized. Nor are the fondest hopes met. Liam, for example, began to lobby for a little brother or sister from the time he learned of his dad's impending remarriage. "Of course I love him," he bubbled at the hospital, "he's my brother." Yet when Liam's infant brother was two weeks old, he answered his teacher's question about the baby's welfare with "Oh, he died." While Liam, at seven, is more direct than most, ambivalence weighs heavily in the mix of ingredients in the relationships between half siblings. The emotional potpourri is seldom separated into its components: jealousy that parental affection may be spread thin, love for an endearing infant, envy of the mutual child's good fortune, and a protective wish that the new child be spared the pain and loneliness of a parental divorce or bereavement.

My husband remembers predicting his boys' response to our son's birth: "I knew it was going to do things that they didn't expect. They expected a baby, they didn't expect a brat, which all little brothers are. They expected a baby, they did not expect parents who were desperate to get some time to themselves. And they expected a baby, they didn't expect a priority, and babies tend to prioritize things that happen in a household."

How you tell children about the impending birth has much to do with what they expect. Parents who are apprehensive about the children's reactions can communicate their distress, signaling that the changes about to be wrought are ominous. One father, so guilty about remarrying and having another child that he postponed informing his children, ended up with hysteria at the dinner table of family friends who, unwittingly, conveyed the news most inopportunely. His fourteen-year-old daughter was antagonistic to the idea of a pregnancy and horrified at the baby's birth.

Preparation and education about how having a baby will affect family life, and a commitment to minimize changes for the older children, can ease the transition, but there is no way to totally anticipate the shifts in relationships that will ensue. The variables are multiple: What else is happening at the same time is critical, as a half sibling can be scapegoated by older children as the cause of disruptions occasioned by changes in a parent's work schedule, in neighborhoods, in schools, or in custody. The temperament of the mutual child is also a major ingredient, as an easy baby minimally disrupts family routines while a demanding one turns everything upside down. And the ages, gender, and birth order of the children of prior marriages are, of course, central, as is custody.

If a new baby arrives when the remarriage is still in its early stages, as was the case for more than half of the families I interviewed and for stepfamilies in general, family members have not yet had the opportunity to accommodate to one set of changes before another set is ushered in. Children still hope their parents will reunite and have not yet accepted a stepparent as a member of the family, with both rights and obligations. As the stepparent strives to feel like an insider in the new family, the children are fighting against being the new outsiders. A baby who is clearly on the inside track with both adults can be perceived as a usurper, or a replacement, especially when the older children are not regular members of the household.

Even in a middle-stage remarriage, adding a mutual child can delay or even impede stepfamily integration, as stepparents, diverted by the instant gratification of taking care of their own infants, retreat from the more difficult challenge of becoming "intimate outsiders" to their stepchildren. It is only when intimacy and authenticity in steprelationships have been achieved that the mutual child is received much as any other younger sibling would be: as a mixed blessing whose very existence introduces an unknown into the equation.

While the stage of stepfamily integration at the time of the mutual child's birth is a critical factor in how he is received by his siblings, the children's ages also come into play here.[3] Some age differences between children of past and present partnerships are clearly more favorable than others in setting the stage both for the initial welcome of the baby and for future relationships among half siblings.

Some intervals between children tend to be benign and others tend to be more risky. Such generalizations are, of course, not true for all pairs of children, since not all children develop at the same rate. Some intervals work particularly well at one time, only to become more difficult some years later. Barry, at ten, for example, was an attentive older brother when Eddie was born to his father and stepmother. Two years later, when the older sister who had responded with disgust to his birth became more interested in Eddie, Barry stepped back a bit from his half brother. "It was also the ages they were going through," said Elizabeth, Eddie's mother. "When Barry was twelve or thirteen, he didn't want to be identified with the little kids, right? He didn't know how to deal with a two- or three-year-old kid who was being bratty. Betty, at sixteen, seemed to be able to relate to Eddie from a more mature perspective. If Eddie wanted to play with Barry, he wouldn't give up, like most two- or three-year-olds, who want what they want, and keep pushing. Barry would just keep saying 'No, Eddie' and finally just push him off and get real cool toward him. Betty, even if she didn't want to do the thing, she might do it for two minutes and that would appease Eddie, and then he'd leave you alone. She could see it from that perspective."

The Preschool Child

Because most children in nuclear families have a sibling within five years of their age, the child who is five or under when a half sibling is born comes closest to the norm. Stepchildren are usually beyond their preschool years by the time stepfamily development has proceeded beyond the early stages of fantasy and "immersion." Of the families I spoke with, there were a few children who were five or under when their half siblings were born in early remarriage, two who were this age in middle remarriage, and none who were this young by the time the remarriage was established.

The stepchild who is of preschool age at the time of the birth of the mutual child is usually a youngest or an only child of the earlier marriage. In new stepfamilies, the parent–only-child pairing can remain very intense, carrying over from the days of single parenthood when it was "you and me against the world." For the preschool child, being alone with one parent may be all the child remembers, so that the parent's finding a partner may mean having to share previously undivided attention. If a baby comes along shortly thereafter, the dilution of attention can come as quite a shock. When the custodial parent, especially, has a baby, the older child can feel very much like an abandoned lover or "dethroned princess."

Denise is an example of an only child raised by a single mother from birth. Together they had crossed an ocean to make a new home; they had been everything to each other, done everything together. It had taken both of them a great deal of getting used to the fact that, in Denise's words, "There was a man in the house and she was actually married to that man." Denise was three and a half when her mother and stepfather set up housekeeping, and five and a half when her brother was born. From the outset, she was displeased by the baby's impending arrival. "I probably didn't like it," she told me, "because I guess I was small and really wanted things for myself." A friend who was an experienced big sister had warned her that it would be no fun; both girls agreed that once the baby was born there was not enough attention directed their way. "People would come over to see my brother. They would say 'hi,' and then go to see him." Hurt and angry at her mother's reduced availability, she was open in expressing her distress.

Her mother, Leslie, recalls breaking the news to Denise: "We said, 'We're going to have a baby brother or sister for you.' She laughed hysterically, jumped off the bed, and said, 'Wonderful, I'll stab it with a knife.' Everett and I nearly died. I think it was hysteria." After this initial outburst, Denise became more conventionally excited about her mother's pregnancy, wanting the baby to sleep at the bottom of her bed, offering to give it her clothes, and making plans for what she and the sister she hoped for would do together. When her mother's pregnancy took a difficult turn and miscarriage was raised as a possibility, she was fiercely protective and already attached: "Not our baby," she protested, "we want our baby."

When Oliver was born, Denise was initially a happy and excited "Mother's little helper." But when Grandma left to return home after five weeks of helping mother and children, Leslie went into a depression that further reduced her availability to her daughter. While Leslie remained depressed and withdrawn, Denise had trouble containing her aggressive impulses toward baby Oliver. She would ask to hold him, to feed him, to play with him, and then suddenly insist that her mother "take him back. Now. Right away." One day she told her mother, "You know, Mommy, I really want to hold him, but when I hug him something inside my head—it's not me, but something inside my head—gets all scrunched up, like this, and says it wants to bite him and punch him and kick him. So I say 'take him away,' cause he's just a little baby, and it would hurt." Leslie marveled at Denise's ability to acknowledge and describe her jealousy, appreciating that her daughter's articulateness made it possible for them to deal openly with the jealousy and for her to change her own behavior to better meet Denise's needs.

Very young children are the most open in expressing the negative side of their ambivalence to a new baby in the family. Frequently, they are very excited about having a sibling until after the baby is born and it becomes apparent that he really isn't going to be a playmate for what seems like a very long time. Three or four years later, the child may no longer remember her initial reaction to her half brother's birth. Her father may describe her as a "thrilled . . . little mother," and her stepmother recall her as essentially uninterested after the excitement of the first week: "It was like bringing a little puppy home. I was surprised she was not either more jealous or more involved. Everybody that she knew who had a brother, had a *brother*. One that could walk and talk. She said she thought she would have someone to play with."

It is for this group of very young children that it is less disruptive when Daddy has another child than when Mommy does, especially if, as is usual, Mommy is the parent to whom the child is closest. One solution to sharing Mommy is to share the baby as well, helping Mommy with the baby as a strategy for staying close to her.

The very young tend to express ambivalence about yet another change in the family by what they do, rather than by what they say, making their own dependency needs very apparent. One five-year-old, for example, spent her mother's pregnancy clinging to her: telling her how much she loved her all the time, wanting to sit by her and throwing her arms around her all the time. When her mother and stepfather argued, she became panicked, letting them know in no uncertain terms that no further changes would be tolerated.

Preschoolers in middle-stage remarried families have the advantage of having become more accustomed to sharing a parent with a stepparent before a half sibling is born. The earlier in a child's life he connects with a stepparent, the more receptive, open, and endearing he will be, making for greater mutual acceptance and deeper attachment. Unlike, for example, a young stepmother who enters the life of a teenager, the stepparent who is with a child from his earliest years will have an authority that is earned by providing nurturance before asking for obedience. Although they may test limits with all adults, toddlers and preschoolers are more ready to accept that adults, all adults, are in charge. Two to four years after the remarriage, children who are still preschoolers may well perceive their stepfamilies as firmly established. While all of the younger children, and many of the older ones, resent being disqualified as a "real" or full sibling to the baby, this is even more true for children in this group, who, like one four-year-old, can be devastated by a friend's remarks that the baby is "not your sister, she's your half sister."

As the Years Go By

When children are five or fewer years apart the half sibling relationship can be most "like a brother-sister relationship, like I remember with my brothers and sisters," in the words of one woman, who describes how her four-year-old son and nine-year-old stepdaughter "play great together," inventing things like an improvised seesaw in the backyard or a playhouse constructed of sofa cushions.

The most difficult time for children this close in age is when the mutual child is two and three years old. Eager to assert their own autonomy, two-year-olds are notorious for being strong-willed and oppositional, and for testing limits. Coming to terms with being a separate self, the two-year-old can snuggle cozily, only to push his parent or sibling away relentlessly. Indeed, even toddlers as young as sixteen months clearly know how to irritate their older siblings.[4] At its worst, the struggle for autonomy is concentrated on keeping rivals out. An older child who is protective of her ground can be both a challenge to the toddler's self-determination and a ready target for his obduracy. The emotional ups and downs of the two-year-old, his changeability and willfulness, the provocation of his testing the limits of his ability to make an impact on the world, especially the world of his family, can easily try her patience, making firmness and tolerance an impossible stance for the school-age child to adopt.[5]

"It wasn't until Ollie got to be about two that he got to be a real pain in the neck for Denise, who was then seven," said Leslie, the mother of both children. "He harassed her to death. It was awful!" What had he done? "I mean he was a normal two-year-old child. She was just distraught that he would come into her room and break things and make a mess. She's a gentle kid, and she would never hit him back. So, he'd go over and he'd pull at her. He wanted her to come into his room and play with him. He was nipping at her, nonstop. We weren't letting him harass her, but he did it every time our backs were turned. We said, 'Tell him that you're not going to let him do that to you.' She had a hard time saying that."

"I think he was jealous of her," Leslie theorized. "Because she's big, and she gets to do things he doesn't get to do. 'Why does Denise get to stay up late?' 'Why does Denise do this?' He just wanted control over everything. He was at that age, when everything had to be his. Her room was off-limits, and it drove him crazy. They were really great enemies the whole year he was two. They didn't like each other one bit. They had nothing in common: They're different sexes, different ages, different interests. She loves to read, and all he'd want is for her to play fire engines with him. And I felt, 'Well, they're just not going to be friends.' It made me sad, but I couldn't force them."

A year later, however, the worst of their conflict had worked itself out. Denise became braver. She locked her door and when Ollie barged in, she was more willing to push him right out again. "I think it was because he was no longer a baby," said their mother. "She didn't want to push him about because he was little. She felt like 'he's only little, I might hurt him,' and she knew we'd get mad if she did." As a strong-willed and sturdy three-year-old, he no longer seemed as if he would be injured by her anger, and she began to say "no." Because she can say "no," she can also say "yes" in a way not available to her earlier. At nine, she voluntarily goes to four-year-old Ollie's room to play. They play school, and he'll play dolls with her. "Still," Leslie continued, "he is a pain in the neck. Let's face it, what a nine-year-old wants and what a four-year-old wants are not often the same. Sometimes she'll say 'Oh, drag off' too."

While children seem to pick on one another most frequently, according to parents, when the mutual child is two to three, the older child is not always the chief target. Denise was inhibited in expressing aggression because of earlier fantasies during her mother's pregnancy of stabbing the baby, and later, in his infancy, had quickly handed him back to their mother when her aggressive impulses toward him frightened her. Because of this history, she was probably less willing to set limits with her half brother when she saw him as especially vulnerable.

Patty, on the other hand, was described by their father as "downright cruel" to Ivan, four years her junior. Her stepmother dates the turnaround to her son's growing autonomy: "He became more of a threat, more of a rival, when he was about three. Now he was becoming a child who could have real kid toys. He was a person in his own right, putting himself places, instead of being schlepped." Tim remembers many ups and downs in Ivan's five years. "On his part, it's always been a puppy dog adoration of his big sister. He would always have this thing where Patty was God, and she'd go from being just very mean, rejecting of him, putting in sly little digs and things. Other times she'd be real loving and helpful to him, teaching him to do things, show him how to count, teach him ABCs.

"The last year, they've been establishing a more equal relationship," Tim continued. "She's very accepting of him, very affectionate. She'll still play stunts like she'll trade him for things she doesn't want. So, we have to step in so he doesn't get screwed over. She's the bones of my body but I can see her being a very cold dealer in some ways." Patty, not surprisingly, differs from both adults in naming the time in Ivan's life that was most difficult for her, perhaps because present hardship is most vivid. "He was cutest when he was about two, and he's most pesty now," she told me, when they were five and nine, "because I have to share more things with him, and I have to take care of him sometimes. If I go outside, he wants to go bike riding with me, too, then I have to look after him when we go around and make sure he doesn't get hurt."

As the mutual child gets older and learns to play games, ride a bike, skate, or otherwise develops skills and interests similar to those of his older half sibling, they are more likely to engage in shared activities than are children separated by a greater span of years. Those half siblings who spend a great deal of time together become friends in a way that is not unlike that of full siblings. After years of being picked on by her remarried mother's first mutual child, Jessica has forgotten ever being mad at her half sister. The girls became very devoted to each other when Annie was four and Jessica almost ten. They began to play games together, and later Jessica could help Annie with her homework more effectively than either of her parents.

Most parents and stepparents of children this close in age describe their competition as "garden variety sibling rivalry," with the older child feeling pursued by the younger, who asks too many questions, wants to play, and won't leave the elder alone, even when his friends are there. When the older child wants to play, he will, but only when it suits him. Even their complaints of one another are the standard sibling complaints of older children who resent tag-along younger brothers and sisters, and younger children who feel unappreciated and shunted aside by their elders, protesting that being given lesser rights and privileges is "unfair." How closely relationships between half siblings five or fewer years apart approximate those between children who share both parents will depend on how much time they spend together and how well integrated their stepfamily has become.

Primary Age Children

Despite their greater understanding of family roles and realities, children between six and ten are more likely than their younger brothers and sisters to suffer a conflict in loyalty when a divorce remains contentious. Children in this age group are especially vulnerable to the stress of a custodial parent's remarriage.[6] All of the children in my study who had the most difficult time adjusting to a mutual child were between six and ten at the time of the birth.

Yet despite the greater vulnerability of children at this age, their family situation is still more important. Dramatic differences in welcoming a mutual child occur for these children, depending on how long the parent has been remarried. For those who are presented with a half sibling shortly after having to accommodate to a stepparent, the demands of yet another change can push them beyond their limits. In contrast, the child in an established remarriage, or even in the middle stages if the child was young enough when the stepparent entered the scene, has already accepted that stepparent as a part of the family and can much more readily make the leap to being a big brother or sister.

Tamara was eight and a half when her mother and stepfather had a baby girl in a recent remarriage. Describing her reaction to the news of the pregnancy, she waxes dramatic, using the kind of voice I expect my parents had in mind when they called me Sarah Bernhardt: "I had mixed feelings. First it was like, 'Oh, great, I'm going to have a little brother or sister.' Then it was like, 'Oh, God, a little twerp, and we're going to have to baby-sit all the time and change its diapers, and it's going to get all the attention. How boring. I wish she'd have an abortion or something.'" After Ilona was born, Tamara vied with her stepfather to be the family member who paid the most attention to the baby, even as she successfully let her mother know that she wanted more attention for herself as well.

The birth order of the children of the first marriage has much to do with how they view the prospect of a half sibling. Only and youngest children, because they have never experienced a new baby entering the family, are more likely than middle and oldest children to feel the most conflict about the change. As the younger of two children, Tamara wondered what changes her mother's pregnancy would bring. "I thought it would be maybe a hassle or maybe fun. It has turned out to be both," she reports.

While more concerned about having to share a parent with a still younger child and having to accommodate to a new family role when they are no longer "the baby," youngest children can be intrigued and curious as well as apprehensive about experiencing the unknown. Perhaps the greatest attraction is moving up a step on the ladder to the "more statusful" position of big brother or big sister. Four years later, one boy, for example, reports that at seven he was happy to get a chance to be "the oldest, older, instead of younger like I was before. I was always babied before and told to 'grow up' and stuff. This gave me a chance to play a different role."

Middle children are even more welcoming of a baby who will dethrone the reigning "baby" of the family, depriving a long-standing rival of his competitive edge. And oldest children, whatever the changes the mutual child brings to the household, are unchallenged in their position as firstborn and top of the pecking order. While many of the youngest and only children in this age range claimed that they were excited about the coming of the mutual child until it became apparent that there would be less attention for them, not all six- to ten-year-olds experienced the dilution of attention as a negative. One child, both of whose parents had remarried, was clearly relieved finally to have another child in his column after being the exclusive focus of four adults.

For most of these children, the new baby brings both fun and hassle. The fun lies in the entertainment value of infants. "It's nice to be around her," Tamara says of Ilona, "we don't get bored watching her." Other six- to ten-year-olds look to the baby as a resource against loneliness, resorting to playing with him or reading to him when they have nothing better to do. The hassles boil down to less attention and more chores. Cleaning up the baby's mess, or watching him while the adults are doing household tasks, feels like Cinderella drudgery to the primary age child who feels that being asked to do more than the baby can do "just isn't fair."

But there are other, unnamed hassles that have to do largely with the lack of progress along the remarriage developmental cycle. When a stepparent has his own child before he has been able to gain acceptance from and authority over, much less the affection of his stepchild, the baby can be a welcome distraction from the hard work of creating a family culture in which all can feel like insiders. In early and even middle remarriage, it is children in this age group, not young enough to require the kind of hands-on nurturance that facilitates bonding, nor old enough to get by without being babied from time to time, who have the hardest time not feeling displaced by a child being born to the remarriage. It is difficult to isolate the source of stress for Greg, age eight: the birth of a baby girl to his father and stepmother; missing the mother with whom he had lived until then; and a new teacher he hated, in a community that was new to him. "But I remember that her being born was not a good experience," he told me. "I was an only child and not used to having another person around. Annette became much less of a mother to me, because now she had her own kid to mother. And I was getting older, and I no longer needed attention as much as the baby did." True enough. He didn't need it as much as the baby did, but he needed more than he was getting as a newly transplanted eight-year-old. As a result, it was hard for him to welcome his half sister.

Contrast his response to Pamela's description of how she and her closest friends greeted her mother's and stepfather's baby: "We all used to play with her. We all used to worship her. We'd carry her around by her neck. It was probably too rough for a baby, but we were just trying to include her." The baby had arrived when Pamela was seven. Six months later her father and stepmother also had a girl. Both couples had been together more than six years before having a mutual child.

Even after three to five years, in stepfamilies that are not yet fully established, an older child can think of a baby as an impediment to his parents' reunification. Fears of being replaced are especially active in stepchildren who do not live in the household that is expecting the new child. Strategies for including such children are vital for the children to feel secure in their parent's affection and related to the mutual child. Parent after parent recounted calling from the recovery room, announcing the birth to their children even before they told their own parents, and arranging for early visits to the hospital, so the children could make a connection to the baby as soon as possible.

Although a child who spends relatively little time in the stepfamily has more fear of being replaced by the mutual child, children whose family membership feels ambiguous for other reasons also share this worry. By the time his half brother was born, Jason, at nine, had been lobbying for years for a brother or sister, having asked his mother and father, although divorced, to have a another child that would go back and forth between their households, as he himself did, an idea his father had dismissed as unworkable: "We were just not on sleeping terms with each other."

Jason's initial reaction to the news that his father and stepmother were expecting a baby was joyful excitement. Soon, however, fantasies that the baby would replace him became evident. His stepmother, Irma, recalls making "a dumb turn" while driving when Jason was on the side of the car that almost got hit. She remembers him commenting, "Well, if I get hit there'll be another baby. You'll have somebody else." His concern about being displaced may have been amplified by the delay in stepfamily integration in this family that resulted from the natural parents' exclusiveness in making decisions about Jason, as they kept both stepparents peripheral to the original triangle of mother, father, and child.

As the Years Go By

Not surprisingly, the relationship between half siblings continues to be most ambivalent when they are between six and ten years apart in age. Unlike half siblings more closely spaced, the older child's initial reception of the mutual child seems to set an enduring tone, with greater consistency between their initial relationship and how they get along later.

Contrasting his relationship with his father's son to his cousin's relationship to *his* younger brother, Jason observes that becoming a big brother for the first time is "much more drastic" at nine than it is at five, "because I had an established personality, it was much harder." From the perspective of greater distance, Larry, thirteen when his half brother was born, thinks that it helped that he was old enough "to probably realize that my parents might not get back together, so I better make the best of it. If you're seven or eight, you think of this new kid as taking away all the attention. Your dad can't go to the park with you, because he has to take care of the new baby brother. Your stepmother, you know, you blame it all on her, and then you take it out on that little kid. It could work out, but that's kind of the stereotype." This stereotype is, of course, more closely realized in early remarriage.

By and large, children this much older than their half siblings are the most vociferous in their complaints that they are discriminated against when they compare how they are treated with what happens with the mutual child. Jeremy, like many first children, feels that his mother has learned how to bring up children from her mistakes with him. "I feel that my mom is more lenient toward the younger kids in more ways than just age," he said. "My mom sometimes gives in to my younger brothers and rags on me all the time."

While six- to nine-year-olds seem to have the hardest time accepting an infant, with girls readier for a half sibling sooner than boys, the disruption caused by the mutual child's birth pales before what is to come when the mutual child reaches the "terrible twos" or the "defiant fours" just as this stepchild reaches preadolescence.

Even children who are pretty pleased about the birth of their half sibling agree that they begin to be "brats" at two, three, or four. With an infant, an older child can tell that the younger one has to be treated differently. When the little one begins to walk and talk and want to play with things like Legos and Matchbox cars and Barbie dolls that still interest the older child, big kids tend to treat the little ones more as peers than their development warrants. Unlike children still closer in age, those who are six to ten years older than their half siblings challenge the little ones to reach beyond their limits, tackling activities that may be too difficult or too dangerous. Unlike the still older children with more developmental savvy, these "big kids" refuse to indulge the immaturity of the little ones, insisting that all players abide by the same rules.

Noting that her son and his twelve-year-old half brother hang out together more than they did earlier, Amelia finds that there have been conflicts between her and her stepson about what it is appropriate to tell a three-year-old to do, even though Kevin is "fantastic" with Owen, taking care of him and playing with him: "Kevin's judgment about that is not the greatest. He'll pile up pillows and tell Owen to jump off the desk into the pillows. I'm always concerned that he's going to hurt himself. Working him up into a complete frenzy roughhousing, throwing him around and wrestling. Playing with guns, pellet guns, and things like that. He sort of has the assumption, since Owen is very verbal, that he's older than he is. He treats him more like one of his peers instead of a three-year-old. And, of course, Owen will do anything Kevin tells him to do, so that's a little nerve wracking."

When the older children are boys, and even more so when the mutual child is a little brother, parents tend to worry more about injuries to the little one, intervening in their brotherly battles in a way that serves to perpetuate the conflict. Mike, the father of three boys, now thinks that he and Irma made a mistake early on by intervening too much on the side of their mutual child, Ethan, who is nine years younger than his son, Jason. "When Jason was ten, eleven, twelve, he could not learn to be a gentle brother. As Ethan was moving into the twos, the terrible age, supposedly, Jason was reaching that kind of self-centered, arrogant, know-it-all period that kids get into." It was at that time that conflicts between the two boys grew. And Ethan learned, as a two- and three-year-old, that to get even with Jason all he had to do was scream, whereupon his parents would jump all over Jason, whether Jason had done something or not. And the cycle would repeat itself, with Jason taking his own revenge in turn.

From the perspective of a few more years, Jason, at fifteen, looks back at that time with an ability to think abstractly about himself that was unavailable to him at eleven: "I felt he was very spoiled and demanding of my parents' time. A lot of little things, like he would go into my room. He wouldn't understand what he was doing, but he'd do things that pissed me off. I'd pick him up and throw him out, and he'd start crying. My parents would, of course, say, 'Jason, you don't have to get that angry, he doesn't understand.' And I'd say, 'That's not true, he does understand.' And, you know, I didn't know any different."

Witnessing the development of Ezra, born when he was fourteen, has also helped Jason come to a new understanding. "I watch Ethan with Ezra," Jason said, "and I know that Ezra doesn't understand. It was hard to accept then, because it was always brought up in my face: "Act your age. Don't act like a two-year-old, don't bring yourself down to his level.' It was hard to understand what they were talking about, and it infuriated me. It's like, 'Damn you, I'm acting my age, I'm just getting in a fight with my brother.' "

There is something to the older children's belief that the needs of the little ones take priority. As children tend to attribute control beyond their years to their preschool siblings, so, too, do parents often expect too much maturity from teenagers, leaving parents frustrated and teens resentful. Especially when there are young children at home, parents can forget that teenagers are not really grown up. Even when teenagers are willing to be helpful when asked to lend a hand, they are perfectly capable of sitting there in the midst of chaos without seeing that something has to be done. Nor will it be apparent to a teenager that stirring up a small child with tickles and wrestling will charge up the little dynamo so that sleep or quiet play become impossible.

As the mutual child enters school and his half sibling approaches or is well into his teens, distance between them grows. The older child moves more into the world of his peers and the younger, too, becomes more involved in activities outside the family. There is usually less conflict at this time, with "the usual sibling stuff" becoming more prominent than residual stepfamily issues. "She's really interested in her own life, her own activities," said Eleanor, stepmother of fifteen-year-old Pamela. "She both hates and kind of likes that the little ones tease her about her boyfriend. She'll stand there and look absolutely mortified, but she's getting a big kick out of it. She knows they all look up to her. She's the teen idol. They love her earrings and her makeup. They get the biggest pleasure out of eavesdropping on her, when she has slumber parties. They come downstairs and giggle: 'Pam's talking on the phone to a boy. Hee hee.' "

Pamela herself agrees: "I'm in a totally different place in my life than my little kids. I always call them 'my little kids,' " she says, referring to her father's and stepmother's mutual children, born when she was seven, nine, and eleven. "If I have something I'd rather be doing, then I don't want to see them. But if I'm just home and not doing anything, I'll spend time with them. If I'm bored, then they can come up to my room and I'll play with them, but I can think of things I'd rather do."

While she enjoys watching them grow up, Pamela has her pet peeves: "I bring a new boy to the house, and Alissa, who's eight, will mistake him for the last boyfriend. That's really embarrassing," she said. "Or Isaac, who's four, will sit out there and chant 'Pam has a boyfriend.' Or I'll come downstairs with a boy and they'll ask, 'Did you kiss him, Pam?' And he's standing right there, and we'll be just really embarrassed. But that's mostly in fun, and I think it's kind of cute, pretty much."

As the stepchild becomes more comfortably settled into her own identity, the younger children are less able to derail her with affectionate teasing. By the time the stepchild is into her middle teens, the mutual child who is six to ten years younger is a familiar part of the background in her life, no longer the focus, in most instances, of resentment and longings that would rewrite the past. Instead, the teenager is looking to the future, to her own life as an adult. As she moves into her late teens, she sees herself as a model for the younger children, an opportunity for them to preview their own growing up, and a link between the generations. As one twenty-year-old, who enjoys being something of an idol to his eleven-year-old half sister, says, "As Amber becomes more of a teenager, I know I'll be looking out for her to make sure she doesn't make any mistakes. I'm not going to be condemning or anything, but I will be protecting. I can talk more and more every day about adult things with Amber. As she becomes an adult, I'll treat her as an adult."

The Preteen Years

Although the cautions that apply to having a mutual child in early remarriage still stand, ten- to-thirteen year olds are in many ways the most receptive of all stepchildren to the prospect of a mutual child. If the developmental tasks of the previous period, a focus on acquiring new skills and moving from a family-centered life to more activities with peers, have been successfully mastered, the preteen is ready to give up being "the baby."

Ready to feel "grown up," only and youngest children, especially, like the feeling of being the older person and that there is someone to whom they have something to teach. When the mutual child is still an infant and toddler, the age gap between baby and preteen is big enough for the older child to have some developmental perspective on what the baby needs and what to expect from him. It is at this age that the older children were the most nurturant. One twelve-year-old, an only child until both his mother and stepmother had babies within five months of each other, talked of his reluctance for them to have more children soon, although he is devoted to both babies: "I wouldn't love having more right now, because it would be one baby in each of my arms, instead of one in both arms and one walking around and doing something." His response underlines how much he thinks of himself as a nurturer of his half siblings. Other preteens are described by parents as "baby-happy" cuddlers and caretakers, happy to put the infant in a Snugli and show him off to friends.

When my son was an infant and going through a colicky period, crying for two hours morning and night, Antonio, then ten, would walk up and down, carrying David in his arms and singing to him. David was frequently comforted by this, and Antonio looked calmest and most content as he soothed his baby brother. Preteens are often skittish about cuddling with parents, feeling that to accept nurturance from adults in this way has a regressive pull that threatens their aspirations to maturity. Babies, however, provide an avenue to physical closeness that gives comfort even as it saves face: Because the older child is the giver of care, rather than its recipient, he can experience the reassurance and comfort of contact without appearing needy. Part of the attraction of babies for this age group, no longer cuddling much with parents and not yet cuddling with dates, is the opportunity they provide to nurture and, in doing so, be nurtured.

Another by-product of taking care of infants is the feeling of being grown up it confers. The pleasure of taking care of infants and the feeling of pride in changed status can occur independently of the stage of the remarriage. When the baby quickly follows the recoupling, however, the pleasures are mitigated by having to accommodate to too much too soon. "There wouldn't have been so much jealousy with a full-blooded sister," Nathaniel said of the half sister born when he was eleven, "because you wouldn't feel like your mother was taken." But further inquiry revealed that the person who he really felt had taken his mother was not his baby sister, but her father. Accepting a stepparent takes longer for children in this age group than for their younger brothers and sisters, and the rapid arrival of another child can feel like a further encroachment on his access to his parent.

One strategy that preteens whose mothers and stepfathers have a baby in early remarriage use to counter their fear that the family is forming in another corner is to vie with their stepparent for the third position in the triangle with mother and baby. Eliot remembers how his stepson George, then ten, would fight with him about who got to hold the baby. "I would say, 'It's my first baby.' And he would say, 'It's my sister.' " Eliot recognized that by taking the baby from him and giving her to his mother, George was "forming the family with Maggie and the baby, because there was this relationship with me that was not quite the same as it was to the new baby." The mutual child, as the only blood relative of all stepfamily members, belongs to everyone. The older child knows that the baby legitimates the stepparent's role in the family in a new way. Wooing the baby is his insurance against his own exclusion.

Although girls as well as boys were competitive with stepfathers as nurturers of their infant half siblings, boys were more likely to nourish fantasies of replacing their stepfather as the baby's other parent. Julia remembers how her son, Jeremy, used to pretend he was the father of both of his half brothers when they were little. "I would just overhear it," she said. "He would tell them to call him 'Daddy.' Talk about little Oedipus. He didn't do it in front of anybody else, but before the kids were verbal, he would play little games with them, where he'd say 'Come to Daddy' and pick them up." Jeremy himself recounts how he learned of the first baby's arrival: "I was at my uncle's. And he came in and said, 'You've had a son . . . a son, you've had a brother.' "

Girls who are especially close to Daddy can also compete with their stepmother over who is to be the third in a family triumvirate. While she attributes her desire to take over the care of her half sister to her own hunger for love, following her mother's death, rather than to a desire to feel that Daddy's baby was also hers, Joanne embarked on an inexplicit strategy of giving to the baby what she wanted for herself. As an adult, she recalls, "I think I started taking that baby over just about as soon as she was announced. My fantasies weren't specific, they just had a warm, snuggly feel to them. I just wanted that baby . . . to hold and play with." Her voice became tender as she told how tiny the baby was, how often she fed her, how much she worried the baby wasn't eating enough. "I remember feeling, not sibling rivalry, kind of the opposite: some kind of rivalry with my stepmother over possession of her. And I couldn't win because I had to go to school every day, and also because I had ambivalence. I also wanted to play with my friends and go places. And I was becoming an adolescent. I felt she was mine, and I wasn't getting to have her enough. A lot was getting worked out through this relationship, it was a good thing that the other babies came along soon. To save her from my clutches."

Preteens in established stepfamilies also seek to fill their needs for love and closeness by becoming special caregivers to the children of those remarriages, but they tend to feel less "needy" than those for whom the sequence of changes has been rapid. These children are generally described as helpful and curious about babies, celebrating their arrival.

It is important to remember that two children of the same age, same custody arrangement, same gender, and even same family can have markedly different responses to a parent and stepparent having a child together, based on the patterns of alliances in their first family. In general, however, in the established stepfamily, all of the themes of preteen enjoyment of babies, common even in earlier stepfamily stages, are amplified. It is for this group that the relationship between half siblings, if they live in the same household, more closely approximates the relationship between any two children in the same family who are separated by this span of years. As in any family, the "kind of baby" makes a difference. With a baby that goes to sleep in the evening and sleeps all night, the parents' time with an older child may be little affected. When luck smiles in this way, the baby's arrival does not detract from the attention a child in this age group needs and enjoys.

As the Years Go By

While there are ups and downs in all sibling relationships, siblings separated by ten to thirteen years tend to weather the squalls of development with enough distance to allow for some equanimity but not so much as to produce remoteness. Eleven years older than her half sister, Paula, at eighteen, finds that age difference has worked out well: "If I were younger, we would have run into more problems. I would have been a bit too close. I'd still be more of a kid. I hadn't reached teenager yet, so there wasn't that big difference in terms of being a kid and someone trying to be an adult. The only disadvantage of the eleven years between us is that Angela doesn't get to have siblings close to her age. When I was her age and my friends would tell me that they had older brothers and sisters who were off in college, I would always think, 'Oh, they don't count.' So if I were any older, I think she would have missed out, and it would have been a lot more work to get to know her if I hadn't had those few extra years with her."

Because they consider themselves in a different league than the little ones, competition is less intense than when the stepchildren are younger at the mutual child's birth. At this age they are more likely to attribute differences in the way they are treated to the age gap than to insist that fairness means that all the children receive the same goods and perform the same services. Even the hassles of accommodating to life with a small child are expressed in matter-of-fact terms, taking the disadvantages into account, but without a great sense of deprivation.

Veneration by the little ones enhances the sense of competence and maturity of those a decade or so older. "I'm like a God to her," said one eleven-year-old about her toddler sister, "and she's a little munchkin." "I can see myself going off to college, and I can see him looking up at me with awe," said Michelle at twelve about eighteen-month-old Evan. Her full brother Vincent, just two years younger than she, never holds her in awe. "I don't want Evan to be older," she continued, "because I like being big." She knows she is, and enjoys being, "one of his favorite people in the world," according to his parents.

Although the feeling that their station in life is impressive to the much younger mutual child is an advantage for the ten- to thirteen-year-old, there is also the attraction of being able to regress comfortably, with a good excuse. Susan describes how Carl and his friends, at twelve, thought two-year-old Eric was "a kick. It allowed these pre-pubescent boys to have a kind of second childhood. They'd get down on the floor and play with him, and they played with his toys when Eric wasn't even there. It gave them a chance to be little kids again. An excuse. He kind of allowed everybody to have some fun." I saw the same scene at our house, where ten-year-olds occasionally enjoyed drinking from baby bottles and twelve-year-olds would squeeze themselves into a pint-size rocker or behind the wheel of a Big Wheel, or sit happily watching cartoons from atop a Fisher-Price School Bus.

As with most siblings separated by many years, however, time together is usually spent with older ones taking care of the little ones, teaching more than playing. Although they can and do play together, the age difference makes them more like "an older sister-auntie," in Paula's terms, rather than siblings who are playmates. The analogy between older half siblings and uncles and aunts is one that comes up frequently. Yet asked to choose, the older children do, in balance, feel more sisterly and brotherly than avuncular to the mutual child. "They're so much younger than me," said one young woman, twelve years older than her oldest half sister, "at the same time they're sisters, and they can irritate the hell out of me. They feel like sisters, not like cousins or somebody else's kid. I tell them what to do, and they listen to me, but we still talk like we're sisters. Like, 'Shut up,' 'Leave me alone.' I think I'd treat a niece differently. I wouldn't feel so much like I could tell them what to do."

The disadvantage for the older children is that the demands of the younger child can be so much more compelling that "the progress of the newborn would become a greater point of focus than the progress of the teenager." This is especially true in large families. "A new child is very dramatic about his or her wishes and needs," said Kathy, twelve years older than her half sister, "they just scream." Knowing how busy her parents were, she thinks she got in the habit of putting her own needs on hold. Her advice to others in her position is to be more assertive than she herself was: "Parents should tell the twelve-year-old to stop and think, 'Is this a time when I've got to say "Mom and Dad, listen, I've really got to talk to you. I don't care how busy you are." Or is this a time when I can just let it go by?' "

Notwithstanding the increasing demands on parents of a new child, the unabashed adulation a baby or toddler has for a sibling ten or more years his senior is often a palpable benefit to the older child, who basks in the sunlight of such uncritical acceptance at a time when his own uncertainties and occasional truculence make parents a less consistent source of approval. It is only when the mutual child becomes more of a person to be reckoned with, walking and talking, that the picture becomes less one-dimensional. Carl dates the shift in his relationship with Eric, ten years his junior, to the time that Eric learned to talk. "Every now and then he gets on my nerves," he said, "when I'm trying to do something. He's just into disagreeing. You say something that's true, and he'll say, 'No, you're wrong.' " The preschooler is experimenting with experiencing himself as an agent in control of his own life. Just making a counterassertion to one of the more powerful people in his family can feel like a badge of courage, a declaration of independence. No matter that it is arbitrary and ill-informed. It is his flag, and he hoists it up the flagpole, demanding that all salute. No wonder that the early adolescent, himself dealing with identity and autonomy issues at another level, finds the three- and four-year-old a particular pest.

Unlike those of children separated by fewer years, the hassles between preschoolers and young teenagers are likely to be less protracted, with more nurturing interludes. Once the fracas is over, a fourteen-year-old is more likely than his twelve-year-old brother to put his cognitive skills to good use and recognize that a four-year-old is not his peer and can't be expected to demonstrate the same level of maturity. Slight irritation, rather than a battle royal, can be his response to the intrusions of a little hanger-on.

Perhaps, too, the stepchild who is fourteen or older by the time the mutual child reaches "the brat age" is less affected by the younger one's willfulness in that the teenager has become more involved with what the rest of the world can provide and is striving not for a bigger slice of the pie of parental attention, but for more latitude to make his own decisions.

Even when they are happy to pursue their own interests in the world of their peers, teenagers who see the younger children, rather than their own evolving desires, as the reason for their getting less attention from their parents can come to resent the early childhood focus in the remarried family with young mutual children. "They were *Sesame Street* and I was rock 'n' roll," said one woman, thinking back to when she was a teenager and her half sisters were preschoolers. "Everything revolved around them. The TV was always tuned to *Mr. Rogers' Neighborhood* or *Sesame Street.*"

The level of competition between siblings more than ten years apart will depend partly on the number of children in the family, the size of the pie to be divided among them, and the arena in which competition arises. Between three and five, children are consolidating their sense of what it means to be a boy or a girl, and with the rigid zealousness of a convert, they divide the world into boy toys and girl toys, boy behavior and girl behavior, insisting on a consistency that frequently cannot be matched in either home or community. Part of learning about gender is getting to know themselves as sexual beings, playing at courtship, and directing their affection, typically, at the opposite-sex parent, whose role is both to acknowledge their sexual identity and to graciously decline to be a partner in the child's fantasy of "marrying Mommy or Daddy." Seeing a younger child of the same sex flirt with the opposite-sex parent can awaken old longings for intimacy with the parent at a time when a teenager's developmental task is to make a romantic choice outside the family.

With children separated by ten to thirteen years, by the time the mutual child enters school the older children are in their middle to late teens. For most families, this is a time of decreasing rivalry and, even when they share a household, decreasing contact. The younger children have moved out of what the older ones consider the "brat stage" and settled into acquiring skills, learning, striving for mastery. And the older children are concerned with trying out who they are to be in the larger arena of the extrafamilial world.

As the younger children themselves become preteens, the age that the older children were when they were born, they again become more interesting to their newly adult big sisters and brothers, who see them with fresh eyes. Instead of being part of the scenery in their parent's home, the mutual child is now embarking on his own quest for identity, with more of his own ideas and opinions, and frequently, a more explicit desire to make contact with the sometimes elusive figures that the children of a parent's earlier marriage have been in their lives, especially when contact has been minimal.

Jane, at twenty-three, was shocked by eleven-year-old Amber's re-membering to bring to her a book she had asked to borrow and then forgotten. "Maybe she has a lot more invested in the relationship than I do," she wondered. "Maybe she would be the one who was more likely to make the first move in trying to maintain some kind of friendship." Thinking back to her own childhood, she remembered that, as an oldest child, she had always wanted an older brother or sister. "There's that fantasy, you know, that every older sibling must have. She's almost an adolescent and maybe knowing older people, having access to the adult world is important to her. My brother and sister and I would be easier to access than her parents, because we're certainly closer in age to her. This is all hypothetical."

From the point of view of the mutual child, Jane's hypotheses have merit. As preteens, beginning to question "official" versions of family history and to work out for themselves just who each person in the family is to them, they find themselves fascinated by their half siblings: who they are, what their example teaches, and what is possible between them. The older children's lives provide a model for thinking about their own lives. It is by watching these much older siblings that they learn what it is like to date, to work, to leave home, to marry, and to have children. In watching the big kids move through their develop-mental paces, the little ones rehearse what it will be like when they themselves come of age. They sift the choices they'd like to emulate from those they'd like to avoid. And they seek to get to know better the half siblings whose lack of interest in them often feels like an undeserved rebuke.

Teenagers

Older teens, more involved in separating from the family than jealously guarding their place in it, are, even in early remarriage, less apt to feel displaced by a new baby than are their younger brothers and sisters. For an only child, the mutual child can feel like a belated fulfillment of an abandoned dream. While Sol was concerned that, after seventeen years as an only child, Dan would have difficulty in accepting his having another child with his new wife, Dan reports feeling "intrigued, so slightly positive, I think I had a lot of joy for my father." Sol remembers that Dan came back from the walk during which he was told of the pregnancy and embraced his stepmother. Later he became very attached to the daughter she gave birth to. "Esther's my sister," Dan told me. "She's the closest person in my new family to me. I have great admiration for her and love her and would do anything to see that she is happy and successful when she grows up."

For Dan, who had never had a brother or sister, the benefits of being an older brother clearly outweighed any continuing tension with his stepmother, allowing him wholeheartedly to embrace her daughter. In contrast, a boy of fourteen, already an older brother, had difficulty transcending the blame he placed on his stepmother for his parents' divorce in his initial response to the child she had with his father. On learning—alas, from his mother—that his father's girlfriend was pregnant, his immediate reaction was that it was a mistake that would be ended in abortion. When that did not happen, he concluded that the marriage that then occurred, although planned before the pregnancy, was a shotgun wedding. Although he denies resenting the baby, he described him in extremely unflattering terms: "He was a fish. He was the ugliest kid. He's totally changed now, but that's my first memory: a no-good kid." Slowly, his curiosity and intelligence led him to get to know his half brother. "It's hard to explain the feeling when you see a brand new baby," he told me. "It's kind of interesting."

More aware of the pragmatic matters of child care and family finances, teenagers receive the news of another child with a view to what it's going to mean in their own day-to-day life. Those who already have a brother or sister are less excited than those who don't, and the more children there are, the more these youngsters become concerned about lack of space, lack of money, and lack of a parent's time. Although loving both his half sister and half brother, one man felt that the strains on family life were more exacting in his father's remarried family with six children than in his mother's family when she had a third child with her new husband.

Perhaps more than any other age group, teenagers are uncomfortable thinking of their parents as sexual, as they themselves begin to explore their own sexuality. Pregnancy and birth are obvious reminders that their parent is having a sexual life. Disgust is not infrequent as an initial reaction to news that a parent is about to reproduce again. Fifteen-year-old Gwen was riding in a car with her father and stepmother when the radio revealed the news that Frank Sinatra and Mia Farrow had just married. "I went on and on about how disgusting it was because he was so old and she was so young and what if they ever had a baby," Gwen remembered. "And in the next breath, my father told me that my stepmother was pregnant."

While girls who are allied with their mothers, especially if their parents' marriage ended in divorce, may persist in feeling disgust for some time, those girls who had always been "Daddy's little girl" sometimes find themselves fantasizing that the baby is theirs. Gwen's initial response to the news of her stepmother's pregnancy was to be "in shock." She focused her distress at the news by developing an obsession with the sex of the baby: Unconcerned about a baby boy as a source of competition, since her father had been far closer to her than to her brother, she dreaded the possibility of another girl. When the inevitable came to pass, and her half sister was born, she was very upset. Her response, more dramatic than most, was to become pregnant almost immediately.

In some ways, she confuses the two pregnancies: "When my stepmother was pregnant . . . actually it was when I was pregnant, I came out with a Freudian slip about it being Daddy's baby." Although the high school guidance counselor to whom she was talking at the time had to call her attention to what she had said, her own mother did much to support the notion that it was her father who was responsible for impregnating her. When Gwen's mother found out about her daughter's pregnancy, she immediately got on the phone with her ex-husband and started screaming at him that it was all his fault. In fantasy, Gwen expressed her wish to remain close to her father, reversing the betrayal of his abandonment by playing out her identification with her stepmother. In reality, she succeeded in getting him to take care of her, as it was he who arranged for an abortion in the distant state to which he had moved, therefore allowing her to see him for the only time that year.

It was when she was there for her abortion that she met her father's three-month-old daughter. To her surprise, she found that she was no longer upset that he had another girl: "She was a baby, and I couldn't hate her. I think I sort of projected on her all this malicious intent to take him away from me. And when I saw her as an infant, it was obvious that she wasn't doing anything malicious." If anything, her own observation and her stepmother's report convinced her that her father was nowhere near as attached to the baby as he had been to her. Ironically, she ended up pleading with him to be more attentive to the baby, whom he would abandon five years later.

Two years later, when Gwen moved in with her father's family, being a sister meant something else again. While she enjoyed playing with the two-year-old, Gwen found that "strangers thought she was my baby," a reaction she found peculiar and difficult. By this time, she understood how her pregnancy had been connected with her father's having a child. "So then to be out in the world and have people make that association was hard. It was embarrassing, almost as if people were aware of this secret."

Even young women who have neither been pregnant nor fantasized about having Daddy's baby find it uncomfortable to be mistaken for the baby's mother. It suggests forbidden wishes. While one thirteen-year-old loved to parade down the aisles of the supermarket with her half sister in the basket, hoping people would think it was her baby, several of the seventeen- and eighteen-year-olds, for whom such a mistake comes closer to possibility, found the suggestion humiliating.

Despite Gwen's experience, parent after parent told me that having a child has been "the ideal teenage birth control program." The young people see firsthand that babies, while cute, "are a hell of a lot of work." And the teenagers themselves emphasize that that lesson has been driven home. Several volunteered that one side effect of the mutual child has been their own decision to defer childbearing until they feel ready to take on responsibilities whose multitude and weight are clearly etched in their minds.

Later in the remarriage developmental process, teenagers' response to a new child depends primarily on what else is going on for them in the stepfamily. While most teenagers deny that their relationship with a half sibling has anything to do with how they feel about the parent and stepparent who are that child's mother and father, conflict between teenager and adults strongly influences how much contact there will be between the new child and the older ones. Teenagers who are not getting along in custodial remarried families tend to leave, either to live with their other biological parent or to emancipate prematurely.[7] Teenagers who are already on a visiting basis with a remarried parent visit less frequently when conflict persists. In either case, the child born into the remarriage has minimal contact with those who are so much older than he that, biologically at least, they could be his parents.

Even when the remarriage is fully established, and relationships between stepparent and stepchild are affectionate and open, the mutual child is not a particularly momentous event in the life of children this much older. Sharing a roof or, more important, being a last chance at having a brother or sister makes the baby more compelling, but most middle and late teens minimize the impact of their parent's having another child on their own lives. Bonnie, almost seventeen when her half sister was born, remembers that she was "not all that interested, probably my usual, 'Sure, why not? If that's what you want to do.' " In retrospect, she thinks she might also have worried about whether she and her sister would be less important to her father now that he had another family. "I remember thinking those things when he got married, so I probably thought it again when he had children." But whether it is an affectation or not, many of the teens who are ready to move out and move on with their own lives take the stance, with Ken, that "you just expect a new baby to be around. If you're the parent you have to worry about it, but if you're just the brother there's nothing to it."

As the Years Go By

The stepchild whose remarried parent has a mutual child when the older child is well into adolescence experiences the pulling inward of the nesting couple and its new young as at variance with his own developmental agenda. The teenager's need at this point is to stay connected, even as he ventures farther and farther from the nest. The danger is that the boundaries of the stepfamily, ordinarily firmer and more protective when the children are young, will create so much of a cloister that the adolescent is either developmentally delayed, staying inside to guard his place in the family from real or anticipated encroachment, or prematurely shut out by an impermeable fence that seems to demand that he be either wholly in or altogether out.

Late teenagers who already have siblings tend to be minimally involved with a mutual child. My stepson Sean was nearly seventeen when David was born. Their father described Sean's attitude toward the baby as that of a Victorian uncle: He liked to pick David up, throw him in the air, and then hand him to someone else to take care of. Judy liked babies, and was interested when her mother had her first mutual child when Judy was twelve. By the time the last of them arrived, she was seventeen and "they were more like dolls," someone to play with briefly before moving on to her own interests. A sixteen-year-old boy was intrigued by his half brother, "but sort of as a stuffed animal," according to his stepmother. He'd dress him up and do silly things with him, but become very irritable when the baby cried or distracted him from his conversations with the adults.

Even with fourteen or more years between them, the mutual child is most unpopular with half siblings when he is between two and five. Especially protective of their privacy, the older children don't appreciate the youngster's difficulties in respecting closed doors. Just having a family can seem an embarrassment to older teenagers, who would prefer to think of themselves as completely independent.

Visiting stepchildren find the age difference an impediment to the kinds of activities they had previously enjoyed with the adults. On a vacation with her dad and his three-year-old daughter, for example, one seventeen-year-old complained that "there were a lot of things my dad and I could have done, go out for late dinners, go out in the evening, that just weren't possible with a younger child around. The activities were very child-centered, and it just wasn't fun." Openly resentful of the attention showered on toddlers, teenagers nonetheless often ward off parents' attempts to be more involved with their older children, asking for more attention and yet avoiding contact. A sixteen-year-old boy, for example, hated the way his colicky baby half sister and her toddler brother cried. He opted out of family dinners, because of "the way the conversation was dominated by the needs of the kids," yet he was unwilling to reserve time to be alone with his parents, preferring to be with his peers. While this can be frustrating to parents, who feel "damned if they do and damned if they don't" pay attention to the older children, it fits with the adolescents' need to regulate their intimacy with parents.

When fourteen or more years divide a parent's first set of children from the children of remarriage, both sides of the divide find the gulf hard to bridge. A mutual child, just graduated from high school, observed: "To start off with, my oldest sister is twice my age. She was my age when I was born, and that is a *big, big* gap. She never really tried to find out what was going on in my life and to really be around me much. I can't blame it on her. I think I have a lot to do with it too, but I also feel that, when I was thirteen, I didn't know to try. I just know I felt put off."

Her father's oldest daughter, the sister in question, also felt the distance: "In a way she felt like she could have been my child, because I'm so much older. For a while I had stepchildren who are older than she is, and I only lived in the house for about six months after she was born. I don't feel I know her as well as I'd like to. There are a lot of areas of likeness, but they haven't been exercised very much." Although both women feel saddened by their lack of contact, over the years each experienced the other as more or less uninterested in reaching out.

Knowing that for very young children it is hard to maintain a sense of attachment over long separations, their older half siblings worry that ordinary developmental transitions will create insuperable obstacles to having a continued relationship. Jason, at fifteen, looks ahead to leaving home to go to college, and is troubled by what that may mean for the younger of his father's two mutual children, fourteen years his junior. "By the time Ezra's become a personality, I'll be in my last year of high school," he said. "I'll be off on my own and a man by then. I think that will be a problem in terms of the two of us being close." Because Ezra "is at an age when he could tend to forget me some," Jason plans to attend a college that is less than a day's drive away, "where it won't cost a fortune to call."

These very much older half siblings can begin to feel like "parent-brothers, more on the brother side," as one sixteen-year-old put it.

Speaking of his mother's son, born when he was seventeen, a young man said, "I could be his father. I never fight with him. There's a big enough gap there so that most of that strife and jealousy, resentment or whatever, just isn't there. I mostly take care of the kids when I go over. It's not like being an uncle, I'm more a part of the family than that. The only thing is I don't live there."

Even when there are a great many years separating the children of each of a parent's marriages, if there is continued regular contact, both sets of children can feel enriched by the more complex generational texture of the family. Andrea, at seventeen, has a nineteen-year-old sister, and a half brother and sister, thirteen and fifteen years older than she is, who spent little time in the same household. "I think it's neat to have a brother and sisters so much older than you are," she says. "They're more people you can look up to but without the obligation of disciplining you. They can take care of you, but they're not like your parents. Because they're so much older, you don't fight with them the way siblings do, but at the same time you're closer to them than you are to extended family, like grandparents or something." Very much a *second* mutual child, she concludes, "I don't think it changes a family that much."

Don't Tread on Me

While optimal spacing between half siblings may not be possible for any number of reasons, some age differences between half siblings seem to work better than others. The following chart presents a summary of how the age of the older child and the length of the remarriage combine to make the timing of the mutual child's birth either more auspicious or more problematic.

The chart refers to "varied" outcomes when it is difficult to collapse the range of either ages or marital duration to come up with a consistent prediction. For example, a three-year-old whose parent has been remarried for two years, or a six-year-old in a stepfamily that has been together for five years when a half sibling is born, would have a relatively smooth time adjusting to this change in family membership. In contrast, the five-year-old in a brand new stepfamily or the nine-year-old whose parent has another child only three years after remarrying can be expected to have a more difficult time of it. As a rule, the

Probable Outcome for Each Stage of Stepfamily Development at Mutual Child's Birth

Age of older child	Early Remarriage (0–2 years)	Middle Remarriage (3–5 years)	Established Remarriage (4–7 years)
2–5 years	Varied	Fine but infrequent	Optimal but rare
6–10 years	Very difficult	Varied	Better
10–13 years	Difficult, but better than for most ages	Better	Optimal
14-plus years	Difficult	Better	Okay

younger the child and the longer the remarriage, the better the predicted outcome. While this may sound contradictory at first, it means that younger children require less time to feel established in stepfamily life.

All of the more conflictual half sibling relationships occurred between a first mutual child and the six- to nine-year-old stepchild who had been his parents' youngest child. Boys in this age group seemed to have a particularly hard time welcoming a new addition, and conflict was most intense when both of the children so spaced were male. When half siblings are between ten and thirteen years apart, however, the older children seem ready to take a more nurturing stance toward the younger and are intellectually better prepared than their younger brothers and sisters to have developmentally appropriate expectations of a new baby. Unlike even older children, whose interests and intimacy needs are directed still more outside the family, the ten- to thirteen-year-old typically takes the opportunity to spend more time with a new baby, developing an attachment that can be very gratifying to both older and younger child.

The age of a stepchild when a mutual child is born is inextricably linked to when in her developmental history other important family transitions occurred. For example, the child whose stepfamily has a baby by the time she is five has typically experienced her own parents' separation very early on. She often does not remember a time when her parents lived together, nor does she recall the more trying times of the marital disruption. Her stepparent arrived on the scene well before she entered kindergarten, making for what is typically a readier acceptance of another nurturing adult. This does not mean that her adjustment to having another child in the family will be a piece of cake, but rather that the added stress of stepfamily life will not be a major aggravation of the normal, expectable difficulties that children in this age group in nuclear families have in accommodating to the birth of a sibling.

Perhaps what makes it more difficult for six- to nine-year-olds to have a half sibling is not that they have lived six to nine years on this earth, but rather how old they were when they experienced parental death or divorce and remarriage. Again, thinking of the boys who had the hardest time feeling secure in their own place in the stepfamily and accepting the baby with relative equanimity, most also had experienced parental death or divorce when they were four to five years old, a time that is traditionally characterized by increased rivalry with the father and affectionate closeness with the mother.[8] To have a parent disappear at this time, or to seem to be the victor in a competition over who will be included in the most intimate twosome in the family, can leave a lasting sense of anxiety and give rise to fear of their own replaceability. For children of this age, it is a nearly impossible task to see a parent's departure as not directed at them. When remarriage has accomplished the substitution of one partner for another, the child still struggling with these themes may not be able to transcend a view of the world that casts the mutual child as his own replacement.

Still older children have the conceptual tools, although they do not always use them, to disentangle the strands of perception, appreciating that point of view creates the angle by which reality is constructed. The egocentrism of the young child, the belief that all acts revolve around him, is replaced by an ability to interpret events in terms of context, so that personal impact is not the be-all and end-all of explanation: Now parental divorce can be seen as a reflection of the relationship between the parents, not that between parent and child, and the birth of a child in remarriage can be accepted as an understandable choice having to do with the marriage itself and not a statement of dissatisfaction with existing children.

9

Growing Up as a Mutual Child

Joseph in his coat of many colors, wrapped in the symbol of his specialness, is nonetheless left to die in the desert pit in which his brothers abandon him. Imbued with a sense of mission, that it falls to him to save his family, indeed, the larger tribal family, he puts to use the confidence born of being much beloved and the psychological acumen derived from studying family politics to ingratiate himself in the household of the pharaoh as counselor and reader of dreams.

Like Joseph, the mutual child, especially a first child of the current union, has a set of relationships to both parents and siblings that set him apart, creating a unique social setting for his development.

The mutual child often has a sense of being special, the fulfillment of a romantic dream. Perhaps he even accepts family cohesion as his mission, taking on the psychological task symbolized by his genetic endowment as the only family member with a biological link to all the others. For instance, eighteen-year-old Ariella, the only mutual child in a stepfamily to which both parents brought children, repeating the family legend about her birth, has a mythological sense of her role in the family romance: "My father always agrees, but my mother still tells me all the time how thrilled they were, how amazing they thought it was that this little baby was a creation of my mother and father. They all wanted to always play with me, and they all felt I was really neat. . . . I think having the baby, me, together brought everyone closer. I think it brought my parents closer. I don't know if they would have been able to make it without the baby, because there were so many problems."

Many mutual children have been told that they brought great joy and have served as a rallying point for their families. Family myths—legends, not untruths—are handed down and become part of the mutual child's legacy of self. Isadora, now an adult, grew up being told she was her parents' "love-child," creating "this incredible bonding in this triangle of my mother and my father and me. There was no other constellation like that in the family," she believes. Surely her mother's daughter and her father's children were not part of the romantic idyll that enshrined her as the culmination of her parents' hopes and dreams. She imagines that being on the periphery of this warm, tender center of the family must have been hard for the older children to take.

Feeling especially cherished by both parents, the mutual child is often especially attached to a parent who has previously been a stepparent only. Delighted finally to have a role that is unambiguous and in which acceptance is not at issue, the stepparent becoming a parent for the first time bonds intensely with the first mutual child, creating a relationship that is enmeshed, overprotective, and sometimes volatile and passionate. Nor is the repeat parent immune from the pull toward intensity with a mutual child, who may be the only child a parent raises from birth to maturity, or the only child who is not the object of competitive conflict with an ex-spouse. Most of these children have a sense of being loved and nurtured in a way that they, at least, see as different and special.

If both parents have had children the mutual child is likely to become more closely wrapped in a tight twosome with the parent who has the most difficult time with his stepchildren. This closeness can take the form of a child's identifying with the parent seen as under siege, defending instinctively and finding it more difficult than her half siblings to feel separate or think critically about this parent. Or it can take the form of special permission to fight it out, challenging authority and arguing vehemently, secure in the knowledge that the bond is strong enough to weather conflict. Many older children commented that mutual children battled with their parents in a way that their stepchildren never did, indeed, never dared to do. "We have a much more volatile, even passionate relationship sometimes," said Isadora, comparing her relationship with her mother to those between the older woman and her other daughter or stepchildren. "She's incredibly protective of me, even frenzied about my well-being. We're very much enmeshed and attached, but she was not the first person I would run to in times of crisis, because she had a tendency to overreact to things."

Whether because the mutual child was a first-time parent's ticket of admission to the stepfamily or a second-time parent's dream-child, the fulfillment of a romantic idyll designed to erase the mistakes of past failures, he is often made well aware that he is central to that parent's life. "My mother has always dedicated her life to my interests," said Isadora, now in her thirties. "In almost every area of my life, she's in there, and she knows what it's about. She's joined groups and jumped on bandwagons. I'm also a lesbian, and when I came out to them, my mother immediately got involved in our church's Parents of Gays and Lesbians group. I really think she sees a lot of me in her, as well as a lot of my father. The idea of my mother and father's bond and me being an extension of that also held true for him."

Again and again the children of remarriage who refer to a special intensity with one parent mention their mothers. Although stepfathers who became fathers at long last can and do develop an especially close relationship with their first child, only one family I interviewed demonstrated this pattern, and the mutual child was too young to comment on how her father would move heaven and earth for her, taking his toddler off for the weekend so his wife could have time to herself. More often it is the mother who becomes the primary parent to the mutual child, whether because of the traditional division of labor in the family, giving women a greater investment of identity in being a parent, even if not for the first time, or because of the greater stress of being a stepmother.

While it is the passion of this attachment, rather than outward signs and symbols, that stepchildren are responding to when they label the mutual child as "spoiled," parents tend to agree that they do, at least sometimes and in some ways, "spoil" the child of remarriage. Frequently citing changed material circumstances for the privileges given to the younger child—more household income, more space once older children have moved out, fewer people's needs to juggle in deciding what can be done where—parents agree that a mutual child may have his own room, a bicycle, a later curfew sooner, and fewer household responsibilities. "She certainly received more materially than the others," said Marilyn of her youngest, the only child of her remarriage. "It simply wasn't there before."

In addition to having greater means to indulge a child born later in life, when the pie can be divided into fewer pieces, parents who are especially close to a child often have a harder time setting limits for that child. "Being younger, I get away with more things," admits Angela at seven, "and it's easier for me to do things." "It's sort of a Chinese menu, she can do whatever she wants," commented her father. In his view, she is still having trouble sleeping through the night in her own bed because of her mother's deep conviction that a child should not have to cry herself to sleep. The mother would go into the other room to comfort her infant, who as an older child would come to their bed in the middle of the night.

Holding On and Letting Go

How then does being more tightly bound to, typically, one parent and being seen as the icon of family unity affect a mutual child's development? Psychologists typically look at the child's early relationships with caregivers as laying the basis for future ways of relating to other people. If parents are loving and dependable, children will grow up to expect that other people will be receptive and trustworthy. Secure attachment lays the foundation for greater ease of separation, when development requires that the child become more independent, willing to venture from the haven of parental protection to explore the greater world.

There are two ways in which this early foundation can be compromised. First, if parents are erratic in their care, frustrating the infant's early needs, they will convey the message that the world is unsafe and undependable. The growing child will then view other people with suspicion, electing not to explore when he can't be confident that hearts and hearths will be open to him on his return. But there is also a price to pay for "too much" love. The child who is held too tightly, doted on and overprotected, can begin to feel smothered or engulfed by the parent. He pays more attention to external cues than to his own feelings, finding it more difficult to discern where he begins and his parent leaves off, compromising his sense of self and making relating to others dangerous in a different way: Unlike the child with unreliable, inattentive parents, who fears being abandoned in later relationships, the overparented child retreats from later intimacy because he fears he will lose himself. An optimal outcome of early attachments is a child who trusts himself and the world, so that he can enter into mutual dependencies, seeing his lot in life as inextricably, and happily, connected with that of others.

In her role as the embodiment of parental dreams and the hub of the family circle, the mutual child is at risk, if anything, of this superfluity of love and attention. Whatever the stresses of stepfamily life, and the triangles that develop as she begins to become more autonomous, actively entering into the complexities of family politics, in the first year of her life, the mutual child, typically, is much beloved and well cared for: by the parent whose family credentials she establishes, the parent whose mistakes she provides an opportunity to repair, and the children who, however ambivalently, see her as connecting them to family members who would otherwise be considered "not related." The mutual child in an enduring stepfamily knows that she is valued. The risk to her development comes from feeling valued for her *function*, as opposed to being valued for her *person*. Her role in the family threatens to eclipse her own needs for autonomy. Secure attachment requires a recognition of separateness: A symbiotic parent-child pair are not attached, they are merged, and the child's sense of self is severely compromised.

What is distinctive, in terms of attachment and separation issues, for the mutual child, as perhaps for any child much younger than a group of siblings, is the development of multiple attachments in infancy and childhood. Despite the intensity of the bond with one or more parents, the mutual child typically forms very intense attachments to half siblings with whom contact is frequent. Shuffled easily from one set of arms to another as an infant, the mutual child can feel like "a pygmy among the giants" if there are much older half siblings, who appear more like parents than peers, telling him what to do, so that he may confront five "bosses" instead of two. When asked to draw his family, Eric, at five, for example, drew three large figures, which he left unlabeled, and one smaller figure, under which he wrote E-R-I-C. The sense of having three important nurturers is underlined by his responses to my questions about who reads to him, puts him to bed, prepares his meals. "My parents," he said, not differentiating one from the other, "and my brother when he baby-sits."

With attachment comes distress at separation, and as much older siblings tend to leave more frequently than do parents, their comings and goings can be a source of stress for the mutual child. Many of the parents reported that their infants and toddlers displayed obvious distress, with tearful departures, when half siblings left for their other parent's house. Real mourning accompanied prolonged separations, which were followed by gleeful reunions. Parents of children as young as ten months report that the babies show signs of depression, crying, with "mopey, pleading looks," when siblings are gone for long periods. Absent siblings are constantly inquired about, and even when the mutual child is old enough to understand the reasons for their absence, he does not like it, protesting, "I don't want them to go." Visitation and custody arrangements make for more frequent partings between half siblings than is the case for the much younger child in a nuclear family, whose siblings leave home eventually, but not continually. Even with consistently devoted parents, the comings and goings of beloved siblings can erode the mutual child's security in attachment and create a sense of anxiety about the stability of the family. Misunderstanding can compound this insecurity, as with the four-year-old boy who inquired whether he, too, would have to go back and forth between two homes when he got big, like his half brother.

Nor is the mutual child's distress at sibling departures confined to the traditional crisis points in separation anxiety during the first eighteen months. When Sean, my oldest stepson, was leaving home at nineteen, David, then two, started to remove Sean's belongings from his car-trailer. Shorter separations are also upsetting, especially before the children have the intellectual tools to understand why the older kids are leaving and that they will return. Amelia tells how, before her son Owen was three, he had a hard time understanding his brothers' joint custody arrangement. "When he was younger, he couldn't understand why they would leave. When they went to their mother's house, he would stand in the window and cry. Now, he just says 'They went to Barbara's house.' They come back enough that he knows they're going to come back. Now it's just part of life. He's learned to accept it, but when he was under two years old, especially when he was just under a year, and again at eighteen months, he couldn't understand why they would leave. We explained to him, at each different age, in words that he can understand, what the story is. That Larry and Kevin have a different mommy, and they all have the same daddy. It's helped that he's been over to their mom's house and met her and seen their cat and dog. He's doing much better because he understands more."

In another joint custody family with three mutual children, their mother reports that all were about two before acquiring even a rudimentary understanding of why their older sister was only in their home half time. "She's at her mom's house," their parents had to repeat over and over again. The children's response was sometimes to get mad, protesting, "Why isn't she here all the time?" "Why does she have to go there?" and "I don't want her to go there." When she returned, they would punish her for being away, withdrawing for a while. Fed up with "all the to-ing and fro-ing," they may act out their distress at partings, like one three-year-old who punched her adult sister in the stomach as the young woman bent down to kiss her goodbye, saying later "I can't stand how she keeps leaving."

Another mother described her seven-year-old as "royally indignant," when one and then the other of her older half sisters left for college. "It's real hard for her," said Alice. "She asks 'Why did they have to go?' questions that she knows the answers to. Sometimes she gets angry. Sometimes she gets sad. She doesn't talk about it a lot. She's bouncing off the walls waiting to see them. Then what happens is she'll become an absolute creep, she just gets real fragile when they're about to leave. This Thanksgiving weekend, she was obviously real edgy and kept asking 'When are you leaving?' 'When are we going to the airport?' "

Even as adults, they have vivid memories of standing on the doorstep crying when an older child drove away to college. All family members agree that sibling departures are hard for the mutual child, especially if he is the only child left at home. According to her mother, Anita cried and appeared to be very lonely as each of the five older children left. Her next-oldest sister, Kathy, remembers: "She was really attached to each of us, in one way or another, and seemed to have really deep feelings for all of us. She seemed to go through a lot of pain when they would leave, and probably has the sense of being deserted." If anything, this sense of being left behind by beloved older siblings pushes the mutual child still closer to the parent whose membership in the family he validates.

Stepping on the Gas, Putting on the Brake

Having much older half siblings can be both a spur and an impediment to growing up fast. One pull for maturity is the constant stimulation the older children provide. Because the resulting complexity creates a more varied home environment than would otherwise be the case, the younger ones are challenged to develop skills that match the richness they experience.

Trying to keep up with a much older sibling can help a youngster be "the kind of kid who at this stage in his development seems more mature than my other kids were," in the words of one father, but only if he is not made to feel that his constant efforts to try to catch up and "be one of the boys" are doomed to failure. If parents and siblings are receptive to his efforts to model himself on them without belittling his efforts, the much younger child can become verbal, creative, energetic, enthusiastic, and precocious. According to their dad, Owen has an ability to "pay attention to the world around him, whereas the other kids seemed to stay kids more." Part of his precocity may stem from his spending more time with his parents, whereas his brothers had each other as playmates when they were small. However, unlike the true only child, who is also precocious, some of the sophistication of the mutual child comes from direct imitation of the older children. Commenting on his father's seven-year-old, fifteen-year-old Scott judges him to be "real mature: He matured really quickly because he always tried to keep up with us. He started to ride a two-wheel bike when he was four, he was taking jumps in the dirt road. He always wanted to come with us." Justifying his need to get a break from the younger boy, he continued, "He does pretty well for his age, but he's not fifteen, or whatever."

There is no question that the mutual child learns from the stepchildren's experience. A vigilant witness, he watches them hoe their row in life and learns what he does and doesn't want to imitate. The older children's lives provide models that are more accessible than the examples provided by parents.

"I was able to see my life in vague sketches, ten years from now," said Emily, "so that may have made some things easier for me to deal with. Understanding that my life isn't just now, that I will go through these periods also. Hearing my mom talk with my sister sometimes about boys, understanding physical relationships maybe before my peers did, so maybe I was able to deal with it more, when it came my time to deal with it, because I'd seen people go through it. I'd seen the problems they'd had in high school, what it was like to be friends when you were in high school. I saw what it was like moving out into an apartment, to be on your own. It gave me ideas about what life is like when you get to be your own person. I understood what working was, what it was like to have a job. I can look at her relationship with John, see how much love they have, and what work they have to go through, what it's like to have a kid. Understanding all these things can be great. I have a little preparation for when I get to be that stage."

Conversely, being seen as a plaything, an entertainment or distraction, can keep a child young. One fourteen-year-old delighted in teaching his three-year-old half brother to say things like "in your eye with a piece of pie" or call people names until he gets a laugh. When these tactics of getting attention become habitual, the child learns not to take himself seriously and seeks the attention and approval of others by being a clown, tailoring his actions to the reactions of others, rather than becoming an initiator. Another way of making a child younger than his years is by doing for him what he is capable of doing for himself. Having a parent or near-parent at every turn can so habituate him to being entertained that he may decline the risk of failure that trial and error entails, limiting his attempts at mastering new skills and developing both competence and confidence.

Feeling that he can never keep up can also inhibit the mutual child who sees the older children as more important and more impressive, resulting in a sense of himself as at a consistent disadvantage. He may feel like a spectator on the sidelines as the activities of the older children appear more compelling and unemulatable. When the child of remarriage tries to overcome this remoteness, his efforts to impress are frequently disparaged by the siblings he views as "exotic" and "neat"; from their vantage point his efforts to compete in an arena in which all the players are much larger are seen as "brattiness," an embarrassing occasion to avoid him. "I wanted to be grown up like them," remembers a newly adult mutual child. "I always idolized them. They didn't have to live at home, and they got to drive cars. They were always really exotic in a way. I wanted to grow up faster. I wanted to impress them, and they didn't see it." Not only did they fail to see how much she wanted to impress them, what they saw was a labored precocity that discouraged contact, leaving her trying still harder to do the impossible: be a peer. Being a Lilliputian among the giants can thus indelibly impress a mutual child with his inferiority, especially when he picks up, even subliminally, that his half siblings are resentful of his very existence.

Later, because she has been a child when her half siblings are long grown, the mutual child may have difficulty in having her own adult-hood recognized, as they continue to treat her as "the baby" when that is no longer appropriate. "For a while, it was neat," recalled Anita, "when I was little, having these brothers and sisters so much older than me, they were practically like parents. Vicki could be my mother, technically. But I got tired of it. I saw them treating each other as equals, but I was always the baby sister. They would be having a discussion, and I would walk in, and they'd stop talking or change the subject. And I never understood, because I was their sister, too, why they had to stop talking." At eighteen, it is troubling to her that she is still not accepted as in the same category with the others, all over thirty. "I think a few times I've said 'Wake up, I'm your little sister, but that doesn't mean I'm not older than I used to be.' "

Who Am I Anyhow?

In developing a sense of his own identity, separating himself from his childhood dependencies and finding his adult niche in the world, the mutual child confronts his greatest challenge, overcoming the centripe-tal pull of his role as the creator of stepfamily cohesion. In our culture, adolescents are faced with two central tasks. One is to develop an identity that is embraced, if not invented, rather than inherited, so that the young person is equipped, upon leaving home, with a sense of self that is continuous and coherent and provides a direction for the future. The other is to fall enough out of love with his parents that he can fall in love with someone his own age.

It is hard to separate from parents, however, when you are the glue that binds them to each other, or that connects one of them with a whole contingent of other stepfamily members. Sociologist William Beer, noting that the centrality of the mutual child brings with it both extraordinary benefits and heavy responsibilities, cautions that this can lead to overconformity, unreasonably high standards, obedience, and a stress on performance.[1] Katherine Baker, a family therapist based in Washington, D.C., argues that because the mutual child's primary role is to enhance family togetherness, "loss of self" choices tend to win out as he progresses through Erik Erikson's stages of identity develop-ment.[2] Thus, an overriding allegiance to family identity can severely compromise the individuation of the mutual child. Overidentifying

with parents, which we have seen to be a specific liability of this
position in the family, is one of the ways that identity formation can
be impaired. Because a secure sense of identity is a prerequisite for
psychological, if not sexual, intimacy, its lack can also create obstacles
to becoming close to people outside the family. The young adult who
remains overinvolved in the family that has raised him will have a
harder time gaining the psychological space to explore becoming intimate with someone who might be a partner in creating a new family.

In the mutual child's developmental journey through identity to
intimacy, the legacy of feeling special, with respect to both parents and
half siblings, can make it difficult for him sufficiently to differentiate
a sense of self that is not constrained by obligations for keeping the
family together. Conceived to be the emotional glue that will make the
remarrying parents and their children one family, even a young mutual
child can demonstrate an awareness that he is the linchpin on which
the very existence of the stepfamily is felt to hinge. Toddlers reveal
their closeness to the emotional pulse of the family by making peace
between parents battling with their stepchildren: endearing, placating,
and comforting in service to their appointed mission in life.

"She had a bizarrely acute sense," said a much older half sister
about Elinor, "and a way of kind of balancing a member of the family.
When Carol would pull something at the dinner table, I remember
Elinor sort of balancing the upset of it. Carol would lash out, and I just
remember Elinor, as a little kid, kind of reaching over to Carol in some
way, or saying, 'Are you okay, Carrie?' something that kind of quieted
things down." And my son David, as a two-year-old, sidled up to his
nine-year-old brother, who sat crying on a friend's staircase during a
party, patting his knee and saying, "I'm Brian's friend, I love Brian."

The older they get, the more conscious they become of the peace-
making role that they assume almost instinctively even before they can
speak. "Sometimes I think I play the mediator in the family," said
Emily at twenty, citing recent occasions when she had smoothed things
over between her mother and her younger sister, her mother and her
father, and her parents and her older half brothers. "When things
happen, I'm usually in the middle," she continued, "saying, 'Maybe
you don't see this side of things?' 'Maybe you don't see this side?' I like
to talk a lot about things, and I don't get as upset. So sometimes I'm
a balancing factor. Sometimes I feel like I'm on a balance board,
because I'm in the middle."

Looking up to her big brothers and sisters and very close to the parent who is a stepparent to them, the mutual child, whatever the shelter of position, is very much in the middle when tensions flare between the stars to which she's hitched her wagon. While very attached to and identified with her parent, as a child she also empathizes with what it means for her half sibling to be a stepchild. Despite having the security of one set of parents, she is, as one mother described it, "exposed to the pains, the torments, or stresses of the girls' tragic loss and the boys' tragic loss." "I didn't find out until I was nine years old," said Aline, "that my brother had not come from the same mother. When I was told, I was devastated for him. My heart broke for him that he lost his mother. I could barely fathom it. And I became very protective of him." Fifty years later, she still does not confront her brother, or if she does, takes a half-humorous tone. "I worshiped him, without any question. I just didn't want to believe he wasn't perfect. I know the core was that he had lost his mother as a child. I felt so sorry for him that I couldn't hurt him by admitting that he didn't do everything right."

Empathic with the older child, the younger examines his own parent for signs of wickedness once he is identified as that villain from folklore: a stepparent. Even those who see no signs of any mistreatment worry that anyone with that job description, even a beloved mother or father, must be scrutinized closely for occupational failings. While most of the children of remarriage staunchly defend their parents as stepparents, they are also strongly affected by prolonged conflict between a parent and his stepchild.

Remembering the "awful, awful times" her mother and her half sister had, seventeen-year-old Ariella claimed "it didn't have an effect directly on me, except that I saw my mother being very hurt. I didn't understand why my sister got so upset with Mom. I don't think when I was little I understood that she was a half sister." Sympathetic to the plight of the older girl, whom she has never directly challenged, Ariella is still drawn to defend her mother, whom she sees as unfairly blamed for unfortunate turns in Rhonda's life over which her stepmother had no control. "Rhonda gave my mom a very, very hard time, because I think she felt that my mom was coming into my father's life and saying, 'Okay, I'm the new mom.' I doubt my mom would do that. I think my mom's position was, 'Okay, I'm marrying your father. I'm here for you if you need me, but I'm not going to push myself on you.' She would

always say things like 'my father this' and 'my stepmother.' She still
sometimes, even now, calls my mom her stepmother, which is really
hard on my mom, because my parents have been married nineteen
years, and that's a long time."

Despite her disclaimers, she later revealed that these scenes "really
upset me. I didn't understand. I couldn't see what my mom was doing
to upset her. Rhonda would walk into the house and say things to my
mom. I just know that my mom would end up going upstairs and
crying. I was always on my mom's side, because I couldn't actually
believe that she would do something bad. I finally started seeing that
my mom wasn't helping the situation either." In the interim, seeing
her mother as already besieged, her stance was to avoid "causing trouble," protecting her mother from any conflict that might be occasioned
by her own adolescent search for identity. This choice, being the "good
girl" or "good boy," while making for a more peaceful family hearth,
can circumscribe the mutual child's opportunities to make mistakes
along the road to self-definition, precluding choices when their consequences are not straightforward and predictable, and resulting in an
overcautious approach to experience.

While feeling trapped when there is crossfire between a parent and
an older sibling can produce a stressful case of competing loyalties for
the mutual child, at no time is his role as the guardian of family
togetherness more apparent than when stepfamily tensions create a
split between his parents. Adelle, for example, while still a child, was
explicitly, if not actually, made the arbiter of the family's continued
existence.

"Most of the time," she told me, "my parents presented a picture
of complete harmony to me. They almost never fought, they were very
affectionate. It was a real nice family, and they really took good care
of me." One night, however, they came home to find that her half
brother had been hanging out at the house with one of his girlfriends,
instead of spending the weekend with his grandfather. Her parents
started a fight, interrupting it briefly to put Adelle to bed. Scared, the
little girl opened her door and overheard: "My mother at one point
commented to my father that he didn't feel in his heart the same way
for me as he did for his son. My father exploded and said that that
wasn't true at all. And it wasn't. I was my father's favorite. Fathers and
daughters always have a special relationship. And after the fight was
over, she came into my room and asked me if I wanted to go away with

her. And I said, 'Is Daddy coming too?' And she said, 'No, he's not.' Then I said, 'Then I don't want to go.' And I never heard anything about that again."

While seldom faced with something this explicit, the mutual child frequently feels that the family's emotional well-being hinges on his fulfilling his parents' hopes: to hold together pieces of former families and make them one, to be the dream-child who has no problems and is not a troublemaker. His fantasy is that if he falls down on the job, the family will dissolve. When, like Adelle, he perceives that he is being handed the power to decide the future of the marriage, the burden is enormous. Luckily Adelle, like most mutual children, while protective of the parent who is a stepparent, is not completely inducted into her mother's persecutory vision of the family. Like her mother she is angry at both her paternal grandparents and her brother's deceased mother's family for treating them both like interlopers. Because, however, she always felt confident she was "Daddy's girl," she does not include him in the ranks of those who oppress her and her mother. She will protect her mother from the dangerous in-laws but will not be enlisted as an ally in the parental struggle over a stepchild.

The young adult's finding someone outside the family to be intimate with depends, in large part, on how successfully he has negotiated the launching stage of family life. Choosing who and what to be and who to be with—Freud's twin objectives of love and work, Erikson's tasks of achieving identity and intimacy—are the tasks at hand for the young adult leaving the family hearth. In establishing a sense of identity, the adolescent and young adult acquire the confidence that they can stand on their own two feet. But leaving home also generally requires the child to have confidence that the home will survive without him. To become intimate with a peer, he must not feel guilt that he is abandoning a partnership with a parent. For the child of remarriage, whose emotional centrality has been an important force in stepfamily cohesion, achieving this assurance can be difficult.

Katherine Baker reports her clinical experience that mutual children have difficulties in separation, moving in and out of the family home, and have trouble making a career choice and forming an intimate relationship that will lead to the formation of a new family.[3] Perhaps the hardest step is gaining some distance in the tight twosome of mutual child and previously childless parent, a task that typically begins in adolescence. One young woman, for example, remembers that by her midteens, she didn't want the older children to identify her with her mother. "I remember getting angry at Mom," she reports, "when she would say something stupid around my brothers. And then getting angry at Robert, when he would bait people. It would make me uncomfortable both for my mom and for myself, cause I would feel linked to her. And then want to separate."

Parents report that their mutual children have a less tumultuous adolescence than their older children, a happy turn of events that they attribute to their own greater wisdom, born of the experience of having successfully raised the children from past unions. When they are pleased with the adults their older children have become, they are more relaxed with their younger children who are grappling with the identity issues of adolescence. Having been there before, they can be confident that the travails of the moment are part of the process, and in the most trying moments can take the attitude that "this too shall pass."

Comparing the teen years of her youngest daughter, a mutual child, to those of her other children and stepchildren, Marilyn quickly sums it up: "Hers were much easier. Never had a problem. Kept waiting for problems that everybody else was talking about. I attribute that to the fact that we were older. We had a lot of experience, and I think what we gave her was the best thing we could give her, trust and respect. That doesn't mean she didn't try things. I'm now learning about the things she tried. But there was always some kind of solidity there. She knows that there was never a super-serious problem among her siblings, and I think that success affirmed that the parents are not so bad."

While greater experience, and the wisdom to learn from past mistakes, go a long way toward explaining why parent-child conflict is less when it is the mutual child who is the teenager, other factors come into play here, too. Having seen one or both parents in conflict with teenage stepchildren, she may learn to avoid conflict, resolving not to be a troublemaker, so as to avoid the scenes she remembers seeing as a small and vulnerable child. Identifying with her parent's pain as a stepparent to teenagers, she curbs her own rebellious impulses, protecting her parent and limiting herself.

Isadora's memory is that the triangle including herself, her mother, and her father "intensified, intensified, intensified, and the other kids were just kind of cut loose." Research shows that stepchildren do leave home earlier than adolescents in nuclear families.[4] No studies to date have tracked the development of children of remarriage; indeed, because they have been raised by both their parents, many do not identify themselves as stepfamily members even when they seek counseling. Nonetheless, both clinical reports and my interviews indicate that if stepchildren are likely to emancipate earlier than the norm, the mutual child is likely to stay closer to the family longer than his peers in first families.

Any youngest child faces a qualitatively different situation in leaving home than did his older brothers and sisters. The older children left a family that stayed a family, a household with two generations, parents and children. The departure of the youngest child, on the other hand, creates an empty nest. If he suspects that his departure will precipitate the dissolution of his parents' marriage, he dare not go. In *Leaving Home*, Jay Haley writes of the difficulty young people have in getting on with the business of becoming adults when they are worried that there will be no home to which to return.[5] When the youngest child is also a first mutual child, long accustomed to playing the role of family mediator and assuming responsibility for keeping one parent connected to the rest of the family, the pull to stay at home can approach the force of gravity.

"I always had trouble with my mother because since I was the only child of hers, she had great expectations of me," said Adelle. "It upset her that I wasn't perfect." Originally planning to attend a college close to home to which she had been admitted early, she changed her plans when her mother expressed her delight about being able to visit every weekend. Instead, she spent another year in high school and chose an equally prestigious school far enough away that her parents could not "pop in" on her. Twenty years later she dreads visits home because her mother is "expecting the day that I leave from the moment I arrive, so she is very sad most of the week."

Contrasting her leaving home with the experience of her half sisters, one her mother's child and the other her father's, Isadora sees a marked difference: "When the other girls became eighteen and left home, my mom really cut them loose. It's been an ongoing process for my mother and me to figure out the boundaries. Here I am thirty-one, and it's still not clear. I've never been cut loose in the same way." When the older girls were in their teens, the emotional intensity in the family was concentrated in the triangle of mother, father, and Isadora, and the older girls were allowed, perhaps prematurely, to emancipate. When Isadora was the same age, and continuing through her young adulthood, her mother "dedicated her life" to her youngest child's interests.

In looking back at how each of them fared as adults, Isadora sees herself as more assertive than her brother and sisters, but less eager to be intimate. "I think I've got a much greater sense of being able to do it on your own, to kind of make it in the world," she told me. Here cultural history plays a role, as this is partly due to the almost twenty years that separate her from her parents' older children, so that she came of age in the seventies when women's expectations were higher. Yet when I asked her how she reconciled her assertion of greater independence with being clasped tightly to the family bosom while the older children were cut loose early on, she pointed to their adult lives as a reflection of the different impact of family realities on each of the children: "Jane just went from one man to another to another. I've never had relationships like that. Mary hooked up with her high school sweetheart. They've stayed together ever since and had kids. I've not had those urges. Even my brother was always involved with somebody. It's only been four years that I've been in a long-term relationship, my first. Even before that I did not connect up easily. I think developing a close relationship with another person has been hard for me."

For the stepchildren in this family, the search has been for connection, for the mutual child autonomy has taken precedence. Prematurely separated from the family, Isadora's half siblings readily transferred their need for closeness to a romantic partner or partners. Although they have met with varying success in finding the intimacy they sought, they have been less venturesome in other areas of life, taking fewer risks. For Isadora, the challenge has been to be close without becoming overwhelmed, maintaining her integrity in an intimate relationship.

For both Adelle and Isadora being an *only* mutual child was part of the pressure in trying to separate. "I'd always hoped that she'd have another kid," said Adelle, who was her mother's only child, "because she drove me crazy." Isadora remembers wishing that "two of us had been born," even though both of her parents already had much older children. "It would have taken some of the pressure off me. There'd be at least two of us to involve with the other brother and sisters. At least we could have talked with each other about what we were feeling." Like children who are their parents' only child in a first marriage who go on to be stepchildren, they long for someone who would be in the same boat.

In the search for a comfortable and fitting identity, understanding where he stands in the family, as well as in the larger world, figures prominently in creating a self-portrait that the adolescent can behold with pride and assurance. Siblings play a significant role in identity formation, although researchers and theorists are not in agreement on how sibling constellation affects development.[6] In any family, part of how each child figures out who he will be is by comparing himself with the siblings who differ from him in age, sex, temperament, personality, and interests. By seeing how he is both similar to and different from others growing up in the same family, he constructs a sense of self that is both related to and differentiated from his siblings. It is almost as if there is a menu of identities and each selection can be made only once; those who come to the table later must choose from what has not yet been tasted.

Younger children ordinarily are more aware of and involved with their older siblings than vice versa. Speaking, for example, of her four-year-old son, Oliver, and her nine-year-old daughter, Denise, Leslie says: "Ollie is quite affectionate with Denise. Everything is him and Denise. Let's say I have to go out, he'll say, 'Who will mind me and Denise?' It's always both of them he thinks about. When Denise gets a chance to speak she usually tells us what's going on with her, rather than waste her precious moments speaking about him."

When there are more years between the mutual child and his half sibling, he may identify himself more as an only child than as a younger brother. Psychologists who study birth order find that sibling position is an important contributor to personality formation.[7] A firstborn child, for example, is more likely to assume an exaggerated sense of responsibility and to take care of others, both in the family and in later occupational choice, while youngest children are more likely to be socially expansive and carefree, expecting to be taken care of. Only children, on the other hand, partake in characteristics of both oldest and youngest, with a tendency to more closely resemble an oldest, who was, after all, an only for some time. Only children tend to be more socially independent, less oriented to peers, more like little adults at an earlier age, and more attached to their parents throughout life.[8]

The child of remarriage who is separated either by many years or by many miles from her half siblings is liable to see herself mirrored in descriptions of the only child, as did Isadora, who told me, "Whenever I would find other kids who were only children, it was very validating." Birth order factors play a kind of mix and match game here, so that the child of remarriage may resemble first children in some ways and middle or later children in others. Speaking of her firstborn son, Elizabeth said, "Although Eddie was a third child for Tom, he was young enough that it was like being a first child, because Barry was ten years old, which was certainly like an adult to this baby. I'm sure that Eddie came into this world feeling that, experiencing everything as a first child does. He has this first-child syndrome, of wanting to be in charge, in control of things."

Only when there has been little contact, however, does the mutual child discount the influence of his half siblings in determining his own position in the family hierarchy. Emily, for example, talks about feeling like both a firstborn and a later-born child: "It was weird being both a fourth child and a first child. When I'm the first child, I'm very much achievement-oriented, get out and do your thing, be an example. It's more pressure. I like being the fourth child. The pressure's off me, I feel like I'm having more fun. I'm a more whole person. I'm very much an overachiever, and I have a need for control, that's from being a first child, and I don't like it as much. So, it's been good having the older brothers and sisters. They make me part of this larger family and ease me up. As I get older, as I get to know them as friends, I can be in a community. I think it's strengthened my relations in other groups. It's relaxed me, now that relations are much better. To be part of the whole, instead of feeling that you have to lead the pack or something." In part, this split reflects changes in the family over time, with more integration between the two groups of children in recent years, as two of the older children established homes in neighboring communities and the third is only hours away.

For the mutual child, as for other youngsters, adolescence is a time of reckoning, of coming to terms with family politics, applying new-found cognitive skills to make sense of who he is with respect to siblings and half siblings. Several young adults described how they started to wonder how they fit in when they were about twelve or thirteen, making efforts to get to know their now adult half siblings, and said that by their middle teens they were even more dedicated to making sense of their place in the family.

Privilege and Paranoia

While no sibling relationship is truly equal, the half sibling pair has more imbalances than most. When the children of past and present marriages have ample opportunity to interact, being closer in age or sharing a household for longer periods of time, the mutual child most frequently is described by parents as adoring or idolizing "the big kids." When the older children are "acting up and carrying on," he may criticize his parents for "giving them more attention for being bad than I'm getting by being good," but his attacks stem from his hurt at feeling abandoned or being turned on by his idols. If he knows the older children have taken care of him as an infant, he may feel he owes them a debt he can never repay. The older children, like most older children, are typically more interested in exploring the larger world when the younger ones still feel that it is an adventure to plumb the interior of the family. But more than older siblings who share both parents, they are likely to see the younger child as a symbol of a set of family circumstances they wished had not come to pass, often to be resented, perhaps to be wished away.

This nonreciprocal relationship between half siblings sets the stage for the act in the drama that I call "privilege and paranoia." Because of their empathy for the older children's loss, whether of a parent or of a family unit, mutual children become acutely aware of their own relative privilege and the envy it excites, whether expressed by or projected on those for whose acceptance they clamor.

Most mutual children are aware that for them life is easier than it was for their older half siblings. Anita, at eighteen, is typical in this respect: "I always had both of my parents right there, all the time. Nothing ever happened when I was little. I know I had it easier . . . we never moved, never did anything, so it was always very steady."

But being the offspring of a second or later marriage does not guarantee relative privilege. The divorce rate for second marriages exceeds that for first, and several studies have shown that children in conflict-ridden nuclear families are more poorly adjusted than children in well-functioning single-parent families.[9]

Barry, for example, thinks that he and his sister were much better off than his younger half brothers, in having a better relationship with their mother and less tension and interference from their stepfather. "It's a really snotty thing to say," he volunteered, "but she was less successful at raising them than raising my sister and me. But that's largely due to the fact that my mother and stepfather had such a bad relationship that adding more people to it just increased the damage possibilities. They were never in agreement on how to raise children, and while he wasn't around a lot, when he came home he'd undercut her authority."

Nevertheless, while the marriage exists, whatever its difficulties, the children of that marriage usually feel at a relative advantage vis-à-vis their older half siblings. It is they who live with both their parents, they who have not weathered the storms of parental separation or death, remarriage, and accommodating to a stepparent. They know from vicarious experience that these can be painful and difficult transitions, but knowing they don't want to follow in the older children's footsteps in this regard presents them with a dilemma. While they do not want to experience the loss of a parent or the acquisition of a stepparent themselves, neither do they want to be seen as different from the other children.

"Except for my brothers and sisters," said one newly adult mutual child, "my emotional life was pretty stable as a child." Except. Whether the gap in age is relatively narrow, and the older children directly inform the younger of their envy, or the difference in age is so great that the envy is usually merely inferred, mutual children do their utmost to minimize differences. They care so much that their mostly adored big brothers and sisters accept and love them that privilege feels like a handicap in sibling relations. "I didn't like it so much that my parents gave me so much attention," said Anita, "I didn't want to be treated differently than my brothers and sisters."

Alexander, at twelve, describes his struggles, which he insists are now in the past, with the expressed envy of his half siblings, both seventeen: "I know that sounds weird, but it is kind of a disadvantage to have both parents when you have brothers and sisters that don't. When you're in my position, they really get jealous and say, 'He's such a great lucky duck, he not only has all the attention for being the youngest, but he also has both parents.' I'd think, 'Oh, I wish they wouldn't give me so much attention,' because I wanted to be real close to my brother. I'd feel like a little runt, the runt of the pack."

What the mutual child experiences is a form of survivor guilt: conflict-ridden guilt and relief at escaping from the casualties inflicted on one's fellows. As small children consider themselves responsible either for holding together or rending asunder their parents' marriages, so too does their egocentrism lead them to internalize their siblings' resentment, blaming themselves for the others' pain. Emily, at twenty, recalls herself at eight or nine, picking up on the resentment that her older half siblings expressed, however indirectly: "I think kids are real sensitive, and I think that as a little kid you don't understand that it's not something you did. Sometimes you put it on yourself, and you don't know why." In response, she developed a vigilance about how other people are responding to her: "I always internalize other people. If I think they may be bothered, I internalize it, and it makes me a little bit apprehensive in terms of doing things."

Ever mindful of how much easier her lot in life is than the older children's, she recalls an experience when she was sixteen that heightened her awareness of her position in the family: "I was practicing the violin, and Delia was sitting on the couch. Suddenly I was just looking at her, and realizing that my mom was talking to me about something. And just realizing that my mom was my mom, and wasn't Delia's mom. I internalized just a real hatred of myself. Well, not a real hatred, but I didn't like my situation. I felt bad for Delia at that point, and just didn't like myself, because I had my own mom, and I had my own sister, and I had a lot of things that she didn't have at that point. It was just really sad, because her mom had died. I could just feel her looking. It must be really hard for her. I think they are close in some ways, but there's always going to be a little bit of a limit, because my mom is not her natural mother. There was just kind of a yucky feeling inside of myself that I was the one occupying this position, where I had something that she didn't have. And that's reflected in a lot of things with my friends. If I could sing better than they could, or something like that, I always felt incredibly bad. Unnecessarily guilty, and I couldn't figure out why. Maybe this is a little bit why, just growing up feeling I had all these things, accidentally, for no reason or anything, and feeling bad about it."

At about the same age, sixteen, she describes feeling "this very strong urge: 'I have to get to know Delia.' She had just gotten married. It was really important to me to get on good grounds with her before she had a child. To talk to her. A lot of it was that I needed so badly to know where I stood with her."

When the older children are much older, the envy is usually inferred rather than explicit. Isadora, for example, reports that while she was told that her mother's daughter and father's children were delighted by her birth, she has lived her life "pretty paranoid" about that, starting with the first time she heard, "Oh, gee, they sure are a lot looser with you than they were with us." "I began to think," she told me, "that would make me mad if it was reversed. And then I started thinking about what it must have been like for me to appear on the scene, and with a heart condition, so that all this attention and energy went into me. Then also I seem to have been given so many opportunities. And there just seemed to be this incredible bonding in this triangle of my mother, my father, and me. There were no other constellations like that in the family. That just sort of clicked it. I just imagined that must be . . . disappointing, and hard to take."

What are the consequences for the mutual child of this dual legacy of privilege and paranoia? One is a finely tuned empathy, a caring concern for the pain of others. In social situations, they are likely to find themselves in the role of peacemaker or mediator, balancing competing demands and trying to come to an accommodation to meet the needs of all, an extension of their role in the family. Another consequence, reported by all of the mutual children old enough to reflect on their experience, as opposed to simply reporting it, is that sibling relationships continue to have great salience, eclipsing parent-child relationships as a source of continued conflict. "It's the kids who have their relationships to work out," said one young woman, "probably because I feel very secure with my parents, I haven't had to think about them as much."

Moreover, experience with siblings seems to generalize to relationships with peers. Emily, for example, is aware that her perception of her half siblings' resenting her inhibits her with other people. Feeling that she is privileged, she strives for homogeneity through self-deprivation. Feeling that she was always on the sidelines, watching the older children's lives, also made it difficult for her to relate to others in their age group: "I would really have a hard time, speaking to them. I just didn't know where I stood." As a result, she feels, she became more interested in people's motivations. This heightened consciousness of interpersonal acceptance issues can be both an asset, developing children's capacity for empathy and sensitivity to others, and a liability, inhibiting their sociability and their best efforts in their own behalf.

The portrait that emerges of the mutual child, then, is of a youngster made to feel special from early on, developing a clear sense of self-worth, but whose specialness carries with it a mantle of responsibility for family cohesion. Vested with a mission for mediation that generalizes outside of the family, she develops an acumen in observing social relationships that develops both a capacity for empathy and an overconcern for how others respond to her. Privileged and precocious, with a sense of competence sometimes shaken by the long struggle to catch up with far larger players, she nonetheless plays down her own accomplishments for fear of alienating others who she anticipates will be envious.

Separation can be difficult for the mutual child who, overidentified with one or both parents and seen as the stepfamily linchpin, may fear that his independence threatens either one parent's family membership or the stepfamily's very survival. Half siblings who come and go frequently can stress his security in attachment, so that fear of abandonment, as well as apprehension about engulfment that comes from overinvolvement with a parent, can become obstacles to intimacy in adult life.

Although parents and children alike stress that the mutual child is related to all of them, creating enduring ties between people otherwise more tenuously connected, biological relatedness may not be as important to his centrality as *equi*distance to all stepfamily members. William Beer underlines that it can be just as important for the mutual child to be linked genetically to nobody as to everybody.[10] Although I have only anecdotal evidence to this effect, a child adopted into a stepfamily as an infant occupies a similarly central position, representing the unity invoked by the remarriage, with many if not all of the accompanying dynamics described here.

Neither the developmental assets nor the liabilities discussed in this chapter are, however, universal for all children born into a stepfamily. In discussing how being the child of a remarriage affects the developmental course of the mutual child, it is important to note some of the factors that either exaggerate or minimize the effects described in this chapter, most of which have been elaborated in previous chapters. By and large, the following trends obtain, always in interaction. The extent to which the developmental picture presented in this chapter applies will be:

- Less in stepfather families than in stepmother families.
- Less in families in which both parents have previously had children.
- Less when there is only one child from each marriage.
- Less when a stepfamily has had time to "ripen" before the child is born.
- More when stepchildren are living in the home full-time or half time.
- More when there is a highly conflictual stepparent-stepchild relationship.
- More when there is an incomplete divorce or another triangulating family figure who enters into a coalition with an older child against a stepparent or the mutual child or both.

Some of what is described here is true of any child much younger than his brothers and sisters, rather than particular to the circumstances of a child born to a remarriage. The much younger child in the nuclear family may also be especially cherished, precocious, and overparented, enjoying a superfluity of role models in his older siblings and suffering when they leave home. He does not, however, represent a different family to the older children when all share both parents. He is not "other" but one of them. No more than they does he bind parents to each other, and neither parent is dependent upon him for legitimation as a family member. Siblings are, therefore, less ambivalent toward a much younger full sibling. There is not the resentment that he plays a role in the family that they cannot.

Later-Born Mutual Children

In addition, second or later mutual children are insulated from stepfamily realities by their oldest full sibling, who like the youngest stepchild lives on the frontier where past and present families meet, for it is at the frontier that most of the action takes place. Asked what it is like to have much older sisters and brothers, younger mutual children are likely to just say, "It's nice," comparing their half siblings favorably with the other slightly older children who lord it over them. "When they're younger like Annie, they're mean," said one six-year-old, referring to her ten-year-old sister. Amy, at eighteen, says that her life may have been somewhat easier than those of her older half siblings, but she minimizes the differences, explaining them by changes in the times and the population of the household. Not even two years younger than her full sister, her awareness of the sensitivities of the older children is in marked contrast to Emily's. While the older girl is keenly aware of the complex emotions that characterize the relationships among the siblings and the stresses on her own position as the first of the mutual children, Amy feels almost untouched by the early adjustments to stepfamily life and their residue: "I was probably the least affected by it in the family. I was so young, and I don't remember that much. I'm sure it was hard for the older kids, because their mother died and they had to accept a new mother. If the older kids went through anything, it happened when they were younger. I don't think it bothers anybody really." While the family today is warm, affectionate, and exceptionally well integrated, only from the vantage point of having an older full sibling can she assume that all issues are long buried.

Hoping History Doesn't Repeat Itself

With or without this layer of insulation from the front lines of stepfamily politics, despite his empathy with his half siblings' loss and his own efforts to reduce differences and strive for sameness, acceptance, and inclusion, the mutual child is not eager to follow in their footsteps. If anything, empathy with siblings leads to a fear of repeating their fate. Even in the best-integrated and best-functioning stepfamilies, the very existence of a steprelationship makes the repetition of the events preceding and precipitating the stepfamily formation a possibility to ponder. Eric, for instance, at five, announced to his parents that he hoped they wouldn't ever divorce, but if they did, he would want them to live next door to each other, an arrangement some neighbors had currently put into practice. His mother said: "I told Eric that arrangement probably wouldn't last, but he said, 'That's what I would want.' I don't think he said, 'I don't want to be like Carl,' but I'm sure that was in his mind: 'I don't want to go on a plane and be so far away from my mom and dad.' "

When their half sibling's parent has died, they may have even more concern than usual that they, too, will be deprived of a parent, although they may not make the connection with what has happened to their older brothers and sisters. "When I was in the third or fourth grade," said Amy, "I would get real scared, just the thought of one of my parents' dying, but I never thought it could have anything to do with it happening to their mother." When they do think of how difficult it must have been for the older children to endure such a grievous loss, they are quick to reassure themselves that their own parents are particularly hale and hearty specimens. Anita, for example, "never worried about my mom's not coming home, or getting sick, or something like that. She was always the strong one. I did worry, but I don't know if it was any worse than any other kid would worry. I sort of figured that since my mom wasn't related to their mother that it wouldn't affect my mom."

Children born into postdivorce stepfamilies, however, are more often confronted with concrete reminders of the problems that entails for children. "We all understand it's hard to go back and forth between parents," said Andy, at twelve, referring to his mother's son and father's daughter, who have either moved from household to household or periodically visit their absent parent. "I understand how they feel, because I'm there every time they go, and I'm still here."

While their experience with having parents who are no longer together is secondhand, they cannot be entirely assured that lightning will not strike twice in the same household. Even parental reassurances are not wholly convincing. As Andy told me: "Both parents say, 'We'll never split up.' But I still do worry a little bit. I still think about it a lot. I don't think they will any time soon, because there's really nothing that's pulling them apart right now. It may happen in the future."

Why does he think so? "Because times are getting harder. It's harder to keep a family. A lot of kids grow up without both parents, and it tears down our society. The kids aren't as well balanced out. It would be much easier for everyone in our society, for kids, if they're not going to stay together not to have children. It's tearing down society. It's making it harder for everybody, and it's making our school system even worse, especially in Philadelphia. Most of the kids in my school don't have a father, 90 percent of the kids in Philadelphia don't have their fathers. They don't really care. 'Oh, what can you do? I can't be beaten, that's child abuse.' So they don't do their homework, use drugs and stuff, and mainly, their reason for it is from single-parent homes. I'm lucky that I have both parents. I'm glad that I do."

Even a mutual child who thinks his own parent is loving and

evenhanded as a stepparent does not want a stepparent for himself. Now that her mother is widowed, one young woman dreads the possibility of her remarrying, as she remembers how hard it was for her mother and half siblings to get along, despite what she sees as valiant efforts by her mother. Growing up in a stepfamily, even without being a party himself in any steprelationship, convinces the mutual child to do his utmost to avoid repeating the circumstances and the struggles of his older half siblings, even as he is ever mindful that the mutual child of this marriage may well be the stepchild of the next.

10

Half Blood

The Politics of Sister- and Brotherhood

In trying to determine how being a half sibling differs from being a full brother or sister, we encounter the limits of knowledge about siblings in general, as sibling relationships are probably the least studied and most underestimated of family relationships. Researchers do agree, however, that brothers and sisters are powerful influences in each other's lives, helping to develop one another's identity and self-esteem, shaping one another's ideas about the outside world, teaching one another about fairness, justice and cooperation, bargaining and negotiation, and mutually regulating behavior by keeping a close eye on each other.[1]

Many factors affect how close or distant half siblings are. In Chapters 4 and 5 we saw how the older children's relationship to their mutual parent and to their stepparent, who is a parent to the younger kids, influences how half siblings feel about each other. Chapter 6 showed how the lobbying efforts of important other relatives must be factored into the stepfamily equation. And Chapter 8 examined how the number of years separating a stepchild and a mutual child helps shape their relationship. This chapter focuses on other ingredients in the complex politics of half sibling relations: how parents filter out the shadings in a multitoned picture of love and resentment, the impact of sex and residence, and how the number of children in each group affects relationships among all.

From their parents' point of view, the "half" qualifier to a sibling relationship can be a meaningless abstraction, especially if the children are raised under the same roof. "Nobody has ever referred to my kids as half brother and half sister," said one mother. "That shocks me when I think of that, I suppose because I'm the parent of both." Even when custody is shared, the parent of both children tends to minimize the difference in bonding between full and half siblings.

When half siblings have little contact, the sibship, not the "half," may feel like the abstraction, so that the mutual children enjoy what one father called "the fiction of having older sisters." He continued, "I mean it's a reality that they have older half sisters and a half brother, but it's mainly a fiction, because they spend relatively little time with them."

Seldom, however, do parents' accounts of half sibling relationships get unqualified confirmation by the children themselves. Rarely is their contact as inconsequential as some parents imagine. The children's own version of how they get along is neither as unremittingly hostile as their strife sometimes appears, nor, in most instances, as unreservedly accepting as other parents would like to believe. "There is that edge between us because we don't share the same mom," said one adult stepchild of her much younger half sister, to whom she is, nonetheless, close.

Boys or Girls Together

Similarity of temperament and weathering crises together can forge bonds that surpass the biological in creating special intimacies between half siblings. Gender, too, can be a basis for solidarity that crosses the divide of having a different parent. While parents are almost unanimous in anticipating that having a mutual child of the same sex will be more "threatening" to an older child who is in a steprelationship with one of the adults, most children play down this consideration. Whether or not they are young enough to envision the baby as an eventual playmate, unless there is a run on one sex within the family, children would vote for the baby to be as much like them as possible. Being the same sex, then, becomes a basis for shared activities and interests, of forging a bond despite the distance in years. Although she is now closer to her twelve-year-old brother, for instance, a ten-year-old girl thinks that as adults she and her baby half sister will be more likely to be friends, having lunch together and sharing interests, while her brother, as a male, will be thinking and doing things that will feel foreign to her.

Almost all of the most difficult half sibling relationships I observed were those between boys and their baby brothers. For these children, having the baby be the same gender as they further aggravated their feeling displaced. Liam, for example, seven when his half brother was born, clearly indicated that any further child added to the family would only be welcome if female. Same-sex siblings are both more likely to become close and more fiercely competitive, but aggression is not equal to lack of closeness.[2] Little brothers who try to be just like their big brothers and little sisters who want to play with their sister's friends can be tag-along pests, yet the greater likelihood of shared interests is an opportunity for closeness.

With the wisdom of hindsight, one stepmother realized that her earlier worries had come to naught: "I think it turned out okay that they were all girls, that they were all sisters together." In addition to the conviviality of greater presumed shared interests, there is an emotional power in seeing your parents raise a child who is the same sex as you are when you are old enough to reflect and analyze how they're doing. Watching her stepmother care for her baby half sister, one teenager found herself thinking of her own deceased mother and how she herself had been mothered. In thinking about parents and stepparents as nurturers and guides, and about how well nurtured and guided they feel, the boy with the baby brother and the girl with the baby sister find a screen on which to view their own emotional histories.

For the younger children, too, gender solidarity can bridge great gulfs in years and experience, both for the future, as they identify the older children's lives as a preview of their own possibilities, and in the here and now. Adrienne, mother of six-year-old Adam and four-year-old Annie, and stepmother of Bev and Judy, nineteen and twenty-three, and Dennis, twenty-two, observes special links between the same-sex children in her stepfamily: "I think Adam has a special fondness for Dennis, and Annie, in her kind of quirky way, is very female-identified. She's always counting the number of women in her family and sorting by sex. So she has a very strong sense of kinship with these big sisters, who she looks very much like. People are always saying 'You're another Miller, you look just like Bev and Judy.' And she loves that."

More than One More

I am stepmother to three boys and mother to one.

Eleanor is mother to three small children and stepmother of a teenage girl.

Ben and Julia each had one child when they married and had their two sons.

The center of gravity of each of these stepfamilies is different. Picture the children of each marriage perched on one end of a seesaw. As the number of children from the present marriage equals the number from prior unions, the seesaw levels out, creating a balance in which neither group outweighs the other. Everything else being equal, which it seldom is, the character of the stepfamily is shaped by where the heft of the children falls: a stepfamily in which the majority of the children are the issue of the remarriage will feel very different to all its members than a family with a group of stepchildren into which a single mutual child is born.

"I'm glad that the new family was not equal in weight until we were all grown up," said one adult stepchild, commenting favorably on her half brother's recent birth. The birth of its second child does shift the balance toward the remarried family, especially with remarried fathers, who may become less involved with a first set of children when there are more demands from those who live with him. "They were more of a representation of the American Family, more toward a suburban, PTA mother, Brady Bunch, more of a traditional family," said Tony, who was fourteen when his stepmother had her second child. The stereotype of the American middle-class family as a two-parent, two-child unit has an almost subliminal power. "I think it's made it seem more like a real family than having a single child," said Sol, reflecting on the birth of his second child in remarriage. "It seems like we're a whole unit with two children that we weren't . . . it just seems . . . the norm, or how families should be. I'm sorry that I didn't have a second child when Dan was growing up."

When still another child is born in remarriage, perhaps the biggest change comes for "his highness the baby," a now-dethroned monarch, the first of the mutual children. Because of the intensity of the connection between a first mutual child and the parent whose first child he is, sharing the parent who was his alone can be difficult for the child who loses his singularity when another child who has equal claim to both his parents is born.

Part of the diminution of rivalry between the older children and a later arrival rests in the baby not being anybody's firstborn child, which may also be what diminishes the rivalry in stepfamilies in which both parents have already had children. Eliot, describing how his stepson George was less excited but tremendously loving with the second of his two daughters, thinks that Ellen was less of a threat than Aileen, who had disrupted George's position as the sole focus of four adults. "The first kid to a first parent is going to be excessively doted upon, for every little twink of the eyelash," he theorized. "There was a little less doting and noticing of Ellen. There she was, a cute little baby who wasn't getting that much attention from either of us, because the girls were only nineteen months apart. George had more space to pick her up. We didn't fight over holding her, as we had over Aileen, because we were generally running like crazy to deal with Aileen and the baby and the household."

Because the addition of a second or later mutual child does not change the position of any of the stepchildren, this baby is frequently welcomed with less ambivalence and is more beloved than her predecessor. Stepchildren who were the baby of their original family have already been bumped from that niche, and their status is unchanged by the new arrival. To those who have had a hard time accepting the first baby born to the stepfamily, the second presents an opportunity to do it differently now that the stakes don't seem so high. Six-year-old Nila was jealous and distant when her father and stepmother had Erica, unlike Polly, then ten, who became their half sister's affectionate caretaker during frequent visits. Five years later, baby Andrew is the apple of Nila's eye. She plays with him more and delights in being able to baby-sit. Clearly more accepting of this second mutual child, she claims him as her full brother, in contrast to Erica, whom she designates a half sister. "She's finally getting a chance to be a big sister," said their father, "in the way that Polly did with Erica."

This coupling of pairs of children from two marriages, oldest with oldest and youngest with youngest, is not an unusual pattern. When the first mutual child is born, it is the first stepchild who retains his position as an oldest child. He may even revel in the comeuppance of his chief competitor, the full sibling who had usurped his own throne. He is also likely to be old enough to take some part in nurturing the baby, making him feel very grown up and capable. In contrast, a youngest child is far more upstaged by the new addition, losing his place as baby of the family.

Mike and Irma remember the early years of Ethan's life as a constant campaign to mute the conflict between him and Jason, Mike's older son. Although he was initially hesitant to have another child, Mike's reasoning has been confirmed by the experience of the first year: Having Ezra has improved how Jason and Ethan get along as well. "My sense of having a third is that it's basically been a real upper, because it confirms that Jason can be a good brother. A loved brother." Jason concurs: "Me and Ezra haven't had, and probably won't go through the same type of scenario as Ethan and I did. I won't be so irritated, because I'm older, and I'll understand that when he throws a tantrum, or whatever he does, I'll be much more able to sit back and watch and just say, 'Don't worry about it.' "

What Jason did worry about, when Ezra was first born, was "that they were full brothers and I was a half brother. I felt left out in some ways, 'cause here they are, and they have that against me. At the time, Ethan and I were not getting along so well. But after talking with Irma, she says she considers me to be a full brother just like I consider myself to be, except for the fact that I don't live full-time over here. By the time it makes a difference, I won't be shifting back and forth. So, I'll be looked at as on my own, and not as, you know, my mom's son. But I'm not into having a contest about it. That's not a relationship, that's a war."

Because the age gap is greater, a second mutual child may be better liked but less known by half siblings than was her predecessor. She will be the "cute little imp," not so much a competitor. Yet even the struggles that may ensue between a first mutual child and his half siblings produce a closeness that is precluded by the developmental chasm that divides the offspring of an earlier marriage from still-later-born children.

Just as the single mutual child strives to become old before his time, trying to keep up with a group of much larger half siblings whose closeness threatens to exclude him, so too can the lone child from an earlier marriage feel excluded by the early childhood focus of the stepfamily with a burgeoning population of tots. Pamela, who is basically very satisfied with both her parents' remarriages, finds only one drawback to her time at her father's house: "All three kids are so much younger than me. It just makes the whole family on a younger level, that's basically because there are three of them and one of me. I mean, our family outings are to the zoo. I used to be very upset, because that's not my idea of a family outing. But I don't think it would be better the other way, because then it would be just my stepmother, my father, and me. Then the family would be way older than me."

The larger the original family, the more negatively the older children seem to respond to the idea of yet another child born to the stepfamily. Audrey remembers that her having a second child made all of her stepchildren angry, although seven years later they report that it made little difference to them. Audrey's recollection, however, is that they were disgusted: "They said, 'What do you mean more children? What do you need more children for? This is terrible. You don't have enough money.' They just couldn't believe it. Money has always been a problem. The older kids get more expensive and our salaries don't really go up. It was tight financially, and I think the kids felt it was selfish of us to put more money into another kid. It put a chill on things. I think the youngest felt it was rejecting that we had another kid. He said, 'You know, I can understand Audrey having another kid, because she only has one, but I can't understand Dad wanting *five*. What does he need five for?'"

In large families especially, adding yet another child can put the squeeze on resources, so that there is less available for each individual. Although parents, as providers, are hard put to support a large number of children, they at least participate in the decision about family size. Children, however, see themselves as excluded from the invitations committee that decides how many people will surround the family table. While willing to concede to their stepparent the right to a single child, they may see further additions as taking the food off their plates. When the second of their children was on the way, one woman was told by her stepchild, "There are too many children in this family. You just don't get enough cupcakes when there are so many."

Even when older children do not see each new child as signaling "less for me" materially, parents' capacity to emotionally support increasing numbers of children is questioned by the older children, who know their own need for parental nurturance is not obviated by their pretensions to adulthood. When the household population threatens to explode, teenagers, especially, do not mince words in expressing their indignation.

By the Numbers

A vital factor in how well mutual children and the children of a parent's prior marriage get along is how many of each there are in the step-family. When there is only one of each, and they are each other's only brother or sister—full, step, or half—the attachment is usually greater than if one or the other is a member of a group of full siblings.

Both of Tricia's parents have remarried. Her father has one child in his second marriage, her mother has two. As a result, Tricia feels closer to her father's daughter than to either of her mother's children: "She's really important, because she's the oldest sister. I don't have any full sisters, so she's the oldest any-related sister that I have, so she's the one I try to be the closest to. She's my sister. She's my friend. We share a room, so we have to be. We fight a lot like sisters of the same age, even though I'm six years older, and then we don't fight a lot. We share each other's secrets."

In contrast, her mother's children form an intense unit, at least in her mind. She is glad there is a large gap between her and the two more closely spaced children. "I think it would be really hard," Tricia continued, "if I was one or two years older than Eva [her mother's next oldest child]. Because it would be more like I would want to be part of that crew, and in a way I wouldn't be, because they're a full sister and brother and I'm not. So it's really good that I'm older than all of them, because instead of being the scapegoat, instead of being pushed out with 'Daddy's our father and he's not your father,' I'm pushed up and looked up to."

Sometimes, however, she does wish that she were closer in age to her father's daughter. "Because there isn't anyone else that she's an-other sister with, so there would be no reason for her to push me out. I would be her sister, and she doesn't have another one, so she wouldn't not consider me one of the crowd." Eventually, she consoles herself that things are probably best as they are, with six- and eight-year gaps in both households, since if she were still closer to her father's daughter it would create an imbalance between the households, making her mother's children feel bad that she was more attached to her father's daughter and, she fears, distressing her mother as well.

What she would really like, her impossible dream, is for her two parents to have had a child closer to her in age, but even more important, "someone who would be in my exact situation." Her biggest complaint, indeed her only complaint, when she contemplates her parents' divorce, is that they deprived her of the chance to have "another kid my age that has both my parents." The benefits that Tricia longs for are validated by those who had what she missed. The stepchild who rotates between households, whether visiting or in joint custody, finds that a full sibling as traveling companion lessens the strain of navigating these transitions. Judith remembers that it was very helpful for her to have had an older sister in dealing with her parents' divorce and subsequent remarriages. "It would have been much more difficult if I'd been an only child. I always felt that whatever else happens, I have my full sister, my sister who's close to me in age. If I felt threatened by my father having another child, I also knew that Bonnie and I had each other."

Divide and conquer can become the order of the day when there are two children from one marriage and only one from the other, regardless of whether it is the first or second union that had the additional child. When there is a single mutual child and two or more children from the first family, the older children rival one another for the affection of the baby and enlist him in their struggles with one another. Even when the two older children are buddies, the arrival of a mutual child can drive a wedge between them, as one becomes closer to the baby and the other feels like "second best" in his efforts to befriend the newcomer.

Although the alliance of the two older children generally remains primary, it can be unbalanced when one is closer than the other to the mutual child. And the little one shows amazing precocity in playing off one bigger kid against the other, exploiting one of his limited resources by playing favorites in bestowing his affection. Even as a two-year-old, my son David could set nine-year-old Brian off and swearing by insisting that Antonio, then eleven, push his stroller or sit next to him. From his vantage point, the two big boys formed a unit: They were large, powerful, engaged in fascinating activities, and traveled back and forth between our home and their mother's. The only way for him to gain entry to the group of brothers was to pry them apart, letting one come close while holding the other off. Obviously, this strategy cannot be rigidly maintained, because even the medium-range effects of alienating a powerful sibling bring retribution, as exclusion is met by exclusion. Every now and then, David would turn his attention to Brian, wooing his favor, only to keep him off balance by returning to shower affection on Antonio, who was not above flaunting David's preference.

When the older two engage in battle, the mutual child can be enlisted in the ranks, usually of the more powerful sibling. Several families reported that one of the big kids would get the little one to hit his rival for him, call him names, or otherwise act as his deputy in sibling rivalry. Alternatively, even in the same families, the little one can serve as a welcome diversion from brotherly battles.

Over the years, alliances can shift, so that the stepchild who was closest to the mutual child as an infant or toddler may not be the one whom he spends the most time with even a few years later. When Eddie was born, it was Barry, then ten, who was most interested in him. His older sister, Kara, had been quite put off by the whole baby business, and had kept her distance from her father's new family. Now that Eddie is five, he and Kara, now twenty, have become "the best of buddies," and Barry has stepped back a little from Eddie. Elizabeth, mother and stepmother of the family, explains the shift: "Now it turns out that Eddie and Kara are very close. They're kind of like birds of a feather. Their father sees the most resemblance between Kara and Eddie. Very high-strung, very emotional, keenly intellectual, super high and lows, emotions in the extremes. Each being the firstborn in their own family, kind of." Faced with this kind of affinity, Barry chooses not to compete.

When it is the stepchild who is the only child of both his parents, the divide and conquer strategy is deployed with even greater sophistication. While alliances are hardly stable, with the older child rallying with one and then the other of the little ones, the most prevalent pattern is for the stepchild to favor the younger of two mutual children, seeing himself as her protector in her rivalry with her immediate senior. Now an adult, Gretchen remembers being very mothering toward the younger of her mother's daughters with her stepfather. "I had to protect her from her older sister, who was always trying to throw her out the window. But it wasn't really fair. It was more child abuse," she said, "because I was five years older than her. Whereas she was always very willing to throw the little one off the balcony, I was always very eager to catch the little one and beat up the older one, who was always ripping my dolls to shreds, and generally having a hard time of it, between the oppressive older sister and the too-adorable younger sister."

With a perspective on their family unavailable to her then, she observes: "I was very much into a power trip with all these younger kids. My mother had a new marriage, and then her husband died. She was completely distracted as a mother. I sort of took over, and I was a real force to be reckoned with in the family. Looking back on it, it must have been a dangerous thing to do to the little ones, because I had my own ax to grind, and there was a lot of time when I was alone with them, trying more to assert my power and control over them rather than helping them develop or cope."

Sometimes the stepchild's use of the power of seniority comes from feeling excluded when the mutual children, united by age and sharing both parents, are particularly close. "Ivy is very attached to Yale," Melanie reports. "Whenever she talks about her best friend, she says, 'My best friend, Yale.' Sometimes when she's whining, like when she's sick or tired or can't have something she wants, Paul will come in in the middle of her whining and run over, put his arms around her. She'll cry and say, 'Get away from me,' and he'll say, 'My own sister doesn't even like me.' It's real hard to watch him invite rejection like that." Paul's response to this completely predictable rebuff is to pick on Yale.

It would be a mistake, however, to assume that attachment always follows full sibling status. Andrew has a half sister from his father's first marriage, and two sisters who have the same mother as he. As a child, he was "factually but not emotionally" aware that the oldest girl was not his mother's daughter. He is closer to Jean than he is to his full sisters. "Jean was wonderful to me, she was my second mama. I was kind of her baby. We're just particularly close. The bond is unshakeable."

When there are two or more children from both marriages, it is more usual, however, for alliances to be made principally within full sibling groups, especially when they do not share a roof full-time. All the children then have someone in exactly the same boat, someone who shares both their parents, is near in age, and grows up under similar circumstances. Finding companions right at hand, children are less likely to cross the divide and become intimate with those who sometimes seem to dwell in a completely different world, especially when half a generation or more may separate them.

Regardless of the eventual numbers on each side of the marital divide, it is the two children on the frontier of the remarried family, the youngest stepchild and the oldest mutual child, whose relationship most plays out stepfamily issues. It is the youngest stepchild who, as baby of the original family, is most vulnerable to feeling displaced by the first mutual child. And it is the first mutual child who, in finding a place for himself in the family, compares himself to his half sibling and discovers that their differing relationships with the adults in the house color what it means to be siblings.

Stepsiblings

In a "his" and "hers" stepfamily, to which both parents bring children from previous marriages, the mutual child can promote closeness among stepsisters and stepbrothers. Earlier research by Lucille Duberman has shown that the birth of a baby improves stepsibling relationships.[3] And it is in these "yours, mine, and ours" stepfamilies that the mutual child, while occasioning some shifts in family organization, is least disruptive. As John and Emily Visher have noted, both adults have already had the experience of being a parent and a stepparent, and all the children involved have already had to deal with sharing a parent with other children.[4] The children have already gotten used to having a stepparent who is another child's biological parent and a biological parent who is another child's stepparent. They have come to terms with the differences in emotional response between each parent-child pair: They know that with one adult they may have an edge, while with the other another child has some advantage. While they may still envy the child who is equally related to both adults, they are more likely to see differences as balancing in the long run.

In the short run, however, they can vie with one another over who is more important to the baby, who, at least at first, is at the family's center. Even when they share a household full-time, there can be competition among the children for who gets to hold the baby more, and who has more claim to insider status with the new arrival. Sometimes the competition occurs along gender lines, with girls claiming greater expertise in baby care than their brothers and stepbrothers, grabbing the baby from less-practiced arms with an accusation: "You'll cause mental retardation if you hold him that way."

Because stepsiblings are usually closer in age than any of them is to the mutual child, age may supersede blood ties in making peers more interesting to one another than a much younger child is to any of them. Both Deirdre and Tony were six when her mother and his father had a son together. "They were really very nice to him, and sweet with him," said Bridget, mother and stepmother. "But after the novelty wore off, and he got a little bit older and started getting into their things and messing them up, you know, he was kind of a pain in the butt sometimes. A lot of times." She laughed, and then considered the position of Alexander, the mutual child. "Sometimes for him it was kind of hard, because they always got to do stuff around the same time, and he always had to wait. So, they would be off, like they could go to the movies alone, and he kind of felt a little bit left out of that one." Meanwhile the bigger kids engage more with one another in the kind of sibling squabbles that Bridget remembers from her own family growing up. "Sometimes they're really close. They get along okay and hang out a lot. Then he'll act real goofy and come on to her friends, and she'll say, 'Oh, he's just acting like a jerk.' Or he'll say, 'Oh, she thinks she knows everything.' You know, the usual sort of stuff."

Taking care of the mutual child can be the way that stepsiblings become better friends, so that the closer each of the older children gets to the younger one, the closer they get to one another. Fifteen-year-old Scott, for example, finds that his mother's one-year-old daughter has been an opportunity to get to know his stepsister, Talia, who is thirteen, while his stepbrother, who is not particularly interested in the baby, remains distant from Scott as well. Stepsiblings are keenly aware that the mutual child belongs to them equally and can feel both empathy and guilt for feeling at an advantage vis-à-vis the mutual child.

Stepsiblings become closer when there is a mutual child only if they have contact with one another. Although the mutual child can feel almost mystically related to a half sibling he barely knows, that sense of instant kinship does not extend to stepsiblings. While Alexander believes that all of his half siblings love one another, Deirdre, his mother's daughter, while close to her stepbrother, Tony, who shares their household, feels no connection with her stepfather's daughters, whom she has barely met. When these adult daughters came to visit, Alexander and Tony had a wonderful time showing them the town, while Deirdre went out with the others only once, felt uncomfortable, and withdrew from their company. Her mother reports that "she felt they treated her funny, I guess because all of those four were related, she felt sort of funny." Twelve-year-old Alexander, on the other hand, although he has seen his father's daughters only twice, feels that they have a deep mutual understanding and "that I've known them as far back as before even they was born. We knew each other when God made us."

Under Two Roofs: Half Siblings Who Don't Live Together

When one set of half siblings is in residence and the others are visitors, it is the absent siblings who are more exciting, their novelty compelling the attention of the mutual child. The excitement generated by the visiting stepchild can be a source of friction between the mutual child and the half sibling who lives with him all the time. When Julia married Ben, her eight-year-old son Jeremy lived with them and his eight-year-old, Josh, came to stay every other weekend. A year later, Ira was born. Julia tells how the triangle among the three boys created this pattern: "Josh had a nice relationship with Ira. He didn't have to live with him all the time. Ira idolized Josh and punished Jeremy. If Jeremy refused to do something with Ira, Ira would say 'When Josh comes this weekend . . .' or when Josh came, Ira would only want to be with Josh. Poor Jeremy felt awful. And then he'd beat up on Ira for the next two weeks, because Ira had just dumped on him. And then Ira would be pissed, so that by the time Josh came, he'd be ready to fawn all over Josh. So Josh got, every other weekend, this baby brother who idolized him. It was something to look forward to at our house." The more Ira moved toward Josh, favoring him over Jeremy, the more Jeremy made daily life unpleasant for Ira, and, completing the cycle, the readier Ira was to wear his heart on his sleeve for the big brother who was seldom there, keeping the battle raging on the home front. Yet, in the midst of this triangular tumult, Jeremy and Josh did become closer to each other than they had been before Ira was born, playing with him as an infant and then tiring of him and going off to pursue eight-year-old fun.

Smoothing transitions for visiting stepchildren can help take the edge off competition among the children about who is most interesting to whom. When an older child visits for the weekend, her stepsister may be looking forward to her arrival as a time when a playmate of the same age will be available to her. When the visitor's priority, as is frequently the case, is to make a connection with the parent she sees only on alternate weekends or, when a mutual child is a new addition, the baby brother she feels deprived of getting to know, the resident stepchild can feel slighted.

Visiting stepchildren, for their part, struggle with feeling that they're missing out on a lot, since "real life," the everyday routines of both parent and mutual child, is what occurs in their absence. Even when opportunities for contact are rare, however, if parents make an effort to integrate the older child, both children can find great meaning in their connection, attaching significance to their relatedness that surpasses the opportunities they are given to explore it.

The mutual child is more often on good behavior with stepchildren who are infrequent visitors, so that "the brat age" is less frequently mentioned by the older children when they don't have to live with a preschooler on a daily or even a weekly basis. The visitor gets much more excited adoration, the "goodies" of being an older sibling, without as much of the aggravation of accommodating to the demands of a much younger child. However, because they are not there to share the everyday routines, the more informal exchanges of family life, older children who spend little time under the stepfamily roof may feel less related to the mutual child than those who are his daily companions.

After the initial excitement, most pronounced in babies and toddlers, the child of remarriage begins to try to make sense out of a relationship that is so intermittent. "Who are these big kids? What are their claims to my Dad? How important am I to them?" At four, for example, Erica is working at coming to terms with the annual visits of her half sisters, ten and fifteen, who live in a distant state. Her mother describes a recent conversation with Erica, occasioned by the older girls' impending arrival: "I explained to her that Daddy used to be married to their mother, and that he's their father, too. When we were driving to school the day before they were coming, she said, 'I want to spend a day just with my Dad alone.' I said, 'Okay, but you're going to have to wait until Polly and Nila leave.' 'Well,' she said, 'I don't want to share him,' and she started crying. 'I don't want them to come.' You have to understand that she feels displaced by our one-year-old, too. I said, 'I'm not saying you shouldn't feel that way. You can. I just want you to try to understand how hard it is for Daddy not seeing Polly and Nila, and how hard it is for them not to see Daddy. It's only a week, and you get to be with him all the time.' My husband said it was going to dissipate as soon as they came, which it did. She couldn't care less about being with him right now."

Several of the mutual children whose half siblings never shared a roof with them volunteered that had they not known that my interest was in families in which there were children from past and present marriages they would not have included the older children in their drawings of their family. Because I asked them to depict their family "doing something together," the children "who didn't live with us because they were so much older" or "lived so far away" were not part of their repertoire of images of shared family activities. When I asked one seventeen-year-old how she thought it would have been different with her half siblings, thirteen and fifteen years her senior, had they lived together, she answers, as would many in her position: "It would have been crazy. It's such a big family, and so many different relationships. And we would have been going through the 'terrible twos' when they were going through adolescence. It would have been more difficult, but I also think that we would have gotten to be closer than we are."

With joint custody, children have both the best and the worst of each world: enough familiarity to feel like siblings and enough distance to keep alive the issues of territoriality. Reentry can be difficult. For the child reentering the home, there is the sense of having missed out on what has been happening without her, wondering if she has been missed, and thinking about what she's missing in the other home. For the child who lives there all the time, sharing space and toys and parents whom he's had all to himself takes getting used to, once again. Closer in age than most half siblings, Patty and Ivan are a good example of how children in joint custody can become possessive, even exclusive about territory. Nine-year-old Patty spends every afternoon in her father's house, returning to her mother's house after dinner, except for the two nights a week she sleeps at her dad's. While five-year-old Ivan "thinks Patty is God," according to both his parents, "she has not always looked so kindly upon him. She sees him as an intrusion," in her stepmother's view, "less so now. She's not here all the time, and he is, so he used to get into her toys. She felt that nothing was sacred. We had to work that one out. She's begun to feel some control, and it became very clear to him that there really were some things that were off limits. When they weren't getting along well a couple of years ago, she expressed it by saying he could never come over to her house again, her mother's house." When she hadn't been able to restrict his access to her territory in the home they shared, she cut off all access to her territory in the home that was hers alone.

Parents, who generally agree that it's "rough" when the children haven't seen one another for a while, observe that bickering seems to be concentrated around the arrival and departure of the children in joint custody. And while adults tend to think that there would be less friction between the children if the older children were in residence full time and didn't have to navigate often stormy transitions, the children disagree. Unable to take a more long-range view, blind to the possibility that more time together could change the nature of the contact and not merely bring them more of the same, they assume that they would fight more if they were around one another more. "I'd probably think of him as more of a brother than as a half brother," said sixteen-year-old Larry about Owen, just three-and-a-half, "if I lived here all the time. It's probably better that we're not, because when they're more your brother, I don't know why, but you fight and get annoyed with them. When you're around somebody all the time, inevitably you get tired of them. So, I think it's good that we're just here half the time."

Baby-sitting

A few years ago, a cartoon in *The New Yorker* showed a middle-aged couple sitting on a couch, their year-old child in a playpen nearby. The caption read: "What do we do now? Neither yours nor mine wants to babysit for ours?" Although most of the older children who have become confident of their ability to take care of young children gained this competence through baby-sitting, there is a vast range of difference in family policy as to who baby-sits for whom, whether they're paid, and whether they can be conscripted or must volunteer.

Parents who employ older children to take care of their mutual child tend to take one of two tacks, paralleling families with children old enough to baby-sit for one another who are not stepfamilies. One approach is that baby-sitting is a voluntary activity, which should be reimbursed, so as to minimize resentment. "We didn't want her to feel like Cinderella," said Eleanor, referring to fifteen-year-old Pamela. "We were very sensitive of not putting Pamela in the position of being the drudge, or doing child care. Occasionally she was asked to help take care, but it was very unusual."

Sometimes this stance emerges as a reaction to criticism of practices in the stepchild's other household. One woman, who tends to make minimal demands on her twelve-year-old stepson, came to this position because she thinks he is asked to do too much by his mother, who also has a year-old child. And when her stepdaughter's mother accused her and her husband of only wanting them as built-in baby-sitters, another stepmother resolved that while they could volunteer, the older girls would never be required to take care of her daughter.

An alternative approach, taken by some parents, is that caring for younger children is an appropriate, unreimbursed household responsibility that an older child owes as a family member. Her husband expects both of his older children, of whom he has joint custody, to be the primary baby-sitters for their children, according to Elizabeth. "He's never given them any monetary reimbursement. This is one of their obligations as a part of the family, that they be available, if they don't already have other plans. We both think it's very beneficial that family members be available and get to spend time with the kids, no matter what the schedule is or what house you're supposed to be at at the time."

Some stepparents, not always in agreement with their mates, are so concerned about not creating a Cinderella that they insist on another baby-sitter, hoping that the older child will choose to go out for the evening, avoiding the awkwardness of having a baby-sitter when a teenager of the same age is lolling around the house. Early attempts at having an older child baby-sit, sometimes during the more explosive developmental "matches" described earlier, sometimes involved so much friction that the adults delay trying again well past the time when the children have worked out their conflicts or the older has acquired enough maturity to competently handle the job. Stepmothers, ever mindful of being thought wicked and more distrustful of their stepchildren, are less inclined to require or even ask their stepchildren to take care of their children than mothers, who are readier to leave their younger children in the care of their older ones. While some stepmothers, especially those who are first-time parents, insist on only leaving their children in the care of adults over twenty or twenty-five, the reason for this can be family dynamics rather than a lack of confidence in the older child's competence. Here the objective may be to avoid the contradictions of being both a stepparent and an employer, since a hired hand is more likely to follow directions and devote his exclusive attention to the care of the children, while an older child, in his own home, may carry on more or less as usual "with an eye out" for the little ones.

Typically, those stepchildren who are not often trusted to take care of their half siblings wish that they had been given more responsibility, while those who are relied upon regularly can feel resentful. In listening to the children talk about what they did and didn't like in what was expected of them, the theme is clearly that they wanted to do what they wanted to do when they wanted to do it.

Among the most burdened was one woman, now in her forties, who remembers being asked to do a great deal, in terms of both household responsibilities and child care, as the oldest of her father's five children, three with the woman he married after her mother's death. Very attached to the smaller children, she resented only that she was not allowed to go out when she wanted to, not because of trust or curfews, but because her stepmother had to care for five kids, three of them under three years old at one point. While she would not have wanted to relinquish all responsibility for the children, seeing them as an important source of affection and connectedness to her father's remarried family, the demands felt excessive.

Paula wanted to take care of her half sister more than her stepmother would allow at first. "She didn't want me to feel negatively toward Angela at all." As a twelve-year-old, Paula had loved playing with the baby and taking her for walks. "I was motherly, and changing diapers didn't bother me. When I was older I wanted to spend time with her, but I didn't care for the assumption that as an older sister you *should* take care of her once a week after school, because 'your little sister really cares for you and she never gets that much time with you.' Not that a sibling shouldn't have to, but because they had promised that I'd never have to. I did enough that I wanted to do, but it was a little bit of 'it shouldn't have to be that way.'" Her chief objection was a perceived lack of choice.

Weathering a Second Divorce

When remarriages end in divorce, as more than 50 percent are reported to do,[5] the relationships among half siblings will depend on how the adults deal with their separation. When they share a mother, and the mother retains primary custody, statistically the norm, the children will be more "in the same boat" than ever. Because they have a relationship with their single parent that is structurally the same for all, half siblings who are all their mother's children, with no stepparent in the home, can be more like "regular brothers and sisters" than they were before the divorce, since none of them has a special tie to an adult within the household. "I never think of him as a half brother," said one twenty-year-old, referring to the child of her mother's second marriage, which had ended more than ten years before, "the family has always been Mom and her kids."

When they share a father, the range of possibilities is greater. At one extreme is Sol, who after his father's second divorce saw his half brother again only once, at the father's funeral, and doubts that he would recognize him if he saw him on the street. When there is more contact between father and children, fathers actively strive to keep their children connected. One man, separated from the mother of his five-year-old son, has worked out a visitation schedule designed so that the two days his sixteen-year-old daughter is with him include at least one day when his little boy is there, too. "They're still very attached to each other," he believes, "but she, at sixteen, is less domestic."

When the remarriage, too, ends in divorce, seeing a half sibling go through what they themselves have experienced can create a bond between children from previous and later marriages. "I feel real connected with her," said Gwen of the half sister born when she was sixteen. When the younger girl was five, their father again moved on, abandoning his younger daughter as he had left his older children seven years before. "I feel she's more than just a stranger. I'd like to get to know her better. I have this fantasy that I can understand her, and she can understand me in a way that's probably unique. Because he did almost exactly the same thing to her that he did to me." Telling of the time that she surprised the younger girl, then twelve, by appearing at their doorstep and announcing that she was the sister whose existence until that time had been a secret, she said, "Within the first twenty-four hours when I found her, she danced for me and we played sports.

And my dad's big things were music and sports. He had encouraged her along those lines as well. I have this idea that she and I share this kind of special parenting, that we had real early. In that sense, I'm glad she's there." There are no negatives, despite her early apprehension that her stepmother's baby would be a girl who would replace her. "He hasn't been there for her either, so I can't really say that she's taken him away, or in any way diminished what I've gotten from him." Instead, their shared experience of abandonment is a basis for solidarity. "When I was getting ready to leave, my sister just got hysterical," Gwen remembered. "I was trying to comfort her, and she just was crying and saying, 'Everybody leaves me, everybody always leaves me.' And I knew exactly what she was talking about."

Strengthening the Bond Between Half Siblings

Everything else being equal, which of course it never is, stepfamilies mesh most when there is one child from a past marriage and one child from a present marriage. With more parental time available to minister to both children's need for affection and attention, there is less opportunity to feel deprived. When a half sibling is a child's only sibling, he is less likely to look for and find distinctions than when he compares a "real" brother to those who are "just steps and halves." Each child has a stake in affiliating with the other: There is no "us and them," it is just "you and me." In contrast, when there are two or more children from each marriage, each child is likely to be closest to a full sibling with whom he shares a history as well as both parents. But however many children there are in all, their relationship depends most on the quantity and quality of their time together.

Growing up together is how brothers and sisters come to feel closer to one another. So, too, with half siblings, which is why children spaced more closely tend to feel more connected. Sharing a genetic inheritance without contact generally does not lead to an enduring relationship. In contrast, children who have shared a roof for most of their childhood, who have grown up with the same cuisine, the same decor, the same neighborhood, the same holiday traditions, and more or less the same child-rearing beliefs and standards have a common heritage that provides a thick weave of connection. In adult life, they look to one another as living witnesses to childhood memories that are enriched and enlivened by having been shared.

When stepchildren come and go, they are acutely aware that most of the family's life together occurs in their absence, and are more fearful that the mutual child, because of his physical proximity to the parent they share, will colonize their emotional territory as well. A parent's time that is exclusively theirs reassures visiting stepchildren that their place in the family, while often unoccupied, is reserved for them alone, even in their absence. Easing transitions for both sets of children involves recognizing that disparate needs can only be met with planning, organization, and clear expectations, creating opportunities to get beyond the excitement of unfamiliarity and providing time to become brothers and sisters.

Parents and stepparents informed about the politics of half brotherhood and half sisterhood can be strategic about how they enter into the children's quarrels. Parents typically underestimate the ability of little children to torment their bigger sisters and brothers. And the little ones soon learn that a strategically placed scream can bring a parent to the rescue, ready to pounce on the older child, who is assumed to be the aggressor since he is, in any case, "older and should know better." In stepfamilies, by the time the mutual child is three or four he has learned that at least one of the adults in the family is likely to see him as in need of protection and will jump to intercede, condemning the elder and soothing the younger. When my stepson Antonio was the mutual child in his parents' remarried family, he remembers taunting his half brother, Sean, seven years his senior. When the two boys were fighting, Antonio would run to his mother for assistance, then stick out his tongue at his brother from behind her back as she scolded Sean. His manipulation was calculated, but invisible to the adults.

Sometimes the use of different status is more explicit. When Annie, for example, was being mean to Jessica, she said, "Why don't you go to Seattle and live with your Daddy?" Even at four, she knew how to use the difference in the girls' relationship to her father against his stepdaughter. The dad in question remembers that "she never did that again. I don't think she dared to, 'cause I'm sure we all said 'Wait a minute!' " Both of her parents clearly let her know that in their family it was not acceptable to use her biological relatedness to both parents as a weapon against her half sister. Their clarity and forcefulness on this issue allowed the girls to work out their disagreements as sisters, each assured of a secure place in the family.

While children who share a roof feel more like siblings than those who spend less time together, when stepfamily politics continue to ravage, less frequent contact reduces the psychological stress for each group of half siblings. The children, left to their own devices, cannot be expected to repair the rifts in the larger family network. Whether conflicts are contained within the stepfamily household or occur between households, children will mirror the larger picture. If the mutual child and his older half siblings are thorns in one another's sides, the would-be Androcles among the adults must look beyond each child for the shadows of larger combatants.

11

When the Children
Are Grown

Sooner or later in the life of the mutual child, the children of a parent's earlier marriage become adults and move out on their own. If all the children have shared a household, the mutual child sees the older children less. If they have lived with their other parent most or all of the time, they may have more contact with the stepfamily now that they no longer have to account to a custodial parent who might feel wounded by the attention paid to the remarried parent's new family.

For the mutual child whose adult siblings come and go, visits can be a confusing and stressful time. The younger children, eager for contact with the older ones, try to monopolize their time. Their half siblings can seem glamorous, exciting explorers of the "awesome" adult world, people they admire, want to emulate, and want to know. As they reach an age, frequently the preteens, when they think about relationships in a new way, they want to build a stairway to the stars to reach these distant idols. The young adults, for their part, are often more interested in spending time with their parents, and may resent the clamor of the younger children for their attention. "They've got Dad all the time, why can't they give me a chance?" they think to themselves.

Alicia, for example, looking back at eighteen, remembers that between eight and eleven she was really sensitive to what her older brothers and sisters thought of her. "We would have family gatherings, and Grant would say something, and I'd end up crying and running up to my room. I don't think he realized I was young. Things like 'Alicia, be quiet, I'm talking right now.' And I didn't understand why he would say that, and they all got a lot of attention. I did, too, but I didn't realize it, because I was here all the time. But when they came over, it would be, 'How's your new job?' 'How's your new boyfriend?' 'What's new?' on and on. I was jealous. I think I was really obnoxious around that age. I was trying to get attention, so around family things I would really be loud and try to act the center of attention. Talia was always saying 'Alicia, be quiet,' and treating me like I was her baby." One of the older children, who genuinely loves her, remembered the same period as "years when I didn't like her. She was a pain in the butt. I don't know if it's because . . . in retrospect, she's felt that she's had six moms and dads, all telling her what to do."

Even when the now-adult stepchildren recognize that the mutual child is acting very much as they themselves did at the same age, they see the youngster as an obstacle to their own contact with their parent. At nineteen, Greg is clear about his priorities: "I go to my dad's to see my dad. I feel some connection to the kids, but being with them doesn't mean that much to me, which is more and more true as I've gotten older. I don't particularly feel the need to see my stepmother and the kids. I don't want to say they're excess baggage," he said, "but they come with the territory." Lately, he's taken to visiting his dad when the two of them can spend most of their time alone together, with an evening with the younger children sandwiched between two days for father and son.

Ironically, adult children whose relationships with their parent and stepparent are more difficult and who visit less may seek respite in focusing on the younger children during visits. "They make it a lot easier to go visit Dad," said one man in his twenties. "My dad and I are really different people. We have different ideas about almost everything that's going on in the world. We get into a lot of arguments, and I don't really have a lot to say to my stepmother. So when I go over for a visit, it's really nice to have the kids around, because I can always play with them. They're a lot more fun to be with than Dad and Astrid."

Most stepparents tend to accept that their stepchildren's prime relationship is with their parent: "When they see him on rare occasions," in the words of one stepmother, "they want to touch base with him." Encouraging one-to-one contact between parent and adult child may fit the needs of the stepparent as well. The children of remarriage, however, are often disappointed and sometimes angry that their parent's adult children are not that interested in them. By the time they reach their preteens, when they are usually most interested in getting to know these elusive, attractive older siblings, mutual children may notice that their adult half siblings see them as "part of the territory," underlining that the younger child's interest in making contact is not reciprocated. Speaking of her father's daughter, now in her early twenties, one eleven-year-old told her mother: "You know, when she comes over, she never talks to *me*. She comes to see you guys. She asks for money, or she brings you these things. Well, the hell with her. You guys drop whatever you're doing and sit down and chat with her whenever she comes over. Why doesn't she say anything to me?"

From her mother's perspective, the lack of interest of her stepchildren has taught her daugher that half siblings are not the same as siblings. "My kids are always making little cards, birthday cards, Christmas cards, always including the older kids. But as the years go by, we see less and less of the older kids. Even the one that we do see isn't very warm toward them."

Another impediment for young adults in welcoming the company of a half sibling is that they take personally the misbehavior of the child and are embarrassed by their connection to him. Nor are they always practiced in making contact with a much younger child. "With a nine-year-old you don't live with," as one woman in her mid-twenties put it, "it's hard to have a sustained conversation on something that the two of you are really sharing. Because you're not there with the personal talks, you're not involved with the projects that she's doing in school, or something like that. Maybe I'll see her once a month, or talk to her on the phone every couple of weeks." Concerned that their father's nine-year-old, whom they see as sometimes acting up when she is around adults, would disrupt her wedding, Bonnie and her sister Judith thought about sitting down and having a very adult conversation with the younger girl about proper behavior. In the end, they did not act the Miss Manners with her, and they were delighted to find that she was "absolutely on the best behavior in her whole life . . . the hit of the party." What made the difference, Bonnie supposes, is talking with Enid about plans for the wedding for a full six months beforehand. "It gave us something to chat about. I would ask her what color dress she wanted to wear. She came with me to the fitting. Maybe in years

I'll look back and see that as something that really made for a big change between us." Being treated like a sister, rather than a potential source of embarrassment, gave Enid a stake in how the wedding would go, creating common ground between children who shared a parent but never shared a home.

Creating common ground seems to be the greatest challenge for half siblings. Being an only child of either marriage increases the motivation for the stepchild, as well as the mutual child, to maintain a relationship with the other. Dan, a devoted older brother, especially to the older of his father's two children with his stepmother, has "always enjoyed the kids," rating them as a positive addition to his time with his father's remarried family. "It might be different if I lived there," he speculated, at twenty-five. "I might want them out of my hair. But when I see them it's always short and sweet. I'm kind of like a goofball uncle who comes over and is filled with love and charm and enjoys being with them. I think the charm would probably wear off quickly if we were together, not that we would have a bad relationship. It's just that it wouldn't be as special as it is."

When they have previously shared a household, young adults are keenly aware of how they serve as a role model for their parent's younger children. Now eighteen, Paula is quite serious about her responsibilities to Angela, her father's seven-year-old. "Sometimes I tell myself, when I see faults in her, that it's not my duty to make her perfect." As a younger sister herself, she is just learning that "older siblings feel a need to take care of a little kid, and I hadn't realized that I felt that, too. We've become closer even though I moved away."

As young adults, many of the stepchildren I spoke with who were considerably older than their half siblings said that being old enough to watch the younger child grow and develop was a big advantage. Judy, for example, contrasted her sisters and brothers, the last of whom was born when she was five, and her half siblings, born when she was twelve to seventeen: "Because I was older when the babies were babies, I've gotten to see them grow up. If you talk about your sibling who's two years younger than you, you don't have an appreciation of what they're like at different stages. You do when you're sixteen."

Even when the age differences are smaller and the contact intermittent, older children cite the fun of witnessing child development as an advantage of having younger half siblings. Speaking of his father's eleven-year-old, twenty-year-old Tony says, "It's been fun being her idol, like when she called me up all the time. It's been interesting seeing her getting into the things preteens get into. She starts caring about her appearance and getting interested in music, not children's rhyme music, popular music. It's nice seeing her grow up to be the kind of person I want her to be like, she seems real open-minded. She's articulate and smart." He is also observant of how his younger half sister, then six, is acquiring new abilities: "Now she has the ability to make her own jokes. She's developed a sense of humor. Just seeing them acquire language skills is fun."

Both boys and girls mention that understanding better what young children are like has made them both better prepared for parenthood and more inclined to postpone becoming a parent. Although Glenn, at twenty-two, is unusual in having taken care of his mother's younger children for three days at a time, he found it a valuable but sobering experience. "It makes me want to wait and not have children until I get a little more patience." When they decide they are ready to have children, however, they are not intimidated by the prospect. Instead, they feel like old hands. Although not yet ready to have the children she and her husband are planning, Kathy, at thirty, is confident about taking care of children: "My body already knows how to hold a kid. I helped raise a child."

Young adults can derive a great deal of satisfaction, too, in the love and esteem in which they are held by their parent's mutual child. At twenty-two, Glenn delights in the affection of his mother's ten-year-old daughter and five-year-old son: "For the little amount of time that I spend with them, they both know very well who I am. They're really enamored with me. I think part of it is that they know I'm not quite a grownup. I have my own house and I work for my own money, but I'm not quite the same as parents and other grownups. Maybe it's because I act silly with them."

Men especially seem to express their protectiveness to their much younger half siblings. Glenn hypothesizes that his relationship to his mother's children "will be more paternal" in the future. And Peter, now in his thirties, is tremendously pleased that his half sisters look to him and his wife as role models, and that they have been confidants to the younger girls. Because his eighteen-year-old half sister lives nearby, at a great distance from her parents, he knows that his father and stepmother appreciate that their daughter has found another home in his house.

As adults, stepchildren who were previously denied responsibility for the mutual child by a protective stepparent are seen in a new light. Now entrusted with their care, however briefly, the young adult no longer feels the need to keep his distance from the kids. Delia remembers how thrilled she was to be given responsibility for the girls she had not been allowed to baby-sit for as a teenager: "I was home visiting, and I had to pick up some tickets. So I said, 'Mom, can I take Emily along for the ride?' In fact, I had both girls. And she said, 'Okay,' and she sort of looked at me as if to say, 'Is it going to be all right?' So I made the girls buckle up, and I wore my seat belt. We drove to Hollywood, I picked up the tickets, and we drove home. And I was thrilled to death that she would allow *them* to go with *me* somewhere, because she was really, really possessive of the kids back then."

Many of the older children, now young adults, report feeling closer to the children of remarriage now that they are out of the home. They miss one another and are happier to see one another now that they do not share, willy-nilly, a house, a table, a television, and their parents. When the stepchildren are grown and on their own, they can have a relationship with the mutual children that does not necessarily involve their parent and stepparent in its every crevice. The younger children may go on weekend visits to the home of an adult sibling, or, more modestly, go on an outing with a half sister and her boyfriend. "We'll get closer as she gets older," said one young woman of her father's nine-year-old, "because we'll be able to spend more time together, just the two of us."

As they develop an independent relationship with the preteen and teenage mutual child, the now-grown children of the first family can mediate between parents and half siblings, as an intermediate generation. "There are certain ways I'm a big sister to her," said Jill, now in her thirties, about her teenage half sister, Iris. "For example, she can talk to me about drugs or sex. And I've often felt between her and my parents in that way, wanting to set limits for her but not wanting to push her away to the extent that she'll feel hesitant to talk to me. So I've definitely catered to the idea that we're contemporaries, so that she can confide in me."

When they are old enough to reflect on the quality of their relationships, the children themselves observe that how well they get along can change with the ups and downs between stepparent and stepchild. Jill, for example, sometimes feels so close to Iris "that I would rip someone with my teeth if they hurt her." Still, "There is that edge between us because we don't share the same mom." And when Jill fights with her stepmother, she feels less close to Iris. "Iris couldn't see my side of it, because she was defending Mom. She's a younger kid, and she needs Mom in a way that a younger kid does. I don't feel free to color her vision really, so there are times when I feel that Iris is not understanding me."

Being seen as firmly in her parent's camp by half siblings who are at odds with that person, who to them is a stepparent, can be a dilemma for the mutual child, especially as a teenager. Wanting to be her own person, to be more with the older kids, to do things with them, she is less interested in being identified with her parents, however much she recognizes and values the ways she is like them. Knowing that the older children may link her to her parents, she struggles with this obstacle to feeling comfortable with and accepted by her half siblings.

People who were formerly distant can also become closer, affecting how each then relates to the third. Time, and the life cycle development of family members, can change stepfamily configurations, bringing stepchild and stepparent together as adults, just when the mutual child is differentiating from his parent during adolescence. Delia, for example, has found a new closeness with her stepmother, now that she is a wife and mother herself. As an adolescent, Delia longed to have the kind of camaraderie with the stepmother who was then her only mom that she fancied her friends enjoyed with their mothers. Instead, she felt her stepmother was "always reserved and pulled back. Since I got married," she recounts, "my folks have treated me differently. I do get the feeling that my mother feels closer to me. And since I had the baby, she has felt even *closer* to me, because she's talked to me about things that she never would before. It's just made it better. There's been a complete turnaround."

The price of the turnaround, however, is that as she gets closer and closer to her stepmother, she feels that her half sisters, in their late teens, have avoided her as a confidante. "I think I am alienating myself from my sisters sometimes. They won't necessarily tell me things that they think I'll tell Mom." Surmising that her brothers know things about the younger girls that she doesn't, she knows that, although she would never tell her sisters' secrets, she is now perceived as in alliance with her stepmother, reversing a pattern of earlier years, when she felt outside the tight circle formed by mother and babes.

As adults, stepchildren more fully appreciate the multigenerational texture of the remarried family with children. Speaking of the ways in which her father and stepmother's children made her life easier or more pleasant, Bonnie said, "For one thing it adds another generation to the family." Elaborating the generational steps in the family, this twenty-six-year-old began: "There's Enid, who's nine, and Andy, who's a baby, and Alexis, my stepmother, is thirteen years older than me and fourteen years younger than my dad. So, when we're all together, I'm sort of the middle generation. You can go back and forth. Get to be the kid when you want, and the grownup when you want. And I now have brothers- and sisters-in-law who are about Alexis's age. It's kind of nice. It's not just having the parents and then the children." Her twenty-four-year-old sister adds, "There'll probably be nieces and nephews soon, now that Bonnie's married. And I'll probably have children before he's too old and that kind of thing." Both sisters envision future family gatherings with their children and their half brother sharing a baby-sitter. Perhaps their half sister will do the job.

Despite some of the early difficulties in accommodating to a parent's having children in remarriage, adult stepchildren are near-unanimous in rejoicing in the existence of those children once they are grown up. "I think overall I like it," said Bonnie's sister Judith, now in her mid-twenties. "In spite of the difficulties that I had in getting used to Enid, I'm glad she's there. Now that I know them as real little people in my life, I certainly would not want to be without them."

Looking to the Future

Siblings' growing up, becoming good friends, and taking care of their parents in their old age is a fairy tale ending that sometimes even comes true. But with industrialization and a highly mobile population, far-flung families make this parental dream less and less a probability. When the children have only one parent in common and, perhaps, never live under one roof, there are more obstacles to continuing to feel and act like "family" once the children are on their own.

Siblings, including half siblings, who are a meaningful part of one another's early lives come to represent belonging, security, and attachment later in life.[1] While adulthood brings with it opportunities for developing the connection between half siblings who have been distant, the experiences they share early on leave indelible impressions. As almost any adult can attest, birth order effects are forever. Eighteen-year-old Paula, in looking toward how her relationship with her older sister will differ from that with her younger half sister, said: "Monica and I will be much more adult to adult, although there will still be always that older sister–younger sister idea, no matter how much we've done in our lives. And with Angela, I think that will be pretty heavily set in. Despite the fact that she may be fifty and I'll be sixty-one, I'll still have eleven years on her. I think it would be neat, at that point, if the three of us can be sitting around the table all as equals."

In early childhood, the mutual child is more committed to lifelong brother- and sisterhood than are his older half siblings. The remarriage's first child, like the oldest of all the children, envisions himself as the sibling who will be the family switchboard, keeping all the others in touch when they have gone their separate ways, making sure they get together for holidays. Imbued with the mission of family solidarity since birth, he carries the banner well into adulthood, unaware that the responsibility is not his alone. An only mutual child may, for example, underestimate the bonds between two sets of half siblings, seeing himself as better positioned by virtue of being related to all by blood, failing to understand that being agemates has created a closeness among the stepsiblings which he does not share.

When they become aware of the older children's relative lack of interest in them, their forecast for the relational future may shift. For example, Amber, at eleven, feels neglected by her adult half siblings. Asked to project how things will be among them when she, too, is grown, she thinks, "It will be farther apart, because we won't be with our parents. They'll probably be living off somewhere, and I don't think we'll see one another even at Christmas or holidays. They'll be visiting my parents, and I might be there at a different time. I don't think we'll cross paths that much."

Amber is responding to the diminished interest typically displayed by those in their late teens and early twenties in being around their families, in general, and younger siblings and half siblings in particular. Concerned with stabilizing their own sense of identity, establishing themselves in work and a love life that no longer centers on the family, these young people characteristically put more distance between themselves and the much younger children who are left at home.

"I deeply regret what happened," said a woman now in her forties, thinking back to the gulf that opened between her and the half siblings she had been very attached to in their earliest years. "Because of my need to lessen the emotional entanglement I felt, especially with my stepmother, and with my father to some extent, I basically stopped thinking about or relating to the kids. When I would go home, I became very aware of the fact that someone who had different values was raising these kids. It was hard to connect to them, and they grew so fast that I really felt I'd lost them. I still loved them a lot, but I visited the family maybe one day a year and felt we had very little in common." It was not until she was divorced and "noticed that I was getting old" that she made an effort to reconnect with her half siblings.

Once well established in adulthood, perhaps with children of their own, the children of the first marriage display a renewed interest in the families from which they come, and in getting to know their younger half siblings "as people." No longer competing for scarce resources, whether emotional or material, they can enjoy discovering what they have in common and being part of a larger family.

Unfortunately, the two groups of siblings may be out of sync when it comes to interest in getting to know one another. As youngsters, the children of remarriage are typically more unabashedly enthusiastic about the older children than the older children are about them. Like Amber, they may feel rejected and retreat, expecting little in return for their clamoring attentiveness. And when the older group turns back toward the family, seeking a new adult relationship with parents and siblings, they may find that mutual children who are in their late teens and early twenties are themselves turned outward, "too busy" to pay much attention to the half siblings who at last have time for them.

Not all half siblings will go on to transcend the separations of up to a generation of years. Adult relationships between half siblings vary enormously with the twists and turns of family circumstances. Several young adults, the offspring of a parent's first marriage, say that their continuing to see their half siblings will depend on a sister or brother who is closer to the younger children and will, therefore, be the future link between the first and second sets of children.

When the age spread is great and common experience slight, it may take an encounter with mortality to provoke half siblings to reestablish contact. Losing one parent, and anticipating losing the other, is an impetus for brothers and sisters to reconnect, yet between the desire to function like a close-knit family and the achievement of that goal lies an investment of time and energy that daunts the more ambivalent. When parents are no longer there to bring the family together, brother- and sisterhood becomes more ambiguous. Barry, for example, "defi- nitely" felt that his younger half brothers were as much family as he and his sister when they were children. At the time, the boys were young and Barry, more than a decade their senior, took an active role in their care, enjoying feeding and changing and playing with them. Now that their mother is dead, and the disparate influences on the two groups of children have led to their becoming very different in their interests and activities, the younger men are less clearly part of his family circle.

For most of the half siblings who spent concentrated time together as children, a lingering sense of relatedness remains. Judy is the second of the five children her mother had with her father before going on to have four more with her second husband. When Judy left her Detroit home thirteen years ago, her half siblings were between seven and twelve. Since then she has seen them only occasionally, with as many as five years passing between contacts. Interviewed just after her wed- ding, which convened all nine, now grown, she mused, "Given all that, it's remarkable that we all sort of feel like siblings, and keep in touch and all that, and like each other. In the last few years, any given visit was kind of a highlight.

"We all do feel like brothers and sisters," she continued, "yet at the same time, there are two different groups. Partly it's based on the other half of our family experience: Theirs is with their father and ours is with our father. They don't know my father real well, but they know who he is. And I certainly know their father. But at the same time, we're all my *mother's* kids, and we all grew up in the same neighbor- hood and had some common experiences." She supposes that in the years to come she will see her full siblings somewhat more, coming together at their father's home as well as at their mother's and seeking one another out independently rather than going home for Thanksgiv- ing and seeing whomever is there.

Leaving home, an event typically thought of as marked by youthful rebellion and parental desolation, can signal the beginning of dramati- cally improved times between stepparent and stepchild. Stepparents report feeling closer to their stepchildren when they no longer share a roof. "I'm much fonder of them," said Adrienne, not untypically, of her husband's three older children. "They're super to be with as long as they're not leaving their wet towels on my floor." And stepchildren find that being outside the thick of things gives them a new perspective on family politics. Delia, for example, remembers moving out of the family home at nineteen as "a real eye opener. I appreciated my parents in a way that I would not have if I'd stayed home."

For stepdaughters of young stepmothers, especially, reaching the age when the older woman became their stepmother can be enlightening. Alexis recounted how Judith, now twenty-four, looked at her and said, "I'm two years older than you were when you were married. I can't believe you were putting up with me when you were twenty-two!" Alexis laughed and added, "Neither can I." Judith, too, volunteered that getting to be the age that Alexis was when she "got us in the package" has made her understand what it was probably like for her stepmother. "Certainly at eight years old I couldn't have cared less what it was like for her," she said. "I thought totally about what it was like for me. I couldn't possibly imagine how difficult it would be to marry someone who had two small children. Now I think I can. We can look back and understand each other better."

The Shrinking Stepfamily

Losing family members, like making room for new relatives, forces a reorganization in the network of relationships among all stepfamily members. And it is not only children who leave home, be it with ease or difficulty. The departure of a parent or stepparent, by separation or death, can give rise to tremors that shake stepfamilies whose foundations are reinforced and deep. When stepfamilies end in divorce, relationships can end precipitously. A man's second divorce, when he has custody of neither set of children, can mean that the children have little or no future contact. One thirty-four-year-old woman has not seen her half sister since their father divorced the younger girl's mother twenty years before, dying shortly thereafter. And while stepparents occasionally assume custody of their stepchildren following a divorce, their right to see the children they have helped raise is generally contingent on the consent of the children's legal parents.

The death of a parent is always an emotional crossroads, but for the stepfamily in which he is the raison d'être for a relationship between his children and his spouse, his passing can threaten to disintegrate the family. What happens between a widow and her stepchildren will depend on what they have built up over the years together. Unfortunately, in the vulnerability of their grief, they can deepen one another's wounds, making reconciliation more difficult. Two years after her husband's death, Joyce finds it too painful to talk about how her stepsons responded to losing their father. Hearing that a boy she had raised from early childhood now considered himself an orphan, she felt invalidated, twenty years of doing the best she could to take care of him thoughtlessly discounted. For the young man, however, having his second parent die made him, in point of fact, an orphan, his stepmother notwithstanding.

Fearing abandonment by stepchildren, even when it is not forthcoming, widowed partners cling ever more closely to the child they shared with the deceased. Whether the mutual child, as the youngest, is the only child still living at home or has already moved on, he continues to represent the remarriage to his surviving parent. He is the reminder of good times shared, the physical embodiment of their union, a life raft to be clung to by a bereaved spouse. After years of a turbulent, enmeshed relationship that included not speaking to each other for long periods, Isadora's relationship with her mother "changed dramatically, drastically" with the death of her father. "We became very, very close," Isadora said, trying to describe the emotional intensity: "It was almost like being a baby again, not in terms of need, just in terms of bonding, connection. We really clung to each other. Of course, that couldn't last. I had to pull back from that. We're both struggling now to reestablish who we are. I grew up a lot. And she exhibited a kind of inner strength and cool and calm that I had *never* seen before, and it was a real relief to know she had. My respect for her went up tremendously. We have a lot more compassion for each other's differences now." Losing a husband and father first brought this "love-child" and her mother closer together and then, finally, allowed them to respect each other's individuality, as each began to see the other as a capable woman, and not the icon of a marriage and its sculptor.

When widow and mutual child are left at home together, becoming individuals can be still more difficult, as they may never yet have been very separate. Leaving a home with two parents is always easier than leaving a parent alone. When parents are together, and solidly so, the child can leave without worrying about abandoning a parent to loneliness. A mutual child, especially if he is the only child of both his parents, may have the added worry that his half siblings will abandon his parent, their stepparent. "I was really scared at first that my brothers would disconnect from my mother when my father died," said Evelyn, who was then sixteen. "I think I finally got it in myself that not only were my parents not perfect, but my sisters and brothers aren't perfect either. They're my role models, so it wasn't easy to see. Gene treated me like a little girl for a *long* time, calling to make sure I did my homework whenever my father was out of town. And when my father died, Gene would call all the time. It drove me up the wall. I was having a hard enough time by myself dealing with my father's death, and he was rubbing it into me. It was as if my mother wasn't around anymore." Gene saw himself as an orphan, and, in becoming more parental toward her, conveyed to Evelyn that she, too, was without parents. Hearing stories about "how the husband died and the wife couldn't live without him and died a year later" aroused her fears of losing her mother, who also clung to Evelyn more tightly as her stepchildren seemed to recede into the distance.

As individuals revert to their "worst selves" under severe stress, reviving discarded patterns of feeling and behaving, so, too, do families fall back into dysfunctional dynamics when stretched beyond their limits by loss. In neither case does the retrenchment represent a collapse of all they have struggled to achieve. Living things do not travel like arrows, propelled by a force beyond their control in an unwavering course that goes in one direction only. With people, and the families and stepfamilies they constitute, change is inevitable but not irreversible, with closeness creating a need for distance, and distance making renewed closeness more possible. Mourning can revive the alliances of earlier stages of stepfamily development, as both children and widow or widower deal with their profound loss. Yet the perspective to recognize this as a transitory response to stress, and avoidance of mutual blaming, can lead to strengthened connections among the grieving survivors.

The Rewards of Effort

Stepfamilies are one arena in which hard work clearly pays off. "It turned out to be a real success story, given where we were all coming from," said Elizabeth, stepmother now of a grown stepdaughter, a soon-to-be-grown stepson and mother of two little boys. "When I think back to how horrible it was, I'm amazed sometimes that I'm still here and that it's worked out to where we just don't have much friction or conflicts in the family." "Some of the things that you work and work and work on, that seem just totally futile, do pay off in the end," said another stepmother. "I can actually see how some of the things I like and respect in my middle kid as an adult come from me!"

With the passage of time, many stepparents and stepchildren come to an appreciation of one another that they did not anticipate in their early years. A stepmother now herself, Ingrid grew up with both a stepmother and a stepfather. "They were both real important to me," she remembers. "My stepmother was a good friend to me. I thought she was *wonderful* My stepfather was everything I could want in a stepfather. He loved kids, and he took me everyplace he went. He was a marine biologist. We looked in tide pools a lot, went to the lab. He was a hugger, very 'come on kids, let's go.' Things were pretty good when he was alive." Both her stepfather and her stepmother, by virtue of being different from her parents, gave her something *additional,* something she would have missed had she had only two parents.

Even stepchildren who have felt crowded by a remarried parent's new children develop empathy for their parents when they are themselves adults, and appreciate the benefits that inhered for all in decisions that in the short view seemed to leave them out. "I think having the kids made them younger in a lot of ways," said one woman, referring to her father and stepmother. "I'm glad they did. They deserved the opportunity to share that with each other. I think it would have been hard on my mother, having to raise three children that were not her own and not have the chance to experience childbirth herself. Having gone through it myself, I think you should have that opportunity, regardless of what situation you've married yourself into. Even though there was a lot of hardship and a lot of heartache. It wasn't always easy for us, and it wasn't easy for them. I remember as a kid, maybe in the first five years of their marriage, I would wake up and I'd hear them arguing. And my dad said, 'I never promised you a bed of roses. I told you it would be difficult.' But I think it made them better parents."

"The good things are that out of broken situations you come out with whole families," her father agrees. "There's a possibility of stronger ties in stepfamilies. You have to work at it more, because it didn't happen naturally. It's got to be better if you struggle and get through the problems. And I'll tell you, at the end it's a lot better than in the middle or in the beginning. We begin to reap what we've sown."

12

Another Entry in the Stepfamily Ledger

Dividing the Pie

To hear stepfamily members at their most impassioned, ask them about their checkbooks. Who pays for what for whom, and how everyone feels about how the financial pie is divided, consumes great quantities of emotional energy, symbolizing commitment and attachment as families subdivide and recombine.[1]

In the United States, most people can always point both to those with far more money and to those with far less. In *Stepmotherhood*, Cherie Burns observes that this is harder to take if they're in your family and "take a chunk out of your budget."[2] Stepparents, however, are not alone in feeling the strain of financial commitments to households in which they have little say. Parents, too, have emotional quarrels with how their ex-spouses spend the money they provide, and question the prolonged dependence of children well into their twenties. Stepfamilies tend to give a great deal of thought to what their financial obligations are and to whom they rightfully accrue. Not only must they figure in disparities in income and number of dependent children, the contribution of the children's other parents, and their beliefs about how money should be spent, but how generous or stingy each tends to be must also be factored in. Only the best and the least well off among them are immune to nagging questions about how love and money go hand in hand.

Financial Merger

The arrival of the mutual child can consolidate the remarried couple as a financial as well as a parental team. Less likely than first marrieds to throw all their earnings into a common pot, drawing from it to pay the family bills, remarrying couples often maintain separate funds, at least at first. Having been through one property settlement, the divorced are cautious about throwing in their economic lot with another person, however beloved at the time.

For most of these families, however, as the years creep by, the financial boundaries begin to blur. Whether or not the connection is explicitly made, most of the families that did keep finances separate at first moved toward more blending of accounts during the pregnancy leading to the first mutual child or at her birth. As childbirth frequently puts a crimp on the woman's earning power, expenses require the deployment of all available funds. Couples begin putting most of their income into their joint accounts, reserving only some modest discretionary income so as to be able to surprise each other on birthdays and holidays.

Several stepfamilies made this shift at a time that coincided with the birth of their first mutual child without explicitly tying the two events together. Bridget, for example, tells that "for a long time it was his money and my money, then it was just money. It happened after Alexander was born, don't ask me why. I think that the first wife needed some extra money in a crisis for one of the girls, and we kind of chipped in and gave it to her. Then after that it just kind of stayed that way. It wasn't agreed upon verbally, it just happened." What just happens is that, having had a child together, even wary remarriers recognize that, willy-nilly, their economic fates are commingled. The child is a living, breathing reminder that at least one of their financial obligations will be a mutual one for quite some time.

Obligations to their children, both original and mutual, can also make it socially and emotionally acceptable for full-time caregivers to accept support from their spouses. "I think we're both real clear," said Julia, "that I have not worked out a career, at making a career outside of being a mother and wife, homemaker, a supporter of everybody, because we had the boys. The kids give me an incredible sense of financial security, in terms of being able to relax into the marriage and not work. It's an economic stigma. It was terrifying to me not to work anymore. I prided myself on supporting myself through college with a kid." She credits her comfort with this arrangement to her husband's uniqueness in abjuring to call the tune even though he pays the piper.

As income tends to become concentrated in one pot, how that pot will be apportioned among the needs of family members can be a point of contention. Having more than enough money for everyone's needs minimizes stepfamily strife about who gets what. "When we first got married," said Alexis, "we had no money. The alimony and the child support were more than we were paying for rent. It was awful, and I was resentful. Then, if you're lucky," she continued, "it gets better."

Alexis and her husband, Bill, were lucky. "My policy," continued Alexis, "has always been to argue for major generosity toward the children, whether it's gifts or weddings or whatever. It works because there's enough money. If there weren't, all the old resentments would pop up. We would have to make choices, and I wouldn't like that. The children would come first, and I would concur intellectually and be glad that I had an equal number of children. As long as there are resources, it's easier to say, 'Oh, let's give the children this or that,' or, 'Let's make sure they come with us on vacation.' "

When, as is more usual, having a second family puts a considerable strain on the ability to support both, the resulting tension can further complicate relationships between stepparent and stepchild. Another couple live modestly on his income as a firefighter while she finishes school, preparing to teach. They have two boys, and his two older girls live with their mother in a distant state, visiting their dad's home yearly. "When I had my own kids," Uta said, "I learned that my own kids were number one. While I enjoy the girls when they're with us, I'm not always proud of the feelings that get stirred up by it, but they crop up at unfortunately the worst times. I wish I weren't so territorial in terms of my kids versus his kids. I wish I had the luxury to consider them a little more and not just myself and my boys. There are people who have large amounts of money, have optimum situations, and obviously there's going to be less stress and less problems. If I have a four-bedroom home and plenty of money, 'Come for two weeks, sure I'll fly you out. What's the problem?' "

When difficult economic choices must be made, couples find that their priorities are not the same. When the financial needs of one set of children are counterposed against those of the other, negotiations that allocate even scarce resources equitably, so that each parent is assured that no child is being shortchanged, are the only means to achieve continued couple solidarity.

Children Keep Tabs on the Family Ledger

The disposal of income within the stepfamily is also a pressing concern for its children. "My dad gives them money all the time," said one eleven-year-old, referring to her older half siblings, who themselves feel financially disadvantaged by their father's second family. The added responsibility of the new child or children is part of what keeps the stepfamily budget a tight one, deferring plans for retirement, perhaps, and making for less slack than would otherwise be the case, so that young adult children may have less help from their parents than do their peers. "It's them over us every time," said one young woman, referring to the children of her dad's second marriage, whom she sees as getting whatever they need, while she and her full siblings have received no help from him in financing their college educations. Her sister concurs that the only disadvantage to their dad having a new family is "the money situation: My dad probably wouldn't be so stingy with us if they weren't around, but I sure don't lay any blame on them. Not saying that we *should* be able to go to him, but we're sort of upper middle class, and our friends can go to their dads if they need help, and we can't. I'm not saying he gives more to them than he does to us. It's just that because they're little, they need to be supported by their parents."

Even when all the children share a household, stepchildren can pin their feelings of deprivation on the younger children, resenting that already scarce resources now must be divided six ways instead of four. In high school, getting two new school outfits when her girlfriends get several can easily lead a teenage girl to blame the existence of her baby brothers for the thinness of her own wardrobe. When stepfamilies include children from both parents' prior marriages, the size of the expanded family, rather than the mutual child per se, is the target of resentment, as children compare their current share of the pie with what they had before or think they otherwise would have. For Scott, now fifteen, his mother's remarriage added a stepbrother, stepsister, and half sister to the lineup of children, which had previously consisted of just him and his brother. "You don't have as much privacy, and it takes privileges away," he said. "Like you get less allowance. When it was just me and Bruce, my mom didn't have to spend all her money on food, and she could take us out to the movies and stuff."

In the natural evolution of family life, stepchildren mature and leave home, leaving the mutual children a smaller group of dependent minors. There may be more to go around for the children of remarriage because there are fewer mouths to feed, and as they become older and more expensive, their half siblings may have become self-supporting. Or parents, more established in their careers or with the benefits of seniority on the job, may have more economic stability. Without opting to give preferential treatment to the children of remarriage, the parents may, nonetheless, be able to provide more to the second family. With a house full of children, doubling or tripling up on bedrooms may have been the order of the day, with no possibility of exceptions. Yet the house that was crowded for eight people is spacious for three, leaving the mutual child with his choice of rooms. And even when the family finances remain pretty grim, when there is one child and not many, that one gets more of what little there is.

At holiday times, families on a tight budget may choose to give more substantial presents to their offspring who are still children, while presenting the young adults with gifts in which 'it's the thought that counts.' "Intellectually," said one woman, "I knew we had had our chance, but then again, I'm not sure that it had been such big deals. It felt a little like, because there was such a large family, and because there was a child, we had been graduated out of being children completely."

Seeing the children of remarriage as the recipients of a bounty, however modest, that contrasts with their own lesser fare, their half siblings see the younger children as insufficiently appreciative. "They've had a lot of things we haven't," said Dinah, "because Dad couldn't afford it when we were growing up. The boys were able to receive the benefits of having three of us out of the house. So I guess I think that they should be a little more thankful, instead of taking some of these things for granted, that we never had that they had. Sometimes they don't treat my parents . . . as gratefully as I think they should."

When children in a family don't all have the same parents, or the same grandparents, resources available to each can vary widely. A father may elect to "starve" in order to pay for the kind of education he wants his daughter to receive, while guiltily acquiescing to his stepchildren's going to schools he considers substandard because he doesn't have the money and their parents do not see the same need. Grandparents may leave money to grandchildren, who can then afford to live on campus while their older half siblings had to commute. But a financial advantage does not always favor the mutual child. Children of the first marriage, too, can be the beneficiaries of windfalls that their younger half siblings have no claim to, as when a father who is better off than his ex-wife's new husband sends his daughter to an expensive Eastern college while her half sister looks forward to a state university.

Typically, however, the mutual child is more accepting of these differences as inevitable. Whereas the older children feel entitled to share in the assets of the stepfamily, as well they should, the mutual child has no sense of entitlement with respect to the resources of those who exist on the periphery of his awareness: the older children's other parent and the grandparents they do not share. Not feeling deprived by virtue of his position in the family, he is not as likely to compound a sense of deprivation by examining the family ledger, demanding a strict accounting.

I Hereby Bequeath . . .

Death can highlight rather than end distinctions among the children in stepfamilies when they do not all share the same parents. While not alone in avoiding thinking about their wills, remarried couples encounter layer upon layer of complexity, as they struggle with the question of how to balance differences in attachment with difference in eventual resources to come up with a disposal of goods that leaves all feeling cared for. By far the most common response to my question "Do you have a will?" was "No, and we really should get to it."

The less a family has to leave, the less they are concerned about what to give to whom. "Oh, we'll divide it equally," said one mother, "all twenty-five cents." And a father, who labeled himself insolvent, said each of his children would inherit from their respective mothers only, making things clear and simple. Yet even when there is very little, children are themselves very aware that their own legacy may be diminished when their parent has additional offspring. At the other end of the spectrum, the beneficiaries of a trust fund bequeathed to all their mother's children may be concerned that the more children she has, the less they will eventually inherit. Even an older child who stands to gain only some few personal effects may wonder, now that he has a half sister, whether she will get it all.

While their share of the wealth, whether large or small, is a part of their concern, still more important is what the bequest symbolizes of the relative position of each child in the family. Now in her forties, the oldest child in a stepfamily that includes two children from a first marriage and three from her widowed father's remarriage decries the tension generated in her family by speculation about their parents' will: "The reality of inequality still exists today. There is an ongoing controversy about who's in the will in what way. I still don't know the truth of it. My father tells me one thing and my brother another. My father tells me we're all treated as equals in the will, and my brother sees me and him as being discriminated against. I think they're both actually saying the same thing, but interpreting it differently: that my father's half of their estate will be divided five ways and my stepmother's will go to her three. I haven't looked into it further, because I don't want to get focused on it, but I hate it all."

Most of the parents try desperately to be fair, and sometimes equality does not seem fair. The question of guardianship, for example, seems to come up for the children of remarriage, while the children of an earlier marriage that ended in divorce are presumed to have another home to go to. Having grown up without her father, who was killed in World War II, Susan is aware that there are risks she doesn't take because she has children. Because the chances of her dying at the same time as her ex-husband, who lives three thousand miles away, are "more than bizarre," her sense of responsibility is somewhat less profound for her older son than for the child she has with her current husband.

In thinking about possibly dying together, remarried couples whose ex-spouses are still alive see their mutual children as needing more because they would not have a surviving parent. Parents who plan to divide everything equally if all the children are adults when they inherit see the need to set aside funds for the guardian to a minor child who would be orphaned by their passing. Appointing a guardian can also be made more complicated by parents' wanting their children to stay close to their half siblings if anything happened to them. An aunt and uncle living halfway across the country, ordinarily a first choice to care for the children of remarriage, can seem a less desirable solution when it would mean compounding the hardship of losing parents with losing brothers or sisters as well.

Even when planning for the more probable eventuality that one adult will die before the other, many couples recognize that whichever of their children are minors at the time, more likely the children of the remarriage, will need more than those who are adults. Sometimes, in thinking about how to be evenhanded, the expenses of having already raised the children who are adults are figured in. Alexis, for example, tells that in rewriting their wills to reflect the arrival of their second child, she and Bill are trying to make them equitable. One way that they see of ensuring that the overall estate is divided equally is to provide for the additional care of the younger children, "those expenses that have already been paid for the older children—education, camps—that if Bill died tomorrow, they've already benefited from." Some families provide for this possibility by temporarily setting aside special funds to go to the guardians of their younger children, with a provision that everything will be divided equally once all the children are launched.

When resources are limited, the very real need to provide differently for a minor child than for his grown half siblings can still feel like deprivation to the adult children. While the rational side of an adult can recognize that a sixteen-year-old needs more financial help than a twenty-five-year-old, the bereaved child that dwells inside the adult can feel slighted.

When there is a single child from a previous marriage and the remarriage has been a long one, a live-in stepparent is apt to be more inclusive in his bequests, counting all the children and dividing the estate into equal portions. "Eleanor thinks of Pamela as one of her children," said Rick, whose wife has taken care of his daughter since her infancy. So, too, does Eliot count George as an equal with his daughters in thinking about how to allocate funds among the three. Feelings of relatedness that stem from the dailiness of the stepparent-stepchild relationship and the relative ease of including "just one more" allow for a generosity that greater distance and larger numbers make more difficult. Bridget, for example, clearly differentiates between her stepson, who lives with them, and the stepdaughters she hardly knows: "There aren't that many resources to divide up. I would definitely try to make sure that they were all taken care of, the three of them," she said, referring to her daughter, her stepson, and the child she has with her current partner. "I'm kind of hands off with the two older ones. It's a combination of things. Partly it's that I haven't spent any time with them, but I think it's also their mother's attitude. They can't help but have a little of that too. There's just something there that I'm uncomfortable with."

For a parent, it is harder to differentiate among children who are all equally his. Because Marv was initially so reluctant to have more children, he and Adrienne resolved that their children would in no way take away from the three children of his first marriage. His original plans for his will included a two-tiered system that favored the older children. "He separated what he'd earned and set aside before the time of the little kids' birth as belonging to the big kids," reported Adrienne, "and what he earned and set aside after that would go to all the kids. He was trying to keep that straight, and then he said, 'I can't do that. These are all five my children, I can't do that to the kids.' "

Both parents and stepparents, however, hesitate to be mathematically evenhanded when they foresee that doing so will create an imbalance in the eventual economic fates of their offspring. These families hold that it is essential to look at whether the children of the first marriage stand to inherit from their other parent and grandparents in reckoning how to divide their own estates. Eliot, for example, in asserting that his stepson will inherit equally with his daughters, mentions that one reason for this equality is that the boy does not stand to inherit anything of substance from his father's family. On the other hand, Roger sees himself as leaving selected sentimental items to his older children, with everything else going to his children with Adelle. His divorce settlement with the older children's mother gave her their house, which will be their legacy, worth more than anything he's accumulated since. Laura, too, is comfortable leaving whatever she and Andrew have to their daughters, knowing that her son has already inherited from his father "more resources than anybody would ever get from us." Andrew disagrees, showing how natural parents are not always the more inclusive. Andrew maintains that all three children would be named equally in the will.

Sorting out the emotional message of the will from the financial realities can be difficult. Melanie struggles with how to do the right thing, knowing that her son Paul's dad is quite well off and that Paul is his only natural child, while the two children of her second marriage stand to inherit far less. "I'd probably divide our things between the younger children, and Paul would go to his dad to provide for him. Yet it's not fair to divide the house between Yale and Ivy. It would be saying to Paul that we didn't provide for him or care for him, whereas he'd be better off financially if we weren't here."

Both parents and stepparents who are confident that the children of the first marriage will be well provided for by their other parent's family tend to reduce their share of the stepfamily pot, but not without conflict. "My sense is that on a real survival level, my son is going to be all right," said his father. "He's going to survive. If I had money, I obviously would leave him something out of affection. The kind of estate that I would have would not . . . I would have to leave it to my wife in order for her and the baby to survive, and I would not have that sort of concern about my son, who has his mother's family. Having gone through this with my father, I would also leave something symbolic. I think it's important for my boy." These families search for a formula that will communicate both their love for all the children and their recognition that their economic fates may be different.

Even if the bequests to children of first and later marriages are not grossly out of balance, there is something about their children being shortchanged by being on the receiving end of fewer lines of inheritance that makes it difficult for several stepparents to see equal division of their own assets as fair. "I don't want to exclude my stepdaughters," said one stepmother, "but it doesn't seem equitable to not let her have more from her mother, when the girls will get from their mother and something from their stepmother. It's not quite resolved. I think we decided that half of it would go to our daughter and the other half would be divided between the other two girls." It is this struggle to both be "fair" and communicate messages of love and inclusion that contributes to stepfamilies' procrastination in making a will.

Perhaps because their family is so evenly balanced, with one child each from a previous marriage and two together, Ben and Julia have overcome any concern that they can redress existing inequalities by their own bequests. "Obviously Josh and Jeremy are in a different situation than the little kids," said Ben. "Jeremy is going to have a vast amount of money coming in from his dad's side of the family. Still, for us, we've seen people split it up in really funny ways, and how it really messes up the kids: feeling there are favorites, 'He loved me more than you,' that kind of thing. I don't want to do that to the kids. At least what they get from me will be equal shares. I hope they'll all be able to make an honorable living in ways that are not exploitative of people, ethical and all that. If one of them is rich and another is poor, I hope the rich one will help out the poor one."

There is, however, one exception to even the most scrupulous evenhandedness. After declaring that "it just goes down the middle, there's nothing I have that I wouldn't want to share equally between the two children," Edward made one qualification that was a universal one. All the stepfamilies drew the line, not at sharing funds equally, but at the objects that have become family heirlooms, which are allocated by bloodline. For Edward, the baby spoon and knife that had been his as a child and were presented to his son Eric at his birth would have to be left to his biological son. "What I probably would do is find something that is not so precious as a family object that I would give to Carl. Like if they gave me the family Bible, I would give the family Bible to Eric. One thing that I'm going to get, unless I get disinherited, is the gold watch, which is the moral equivalent of the spoon and the knife. It's the grandfather to father to son kind of trip. I guess I would give that to Eric and find a pair of cufflinks or something like that that were my grandfather's that my father had and give that to Carl. Because those things are given in a kind of trust. They're not exactly freely given. The expectation is that they will pass down, generation on generation." It is here that obligations to ancestors take priority over the very real love and attachment to stepchildren and children alike.

Inheriting Intangibles

It is not only in disposing of their worldly goods that families bequeath to their children what they have inherited from their ancestors. Sharing a cultural heritage, like the distribution of more tangible assets, is an important influence on the stepfamily's cohesion, both in the children's early years and beyond. In writing about how stepfamilies cohere over time, Patricia Papernow talks about "thickening the middle ground," building over time the store of shared experience, the rituals of daily life and celebration, that create a family culture that builds on the past but belongs uniquely to its current constituents.[3] Psychologist and family therapist Mary Whiteside examined how rituals and celebrations crystallize issues of family identity for stepfamilies, requiring that complex decisions about values be made explicit and preconceptions

reexamined, and leading to "innovative experiments in everyday living."⁴ Encouraging stepfamilies not to rush into premature and rigid
simplifications that fail to recognize the complexity of remarried binuclear families, she urges the "explicit planning and careful negotiation"
that make room for all emotionally important family members in both
formal ceremonies and informal traditions. "Under such circumstances," she concludes, "both children and adults can experience a
sense of belonging with both a secure connection to the past and
permission to explore the possibilities of the future."

No easy task this. Indeed, Whiteside found that, especially in their
early years, even stepfamilies that work well had their share of failures
in working out how to celebrate holidays or rites of passage. While it
is vital not to overlook, obscure, or deny differences among family
members, the more cultural similarity there is among stepfamily members, the easier the task of building a family culture that will feel
familiar and continuous to all, helping them to feel like family.

The father of five grown children, the first three born before he was
widowed and the last two since his remarriage, was firm in his conviction that his family is close because he wants it to be close. "I didn't
enjoy a larger extended family," he told me. "Our ancestors were
massacred. My wife and I grew up without this security in our background, without that cushion to fall back on. That's what I'm trying
to build."

His family is closer and more integrated than most stepfamilies, and
it is not only his wanting it that will keep his children a continuing part
of one another's family. Not only did they share a home growing up,
not only were there never more than two parents at a time in any of
their lives, but they also share the Armenian culture that is an important part of their identity, as a family and as individuals. A history of
persecution as an ethnic minority accentuates the coherence of their
community. All the children have attended the same church and gone
to the same camps as they come of age. And all the children look like
brothers and sisters. No clear biological Maginot line marks where one
set of full siblings leaves off and the other begins.

In contrast, "It's clear when I take all the kids to the doctor," said
one Greek woman, "that I am the little one's mother and that the older
kids couldn't be mine," referring to her fair-skinned, fair-haired stepsons. Even when differences in parentage are not apparent to the casual
observer, cultural differences can become a focus for divisiveness within

the family. It is easy to see how one child's wish that his mother's younger children would share his fundamentalist beliefs so as to be able to go to Heaven with him and his sister could easily come between these half siblings. Similarly, the education she receives in her Jewish preschool can make a six-year-old more of an unknown, strange and incomprehensible, to her Christian Science half brothers. When stepchildren, whether out of loyalty to a parent or alienation from a stepparent, seek to distance their half siblings, cultural differences become convenient symbols for feelings of estrangement.

Difference does not have to be alienating, however. Indeed, mutual children, especially, striving to be like the children of a parent's former marriage, are often intrigued by what distinguishes the older children and willing to adopt aspects of their identity given the opportunity. Speaking of her father's seven-year-old, Paula, at eighteen, said: "Angela used to ask about our mother, about being Jewish, celebrating Chanukah. There's a touch of intrigue to her, and she'd like to be Jewish just in the sense of it's another thing to do, another thing to be. But not for the sense that it came down to wanting to be Jewish for the reasons that one is Jewish." What she wants is to be like her big sisters.

For stepfamilies, being culturally similar can help to offset an overload of difference, building on the familiar to create a sense of family. But mingling differing traditions in one stepfamily does not have to be divisive. Differences can be enriching, ways of learning about the world in its diversity. When differences are discussed openly, without competing for an exclusive option on the truth, they can lead to greater closeness.

Conclusion

As I write, I have known Sean, Antonio, and Brian for eight years. I have been their stepmother for six years and David's mother for five. It is not a long time, but much has happened. We have had good times and bad. There have been occasions when each of us, I'm sure, would have been just as happy to see one or more of the others drop off the face of the earth. Yet, as time goes on, and the more tumultuous moments recede in the distance, not having the three older boys in my life has become unthinkable. We are family.

And while I'm sure that the care and concern among us would have developed over time in any case, having David has thickened the connective fibers that weave us together. He is important to each of us, singly and together, a significant if not always sanguine force in the psychological climate. In the most trying of times, his existence has meant that I could not throw up my hands and strike out on my own. Loving his father, and knowing the older boys' pain in not living with both parents, I could not sacrifice David's future to my occasional distress at being a stepmother.

Perhaps because he has a mother who copes with stress through study, David has been acutely aware that he is growing up in a step-family and ever curious about who is related to whom and how. Who he is and how he matures is inextricably tied in with being his father's fourth son and his mother's only child. The complex fraternity of brothers and half brothers in his home sets the stage for the drama that shapes his destiny.

As is true for many of the families that contributed to this book, our life together is more committed, more convivial, and more complex because we have added a child to a stepfamily. I have tried to convey their experience, exposing the patterns, and revealing that how people play the cards they are dealt makes a difference between stepfamilies that work and those for whom the struggle seems unending. What emerges from the variety and the complexity of the interviews is a portrait of stepfamily life that, while not without blemish, becomes more dimensional and vibrant when it includes at least "one that's ours."

Perhaps the most striking theme that emerges from the interviews is how much stepparents and stepchildren wish to feel valued by one another. Behind the conflicts, despite competing loyalties and the too frequent assumption of a scarcity model for the family's emotional economy, I heard the refrain, from both adult and child, "I really want him to love me, and I don't know if or how I can bring that about." Mean-spiritedness, when it arises in all of us from time to time, can almost always be traced to feeling pushed to the periphery of the family, so that we strike out in the despair of isolation. I was most moved by the declarations of appreciation made by adult stepchildren and their stepparents, who look back at harder times and applaud one another's tenacity in struggling through the underbrush of tentative mutual testing to establish a clearing of commitment and concern. Hearing firsthand so many stories from those whose undaunted persistence has clearly accomplished goals that once seemed far off has helped me to persevere through discouraging times.

Again and again, time emerges as the measure of all things. Changes that were difficult in the short run, when recalled from a distance appear as only one of many tricky turns in the road. Remarried parents who were less than enthusiastic when their mutual child was conceived and the stepchildren who blamed the little ones for their own disappointments found that adding a child to a remarried family creates opportunity as well as encumbrance. While some of the older children wonder "what if" their parent had no more children with a new spouse, none who've graduated from childhood themselves say of the mutual child, "I wish he'd never been born." Time has taught them to value the possibilities for connection; regrets center on missed opportunities to strengthen the ties between them.

For stepfamilies having children in remarriage, the dream is to create a center that holds. They seek to repair the wounds of the past, creating a family that will endure, a family that brings together past and present. They wish to have one or more children who allow stepparents and noncustodial parents to feel like "real" parents without abandoning their existing children or stepchildren, whose need for nurturance abides, despite their greater age and even intermittent presence.

Having a child in remarriage adds glue to the stepfamily without guaranteeing that the resulting collage will be pleasing to the eye. It creates an opportunity for greater cohesion but does not guarantee it. Nor is closeness always either pacific or gratifying: Both lovers and combatants can be locked in embrace.

The Coat of Many Colors

Longed for by some and greeted with apprehension by others, the child born to the remarried family is both privileged by his station and burdened by his role in holding together members less connected to one another than they are to him. The coat of many colors, Joseph's mantle of specialness, is part of his inheritance, and it contains all the colors of the rainbow, from bright to dark. The mutual child is both advantaged and made vulnerable by the same set of circumstances. A secure foundation, social acumen, and a sense of self-worth are the benefits of his position, and hypervigilance in social relations and difficulties in becoming his own person are its liabilities.

Easing his way, mitigating his older sisters' and brothers' turmoil, and making his parents' marriage an enduring one all require attention and acceptance of the necessity to balance competing needs of all family members. Knowing what to expect, dispensing with romantic fantasies of how things should be, and realizing that difficulties are not necessarily signs of personal inadequacy help to develop an attitude that makes transformation possible.

The families who found their way into these pages are a varied lot, yet there is a unity to their family concerns. As stepfamilies who have chosen to have children in remarriage, they face many of the same challenges. While the resources at their disposal certainly vary, the commonality of their concerns points to an overall strategy for surmounting problems and taking advantage of opportunities. The greatest danger for those discouraged by stepfamily politics is to personalize difficulties, blaming ourselves and each other for being, doing, and feeling different from our neighbors in nuclear families.

Surrendering the notion that stepfamilies can be just like first families is a first step. Recognizing that there may well be hard times before it gets better, that understanding and trust take time to evolve, helps us to understand what is happening in our homes, instead of feeling beaten by the situation. Sometimes what needs to be done is not comfortable. It may feel easier for ex-spouses to keep the fires of unresolved conflicts burning or allow them to smolder below the surface. It may feel easier for a stepparent to devote himself to his own child and figure that his stepchildren are just as pleased not to have to deal with him. It may feel easier for a child to pick on a new half sibling than to confront her stepparent with her desire to feel important and loved. And it may feel easier for the parent of all the children to stay in the middle, protecting his partner from his children and his children from their stepparent. Avoiding the uncomfortable, however, can perpetuate suffering and preclude the real satisfactions that are possible when each pair within the stepfamily is free to explore and develop the possibilities for affection, respect, and intimacy between them.

We have seen that expecting stepfamilies to feel just like first families leads to disappointment. Allowing relationships to be limited by the "step" qualifier leads to discontent from the opposite route, expecting little and asking less of people who are related to us by a term prefixed by "step." The boy who withdraws from his stepfather, not asking for more closeness between them because he's not his "real" father, and the woman who sees her stepdaughter as impossible because she is "no daughter of hers," rather than because she is a teenager, acting like teenagers often do, cut off whatever possibilities there are for improving these relationships. If what is undesirable is a necessary function of what is immutable, by definition change cannot occur. One father I spoke with conjectured that "part of having a good blended family is having a good *myth:* that it's possible, that the kids will be okay, that you'll be okay, and that it will all work out reasonably well. It's not as if people don't have problems. People have problems. They may not be substantially worse than anybody else's problems. And they probably are not insuperable."

A Fairy Tale Ending

Although there are no fairy tale endings in real life, it is hard to write about stepfamilies without thinking about Cinderella and others like her who instruct youngsters that steprelations are frightening, even life-threatening. While there is no memorable child of legend who is the issue of a parent's remarriage, we can imagine how such a child might be greeted.

Picture, if you will, a festive gathering called to celebrate the arrival of the first child born to a remarried monarch. Among the crowd, the children of the monarch's first marriage mingle: Some are dispirited, others affect a lack of interest, while still others enthusiastically join in drinking to the baby's health.

Three good fairies have come to offer their beneficent spells. The First Good Fairy, a well-meaning sort, approaches the Mutual Child's cradle and offers her gift. "May your life be a blessing to this happy realm. You represent a new beginning, a chance to start over. May your parents love you and each other, fulfilling in this new family the dreams that were dashed in the past."

The Second Good Fairy, although somewhat naive about step-family politics, still recognizes that there are no new beginnings, only later stations on the journey. "May you bring harmony to the family into which you are born," she chants. "May your sisters and brothers find a bond through you. May they be joined to their stepparent by virtue of your being, and may you, for all your days, be the tie that binds all those who suffer the rancors of the past and precipitous change."

Suddenly, the jubilation is marred by the entrance of an uninvited guest, the Spirit of Celebrations Past, the disappointed hopes of the child's parents in their first families. She alights at the baby's side, a crow on the cradle. "Hah," she smirks, "enough of your romantic fancies. Those who would banish the past will find their path crowded with ghostly hobgoblins, creating mischief in their wake.

"May your very blessing be turned into a curse," she sneers in grim invocation. "May you suffer the resentment of brothers and sisters who see you as privileged and spoiled. May you stand between the older children and their stepparent, a target for the children's anger at your parent, who holds you too tightly, in consolation for his pain as a stepparent. May your parent live in fear lest the older children hurt you, and may the children use you as a benchmark of their own deprivation, warding off your claims to fraternity. May you be bound in perpetuity to keep others connected to one another, never finding your own path."

Then, as suddenly as she appeared, the evil intruder is gone. As luck would have it, however, the Third Good Fairy, a family therapist in her off hours, sets about to reverse the damage.

"I cannot undo all that was invoked by our intruder," she begins, "but I can compose a blessing to change the curse to a series of signposts, marking the pitfalls on this child's course, and charting the bridges and tunnels, the detours and byways, that can make my sisters' wishes prevail over those invoked by our ill-wisher. Only when the past is ignored does it become ugly and destructive."

Turning from the cradle to the King and Queen, she speaks directly to them. "My wishes are for you, for it is through your wisdom that this child, and all your children, will be blessed. May you find solace in each other, that your children may grow unburdened by demands to side with one of you against the other. May you each allow the other to come close enough to each child to care for all the children. May you make your peace with the past, so that its memories and its survivors do not continue to haunt you. May you savor the delight of having a child together, without asking that the child sacrifice himself to the unity of the family. May you devote yourself to nurturing the tender and sensitive connections between stepparent and stepchild, so that each may feel at home in the family's interior. So, too, may your child escape being battered by conflicts detoured in his direction, allowing him, and all the children, solidarity forever."

"Well," said the Queen to the King, when fairies and celebrants alike had retired, "I can't say as I like everything we heard. But," she sighed, "even if the territory is not unreservedly attractive, at least we have a map."

This book, I hope, is a map for the rest of us. May it help parents and the professionals who work with them over the rough spots in the terrain, avoiding the sharp inclines that precipitate falls and finding the high road to a stepfamily life that is enriched by and kind to the "one that's ours."

Appendix

Demographics of Stepfamilies with Mutual Children

Because stepfamilies form what the Vishers have called an "invisible" population, it is impossible to state accurately just how many families fit the profile described in this book. Despite the predictions that by 1990 there will be more binuclear families than nuclear families in the United States, we cannot fully describe the demographics of this growing segment of our population.[1] For one thing, the census did not inquire until 1980 whether respondents have children who do not live with them, so there is little information on stepfamilies formed by the remarriage of a noncustodial father and no information about whether grown children share both parents with children living in the household. According to a 1985 report by sociologists Andrew Cherlin and James McCarthy, nearly 10 percent of all the households in the United States consist of couples in which at least one member is remarried after a previous divorce: Of these, 30 percent were marriages of divorced women to men who were marrying for the first time; 35 percent were first-time brides marrying divorced grooms; and the remaining 35 percent were remarriages for both parties.[2] This leaves out the 3 percent of all marriages that include a widowed partner, as well as the marriages of never-wed people who are nonetheless parents, both of whom fall into our understanding of what is a stepfamily.

Slightly more than half of all couples have children at the time of a divorce, accounting for more than 1.2 million children whose parents divorce each year. Demographer Paul Glick, extrapolating from these figures, estimates that by 1990 approximately one-third of all children will encounter a divorce before reaching the age of eighteen, and when separations that are not formalized by divorce are included, this figure jumps to two in five. More than half of these children will see the parent with whom they live remarry, so that one child in four will grow up having more than two parents.[3] When we factor in those children whose noncustodial parent remarries, and those children who acquire a stepparent through the marriage of a never-wed parent or the remarriage of a widowed parent, the numbers of children who will have a stepparent during some part of their growing-up years are staggering.

Trying to tease out from the available statistics just how many of these stepfamilies will have children in remarriage is a difficult task. In a 1984 report, demographer Larry Bumpass estimated, on the basis of the 1980 census, that 66 percent of children entering remarried families are likely to have a stepsibling or a half sibling, with 30 percent, or two million children, acquiring a half sibling within four years of their mother's remarriage. Most of these children will have *either* half siblings *or* stepsiblings, however, because a remarrying parent is more likely to have a mutual child if his or her new spouse has not previously had children. Only 16 percent of all children whose parent remarries have *both* stepsiblings *and* half siblings. Of stepchildren with a stepfather who was not previously married, for example, 44 percent have a half sibling, whereas only 26 percent of the children whose stepfather had been married before have a half sibling.[4] Comparable figures are unavailable for remarried fathers and their previously unmarried brides.

While we know far less about the stepfamilies formed by remarried fathers, there is reason to believe that these remarriages more frequently include a new child than do the remarriages of their ex-wives. Not only do divorced and widowed men remarry in somewhat higher numbers than do their female counterparts, they also tend to marry women who are younger than they by more years than their first wives. These younger women are more likely not to have been married before and more likely not to have had children. Since a woman's youth and a previously unmarried and childless partner demonstrably contribute to greater fertility in remarriage for women, the same factors are likely to apply to remarrying men and their partners.

Cherlin and McCarthy, using figures from the Current Population Survey of the United States Census, have estimated that 1.3 million households consist of remarried couples and their minor children from both past and present partners. For nearly half of the remarried couples with children of the current marriage, neither partner had children under eighteen from a previous marriage. Those stepfamilies in which both parents had minor children from two or more marriages were outnumbered by more than four to one by those in which one partner was a first-time parent.[5] According to Cherlin and McCarthy, two-thirds of all remarriages following divorce do not have children under eighteen from the present marriage, although one-third of these couples have one or more children under eighteen living with them. For nearly half of the remarried couples with minor children of the current marriage, or 16 percent of the total, neither partner had children under eighteen from a previous marriage. In an additional 14 percent, only one of the parents had minor children from a previous marriage, leaving only 3.3 percent of these remarriages that included children under eighteen from both partners' previous marriages and from the current union.

There are many ways in which these figures underestimate the number of stepfamilies with children from both past and present unions. First, they fail to take into account remarriages of both widowed parents and previously unmarried adults who are, nonetheless, parents. Second, they do not consider any children over eighteen years of age, whether they are the issue of a first marriage or of the current partnership. As a result, stepfamilies in which all of the children are grown are not counted. Similarly, mutual children under eighteen who have adult half siblings are counted along with children who are truly the first for both parents as part of the 48 percent of the families with children from a present marriage only. Therefore, we know only that the estimate of 1.3 million stepfamilies with both stepchildren and mutual children significantly underestimates the numbers of stepfamilies with children from both past and present unions.

Methodology

I interviewed whole families, talking with all available family members over the age of three. In all, I interviewed 150 people, representing fifty-five remarried households. Included are twenty-five families in which I met with between four and seven family members, and, in an additional six families, I spent time with either two or three informants. Some individuals represent more than one remarried household, for example, when the mother and stepmother of a family in which several members were interviewed is also an informant on the family in which she grew up as a mutual child, or when a child is interviewed about the stepfamilies formed by both his mother's and father's remarriages.

All interviews were done individually. In most instances, I met with people in their own homes. Occasionally, I had the opportunity to interview the stepfamilies formed by the remarriages of both ex-spouses. In addition, I spoke with a few parents, themselves not remarried, who could offer the perspective of the child's other parent in a single-parent household, monitoring changes as a former partner has a child with a new spouse. And I spoke with a few whose second marriages had also ended in divorce, to learn something about what happens when the first group of children has to deal with yet another dissolution and the children of remarriage follow in their half siblings' footsteps to become children of divorce.

Not included were the nearly half of all half siblings living with their mothers who live with their mothers alone. What put this group outside the purview of this study is that in families of single mothers and their children, be they whole or half siblings, the children are "all in the same boat." While some noncustodial fathers are, of course, more attentive than others, for most of these children the family is "Mom and her kids." All are equally related to their primary parent. None have a stepparent who is more closely bonded to one of the other children. There is no necessity for the fathers of each of the kids to have anything to do with the other children. It is a different dance.

The stepfamilies interviewed for this book are a diverse group of people ranging from the working poor to the wealthy. Most fall somewhere in between, with economic pressure a daily fact of life, but with some choices about how to allot their resources. There are mothers who work full-time outside the home, mothers who work at part-time jobs, and mothers who are committed to being at home while their children are young. There are also a couple of fathers whose income-producing work is secondary to their role as nurturers of their children.

Although professionals are overrepresented in their number, the work roles of the parents and adult children interviewed are many and various: There are white-, blue-, and pink-collar workers; those employed by labor unions and by large corporations, by municipalities and by the federal government; artists and craftspeople; health care and social service workers, and teachers at all levels, from preschool to university. A full list of occupations includes: retailer, political lobbyist, longshoreman, pharmacist, contractor, housewife, musician, baker, social worker, film production assistant, police officer, physician, dancer, businessman, editor, accountant, administrative assistant, artist, psychiatrist, congressional aide, attorney, cabinetmaker, mechanic, physician's assistant, secretary, journalist, graduate student, electronics engineer, municipal employee, seamstress, gardener, social worker, transit supervisor, writer, secretary, anthropologist, labor union official, psychologist, historian, mediator, and preschool, high school, community college, and university teachers.

Most of the families interviewed were Caucasian and native born, but they included blacks, Chicanos, and Asian-Americans, as well as those born in Scotland, Ireland, and Hong Kong, an Israeli and a Palestinian. Among them are those who identify strongly with their ethnic heritage, be it Armenian, Irish, Polish, Arab, Japanese, Iranian, Jewish, or "hillbilly." Most are Catholics, Protestants, and Jews, but there are also adherents of the Eastern Orthodox, Greek Orthodox, and Mormon faiths, and one family that identifies itself as "born-again" Christians. Some practice their religion, and others do not. Many families are "all of a kind," with both partners coming from similar cultures, while others are "mixed" either ethnically or in religious background.

Almost all of the stepfamily parents were married. A few, however, were living together for anywhere from six to twenty years. Because the couples who are living together without marrying have been together for a long time, and because they are not in any other way distinguishable from the other families, they have been referred to as among the "remarried" unless otherwise noted.

All are among the "successes" of remarriage, having passed the four-year mark, by which time two-fifths of all remarried couples have divorced.[6] These stepfamilies have been together between four and thirty-seven years, with a median duration of ten years. Three have suffered the death of one of the remarried partners, after eight, twenty-three, and thirty-seven years of remarriage. Eleven of the fifty-five families represented have ended in divorce, as few as five years or as many as thirty-seven years following a second wedding. And, by the time this book went to print, at least two couples who were together at the time their families were interviewed had since separated.

The largest group among the families was formed by first-time brides and their recycled grooms, followed by stepfamilies created by a remarrying mother and a single man, with the smallest number of families including parents who each bring children from a previous marriage. While there is no way of stating unequivocally that this is the case, there is reason to believe, because of the greater probability associated with a woman's youth and the previous childlessness of either partner, that this reflects the percentage of each of these stepfamily forms that actually go on to have one or more children in remarriage.

The group studied, however diverse, does not strictly reflect all such stepfamilies in the general population. It is hard to say what a representative sample would look like. First, there are many kinds of stepfamilies. Just looking at the marital status of the adults, whether each partner is unmarried, divorced, or widowed, we get eight different types of remarriage, even before looking to see whether it is the man, the woman, or both who have children from a previous marriage, whether those children live with them or not, and whether they go on to have a child together. These factors alone produce sixty-four possible stepfamily formations.

And there is much else to take into consideration. Judith Wallerstein and Joan Kelly have amply demonstrated that a child's age when his parents divorce has important implications for his adjustment to the separation and his subsequent development.[7] In addition, how many years the children spend in a single-parent household, how old they are when a parent remarries, how long the stepfamily has been in existence, the custody arrangement, the number of children from the first marriage, their birth order, a stepparent's age, and whether both adults bring children from a previous marriage, all have bearing on stepfamily adjustment and how it makes room for a mutual child.

While it is difficult, if not impossible, to specify the typical stepfamily, the families interviewed are clearly atypical in terms of how involved the fathers continue to be with their children following divorce. Nearly 20 percent of the families had joint physical custody of the children of the first marriage, with the children moving between Mom's house and Dad's house on a regular schedule, be it weekly, biweekly, monthly, or annually. While most of the other families had the traditional arrangement of living with Mother most or all of the time, spending more limited time with Father on what is commonly called a "visitation" basis, there were a few custodial fathers as well. With the exception of one man, whose daughters came to live with him when they reached their early teens after spending their earlier childhood in their mother's home, all of the men who were primary custodians were widowers.

Not only were the dads in this study more actively involved with their children than is the norm, they were also more regular in their financial support. This is not surprising, since access to their children has been shown to be a big factor in assuring father's continuing support.[8] Unfortunately, this is a departure from the widespread situation of children of divorce. Many studies have shown that fathers typically tend to decrease their contact with the children over time following a divorce. In a Pennsylvania study, Frank Furstenberg and others found that 50 percent of children of divorce had not seen their noncustodial fathers in five years, an additional 20 percent had not had contact for two years, and only 16 percent saw their dads as often as once a week.[9] Later, he and Graham Spanier discovered that contact between a noncustodial parent and his children decreases with remarriage: Two-thirds visit when neither divorced spouse has re-wed, dropping to 40 percent with one remarriage and 34 percent when both have new partners.[10] In a California study, Lenore Weitzman, decrying no-fault divorce as leading to the increased poverty of women and children, found also that 23 percent of California fathers never see their children after the divorce.[11]

In contrast, it was the exceptional natural father in these families who failed to keep up regular contact with his children. Twenty percent of the remarried mothers whose children's father is alive received little or no support, and these children saw their fathers erratically if at all. All of the noncustodial fathers interviewed, however, saw their children regularly and, with an occasional lapse that coincided with unemployment, were reliable in their child support.

Notes

Introduction

1. Jamie Kelem Keshet, *Love and Power in the Stepfamily: A Practical Guide* (New York: McGraw-Hill, 1987).
2. Jessie Bernard, *Remarried: A Study of Marriage* (New York: Russell and Russell, first edition, 1956, second edition, 1971).
3. Emily B. Visher and John S. Visher, *Stepfamilies: A Guide to Working with Stepparents and Stepchildren* (New York: Brunner/Mazel, 1978).
4. Frank F. Furstenberg, Jr., Christine W. Nord, J. L. Peterson, and N. Zill, "The Life Course of Children of Divorce: Marital Disruption and Parental Contact," *American Sociological Review*, 48 (1983), pp. 656–668. Additional support for this lack of agreement about family member can be found in
   Kay Pasley, "Family Boundary Ambiguity: Perception of Adult Remarried Family Members," in K. Pasley and M. Ihinger-Tallman (eds.), *Remarriage and Stepparenting: Current Research and Theory* (New York: Guilford Press, 1987).
5. Andrew Cherlin, "Remarriage as an Incomplete Institution," in *American Journal of Sociology*, 84(3) (1978), pp. 634–650.
6. Salvador Minuchin, *Families and Family Structure* (Cambridge, Mass.: Harvard University Press, 1977).
   Salvador Minuchin and H. Charles Fishman, *Family Therapy Techniques* (Cambridge, Mass.: Harvard University Press, 1981).
7. Constance R. Ahrons and Roy H. Rodgers, *Divorced Families: A Multidisciplinary Developmental View* (New York: W. W. Norton and Company, 1987).

8. Paul C. Glick, "Marriage, Divorce and Living Arrangements: Prospective Changes," *Journal of Family Issues*, 5 (1984), pp. 7–26.

9. U.S. Bureau of the Census, "Number, Timing, and Duration of Marriages and Divorces in the United States: June 1975," *Current Population Reports*, ser. P-20, no. 297 (Washington, D.C.: U.S. Government Printing Office, 1976).

10. Salvador Minuchin, *Family Kaleidoscope* (Cambridge, Mass.: Harvard University Press, 1984).

1. Will We? Won't We?

1. This figure is based on a cover article on infertility in the December 6, 1982, *Newsweek*, based on data from the American Fertility Society. Other estimates dip as low as 10 to 15 percent. See

Felicia Steward, *Understanding Your Body: Every Woman's Guide to Gynecology and Health* (New York: Bantam Books, 1987).

2. Jessie Bernard. *Remarried: A Study of Marriage* (New York: Russell and Russell, first edition, 1956, second edition, 1971).

3. Clifford J. Sager, Hollis Steer Brown, Helen Crohn, Tamara Engel, Evelyn Rodstein, and Libby Walker, *Treating the Remarried Family* (New York: Brunner/Mazel, 1983).

4. Patricia Papernow, "The Stepfamily Cycle: An Experiential Model of Stepfamily Development," *Family Relations*, 33 (1984), pp. 355–363.

5. Paul C. Glick, "Marriage, Divorce and Living Arrangements: Prospective Changes," *Journal of Family Issues*, 5 (1984), pp. 7–26; and

Frank F. Furstenberg, Jr., and Graham B. Spanier, *Recycling the Family: Remarriage After Divorce* (Beverly Hills, Calif.: Sage, 1984).

6. Stepfamilies who have a mutual child usually do so within the first four years, during which 80 percent of the remarried mothers who eventually will have more children give birth. Eleven percent of the children who acquire half siblings have mothers who are already pregnant at the time of the remarriage, and 24 percent acquire a half sibling within eighteen months of the wedding. Although comparable figures are not available for remarrying fathers who have children in remarriage, their greater haste in remarrying makes it likely that their mutual children are born similarly soon. See

Larry Bumpass and R. R. Rindfuss, "Children's Experience of Marital Disruption," *American Journal of Sociology*, 85 (1979), pp. 49–65; and

Janet D. Griffith, Helen P. Koo, and C. M. Suchindran, "Childlessness and Marital Stability in Remarriages," *Journal of Marriage and the Family* (August 1984), pp. 577–585.

2. Tipping the Parental Balance

1. E. E. LeMasters. "Parenthood as Crisis," *Marriage and Family Living,* 19 (1957), pp. 352–355.
2. Carolyn Pape Cowan and Philip A. Cowan, "A Prevention Intervention for Couples Becoming Parents," in C. F. Z. Boukydis (ed.), *Research on Support for Parents and Infants in the Postnatal Period* (Norwood, N.J.: Ablex Publishing Company, 1987).
3. Larry Bumpass and R. R. Rindfuss, "Children's Experience of Marital Disruption," *American Journal of Sociology,* 85 (1979), pp. 49–65.
4. Anne C. Bernstein, *The Flight of the Stork* (New York: Delacorte, 1978).
5. Lucille Duberman, "Step-Kin Relationships," *Journal of Marriage and the Family,* 35 (1973), pp. 283–292; and

    Emily B. Visher and John S. Visher, *Stepfamilies: A Guide to Working with Stepparents and Stepchildren* (New York: Brunner/Mazel, 1978).
6. The source for the information on the decline in self-esteem for most women becoming mothers for the first time is Alice Rossi, "Transition to Parenthood," *Journal of Marriage and the Family,* 30 (1968), pp. 26–39.
7. Diane Ehrensaft, *Parenting Together: Men and Women Sharing the Care of Their Children* (New York: Free Press, 1987).
8. Nancy Chodorow, *The Reproduction of Mothering: Psychoanalysis and the Sociology of Gender* (Berkeley: University of California Press, 1978).
9. Ehrensaft, op. cit.
10. William R. Beer, "Dynamics of Stepsibling and Half-Sibling Relations," in William R. Beer (ed.), *Relative Strangers: Studies of Stepfamily Processes* (New York: Rowman and Littlefield, 1988).
11. Gene Brody, University of Georgia. Cited in *The New York Times,* July 28, 1987. Also

    Brenda Bryant and Susan Crockenberg, "Correlates and Dimensions of Prosocial Behavior: A Study of Female Siblings and Their Mothers," *Child Development,* 51 (1980), pp. 529–544.

3. Parents Together

1. Jamie Kelem Keshet (personal communication, 1986), applying Carol Gilligan's model of rights and responsiveness as moral styles that characterize gender-related approaches, suggests that stepparents frequently take a "rights" approach to their stepchildren, while parents more often employ a "responsiveness" model with their children. Gilligan describes a "rights" orientation as concerned with fairness and equality, balancing the claims of the other and the self,

while a "responsiveness" orientation is based on the concept of equity, which recognizes differences in need and "rests on an understanding that gives rise to compassion and care." A fuller discussion of this theoretical model can be found in Carol Gilligan, *In a Different Voice: Psychological Theory and Women's Development* (Cambridge, Mass.: Harvard University Press, 1982).

2. Gary W. Becker, Elizabeth M. Landes, and Robert T. Michael, "An Economic Analysis of Marital Instability," *Journal of Political Economy,* 85 (1977), pp. 1141–1187. This is somewhat confounded by the finding that marriages in which only one partner was remarried were not significantly more likely to end in divorce than those in which both partners are in a first marriage (8 versus 6 percent); marriages in which both partners had previously been married were nearly twice as likely to end in divorce. These remarriages at greater risk of divorce are also those least likely to have a mutual child. See Lynn K. White and Alan Booth, "The Quality and Stability of Remarriages: The Role of Stepchildren," *American Sociological Review,* 50 (1985), pp. 689–698.

4. Being a Parent to Children New and Old

1. Jill Krementz, *How It Feels when Parents Divorce* (New York: Knopf, 1984).

5. A Basis for Comparison

1. Anne-Marie Ambert, "Being a Stepparent: Live-in and Visiting Stepchildren," *Journal of Marriage and the Family,* 48 (1986), pp. 795–804.
2. For a fuller discussion of the stages in stepfamily development, see pp. 43–44 and Patricia Papernow, "The Stepfamily Cycle: An Experiential Model of Stepfamily Development," *Family Relations,* vol. 33 (1984), pp. 355–363.
3. Brenda Bryant and Susan Crockenberg, "Correlates and Dimensions of Prosocial Behavior: A Study of Female Siblings and Their Mothers," *Child Development,* 51 (1980), pp. 529–544.
4. William R. Beer, "Dynamics of Stepsibling and Half-Sibling Relations," in William R. Beer (ed.), *Relative Strangers: Studies of Stepfamily Processes* (New York: Rowman and Littlefield, 1988).

6. The Hole in the Stepfamily Fence

1. E. Mavis Hetherington, M. Cox, and R. Cox, "Family Interaction and the Social, Emotional and Cognitive Development of Children

Following Divorce," in V. C. Vaughan and T. B. Brazelton (eds.), *The Family: Setting Priorities* (New York: Science and Medicine, 1979).

2. Jessie Bernard, *Remarried: A Study of Marriage* (New York: Russell and Russell, first edition, 1956, second edition, 1971).

3. Constance R. Ahrons and Roy H. Rodgers, *Divorced Families: A Multidisciplinary Developmental View* (New York: W. W. Norton and Company, 1987).

4. P. Lutz, "The Stepfamily: An Adolescent Perspective," *Family Relations*, 32 (1983), pp. 367–375.

5. Clifford J. Sager, Hollis Steer Brown, Helen Crohn, Tamara Engel, Evelyn Rodstein, and Libby Walker, *Treating the Remarried Family* (New York: Brunner/Mazel, 1983).

6. Constance R. Ahrons and Lynn Wallisch, "Parenting in the Binuclear Family: Relationships Between Biological and Stepparents," in Kay Pasley and Marilyn Ihinger-Tallman (eds.), *Remarriage and Stepparenting: Current Research and Theory* (New York: Guilford Press, 1987).

7. Kenneth Kressel, *The Process of Divorce: How Professionals and Couples Negotiate Settlement* (New York: Basic Books, 1985).

8. Marilyn Ihinger-Tallman, "Perspectives on Change Among Stepsiblings," presented at the annual meeting of the National Council on Family Relations, Dallas, Texas, and reported in Marilyn Ihinger-Tallman and Kay Pasley, *Remarriage* (Newbury Park, Calif.: Sage Publications, 1987).

9. Linda E. Campbell, Berkeley, California. Personal communication.

10. Emily B. Visher and John S. Visher, *Old Loyalties, New Ties: Therapeutic Strategies with Stepfamilies* (New York: Brunner/Mazel, 1988).

11. Ahrons and Rodgers, op. cit.

12. Ibid.

7. What's in a Name?

1. Judith S. Wallerstein and Joan Berlin Kelly, *Surviving the Breakup: How Children and Parents Cope with Divorce* (New York: Basic Books, 1980).

2. Jean Piaget and Barbel Inhelder, *The Psychology of the Child* (New York: Basic Books, 1969).

3. Lawrence Kohlberg, "A Cognitive Developmental Analysis of Children's Sex-Role Concepts and Attitudes," in Eleanor E. Maccoby (ed.), *The Development of Sex Differences* (Stanford, Calif.: Stanford University Press, 1966).

4. Anne C. Bernstein, *The Flight of the Stork* (New York: Delacorte, 1978).

5. Constance Ahrons, in describing the two-household family of divorced

parents and their children as the "binuclear family," points out the paucity of our vocabulary for describing the relationships between individuals in the remarriage chain.

See Constance R. Ahrons and Roy H. Rodgers, *Divorced Families: A Multidisciplinary Developmental View* (New York: W. W. Norton and Company, 1987).

8. How Old Was I When You Were Born?

1. Jill Krementz, *How It Feels when Parents Divorce* (New York: Knopf, 1984).
2. Ibid.
3. Mary Whiteside has elaborated Patricia Papernow's model of stepfamily development to describe how children of various ages negotiate the stages in the evolution and consolidation of the remarried family. This chapter employs a similar model to demonstrate how children's expectations and initial responses to the birth of a half sibling are best understood in the context of how settled they are in their stepfamilies. See

   Mary F. Whiteside, "Chapter Seven: Remarried Systems," in Lee Combrinck-Graham (ed.), *Handbook of Children in Family Therapy: The Context of Child Mental Health* (New York: Guilford Press, 1988).
4. Judy Dunn, *Sisters and Brothers: The Developing Child* (Cambridge, Mass.: Harvard University Press, 1985).
5. The discussion how siblings get along at different ages, depending on the age interval between them, relies on the developmental model of Erik Erikson. See

   Erik H. Erikson, *Identity and the Life Cycle: Selected Papers*, Psychological Issues, Vol. 1, No. 1 (New York: International Universities Press, 1959).
6. Judith S. Wallerstein and Joan Berlin Kelly, *Surviving the Breakup: How Children and Parents Cope with Divorce* (New York: Basic Books, 1980).
7. Lynn K. White and Alan Booth, "The Quality and Stability of Remarriages: The Role of Stepchildren," *American Sociological Review*, Vol. 50 (October 1985), pp. 689–698.
8. We can only speculate about why boys in this age group seem to have a harder time accommodating to having a half sibling than do girls. It may be that because fathers are typically the ones to leave the household, parental separations that occur when children are about four or five years of age are more stressful for their sons than for their daughters. Other research has shown that boys are more vulnerable to many kinds of stresses than are girls. Of course, it is possible that

more difficult half sibling relationships among boys six to nine years apart in age just happened to exist in the families I interviewed.

9. Growing Up as a Mutual Child

1. William R. Beer, "Dynamics of Stepsibling and Half-Sibling Relations," in William R. Beer (ed.), *Relative Strangers: Studies of Stepfamily Processes* (New York: Rowman and Littlefield, 1988).
2. Katherine Baker, "The Role of the 'Mutual Child' in Remarried Family Issues," paper presented at the annual meeting of the American Family Therapy Association, Chicago, 1987.
3. Ibid.
4. Lynn K. White and Alan Booth, "The Quality and Stability of Remarriages: The Role of Stepchildren," *American Sociological Review,* 50 (1985), pp. 689–698.
5. Jay Haley, *Leaving Home* (New York: Basic Books, 1980).
6. For a summary of conflicting opinions on how sibling constellation affects personality development see Monica McGoldrick and Randy Gerson, *Genograms in Family Assessment* (New York: W. W. Norton and Company, 1985).
7. Walter Toman, *Family Constellation: Its Effect on Personality and Social Behavior,* 3rd edition (New York: Springer, 1976).
8. T. Falbo (ed.), *The Single-Child Family* (New York: Guilford Press, 1984); and J. Jacobus, "The One Child," cited in McGoldrick and Gerson, op. cit.
9. Mavis Hetherington, M. Cox, and R. Cox, "The Aftermath of Divorce," in J. H. Stevens, Jr., and M. Mathews (eds.), *Mother-Child, Father-Child Relations* (Washington, D.C.: National Association for the Education of Young Children, 1978); and
   Michael Rutter, "Protective Factors in Children's Responses to Stress and Disadvantage," in M. W. Kent and J. E. Rolf (eds.), *Primary Prevention of Psychopathology: Promoting Social Competence in Children,* Vol. 3 (Hanover, N.H.: University Press of New England, 1979), pp. 121–140.
10. Beer, op. cit.

10. Half Blood

1. Stephen P. Bank and Michael D. Kahn, *The Sibling Bond* (New York: Basic Books, 1982); and
   J. D. Schvandeveldt and Marilyn Ihinger, "Sibling Relationships in the Family," in W. R. Burr et al. (eds.) *Contemporary Theories About the Family: Volume One, Research-Based Theories* (New York: Free Press, 1979).

2. Judy Dunn, *Sisters and Brothers: The Developing Child* (Cambridge, Mass.: Harvard University Press, 1985), p. 18.

3. Lucille Duberman, *The Reconstituted Family: A Study of Remarried Couples and Their Children* (Chicago: Nelson-Hall, 1975).

4. Emily B. Visher and John S. Visher, *Stepfamilies: A Guide to Working with Stepparents and Stepchildren* (New York: Brunner/Mazel, 1978).

5. Frank F. Furstenberg, Jr., and Graham B. Spanier, *Recycling the Family: Remarriage After Divorce* (Beverly Hills, Calif.: Sage Publications, 1984). Furstenberg and Spanier cite a 55 percent divorce rate for remarriages as contrasted with a 50 percent divorce rate for first marriages.

11. When the Children Are Grown

1. Judy Dunn, *Sisters and Brothers: The Developing Child* (Cambridge, Mass.: Harvard University Press, 1985), p. 163.

12. Another Entry in the Stepfamily Ledger

1. First, it is important to recognize that the families I interviewed are perhaps least representative of stepfamilies in general when it comes to financial matters. Lenore Weitzman reports that the economic fallout of no-fault legislation has been "the systematic impoverishment of women and children," affecting women at all socioeconomic levels. Weitzman writes: "On the average the divorced women and their minor children in the household experienced a 73 percent decline in their standard of living in their first year after divorce. Their former husbands, by contrast, experienced a 42 percent rise in their standard of living." Although courts set child support payments low in order to encourage fathers to comply, this tactic not only contributes to the reduction in the economic circumstances of both women and children, it also fails in its object: 53 percent of the women who are awarded child support don't receive it.

Only two of the mothers in my study reported that their ex-husbands failed to help support their children, and only two of the fathers reported occasionally missing a child support payment when they were between jobs, perhaps because so many of the stepfamilies in this group shared custody of their children, an arrangement that encourages continued financial support. See Lenore Weitzman, *The Divorce Revolution: The Unexpected Social and Economic Consequences for Women and Children in America* (New York: Free Press, 1985).

2. Cherie Burns, *Stepmotherhood* (New York: Harper and Row, 1985).
3. Patricia Papernow, "The Stepfamily Cycle: An Experiential Model of Stepfamily Development," *Family Relations*, Vol. 33 (1984), pp. 355–363.
4. Mary F. Whiteside, "Creation of Family Identity Through Ritual Performance in Early Remarriage," in Evan Imber-Black et al. (eds.), *Rituals and Family Therapy* (New York: W. W. Norton and Company, 1988).

Appendix

1. Paul C. Glick, "Marriage, Divorce and Living Arrangements: Prospective Changes," *Journal of Family Issues*, 5 (1984), pp. 7–26.
2. Andrew Cherlin and James McCarthy, "Remarried Couple Households: Data from the June 1980 Current Population Survey," *Journal of Marriage and the Family*, 47 (1985), pp. 23–30.
3. Glick, op. cit.
4. Larry Bumpass, "Some Characteristics of Children's Second Families," *American Journal of Sociology*, 90(3) (1984), pp. 608–622.
5. Cherlin and McCarthy, op. cit.
6. U.S. Bureau of the Census, "Number, Timing, and Duration of Marriages and Divorces in the United States: June 1975," *Current Population Reports*, ser. P-20, no. 297 (Washington, D.C.: U.S. Government Printing Office, 1976).
7. Judith S. Wallerstein and Joan Berlin Kelly, *Surviving the Breakup: How Children and Parents Cope with Divorce* (New York: Basic Books, 1980).
8. Frank F. Furstenberg, Jr., Christine W. Nord, J. L. Peterson and N. Zill, "The Life Course of Children of Divorce: Marital Disruption and Parental Contact," *American Sociological Review*, 48 (1983), pp. 656–668.
9. Ibid.
10. Frank F. Furstenberg, Jr., and Graham B. Spanier, *Recycling the Family: Remarriage After Divorce* (Beverly Hills, Calif.: Sage, 1984).
11. Lenore Weitzman, *The Divorce Revolution: The Unexpected Social and Economic Consequences for Women and Children in America* (New York: Free Press, 1985).

Bibliography

Ahrons, Constance R., and Rodgers, Roy H. *Divorced Families: A Multidisciplinary Developmental View.* New York: W. W. Norton and Company, 1987.

Bank, Stephen P., and Kahn, Michael D. *The Sibling Bond.* New York: Basic Books, 1982.

Beer, William R. (ed.). *Relative Strangers: Studies of Stepfamily Processes.* New York: Rowman and Littlefield, 1988.

Bernard, Jessie. *Remarried: A Study of Marriage.* New York: Russell and Russell, first edition, 1956, second edition, 1971.

Bernstein, Anne C. *The Flight of the Stork.* New York: Delacorte, 1978.

Burns, Cherie. *Stepmotherhood: How to Survive Without Feeling Frustrated, Left Out, or Wicked.* New York: Harper and Row, 1985.

Duberman, Lucille. *The Reconstituted Family: A Study of Remarried Couples and Their Children.* Chicago: Nelson-Hall, 1975.

Dunn, Judy. *Sisters and Brothers: The Developing Child.* Cambridge, Mass.: Harvard University Press, 1985.

Ehrensaft, Diane. *Parenting Together: Men and Women Sharing the Care of Their Children.* New York: Free Press, 1987.

Ephron, Delia. *Funny Sauce.* New York: Viking Press, 1986.

Furstenberg, Frank F., Jr., and Spanier, Graham B. *Recycling the Family: Remarriage After Divorce.* Beverly Hills, Calif.: Sage Publications, 1984.

Gilligan, Carol. *In a Different Voice: Psychological Theory and Women's Development.* Cambridge, Mass.: Harvard University Press, 1982.

Haley, Jay. *Leaving Home.* New York: Basic Books, 1980.

Ihinger-Tallman, Marilyn, and Paley, Kay. *Remarriage.* Newbury Park, Calif.: Sage Publications, 1987.

Keshet, Jamie Kelem. *Love and Power in the Stepfamily: A Practical Guide.* New York: McGraw-Hill, 1987.

Krementz, Jill. *How It Feels when Parents Divorce.* New York: Knopf, 1984.

McGoldrick, Monica, and Gerson, Randy. *Genograms in Family Assessment.* New York: W. W. Norton and Company, 1985.

Messinger, Lillian. *Remarriage: A Family Affair.* New York: Plenum Press, 1984.

Minuchin, Salvador. *Families and Family Structure.* Cambridge, Mass.: Harvard University Press, 1977.

———. *Family Kaleidoscope.* Cambridge, Mass.: Harvard University Press, 1984.

———, and H. Charles Fishman. *Family Therapy Techniques.* Cambridge, Mass.: Harvard University Press, 1981.

Pasley, Kay, and Ihinger-Tallman, Marilyn (eds.). *Remarriage and Stepparenting: Current Research and Theory.* New York: Guilford Press, 1987.

Piaget, Jean, and Inhelder, Barbel. *The Psychology of the Child.* New York: Basic Books, 1969.

Rosin, Mark Bruce. *Stepfathering: Stepfathers' Advice on Creating a New Stepfamily.* New York: Simon and Schuster, 1987.

Sager, Clifford, J., Brown, Hollis Steer, Crohn, Helen, Engel, Tamara, Rodstein, Evelyn, and Walker, Libby. *Treating the Remarried Family.* New York: Brunner/Mazel, 1983.

Toman, Walter. *Family Constellation: Its Effect on Personality and Social Behavior.* 3rd edition. New York: Springer, 1976.

Visher, Emily B., and Visher, John S. *How to Win as a Stepfamily.* New York: Dembner Books, 1982.

———. *Old Loyalties, New Ties: Therapeutic Strategies with Stepfamilies.* New York: Brunner/Mazel, 1988.

———. *Stepfamilies: Myths and Realities.* Secaucus, N.J.: Citadel Press, 1980.

Wallerstein, Judith S., and Kelly, Joan Berlin. *Surviving the Breakup: How Children and Parents Cope with Divorce.* New York: Basic Books, 1980.

Weitzman, Lenore. *The Divorce Revolution: The Unexpected Social and Economic Consequences for Women and Children in America.* New York: Free Press, 1985.

Books for Children

Berman, Claire. *What Am I Doing in a Stepfamily?* Secaucus, N.J.: Lyle Stuart, Inc., 1982.

Boyd, Lizi. *The Not-So-Wicked Stepmother.* New York: Viking Kestrel, 1987.

Bradley, Buff. *Where Do I Belong? A Kids' Guide to Stepfamilies.* Reading, Mass.: Addison-Wesley, 1982.

Craven, Linda, *Stepfamilies: New Patterns of Harmony.* New York: Julian Messner, 1982.

Gardner, Richard A. *The Boys and Girls Book About Stepfamilies.* New York: Bantam Books, 1982.

Getzoff, Ann, and McClenahan, Carolyn. *Stepkids: A Survival Guide for Teenagers in Stepfamilies.* New York: Walter and Company, 1984.

Green, Phyllis. *A New Mother for Martha.* New York: Human Sciences Press, 1978.

LeShan, Eda. *What's Going to Happen to Me?* New York: Avon Books, 1976.

Lewis, Helen Coale. *All About Families—The Second Time Around.* Atlanta: Peachtree Publishers, 1980.

Shyer, Marlene, Fanta. *Stepdog.* New York: Charles Scribner's Sons, 1983.

Stenson, Janet Sinberg. *Now I Have a Stepparent, and It's Kind of Confusing.* New York: Avon, 1979.

Vigna, Judith. *Daddy's New Baby.* Niles, Ill.: Albert Whitman and Company, 1982.

———. *Grandma Without Me.* Niles, Ill.: Albert Whitman and Company, 1984.

———. *She's Not My Real Mother.* Chicago: Albert Whitman and Company, 1980.

Index